Common and Scientific Names of Fishes from the United States, Canada, and Mexico

Seventh Edition

Common and Scientific Names of Fishes from the United States, Canada, and Mexico

Seventh Edition

Lawrence M. Page, *Chair*
Héctor Espinosa-Pérez, Lloyd T. Findley, Carter R. Gilbert,
Robert N. Lea, Nicholas E. Mandrak, Richard L. Mayden, and Joseph S. Nelson

Committee on Names of Fishes
A joint committee of the American Fisheries Society and the
American Society of Ichthyologists and Herpetologists

American Fisheries Society
Special Publication 34

Bethesda, Maryland
2013

The American Fisheries Society Special Publication series is a registered serial. The suggested citation format follows.

Page, L. M., H. Espinosa-Pérez, L. T. Findley, C. R. Gilbert, R. N. Lea, N. E. Mandrak, R. L. Mayden, and J. S. Nelson. 2013. Common and scientific names of fishes from the United States, Canada, and Mexico, 7th edition. American Fisheries Society, Special Publication 34, Bethesda, Maryland.

Cover illustration by Mr. Craig W. Ronto

Printed in the United States of America on acid-free paper.

Library of Congress Control Number 2012947049
ISBN 978-1-934874-31-8
ISSN 0097-0638

American Fisheries Society Web site: *www.fisheries.org*

American Fisheries Society
5410 Grosvenor Lane, Suite 110
Bethesda, Maryland 20814
USA

This book is dedicated to our friends and colleagues
Reeve M. Bailey (1911–2011) and Joseph S. Nelson (1937–2011).
Their knowledge of fishes never ceased to amaze us, and their
dedication to the Committee on Names of Fishes
never failed to engage us.

Este libro está dedicado a nuestros amigos y colegas
Reeve M. Bailey (1911–2011) y Joseph S. Nelson (1937–2011).
Su conocimiento de los peces nunca cesó de sorprendernos, y su
dedicación al Comité de Nombres de Peces nunca dejo de fascinarnos.

Ce livre est dédié à nos amis et collègues
Reeve M. Bailey (1911–2011) et Joseph S. Nelson (1937–2011).
Leurs connaissances des poissons nous ont toujours impressionnées, et leur
dévouement envers le Comité sur les noms des poissons
n'a jamais cessé de susciter notre intérêt.

CONTENTS

NAMES OF FISHES COMMITTEE

Héctor Espinosa-Pérez, Colección Nacional de Peces, Departamento de Zoología, Instituto de Biología, Universidad Nacional Autónoma de México, Apartado Postal 70-153, Ciudad Universitaria, Tercer Circuito Exterior s/n, Distrito Federal 04510, México; hector@unam.mx

Lloyd T. Findley, Investigador Titular, Centro de Investigación en Alimentación y Desarrollo, A.C.-Coordinación Guaymas, Carretera al Varadero Nacional, km. 6.6, Colonia Las Playitas, Apartado Postal 284, Guaymas, Sonora 85480, México; findley@ciad.mx

Carter R. Gilbert, Emeritus Curator of Fishes, Florida Museum of Natural History, University of Florida, Gainesville, Florida 32611, USA; carter_gilbert@bellsouth.net

Robert N. Lea, Research Associate, California Academy of Sciences, 55 Music Concourse Drive, Golden Gate Park, San Francisco, California 94118, USA; rnlea@comcast.net

Nicholas E. Mandrak, Research Scientist, Great Lakes Laboratory for Fisheries and Aquatic Sciences, Fisheries and Oceans Canada, Burlington, Ontario L7R 4A6, Canada; nicholas.mandrak@dfo-mpo.gc.ca

Richard L. Mayden, Professor and Endowed Chair, Department of Biology, Saint Louis University, St. Louis, Missouri 63103, USA; cypriniformes@gmail.com

Joseph S. Nelson (deceased 2011), Department of Biological Sciences, University of Alberta, Edmonton, Alberta T6G 2E9, Canada

Lawrence M. Page, Curator of Fishes, Florida Museum of Natural History, University of Florida, Gainesville, Florida 32611, USA; lpage1@ufl.edu

LIST OF FAMILIES

Common names given in parentheses in English, Spanish, and French.

INTRODUCTION

This book provides a comprehensive list of all species of fishes in Canada, Mexico, and the continental United States. All species, ranging from small, secretive or rare fishes to large, sport and commercial fishes, are of importance in documenting and understanding the biodiversity of the continent. Many of the species are used as laboratory experimental animals, are displayed or maintained in public or private aquariums, are used as bait, or are treated as objects of natural history inquiry or aesthetic appeal. Some species once disdained as "trash fish" are commercially harvested and highly valued today. An increased environmental consciousness has focused attention on native fishes as indicators of the condition of freshwater and marine ecosystems, as can be appreciated by the frequency that endangered species are discussed in the media. This book's format should make it easy for those with special interests to use.

A major change in this seventh edition of *Common and Scientific Names of Fishes* is the addition of a common name in French for each Canadian species, rather than only those from Quebec. Although with this change we lose an updated checklist of Quebec species, we gain a checklist for all Canadian species (Canadian-occurring species are provided with a name in French, just as Mexican-occurring species have a name in Spanish). We also, for the first time, record under "Occurrence" those species in the Arctic Ocean off continental North America.

As with past editions, we have adhered to the principle of stability of common names, only changing them for specific reasons documented in Appendix 1. As in the 2004 list, we have carefully attempted to follow the general consensus of what specialists have published; where there are conflicting views, we generally state the basis of our decision in Appendix 1. In addition, as in 2004, we dealt with differences of opinion among members of the Committee on Names of Fishes by voting after open discussions.

Earlier lists were published in 1948, 1960, 1970, 1980, 1991, and 2004 (as American Fisheries Society Special Publications 1, 2, 6, 12, 20, and 29, respectively). These lists have been widely used and have contributed substantially to the goal of achieving uniform use of common names and avoiding confusion in scientific names. This list recommends the scientific names to use and reflects, in our judgment, the current views of specialists. From 570 entries in the abbreviated 1948 list (comprising primarily the better known sport, commercial, and forage fishes), coverage increased to 1,892 species in 1960, to 2,131 in 1970, to 2,268 in 1980, and to 2,428 species in 1991 (in Canada and continental United States). The 2004 edition (sixth), in adding the Mexican fauna, included 3,700 species—3,694 fishes and six newly added cephalochordates ("amphioxins"). The present edition includes 3,875 species.

In this list, as in that of 2004, the joint American Fisheries Society/American Society of Ichthyologists and Herpetologists (AFS/ASIH) Committee on Names of Fishes has endeavored to include common names for all native (indigenous) and established introduced species in the region of coverage, even when the introduced species occur in very limited areas. The number of introduced species found in our area, both through intentional and accidental releases, continues to rise. If there is no evidence that a nonnative species has established a breeding population (although it has been collected), it is not included. Some introduced species previously believed to be established in North America but now thought not to be established are no longer listed. Current information on nonnative fishes in the United States is available at http://nas.er.usgs.gov/taxgroup/fish/default.asp, and for Mexico at www.conabio.gob.mx/invasoras/index.php/Especies_invasoras_-_Peces. Common names for those few hybrid fishes that are important in fishery management or in sport or commercial fisheries are given in Appendix 2.

Most additions to this seventh edition resulted from descriptions of new species and range extensions resulting from marine and freshwater surveys. Arctic Ocean distributions are based on limited sampling, and with further studies and ongoing climate change, we expect the list to grow. Recent systematic studies and reconsideration of past decisions by the Committee on Names of Fishes ("Committee" hereafter) have led to the recognition of species names previously thought to be junior synonyms and, conversely, have concluded that some species names on previous lists are junior synonyms; those latter names have been removed. There are still many cases where there is uncertainty about whether a given taxon should be treated at the species level or at the subspecies level, particularly in the families Cyprinidae, Catostomidae, and Salmonidae. Differences of opinion may result among users employing different species concepts and exploring different lines of evidence (e.g., morphological, molecular, ecological, and behavioral). In accepting species as valid from various works (faunal or systematic), we made little or no judgment on authors' species concepts. Taxa of uncertain status were dealt with on a case-by-case basis. Where there is ongoing research on the question, we prefer to wait until the evidence is published before making a decision. Further discussion on how we have proceeded is given below under various headings.

Comprehensive listing of all species of fishes in the area of coverage in North America was attempted with the following exceptions. Many species for which the adults are known only from beyond our bathymetric (200-m bottom depth) and geographical limits have early life-history stages that have been recorded from our continental shelf waters. These "egg or larvae-only" examples are excluded from this list, as are the adults of many mesopelagic species that may occur over the outer shelf where deep waters occur very close to shore. Further qualifications are given in the next section.

Area of Coverage

This edition includes, as far as is known, all species of fishes known to have, or to have once had, reproducing populations in the fresh waters of continental Canada, the United States, and Mexico and those marine species inhabiting (as adults) contiguous shore waters on or above the continental shelf waters to a bottom depth of 200 m (656 ft). We exclude species known only from beyond continental shelf waters over bottoms exceeding 200 m, even if found in the midwater of less than 200 m. Species from the Arctic Ocean are included. The southern boundary of the Arctic Ocean in North America is defined as extending from the northern tip of Lab-

rador along latitude 61°N to Greenland in the Atlantic and from the western tip of the Seward Peninsula to the United States–Russia border in the Bering Strait in the Pacific. The list of Arctic Ocean species was compiled primarily from Mecklenburg et al. (2002, 2011) and Coad and Reist (2004). As further exploration of the Arctic Ocean is undertaken, additional species will be recorded. Similarly, there are many species known in waters south of Mexico that will undoubtedly be recorded from Mexico in the future. This may be especially true on the Atlantic side, where many species known from Belize have yet to be recorded from Mexico. In addition, several species are known from freshwater in Belize but not recorded from Mexico.

In the Atlantic Ocean, all shore fishes from Greenland, eastern Canada, the United States, and Mexico, including those from the Gulf of Mexico and Caribbean Sea southward to the Mexico–Belize border, are included. Species from Iceland, Bermuda, the Bahamas, Cuba, and other West Indian (Caribbean) islands are excluded unless they also occur in the region covered. In the Pacific Ocean, species occurring over the continental shelf from Bering Strait to the Mexico–Guatemala border, including the oceanic Revillagigedo Archipelago and Guadalupe Island, to a depth of 200 m in contiguous shore waters are included. It is especially difficult to know which species to include for oceanic islands lacking a shelf, where oceanic species may be found close to shore along with neritic species. In such cases, we have included only species usually considered to be "shelf" species. Species from the Hawaiian Islands and Clipperton Island (Atoll), with their highly endemic and largely Indo-Pacific faunas, are not included. Deep-sea fishes, whether benthic or mesopelagic, including vertically migrating species that temporarily enter the epipelagic zone, and strictly oceanic fishes are excluded unless they appear other than as presumed strays in North American shelf waters. Often, in practice, this distinction is difficult to apply and consequently arbitrary. Pelagic fishes that are regularly found over the continental shelf are included. We exclude species that are known in North American waters only from deeper than 200 m, even though they have been captured in extralimital areas where the bottom depth is shallower than 200 m. Users should exercise caution when inferring depth ranges of species (e.g., *Enchelycore anatina*, commonly found in the eastern Atlantic well above 200 m, has been recorded in the western Atlantic only at depths in excess of 200 m, and *Ophichthus menezesi*, described from 169–209 m off Brazil, was found in the Gulf of Mexico off Florida only from 1,200 to 1,400 m).

Key abbreviations in the list provide a general guide to occurrence. An "**A**" denotes Atlantic Ocean and extends to the boundary with the Arctic Ocean (as defined above), whereas "**AM**" denotes occurrence in Atlantic Ocean in Mexico but not in Canada or the United States. An "**Ar**" denotes occurrence in the Arctic Ocean (these species, except for new additions, were listed in previous editions as occurring in the Pacific or Atlantic depending on occurrence either west or east, respectively, of the Boothia Peninsula of Canada). A "**P**" refers to the Pacific Ocean and extends to the boundary with the Arctic Ocean, whereas "**PM**" denotes occurrence in the Pacific Ocean in Mexico but not recorded in Canada or the United States. An "**F:**" indicates occurrence in fresh waters or other inland waters that are saline (e.g., Salton Sea, California). Some species so designated may refer only to historical records, such as *Elops affinis* in the lower Colorado River and Salton Sea. An "F:" designation followed by a "**C**" denotes freshwater Canada, whereas "**M**" denotes freshwater Mexico and "**U**" denotes freshwater United States (contiguous states and/or Alaska). It should be noted that (1) marine species known off one coast shallower than 201 m, but off the other coast deeper than 200 m, are only indicated as occurring off the shallower-recorded coast (e.g., *Notacanthus chemnitzii* is listed as "A" only but is known off California only from depths more than 200 m); (2) although a species may be noted as occurring in both marine and freshwaters, it may be primarily marine or primarily freshwater and occur only rarely in the other; and (3) many species not otherwise noted in the list as "F" have been collected on occasion in estuarine or freshwater.

A bracketed "**[I]**" follows the letter indication of occurrence for any introduced (nonindigenous) species established within our area of coverage and may be used separately or collectively for the "A," "P," "F," "C," "U," and "M" designations (these are species introduced into the designated area via human activity). This symbol is not used for introductions of a native species within a designated area (e.g., the transfer of *Salvelinus fontinalis* from eastern to western Canada) but is employed for a species subsequently dispersing on its own into a country from another into which it had been introduced (e.g., *Scardinius erythrophthalmus*). As with the 2004 edition, we indicate the successful introduction of species from one ocean to another (e.g., *Alosa sapidissima* and *Morone saxatilis* were introduced into Pacific waters from the Atlantic, and their occurrence is thus indicated as "A-P[I]-F:CU"). A bracketed "**[X]**" indicates that the species is considered extinct. Species given in the 2004 edition that are still extant but known only from historical records in part of the former range and probably are now extirpated in either Canada or the United States are still listed (e.g., *Erimystax x-punctatus* no longer exists in Canada but does occur in the United States and is listed as "F:CU"; *Catostomus bernardini* no longer exists as a native in the United States but does occur in Mexico and is listed as "F:UM"). A bracketed "**[XN]**" indicates that the species is considered extinct in nature but is maintained in captivity. Species noted as "A" or "P" and showing a common name in Spanish and/or French occur in the waters of the United States, Mexico, and/or Canada.

The sequence of code letters denoting distributions of species occurring in marine and freshwater habitats may differ in some cases from those appearing in the 2004 list. Differentiation of Canadian and American freshwater species in, and the addition of Mexican marine and freshwater fishes to, the 2004 list led to the use of three corresponding new letters ("C," "U," and "M"), which often appeared in combination and resulted in complex distributional codes. This is further complicated in the present list by the addition of an Arctic category, "Ar." To simplify the distributional codes, occurrence is now coded in the following sequence: "A-P-Ar-F:CUM." For example, *Oncorhynchus mykiss* was listed in 1991 as "A-F-P," in 2004 as "A[I]-F:CUM-P," and in the present list is "A[I]-P-F:CUM."

Family Names

Family names are important in identification and information retrieval. They are widely used in scientific literature, popular books on fishes, dictionaries, and encyclopedias. Although a few family names appearing in earlier editions of this list have been placed in synonymies, the current list shows an increase in the number of fish families over that of the 2004 edition. We have accepted changes in the composition of some families published since the 2004 edition, when the changes seemed clearly to result in monophyletic taxa. However, we preferred not to make arbitrary changes that split a family considered to be monophyletic. For example, we recognize the whitefishes, grayling, trouts, salmons, and chars in one family (Salmonidae) rather than in three families as preferred by some authors (especially in Europe). Families added to the list are annotated in Appendix 1, and appendix notes are generally provided where we declined to make changes suggested in some publications.

Scientific Names

Scientific names of species and higher taxa are those formed according to the International Code of Zoological Nomenclature, a set of rules for the naming of animals. Other names, published or not, are unavailable.

Common Names

Common names of species have a long history, far exceeding that of scientific names, and as long as the public and biologists use them, it is necessary to have a standardized and effective system for them. The Committee has developed a body of common names (a single name in English for all included species and a single name in Spanish and/or French for species occurring in Mexico and/or Canada) that reflect broad current usage and promote the stability and universality of names applied to North American fishes.

Common names of fishes, as used in this list, are applied to individual species. Sometimes these names are employed as "market names." However, market names often apply to several species. In the interests of an informed public, we strongly encourage the adoption of the common names presented herein whether by authors, merchants, or others, even if a name is thought to have little appeal (e.g., we discourage the use of the regional market name "mullet," instead of sucker, when applied to members of

the family Catostomidae). A summary of market names in English, as they apply to fishes (and invertebrates) sold in the United States, is available in *Guidance for Industry: The Seafood List—FDA's Guide to Acceptable Market Names for Seafood Sold in Interstate Commerce*, 1993, revised 2009, United States Food and Drug Administration (see www.fda.gov/Food/GuidanceComplianceRegulatoryInformation/GuidanceDocuments/Seafood/ucm113260). In the present list, many names differ from those used in publications of the Food and Agriculture Organization of the United Nations. We hope that in the future there may be greater agreement.

The common name, as here employed, is viewed as a formal appellation to be used in lieu of the scientific name of a species. We emphasize that common names are not intended to duplicate the power of scientific names in reflecting phylogenetic relationships (see Principle 8 below). History has shown that common names often are more stable than scientific names.

Common names are usually more readily adaptable to lay uses than are scientific names. There is clear need for standardization and uniformity in vernacular names not only for sport and commercial fishes, but also as names for market and aquarium fishes, in legal documents, and as substitutes for scientific names in popular and scientific writing. A few common names in Spanish, newly added to the list in 2004, required changing to reflect actual use.

Providing common names in French for all fishes occurring in Canadian fresh and marine waters requires knowledge of the composition of the fish fauna in freshwaters and the Canadian portions of the Arctic, Atlantic, and Pacific oceans. Because such knowledge is not found in a single reference, lists of freshwater and marine species were compiled. The freshwater list was compiled primarily from the unpublished inventory of the General Status of Species in Canada project completed in 2005 (www.wildspecies.ca). The list of Arctic Ocean species was compiled primarily from Mecklenburg et al. (2002, 2011) and Coad and Reist (2004). Lists of Canadian-occurring species for the Atlantic and Pacific oceans were based on the unpublished inventory of the General Status of Species in Canada project, completed in 2005 (www.wildspecies.ca) and extensively supplemented with data from the

Atlantic Reference Centre collection, Canadian Museum of Nature, Fisheries and Oceans Canada, Royal British Columbia Museum, and Royal Ontario Museum. Common names in French for freshwater fishes were largely based on the 2004 list, Scott and Crossman (1973), and D. E. McAllister (1990, *A List of the Fishes of Canada/Liste des poissons du Canada*, Syllogeus 64). Common names in French for marine species were based on the General Status of Species in Canada project (an unpublished list) completed in 2005 (www.wildspecies.ca) and extensively supplemented by B. W. Coad (1995, *Encyclopedia of Canadian Fishes*, Canadian Museum of Nature and Canadian Sportfishing Productions, Ottawa) and FishBase (www.fishbase.org). For species for which common names in French could not be found, common names in English were translated into French. All common names in French were reviewed by C. B. Renaud and P. Dumont.

Several species have common names in English derived directly from their names in Spanish as used in Mexico and, where appropriate, bear accent marks. The committee was divided on whether to treat these names as "automatically anglicized" and thus not carry over the accent marks or to regard them as properly accented words in Spanish embedded in (transferred to) a common name in English. We concluded that some geographic names, based on widespread adoption into English, can be considered to be already anglicized (e.g., Yucatan versus Yucatán, Rio Grande versus Río Grande), whereas some others, generally not in use in English, as not anglicized. To understand the meaning of accent marks in words in Spanish (which have different meanings in words in French), we provide the following guide to allow the correct pronunciation of common names in English containing words derived from geographic place names in Mexico. In pronouncing unaccented Spanish words that end in a vowel, "n," or "s," as is generally the case, the stress falls on the second-to-last syllable (the second-to-last vowel, e.g., bravo), whereas for words that end in a consonant other than "n" or "s," the stress falls on the last syllable. Words not following this rule carry an accent mark (´) over the vowel of the stressed syllable (often the last, e.g., Zirahuén and Michoacán). As noted above, those few common names in English considered to be anglicized from the Spanish

do not have an accent mark, even though they do in the Spanish, because such punctuation is not a convention of the English language. The guide to pronunciation in English should be based on the spelling in Spanish—thus for *Poeciliopsis scarlli*, the rule for its common name in Spanish, guatopote michoacano (no accent mark for this adjective), would be to place the accent over the second-to-last syllable in michoacano (over the vowel "a"). The same emphasis should apply to the derived name in English (but now, due to a difference in spelling, over the ultimate "a," as Michoacán Livebearer). Examples of where the stress would be placed on other than the second-to-last syllable follow. Species with the common name in English, as derived from a Mexican geographic name in Spanish, having the accent on the last syllable (accent over last vowel) would include Lacandón Sea Catfish, Tamesí Molly, and Michoacán Livebearer. Species with the common name in English, as derived from a Mexican geographic name in Spanish, having the accent on the third-to-last syllable (accent over third-to-last vowel) would include San Jerónimo Livebearer and Cuatro Ciénegas Platyfish.

Agreement on many common names may be reached quickly, but others are attended by complications. Disagreement is especially common for fishes known by market names that differ from those more familiar to anglers, biologists, and others (e.g., what is often called "Red Snapper" on much of the English-speaking Pacific coast may be a species of *Sebastes* [rockfishes] and not a species of a true snapper of the genus *Lutjanus*). The use of different names in various parts of the geographic range of a species creates difficulties that seem solvable only through arbitration. Conversely, a given name may be employed in different places for different species (as shown by the Red Snapper example). Although Committee action on such situations may not be expected to change local use quickly, it is counterproductive to sanction use of one name for two or more species. We emphasize that all users of fish common names are ill served, and perhaps misled, if names are used in an inconsistent manner.

After struggling with common names for many years, an earlier Committee on Names of Fishes realized the importance of establishing a set of guiding principles to be employed in the selection of common names. Such a code permits a more objective appraisal of the relative merits among several names than if selection were based primarily on personal experience and preference. Consideration of many vernacular names of fishes makes it apparent that few principles can be established for which there will be no exceptions. Many exceptions exist because, at the time the Committee began to function, a majority of the larger and more abundant species in the United States and Canada had such firmly established common names that it would have been unrealistic to reject them just to conform to a newly established set of principles. The name for a species may often be decided by weighing the pros and cons among possible choices and selecting the one that best fits the aggregate of guiding criteria. The criteria that the Committee regards as appropriate to the selection of common names of fishes are repeated below from previous lists, with some modification.

Principles Governing Selection of Common Names

1. *A single vernacular name in each appropriate language shall be accepted for each species.* In the 1991 edition, only one fish, *Coregonus artedi*, had two accepted common names; in the 2004 list and in the present list, there are no exceptions.

2. *No two species in the list shall have the same common name.* Commonly used names of extralimital species should be avoided for species in our area whenever possible.

3. *The expression "common" (or its Spanish or French equivalent) as part of a fish's name shall be avoided.* Exceptions are made for long-established names such as Common Carp/carpa común, Common Shiner, tiburón zorro común, cazón espinoso común, and aiguillat commun.

4. *Simplicity in names is favored.* In fish names in English and Spanish, hyphens and apostrophes shall be omitted (e.g., Smallmouth Bass) except when they are orthographically essential (e.g., Three-eye Flounder), have a special meaning (e.g., C-O Sole), are necessary to avoid possible misunder-

standing (e.g., Cusk-eel), or join two fish names, neither of which represents the fish in question, into a single name (e.g., Trout-perch, which is neither a trout nor a perch). Compounded modifying words, especially appropriate to English, including paired structures such as a spot on either side of the caudal peduncle, should usually be treated as singular nouns in apposition with a group name (e.g., Spottail Shiner), but a plural modifier should usually be placed in adjectival form (e.g., Spotted Hake, Blackbanded Sunfish) unless its plural nature is obvious (e.g., Fourspot Flounder). Preference shall be given to names that are short and euphonious. The compounding of brief, familiar words into a single name, written without a hyphen, may in some cases promote clarity and simplicity, especially in English (e.g., Tomcod, Goldfish, and Mudminnow), but the practice of combining words, especially those that are lengthy, awkward, or unfamiliar, shall be avoided.

5. *Common names in English shall be capitalized.* The first letter in each word in the common name shall be capitalized except after a hyphen unless that word requires capitalization as a proper noun (e.g., Pit-Klamath Brook Lamprey, Ragged-tooth Shark, Atlantic Salmon, Dusky Cusk-eel, Tropical Two-wing Flyingfish, and Northern Rock Sole). This is a change from past editions. Common names for taxa above species level (e.g., Pacific salmons, temperate basses) are not affected. A superscript caret (^) is placed in the list after those common names in English that contain a proper noun (or a word treated in the 2004 list as a noun such as "Gulf," where a particular gulf is implied) that always requires capitalization. This notation will be useful to some users because it is sometimes not clear from past lists which names contained a proper noun (e.g., Buffalo darter, Strawberry darter, and Warrior darter) and which did not (e.g., colorado snapper and warsaw grouper).

6. *Names intended to honor persons* (e.g., the formerly used names, Allison's tuna, Julia's darter, Meek's halfbeak, and blanqui-

llo de Hubbs) *are discouraged in that they are without descriptive value.* However, in a few instances, patronyms have become so widely used that they are accepted (e.g., Guppy, Lane Snapper). This principle does not apply to common names in French (e.g., the common name for *Liparis coheni* is limace de Cohen). However, in cases where a patronymic or matronymic common name did not have an established priority, an alternate common name usually was chosen.

7. *Subspecies shall not be assigned common names.* As with the 2004 edition, we have not provided scientific or common names for subspecies. Nevertheless, we recognize that subspecies, with their own evolutionary history in allopatry, have importance in evolutionary inquiry and may be given special protective status and recognized in studies of biodiversity. Some subspecies are so different in appearance (not just in geographic distribution) that they are readily distinguished, and common names for these populations may exist, constituting an important aid in communication.

   Hybrids are usually not given common names, but those important in fish management and that have established common names are treated in Appendix 2. Cultured varieties, color phases, and morphological variants are not named, even though they may be important in commercial trade and culture of aquarium fishes (e.g., the many varieties of Goldfish and Common Carp, the spotted versus the golden color phases of Leopard Grouper and Guineafowl Puffer).

8. *The common name need not be intimately tied to the scientific name.* The periodic and necessary changes in scientific nomenclature do not necessarily require changes in common names. The practice of applying a common name to a genus and a modifying name for each species, and still another modifier for each subspecies, while appealing in its simplicity, has the defect of inflexibility, and risks nonrecognition of a fish by discarding what may be a perfectly acceptable and traditionally used name. That practice is an attempt to recreate, in common names, the scientific nomenclature. If a species is transferred from one genus to another, or a subspecies is shifted to species status in the ichthyological literature and thus would enter the list, the common name should remain unaffected. It is not a primary function of common names to indicate relationship. This principle continues to be misunderstood or rejected by those who advocate that common names of all members of a genus should incorporate the same root word(s) (e.g., that all *Oncorhynchus* be called salmon, such as "rainbow salmon" and "steelhead salmon," and those of *Salvelinus* should be named char, such as "brook char"). The stability of common names outweighs any advantage to be gained in strict adherence to linking common names to scientific names. When two or more nominal species are found to be identical (synonymous), one name shall be adopted for the recognized species. See also Principle 13.

9. *Names shall not violate the tenets of good taste (e.g., names shall not contain offensive words).* Our changes of the names squawfish to pikeminnow for species of *Ptychocheilus*, and jewfish to goliath grouper, were made in the 2004 list with this principle in mind.

The preceding principles are largely procedural. Those below aid in the selection of suitable names.

10. *Colorful, romantic, fanciful, metaphorical, and otherwise distinctive and original names are especially appropriate.* Such terminology adds to the richness and breadth of the nomenclature and provides satisfaction to the user. Examples of such names in English include Madtom, Dolly Varden, Midshipman, Chilipepper, Garibaldi, Pumpkinseed, Flier, Angelfish, Moorish Idol, and Hogchoker; in Spanish, they include bruja, guitarra, chucho, and lacha; and in French, they include tête-de-boule, ventre citron, and truite fardée.

11. *North American native names or their modifications are welcome for adoption as common names.* Those in current use include Menhaden, Eulachon, Cisco, Chinook Salmon, Mummichog, Tautog, puyeki, and totoaba.

12. *Regardless of origin, truly vernacular names that are widespread and in common use by the public are to be retained when possible.* Many well-known fish names utilized north of Mexico incorporate (have embedded) Spanish words or their modifications (e.g., barracuda, cero, mojarra, pompano [from pámpano], and sierra). Examples from other languages include capelin (French), bocaccio (Italian), and mako (Maori). Most of these conform to Principles 14 and 15 below.

13. *Commonly employed names adopted from traditional English* (e.g., chub, minnow, trout, bass, perch, sole, flounder), *Spanish* (e.g., cazón, sardina, carpa, mojarra, perca, lenguado), *or French usage* (e.g., méné and perche) *are given considerable latitude in taxonomic placement.* Adherence to historical usage is preferred if this does not conflict with the broad general usage of another name. Many names have been applied to similar-appearing but often distantly related fishes in North America. For example, we find "bass" and "lenguado" in use for representatives of several families of spiny-rayed fishes, and "perch" and "perca" for even more. "Chub" appears in such unrelated groups as Cyprinidae and Kyphosidae, and "mojarra" in Cichlidae, Gerreidae and other families. The Ocean Whitefish or pierna, *Caulolatilus princeps*, sometimes referred to as "salmón" in northwestern Mexico, is not a salmonid, and the Pacific Pompano (pámpano in Spanish), *Peprilus simillimus*, is not a carangid (as are other species called pompanos), yet each is best known to fishermen throughout its range by the name indicated. For widely known species, it is preferable to recognize general usage. Established practice with original usage should outweigh attempts at consistency. This is not well understood by some ichthyologists who feel that "perch" should not be used for an embiotocid, "trout" for a *Salvelinus*, "sardinita" for a characid, and "cazón" for a carcharhinid. Some problems have been avoided or minimized by joining names in English to create new words (e.g., seatrout for sea trout, mudsucker for mud sucker, surfperch for surf perch); such combinations have gained wide acceptance since they were adopted in earlier lists.

14. *Morphological attributes, color, and color pattern are desirable sources of names and are commonly used.* Sailfin, flathead, slippery, giant, mottled, copper, and tripletail in English; chato, jorobado, bocón, gigante, jabonero, pinto, and cobrizo in Spanish; citron, cuivré, fardé, and fossettes in French; and a multitude of other descriptors decorate fish names. Efforts should be made to select terms that are descriptively accurate and to hold repetition of those most frequently employed (e.g., white [blanco, blanc], black [negro, noir], spotted [manchado, tacheté], and banded [rayado/de cintas, barré]) to a minimum. Following tradition for names in English in American and Canadian ichthyology, we have attempted to restrict use of "line" or "stripe" to mean longitudinal marks that parallel the body axis, and "bar" or "band" to mean vertical or transverse marks. However, that tradition does not hold for names in Spanish as utilized in Mexico, where the term "rayado/rayada" is often applied to such marks.

15. *Ecological characteristics are desirable sources of names.* Such terms should be properly descriptive. English (Spanish, French) modifiers such as reef (arrecifal, récif), coral (coralino, corail), sand (arenoso, sable), rock (rocoso, roche), lake (de lago, lac), and freshwater (dulceacuícola, dulcicole) are well known in fish names.

16. *Geographic distribution provides suitable adjectival modifiers.* Poorly descriptive or misleading geographic characterizations (e.g., "Kentucky Bass" for a wide-ranging species) should be corrected unless they are too entrenched in current usage. In the interests of stability, we have retained such names as Alaska Blackfish,

even though this species also occurs in Russia, and guatopote de Sonora, even though this livebearer commonly occurs outside the state of Sonora. In the interest of brevity, it is usually possible to delete words such as lake (lago, lac), river (río, fleuve), gulf (golfo, golfe), or sea (mar, mer), in the names of species (e.g., Colorado Pikeminnow, not "Colorado River Pikeminnow"; topote del Balsas, not "topote del Río Balsas").

17. *Scientific names of genera may be employed as common names outright* (e.g., gambusia, remora, anchoa, brótula, and guavina) *or in modified form* (e.g., molly, from *Mollienesia*). Once adopted, such names should be maintained even if the genus or higher level scientific name is subsequently changed. These vernaculars are written in Roman typeface (i.e., not in italics as in the scientific name for the genus).

18. *The duplication of common names for fishes and other organisms should be avoided if possible, but names in general usage need not be rejected on this basis alone.* For example, "buffalo" is employed for various artiodactyl mammals and for catostomid suckers of the genus *Ictiobus*, "zorro" (literally meaning fox) is used for alopiid sharks, and "mariposa" (literally meaning butterfly) is employed for chaetodontid butterflyfishes and gymnurid butterfly rays. On the basis of prevailing usage, such names are admissible as fish names without modification.

Relationship of Common and Scientific Names of Species

The objectives of this list are to recommend common names and to provide the generally accepted scientific names for all species of fishes occurring within the geographical boundaries used. Common names can be stabilized by general agreement. Scientific names, on the other hand, will inevitably shift with advancing knowledge of the phylogenetic relationships of species and in accordance with the views of taxonomists. The scientific nomenclature employed has been reviewed carefully with regard to spelling, authorities, and years of original

descriptions. We emphasize that there are many groups of fishes for which there is disagreement on classification or where the classification is poorly known. Also, there are often subjective differences of opinion among workers in designating ranks for taxa (see discussions above under "Family Names," "Common Names," and particularly Principle 8).

Plan of the List

The list is presented in a phylogenetic sequence of families of Recent (Holocene) fishes as it is generally understood. Arrangement of the classes, orders, and families generally follows Nelson (2006), but some changes reflect recent systematic studies. In most cases, we give a single common name for each family in English, Spanish, and French. However, two (rarely three) names are occasionally given when general usage so dictates. Spelling of the names of authors of species follows W. N. Eschmeyer, editor, *Catalog of Fishes,* electronic version, http://research.calacademy.org/ichthyology/catalog/fishcatmain.asp.

Within families, genera and species are listed alphabetically. Part I consists of five columns: the scientific name, areas of occurrence, common name in English (regardless of area of occurrence), common name in Spanish for Mexican-occurring species, and common name in French for Canadian-occurring species.

We followed the latest (fourth) edition of the International Code of Zoological Nomenclature, 1999 (hereafter referred to as the "Code"; www.nhm.ac.uk/hosted-sites/iczn/code/) and employed original orthographies of species names. Accordingly, the endings of some patronymic names have been changed to *-i* or *-ii*, as appropriate. In this edition of the list, we continue to add, after the scientific name, the author(s) and the year of the original published description of the species. Authors and dates are commonly needed by persons who may not have ready access to the original literature. Determination of the correct author and the year of publication can be complicated, especially for names proposed before 1900. Our justifications for the spellings of Delaroche, Forsskål, Lacepède, and Lesueur were explained in the third (page 5) and fourth (page 8) editions. The attribution of names proposed in the M. E. Blochii Systema Ichthyologiae, 1801, by J. G. Schneider was explained in the fourth edition (page 8).

Use of the author's name reflects current interpretation of the Code. In line with those rules, the author's name directly follows the specific name (written in italics). If the species, when originally described, was assigned to the same genus to which it is assigned herein, the author's name is not enclosed in parentheses; if the species was originally described in another genus, the author's name appears inside parentheses. The year of publication is separated from the authority by a comma (and is included within the parentheses if present). For example, Mitchill originally named the Brook Trout *Salmo fontinalis*, in a work published in 1814; it appears here as *Salvelinus fontinalis* (Mitchill, 1814). As noted in the 2004 edition, parentheses are not placed around an author's name in cases where the species-group name was originally combined with an incorrect spelling or an unjustified emendation of the genus name, even though an unjustified emendation is an available name with its own authorship and date (Article 51.3.1 of the Code). Hence, as with the 2004 edition, parentheses are not used for the author of species originally described in such genera as *Rhinobatus* (now *Rhinobatos*), *Raia* (now *Raja*), *Lepidosteus* (now *Lepisosteus*), *Ophichthys* (now *Ophichthus*), *Nototropis* (now *Notropis*), *Amiurus* (now *Ameiurus*), *Hemirhamphus* (now *Hemiramphus*), *Opisthognathus* (now *Opistognathus*), and *Pomadasis* (now *Pomadasys*).

Since the sixth edition was published in 2004, many users have communicated their suggested changes to the Committee, and each suggestion received consideration as we prepared the present edition. Stability in common names was given highest priority, and changes have been made only for substantial reasons. Scientific knowledge of fishes has advanced rapidly since the last edition, with many new species described, many additional species recorded in North American waters, and numerous taxonomic/systematic revisions completed. All new entries and all entries that depart in any way (scientific name, author[s], year of description, occurrences, and common names) from the 2004 edition are preceded by an asterisk (*). Information describing and explaining the change is given for each such entry in Appendix 1, identified by the page number on which the name appears in the list. Information formerly given in Appendix 1 of the 1970, 1980, 1991, and 2004 lists (pages 65–87, 68–92, 71–96, and 187–253, respectively), documenting the changes between editions 2 and 3, between 3 and 4, between 4 and 5, and between 5 and 6, is generally not repeated in this edition.

A plus sign (+) before an entry indicates that although the entry is unchanged, a comment will be found in Appendix 1 under that name. This includes taxa above the species level (e.g., family and order) where the name is unchanged but the composition of the taxon differs from that in the 2004 edition (by removal of taxa or transfers from other higher taxa).

Although most decisions of the Committee have been unanimous, several were made by majority vote, and no Committee member necessarily subscribes to all decisions reached. We realize that not all decisions will be accepted by all colleagues, but we hope that all users will appreciate our efforts. In many cases, information available to the Committee exceeded that found in the current literature. The Committee often struggled to reach decisions regarding inclusion of such information and has been cautious about adopting changes.

Index

The Index includes scientific names and common names in all three languages. Page references are given for common names herein adopted for families and species. A single entry is included for each species; for example, Brook Trout is entered only under "Trout, Brook," and trucha de arroyo under "trucha, de arroyo."

Page references are given for the scientific names of classes, orders, families, genera, and species. Each species is entered only under its specific (trivial) name. For example, *Sciaenops ocellatus* may be located only under "*ocellatus, Sciaenops*," although an entry for "*Sciaenops*" directs the reader to the page where entries in that genus begin. Scientific names of species that are not accepted for this list are generally excluded, except for those that appeared in the 2004 (sixth) edition and have since been placed in synonymy, as explained for such cases in Appendix 1.

Acknowledgments

This list is the result of contributions made over seven decades by the many past and present members of the Committee on Names of Fishes. To all of the former members, we are greatly indebted. Lasting contributions were made also by many specialists assisting with the second, third, fourth, fifth, and sixth editions, wherein their help was acknowledged.

In preparing materials for this edition, we have received assistance and advice with names and literature from many individuals. We are especially indebted to those who participated in Committee meetings, including those hosted annually by the American Society of Ichthyologists and Herpetologists: William D. Anderson, Jr., George H. Burgess, Bruce B. Collette, Matthew T. Craig, William N. Eschmeyer, Karsten E. Hartel, John F. Morrissey, Robert H. Robins, Juan Jacobo Schmitter-Soto, Gerald R. Smith, W. Leo Smith, William F. Smith-Vaniz, Harold J. Walker, Jr., and James D. Williams.

So many individuals assisted our task that it is impractical to list them all. Some, however, have been especially helpful and merit special mention: Arturo Acero P., Eduardo Balart, Carole Baldwin, Henry L. Bart, Jr., Richard J. Beamish, Hugues Benoit, D. A. Boguski, Brian W. Bowen, George H. Burgess, Mary Burridge, Brooks M. Burr, Gregor M. Cailliet, Kent E. Carpenter, Martin Castonguay, the late José Luis Castro-Aguirre, David Catania, Don Clark, Brian Coad, Bruce B. Collette, the late Salvador Contreras-Balderas, Lara Cooper, Walter R. Courtenay, Matthew T. Craig, Margaret F. Docker, Jean-Denis Dutil, William N. Eschmeyer, Richard F. Feeney, Moretta Frederick, Jon D. Fong, Patricia Fuentes M., Anthony C. Gill, Graham Gillespie, R. Grant Gilmore, Adrián González A., D. H. Goodman, David W. Greenfield, Gavin Hanke, Karsten E. Hartel, Philip A. Hastings, Philip C. Heemstra, Dean A. Hendrickson, Mysi D. Hoang, Leticia Huidobro C., Tomio Iwamoto, Robert E. Jenkins, G. David Johnson, Cynthia Klepadlo, J. M. Leis, Andrew Lewin, María de Lourdes Lozano V., Milton Love, Zachary P. Martin, Katherine Maslenikov, John E. McCosker, Catherine W. Mecklenburg, Roberta Miller, Randy Mooi, James A. Morris, Jr., John F. Morrissey, David A. Neely, Leo G. Nico, James W. Orr, Mauricia Pérez-Tello, Frank L. Pezold, Edward J. Pfeiler, Theodore W. Pietsch, Héctor G. Plascencia, Kyle R. Piller, Dennis Polack, Zachary Randall, Stewart B. Reid, James D. Reist, Claude B. Renaud, D. Ross Robertson, Robert H. Robins, Luiz A. Rocha, Dawn M. Roje, Richard H. Rosenblatt, Ramón Ruíz-Carus, Kate Rutherford, Juan Jacobo Schmitter-Soto, Pamela J. Schofield, Jeffery A. Seigel, Randal A. Singer, Gerald R. Smith, W. Leo Smith, William F. Smith-Vaniz, Wayne C. Starnes, J. D. Stelfox, Duane E. Stevenson, Camm C. Swift, Michael S. Taylor, Christine E. Thacker, Alfred W. Thomson, Luke Tornabene, Xavier Valencia D., Albert M. van der Heiden, James Van Tassell, Lou Van Guelpen, Harold J. Walker, Jr., Edward O. Wiley, James D. Williams, and Mark V. H. Wilson.

Travel funds for Committee members to attend three marathon work sessions were provided by the American Fisheries Society. In 2009, the meeting was held at the Instituto de Biología, Universidad Nacional Autónoma de México, in Mexico City, and hosted by Committee member H. S. Espinosa-Pérez. Support for this meeting was provided by Director T. María Pérez and R. Cordero B., L. Huidobro, and X. Valencia. In 2007 and 2010, meetings were held at the Florida Museum of Natural History, University of Florida, Gainesville, and were hosted by Committee members Carter R. Gilbert and Larry M. Page and greatly assisted by local ichthyologists.

We also wish to thank our home institutions for subsidizing our efforts on this project, often including travel funds, secretarial help, duplicating facilities, and postal services, and for providing work space for Committee members.

The staff, particularly Aaron Lerner and Ghassan (Gus) Rassam, of the American Fisheries Society has helped in many ways. We are especially grateful for the dedicated and pleasant help of Deborah Lehman. Throughout the years, the various presidents and other officers of the American Fisheries Society and of the American Society of Ichthyologists and Herpetologists have continuously offered encouragement to the Committee.

The new and revised sections of the Introduction were translated into Spanish by Gabriela Montemayor and edited by Committee members Héctor Espinosa-Pérez and Lloyd Findley, assisted by Juan Jacobo Schmitter-Soto. The translation of the Introduction into French was made with the support of Fisheries and Oceans Canada by Jacqueline Lanteigne, Claude Renaud, and Johannie Duhaime. Much help was received from Claude Renaud and Pierre Dumont with providing common names in French. Jesse Grosso, Florida Museum of Natural History, assisted in organizing the final manuscript.

Key Abbreviations and Symbols for Part I:

[1] **A** = Atlantic; **AM** = Atlantic Mexico but not recorded in United States or Canada; **Ar** = Arctic Ocean; **F:C** = Freshwater Canada; **F:M** = Freshwater Mexico; **F:U** = Freshwater United States (contiguous states and/or Alaska); **P** = Pacific; **PM** = Pacific Mexico but not recorded in United States or Canada; **[I]** = nonnative (introduced or invasive) and established in our waters; **[X]** = extinct; **[XN]** = extinct in nature but maintained in captivity.

[2] Common names in English are provided for all species in the list (several are adaptations of the name in Spanish for species occurring in Mexico), names in Spanish indicate freshwater and marine species occurring in Mexico, and names in French indicate freshwater and marine species in Canada (coverage is countrywide, not only in Quebec as in the 2004 list). **En-**, **Sp-**, and **Fr-** indicate family names in English, Spanish, and French, respectively.

* Change from 2004 list (sixth edition) in scientific or common name(s) or in distribution (other than addition of **Ar**—new in this edition); see Appendix 1 for explanation of change.

^ Superscript caret denotes a common name in English that contains a proper noun (or a word treated in 2004 list as a proper noun, such as "Gulf"); see Principle 5.

+ See Appendix 1 for comment.

INTRODUCCIÓN

Este libro proporciona una lista exhaustiva de todas las especies de peces que habitan en Canadá, México y la parte continental de los Estados Unidos. Para entender la biodiversidad de peces en el continente, es de gran importancia documentar todas las especies, desde las más pequeñas, las poco conocidas o raras, hasta las especies de peces grandes de importancia comercial o deportiva. Muchas de esas especies son utilizadas en experimentos de laboratorio, son exhibidas o mantenidas en acuarios públicos o privados; otras se usan como carnada y otras son objeto de investigación por preguntas de la historia natural o por su atractivo estético. Algunas especies de peces que en otro tiempo eran despreciadas como "basura", ahora se les da un alto valor y son cultivadas o capturadas comercialmente. Un aumento en la concientización hacia el cuidado del medioambiente ha hecho que la atención se centre en los peces nativos, como indicadores de la condición de los ecosistemas marinos y de agua dulce, lo cual se hace evidente por la frecuencia en que las especies en peligro son objeto de discusión en los medios. Para aquellos que tengan un interés especial en estos temas, el formato de este libro facilitará su uso.

Un cambio relevante en esta séptima edición de *Nombres Científicos y Comunes de Peces* es la adición de nombres comunes en francés para las especies de todo Canadá y no sólo para aquellas de la provincia de Quebec. Aunque con este cambio se detiene la actualización de la lista de especies de Quebec, se gana una lista para todas las especies marinas de Canadá (se proporciona el nombre común en francés sólo para las especies que habitan en Canadá, así como se provee el nombre común en español sólo para las especies que habitan en México). Además por primera vez, se registran bajo el rubro de "Presencia" ("Occurrence") aquellas especies que se encuentran en el Océano Ártico cerca del continente norteamericano.

Al igual que en las ediciones anteriores, nos hemos apegado al principio de estabilidad para los nombres comunes, cambiándolos sólo por razones específicas, que se documentan en el Apéndice (Appendix) 1. Como en la lista de 2004, hemos procurado seguir cuidadosamente el consenso general de lo que han publicado los expertos; donde hay discrepancias se establecen las bases de nuestra decisión en el Apéndice 1. Además, al igual que en 2004, las diferencias de opinión entre los miembros del comité se resuelven por votación después de una amplia discusión.

Las listas anteriores se publicaron en 1948, 1960, 1970, 1980, 1991 y 2004 (en las publicaciones especiales Nos. 1, 2, 6, 12, 20, y 29 de la Sociedad Americana de Pesquerías [American Fisheries Society]). Dichas listas han sido utilizadas ampliamente y han contribuido de forma sustancial al lograr la meta del uso uniforme de los nombres comunes y evitar a su vez la confusión con los nombres científicos. Esta lista recomienda cuáles nombres científicos utilizar y, en nuestra opinión, refleja la visión actualizada de los expertos. De 570 registros en la lista abreviada de 1948 (que comprendió principalmente las especies mejor conocidas de peces para pesca deportiva, comercial y especies forrajeras), ésta se incrementó a 1,892 especies en 1960; a 2,131 en 1970; a 2,268 en 1980, y a 2,428 especies en 1991 (para Canadá y la parte continental de los Estados Unidos). Para la edición 2004 (sexta), donde se incluyó la fauna mexicana, se incrementó a 3,700 registros: 3,694 peces y 6 cefalocordados (anfioxos). La presente edición incluye 3,875 especies.

En esta lista, como en la de 2004, el Comité de Nombres de Peces, en conjunto para la Sociedad Americana de Pesquerías (American Fisheries Society) y la Sociedad Americana de Ictiólogos y Herpetólogos (American Society of Ichthyologists and Herpetologists) (AFS/ASIH), se dio a la tarea de incluir nombres comunes para todas las especies nativas y para las especies introducidas establecidas en el área de cobertura, aún cuando las especies introducidas se presenten en áreas muy limitadas. Se sigue incrementando el número de especies introducidas ya sea por liberación intencional o accidental. No se incluyen las especies introducidas que no hayan establecido una población reproductora (aún cuando hayan sido colectadas). Algunas especies introducidas que se creyeron previamente establecidas en norteamérica y ahora se piensa que no es así, ya no se registran en la lista. La información actualizada de peces no-nativos en los Estados Unidos está disponible en http://nas.er.usgs.gov/taxgroup/fish/default.asp y para México se encuentra en www.conabio.gob.mx/invasoras/index.php/Especies_invasoras_-_Peces. Los nombres comunes para unos cuantos peces híbridos que son importantes en el manejo pesquero o en pesquerías deportivas o comerciales se proporcionan en el Apéndice (Appendix) 2.

La mayoría de las adiciones en esta séptima edición resultaron de la descripción de nuevas especies y nuevos registros de extensión de áreas de distribución, a través de exploraciones marinas y en aguas continentales. Los registros de distribución para el Océano Ártico provienen de muestreos limitados. Sin embargo, esperamos que el registro crezca con los estudios actuales y también debido al cambio climático. Algunos estudios en sistemática recientes y la reconsideración de decisiones anteriores hechas por el Comité de Nombres de Peces, han llevado al reconocimiento de nombres de especies, que en otro tiempo se pensó eran sinónimos secundarios (junior synonyms) y, por el contrario, se ha concluido que algunos nombres de especies proporcionados en listas previas ahora representan sinónimos secundarios; estos últimos nombres han sido eliminados de la lista. Existen aún muchos casos en los que hay incertidumbre de si un taxón determinado debe ser reconocido a nivel de especie o de subespecie, particularmente en las familias Cyprinidae, Catostomidae y Salmonidae. Pueden presentarse diferencias de opinión entre los usuarios sobre emplear diferentes conceptos de especie, que exploren distintas líneas de evidencia (e.g., morfológica, genética, ecológica o conductual). Al aceptar especies como válidas resultado de varios trabajos (faunísticos o sistemáticos), ponemos en poco o nulo juicio el concepto particular de especie considerado por los diferentes autores. Los taxones de estatus incierto se trataron caso por caso. Si hay investigaciones en proceso sobre un caso a discusión, preferimos esperar para tomar una decisión hasta que las evidencias sean publicadas. Más adelante, en varios encabezados, se explica de manera más detallada del cómo se ha procedido.

Se intentó presentar una lista exhaustiva de todas las especies de peces en el área de cobertura en Norteamérica, con las siguientes excepciones. Muchas especies, de las cuales se conocen los adultos sólo más allá de nuestros límites batimétricos (200 m de profundidad al fondo) y geográficos, tienen estadios de vida tempranos que han sido registrados en aguas de nuestra plataforma continental. Esos ejemplos de "huevos o larvas" son excluidos de esta lista, así como lo son los adultos de muchas especies mesopelágicas que pudieran estar muy cerca de la costa sobre la plataforma exterior en aguas profundas. Se proporcionan más detalles en la siguiente sección.

Área de Cobertura

Hasta donde se tiene conocimiento, esta edición incluye todas las especies de peces que se reconoce que existen o que se sabe tuvieron alguna vez poblaciones reproductoras en aguas dulces de Canadá, los Estados Unidos y México, y de aquéllas especies marinas residentes (etapa adulta) en aguas contiguas a la costa o en aguas de la plataforma continental hasta una profundidad de 200 m. Se excluyen las especies conocidas más allá de la plataforma continental cuando la profundidad excede de los 200 m, inclusive cuando la especie se haya registrado a media agua a menos de 200 m. Se incluyen las especies del Océano Ártico. El límite sureño del Océano Ártico en Norteamérica comprende de la punta norte de la península de Labrador, y a lo largo de la latitud 61° N hasta Groenlandia en el Atlántico, y de la punta oeste de la península de Seward, hasta la frontera de los Estados Unidos con Rusia en el estrecho de Bering en el Pacífico. La lista de especies para el Océano Ártico, fue recopilada principalmente de Mecklenburg et al. (2002, 2011) y de Coad y Reist (2004). Se aumentarán más especies a la lista mientras se sigan realizando prospecciones en el Océano Ártico. De la misma manera, existen muchas especies en aguas al sur de México, las cuales indudablemente se agregarán a las listas futuras. Esto puede ser expresamente particular para el lado Atlántico, donde muchas especies conocidas para Belice faltan por ser registradas para México. Además, varias especies dulceacuícolas que se conocen para Belice no están registradas para México.

Para el Océano Atlántico se incluyen todos los peces litorales de Groenlandia, el este de Canadá, los Estados Unidos y México, incluyendo aquéllos del Golfo de México y Mar Caribe hacia el sur en la frontera México-Belice. Se excluyen las especies de Islandia, Bermudas, Bahamas, Cuba y otras islas del Caribe (Antillas), a menos de que se presenten en el área de cobertura. Las especies que se incluyen para el Océano Pacífico son las que se presentan sobre la plataforma continental desde el Estrecho de Bering hasta la frontera de México-Guatemala, incluyendo aguas costeras de las Islas Revillagigedo y la Isla Guadalupe, a una profundidad de 200 m. Es particularmente difícil saber cuáles especies incluir para las islas oceánicas que carecen de plataforma, donde las especies oceánicas pueden encontrarse cerca de la costa junto a las especies neríticas. En tales casos, se incluyeron sólo las especies consideradas como de "plataforma". No se incluyen las especies de las Islas Hawaii e Isla (Atolón) Clipperton, con sus faunas altamente endémicas y principalmente de origen Indopacífico. Asimismo, se excluyen los peces de profundidad, sean bentónicos o mesopelágicos, incluyendo las especies que migran verticalmente y que entran temporalmente a la zona epipelágica; así también los peces estrictamente oceánicos son excluidos a menos de que aparezcan no sólo como ejemplares accidentalmente encontrados en aguas de la plataforma continental de Norteamérica. En la práctica, muy a menudo esta distinción es difícil de establecer y por lo tanto es arbitraria. Se incluyen los peces pelágicos que se encuentran regularmente sobre la plataforma continental. Se excluyen las especies conocidas en aguas de Norteamérica que habitan a más de 200 m de profundidad, aún cuando se hayan capturado en áreas fuera del área de cobertura en donde la profundidad del fondo es menor a 200 m. Los lectores deben ser cautos cuando hagan inferencias sobre los intervalos de profundidad a las que se registran las especies (e.g., *Enchelycore anatina*, la cual se encuentra por lo general por arriba de los 200 m de profundidad en el Atlántico oriental, ha sido registrada en el Atlántico occidental a profundidades que exceden los 200 m, y *Ophichthus menezesi*, descrita entre los 169 y 209 m de profundidad en Brasil, la cual se ha encontrado en el Golfo de México cerca de Florida a 1,200 y 1,400 m).

Las abreviaturas clave en la lista proporcionan una guía general para indicar presencia (incidencia). Una "**A**" denota Océano Atlántico que se extiende hasta el límite con el Océano Ártico (como se definió anteriormente), mientras "**AM**" significa incidencia en el Océano Atlántico en aguas de México, pero no en Canadá ni en los Estados Unidos. La "**Ar**" indica incidencia en el Océano Ártico (esas especies, excepto por las nuevas adiciones, fueron enlistadas en ediciones previas como presentes en el Pacífico o Atlántico, dependiendo de si se presentaban en el oriente u occidente de la península de Boothia en Canadá). Una "**P**" se refiere al Océano Pacífico que se extiende hasta el límite con el Océano Ártico, mientras que "**PM**" significa presencia en el Océano Pacífico en México, pero no registrado en Canadá o en Estados Unidos. La "**F:**" indica la presencia en agua dulce o en aguas interiores que son salinas (e.g., Salton Sea, California). Algunas especies así designadas pueden referirse sólo a registros históricos, como el caso de *Elops affinis* en la parte baja del Río Colorado y Salton Sea. La sigla "**F:**" seguida por una "**C**" significa en agua dulce de Canadá, mientras que seguida por una "**M**" indica agua dulce en México, y seguida por una "**U**" señala agua dulce en los Estados Unidos (estados contiguos y/o Alaska). Debe hacerse notorio que: (1) a las especies marinas conocidas en zonas costeras adyacentes de menos de 201 m, pero cerca de otra costa con profundidad mayor a 200 m, se les coloca como si sólo incidieran cerca de la costa con menor profundidad (e.g., *Notacanthus chemnitzii* está enlistada sólo como "A", pero se sabe que está presente adyacente a la costa de California sólo en profundidades de más de 200 m); (2) aún cuando existen especies que pueden incidir tanto en agua dulce como en agua marina, serán principalmente marinas o dulceacuícolas y se presentan ocasionalmente en uno u otro medio; y (3) muchas especies que no aparecen anotadas en la lista como "F" han sido colectadas ocasionalmente en aguas dulces o estuarinas.

Una "I" entre corchetes "**[I]**" contigua a la letra que denota la incidencia de especie, sirve para señalar cualquier especie introducida (no-nativa) establecida dentro de nuestra área de cobertura, y puede ser usada separada o colectivamente para las siglas "A", "P", "F", "C", "U" y "M" (estas son especies introducidas por actividades humanas dentro del área indicada). Este símbolo no se utiliza para la introducción (transplante) de una especie nativa a un área determinada (e.g., la introducción de *Salvelinus fontinalis* del este al oeste de Canadá), pero se emplea para especies que han sido previamente introducidas a un país y que se dispersan subsecuentemente por sí mismas de ese país a otro (e.g., *Scardinius erythrophthalmus*). Así como se hizo en la edición de 2004, señalamos la exitosa introducción de un océano a otro (e.g., *Alosa sapidissima* y *Morone saxatilis* fueron introducidas al Pacífico de aguas del Atlántico y su incidencia se denota como "A-P[I]-F:CU"). Una X entre corchetes "**[X]**" indica que la especie se considera extinta. Todavía se enlistan las especies presentadas en la edición 2004 que aún existen, pero que se conocen sólo por registros históricos en parte de su extensión original de distribución y que probablemente están actualmente extirpadas ya sea de Canadá o de los Estados Unidos, como por ejemplo: *Erimystax x-punctatus* que ya no existe en Canadá, pero está presente en los Estados Unidos y se enlista como "F:CU"; *Catostomus bernardini* ya no está presente como especie nativa en los Estados Unidos, pero incide en México y se enlista como "F:UM". La XN entre corchetes "**[XN]**" indica que la especie está considerada como extinta en la naturaleza pero es mantenida en cautiverio. Las especies denotadas con "A" o "P" y que tienen nombre común en español y/o francés, inciden en aguas de los Estados Unidos, México y/o Canadá.

La secuencia de las letras de la notación que indica la distribución de las especies presentes en hábitats marinos y dulceacuícolas en algunos casos puede diferir de la que aparece en la lista de 2004. La separación de especies dulceacuícolas de Canadá y Estados Unidos y la adición de peces marinos y dulceacuícolas de México provocó el uso de tres nuevas letras correspondientes (C, U, M) que a menudo aparecen combinadas y resultan en complejos códigos de distribución. Esto se complica aún más en la lista actual debido a la adición de una categoría para el Océano Ártico (Ar). Para simplificar los códigos de distribución, la presencia de una especie se codifica en el orden siguiente: A-P-Ar-F:CUM. Por ejemplo, *Oncorhynchus mykiss* estaba enlistada en 1991 como A-F-P, en 2004 como A[I]-F:CUM-P, mientras en la presente lista aparece como A[I]-P-F:CUM.

Nombres de Familia

Los nombres de familia son importantes en la identificación y consulta de la información. Son ampliamente usados en literatura científica, libros populares sobre peces, diccionarios y enciclopedias. Aunque unos cuantos nombres de familia que han aparecido en ediciones previas de esta lista han sido colocados en sinonimias, en esta lista se muestra un incremento en el número de familias de su correspondiente en la edición 2004. Hemos aceptado cambios en la composición de algunas familias que se han publicado desde la edición 2004, cuando los cambios resultan claramente de taxa monofiléticos. Sin embargo, preferimos no hacer cambios arbitrarios que dividan una familia considerada como monofilética. Por ejemplo, reconocemos a los coregónidos, al tímalo, truchas, y salmones en una familia (Salmonidae), en lugar de tres familias como prefieren otros autores (especialmente en Europa). Las "nuevas" familias que se agregaron a la lista actual están explicadas en el Apéndice 1, y las notas que aparecen en el apéndice se presentan por lo general los casos en los que se decidió no adoptar los cambios sugeridos en algunas publicaciones.

Nombres Científicos

Los nombres científicos de especies y taxones superiores serán los constituidos de acuerdo con el Código Internacional de Nomenclatura Zoológica, un conjunto de reglas para la nomenclatura de los animales. Otros nombres, publicados o no, no están disponibles.

Nombres Comunes

Los nombres comunes de las especies tienen una larga historia que excede en tiempo a la de los nombres científicos. Mientras sigan siendo utilizados por el público y los biólogos, es necesario tener un sistema estandarizado y efectivo para los mismos. El comité ha desarrollado una base de nombres comunes (un único nombre en inglés para todas las especies incluidas y un único nombre en español y/o francés para las especies que están presentes en México y/o Canadá), que refleja un amplio uso y promueva la estabilidad y universalidad de los nombres asignados a peces de Norteamérica.

Los nombres comunes para peces, como se usan en esta lista, se asignan a especies de forma individual. Algunas veces esos nombres son empleados como "nombres de mercado". Sin embargo, esos nombres de mercado muy a menudo se asignan a varias especies. En el interés de que haya un público informado, enfáticamente sugerimos que se adopten los nombres comunes aquí presentados, ya sea por autores, comerciantes u otros, aún si se piensa que un nombre es poco llamativo (e.g., desalentamos el uso del nombre regional "lisa" ["mullet" en inglés] en lugar de matalote para miembros de la familia Catostomidae). Un resumen de los nombres comerciales en inglés, así como se les asigna a los peces (e invertebrados) que se venden en los Estados Unidos, se encuentra disponible en *Guidance for Industry: The Seafood List—FDA's Guide to Acceptable Market Names for Seafood Sold in Interstate Commerce*, 1993, revised 2009, United States Food and Drug Administration (ver www.fda.gov/Food/GuidanceComplianceRegulatoryInformation/GuidanceDocuments/Seafood/ucm113260). En la presente lista, muchos nombres difieren de aquellos utilizados en las publicaciones de la Organización de las Naciones Unidas para la Agricultura y la Alimentación (FAO). Esperamos que en el futuro exista un mayor acuerdo.

El nombre común, de la manera en que se emplea aquí, es visto como un apelativo formal para ser utilizado en lugar del nombre científico de una especie. Enfatizamos que los nombres comunes no llevan la intención de duplicar el poder de los nombres científicos en reflejar las relaciones filogenéticas (ver el principio 8 más adelante). La historia ha mostrado que a menudo los nombres comunes tienen más estabilidad que los nombres científicos.

Los nombres comunes son más fácilmente adaptables al uso popular que los nombres científicos. Existe una clara necesidad para la estandarización y uniformidad en los nombres vernáculos, no sólo para peces comerciales o de pesca deportiva, sino también para peces de acuarios y los de venta en los mercados, en documentos legales, y como sustitutos para nombres científicos en escritos científicos y populares. Unos cuantos nombres en español, recientemente agregados a la lista de 2004, requirieron cambios que reflejan su uso actual.

El proporcionar nombres comunes en francés para todos los peces presentes en Canadá,

tanto marinos como de agua dulce, requiere un conocimiento de la composición de la fauna íctica en agua dulce y porciones canadienses de los océanos Ártico, Atlántico y Pacífico. Debido a que ese conocimiento no está sólo en una referencia, la lista de especies dulceacuícolas y marinas fueron recopiladas. La lista de especies de agua dulce fue obtenida principalmente del inventario no publicado en el proyecto Estado General de Especies en Canadá, terminado en 2005 (www.wildspecies.ca). La lista para las especies del Océano Ártico fue recopilada principalmente de Mecklenburg et al. (2002, 2011) y Coad y Reist (2004). Las listas para especies canadienses que inciden en los océanos Atlántico y Pacífico se formaron con base en el inventario no publicado del proyecto de Estado General de Especies en Canadá, terminado en 2005 y complementado extensamente por datos de la Colección de Referencia del Atlántico, Museo Canadiense de la Naturaleza, Pesquerías y Océanos de Canadá, Museo Real de Columbia Británica y el Museo Real de Ontario. Los nombres comunes en francés para peces dulceacuícolas se formaron a partir de la lista de 2004, Scott y Crossman (1973) y D. E. McAllister (1990, *Una lista de peces de Canadá/Liste des poissons du Canada*, Syllogeus 64). Los nombres comunes en francés para las especies marinas se hicieron con base en el proyecto de Estado General de Especies en Canadá, terminado en 2005 (lista no publicada) (www.wildspecies.ca) y extensamente complementado por B.W. Coad (1995, *Enciclopedia de peces canadienses*, Museo Canadiense de la Naturaleza y Producciones canadienses de pesca deportiva, Ottawa) y FishBase (www.fishbase.org). Para las especies que no se encontró el nombre común en francés, por lo general se tradujeron los nombres comunes del inglés. Todos los nombres comunes en francés fueron revisados por C. Renaud y P. Dumont.

Varias especies tienen nombres comunes en inglés derivados directamente de los nombres en español, tal y como se usan en México y llevan acento donde es requerido. El comité estuvo dividido en sus opiniones al querer tomar una decisión acerca de si esos nombres deberían ser "automáticamente adaptados al inglés" y ya no escribir el acento, o considerarlas como palabras en español inmersas en (transferidas a) un nombre común en inglés. Se concluyó que algunos nombres geográficos—basados en una amplia inserción en el idioma inglés—pueden ser considerados ya adaptados al inglés (e. g., Yucatan en lugar de Yucatán; Rio Grande en lugar de Río Grande) mientras que otros términos, que no se usan comúnmente en inglés, no están automáticamente adaptados al inglés. Para entender el significado de los acentos de las palabras en español (que tienen diferente significado en las palabras en francés), proporcionamos la siguiente guía para permitir la pronunciación correcta de los nombres comunes en inglés que contienen nombres derivados de lugares geográficos en México. Cuando se pronuncian palabras en español sin acento que terminan en las consonantes "n" o "s", como es generalmente el caso, el énfasis recae en la penúltima sílaba (en la penúltima vocal, e.g., Bravo), mientras que las palabras que terminan en una consonante distinta a "n" o "s", el énfasis recae en la última sílaba. Las palabras que no siguen esta regla llevan acento escrito sobre la vocal de la sílaba que se enfatiza (casi siempre la última, e.g., Zirahuén, Michoacán). Como se especifica arriba, aquellos nombres comunes en inglés considerados como adaptados al inglés del español no tienen acento escrito, aunque lo lleven en español, porque tales marcas de puntuación no son una convención del idioma inglés. La guía para la pronunciación en inglés debería ser con base a como se escribe en español, así para *Poeciliopsis scarlli*, la regla para este nombre común en español, "guatopote michoacano" (sin acento escrito para este adjetivo), será el colocar el acento sobre la penúltima sílaba en michoacano (sobre la vocal "a"). El mismo énfasis debe ejercerse en el nombre derivado para inglés (pero, debido a las diferencias de escritura, sobre la última "a", como Michoacán Livebearer). Se dan abajo ejemplos de otras sílabas—aparte de las mencionadas anteriormente—donde debe ser enfatizada la pronunciación. Las especies con el nombre común en inglés, derivados de algún nombre geográfico de México, que tienen acento en la última sílaba (acento escrito en la última vocal) incluyen Lacandón Sea Catfish, Tamesí Molly, y el Michoacán Livebearer. Especies con nombre común en inglés derivados de algún lugar geográfico de México, que tienen acento en la tercera sílaba (a la última) incluyen San Jerónimo Livebearer y Cuatro Ciénegas Platyfish.

Se necesita llegar rápidamente a un acuerdo sobre muchos nombres comunes, pero por complicaciones otros han sido atendidos. El desacuerdo al respecto es particularmente común para los peces que se conocen por sus nombres de mercado, y estos difieren de aquellos más familiares para pescadores deportivos, biólogos y otros (e.g., lo que se conoce comúnmente como "huachinango rojo", que en muchos lugares costeros en la costa Pacífica de habla inglesa puede ser una especie de *Sebastes* [rocotes] y no una especie de los verdaderos huachinangos del género *Lutjanus*). Las dificultades que crea el usar varios nombres para una misma especie que está presente en diferentes partes, parecen poder resolverse sólo a través de arbitraje. Por el contrario, un nombre dado puede ser usado para diferentes especies en distintos lugares (como el ejemplo para el huachinango rojo). Aún cuando la acción emprendida por el comité en dichas situaciones no puede provocar un cambio local rápido, es contraproducente el acreditar el uso de un nombre para dos o más especies. Creemos enfáticamente que los usuarios de nombres comunes de peces quedarán mal informados y tal vez confundidos, si los nombres se usan de manera inconsistente.

Después de debatir con los nombres comunes por muchos años, uno de los Comités de Nombres de Peces anteriores se dio cuenta de la importancia de establecer una serie de principios rectores para la selección de nombres comunes. Tal regla permite una valoración más objetiva de los méritos relativos de varios nombres, que si la nominación estuviera basada principalmente en la experiencia y preferencia personal. La consideración de muchos nombres vernáculos de peces hace aparente que puedan establecerse pocos principios para los cuales no habría excepciones. Existen muchas excepciones, debido a que para el tiempo en que el comité comenzó a trabajar, la mayoría de las especies grandes y más abundantes en los Estados Unidos tenía nombres comunes solidamente establecidos que hubiera sido absurdo rechazarlos sólo para acomodarlos a una nueva serie de principios. Muy a menudo, el nombre para una especie puede ser decidido ponderando los pros y los contras entre las opciones probables y seleccionar la que mejor se ajuste a la guía de criterios. Más adelante, con algunas modificaciones, se repiten los criterios (de listas previas) considerados por el comité como los apropiados a seguir para la selección de nombres comunes de peces.

Principios que Rigen la Selección de Nombres Comunes

1. *Un solo nombre vernáculo para cada especie debe ser aceptado en cada idioma.* En la edición de 1991, sólo para un pez, *Coregonus artedi*, se aceptaron dos nombres comunes; en la lista de 2004 y en la presente edición no se hacen excepciones.

2. *No puede haber dos especies en la lista con el mismo nombre común.* En lo posible, debe evitarse el uso de nombres de especies fuera de los límites de nuestra área de cobertura.

3. *Debe evitarse el uso de la palabra "común" (o su equivalente en inglés o francés) como parte del nombre de un pez.* Algunas excepciones (por tiempo de uso) se hacen en el caso de Common Carp/carpa común, Common Shiner, tiburón zorro común, cazón espinoso común y aiguillat commun.

4. *Se favorecen los nombres simples.* Se omitirán los guiones y los apóstrofes para los nombres de peces en inglés y español (e.g., Smallmouth Bass, gobio lomopintado), a menos de que sea esencial para su ortografía (e.g., Three-eye Flounder), o tengan significado especial (e.g., C-O Sole, pargo azul-dorado, chac-chi), o sean necesarias para evitar malos entendidos (e.g., Cusk-eel), o cuando en un solo nombre se unan dos nombres de peces, ninguno de los cuales representa al pez en cuestión (e.g., Trout-perch, que no es ni trucha [trout] ni perca [perch]). Las palabras calificativas compuestas, especialmente en inglés, que incluyen la definición de estructuras pareadas como una mancha a cada lado del pedúnculo caudal, deberían ser usualmente consideradas como sustantivos simples impositivos a un nombre grupal (e.g., Spottail Shiner, ronco rayadillo), pero un calificativo plural debe ser escrito como adjetivo (e.g., Spotted Hake, Blackbanded Sunfish, gobio punteado) a menos de que su

origen plural sea obvio (e.g., Fourspot Flounder). Se dará preferencia a los nombres que sean cortos y fonéticos. La composición de palabras familiares cortas en un único nombre, escritos sin un guión, puede en algunos casos reflejar claridad y simpleza especialmente en inglés (e.g., Tomcod, Goldfish, Mudminnow), de manera que deben evitarse el uso de palabras compuestas, especialmente aquellas largas, poco prácticas o poco comunes.

5. *Los nombres comunes en inglés deben escribirse con mayúscula.* La primera letra en cada palabra en el nombre común debe ir con mayúscula excepto después de un guión, a menos de que la palabra deba escribirse con mayúscula, como sustantivo propio (e.g., Pit-Klamath Brook Lamprey, Raggedtooth Shark, Atlantic Salmon, pero Dusky Cusk-eel, Tropical Two-wing Flyingfish, Northern Rock Sole). Este es un cambio a las ediciones previas. Los nombres comunes para taxones superiores al nivel de especie no son afectados (e.g., Pacific salmons, temperate basses). Se coloca un superíndice (^) en la lista después de los nombres comunes en inglés que contienen un nombre propio (o una palabra considerada como nombre en la lista de 2004, como "Gulf", donde se implica un golfo en especifico) que siempre se requiere escribir con mayúscula. Esta anotación será útil para algunos usuarios, porque en ciertas ocasiones no está claro en las listas pasadas cuáles nombres llevan un nombre propio (e.g., Buffalo darter, Strawberry darter, y Warrior darter) y cuáles no (e.g., colorado snapper y warsaw grouper).

6. *Se desalienta el uso de nombres que tengan la intención de honrar personas* (e.g., los nombres usados originalmente, Allison's tuna, Julia's darter, Meek's halfbeak) *debido a que carecen de valor descriptivo.* Sin embargo, en algunos casos, los patronímicos se aceptan ya que han sido utilizados ampliamente (e.g., Guppy, Lane Snapper). Este principio no rige para los nombres comunes en francés (e.g., el nombre común para *Liparis coheni* es limace de Cohen). Aunque para los casos en los

que no había una "prioridad" establecida para un nombre común de un patronímico, se escogió un nombre común alternativo.

7. *Las subespecies no deben tener nombres comunes.* Así como para la edición de 2004, no presentamos nombres científicos o comunes para las subespecies. Aún así, reconocemos que las subspecies, con su propia historia evolutiva en alopatría, tienen importancia en los estudios evolutivos y puede dárseles una categoría especial de protección y ser aceptadas como tales en estudios de diversidad. Algunas subespecies son tan diferentes en apariencia (no sólo en distribución geográfica) que son fácilmente distinguidas y existen los nombres comunes para esas poblaciones, constituyendo una importante ayuda en comunicación.

Generalmente, no se les asigna un nombre común a los híbridos, pero aquellos que son relevantes para el manejo pesquero y que tienen nombres comunes establecidos se abordan en el Apéndice (Appendix) 2. Las variedades cultivadas, fases de coloración, y variantes morfológicas no se nombran, aún cuando puedan ser importantes en intercambio comercial y cultivos para el comercio de peces de ornato (e.g., las muchas variedades de carpa dorada y carpa común, las fases de color de manchado versus dorado de la cabrilla sardinera y botete aletas punteadas).

8. *El nombre común no necesita estar vinculado al nombre científico.* Los cambios periódicos y necesarios en la nomenclatura científica no necesariamente requieren el cambio de los nombres comunes. La práctica de asignar un nombre común a un género y un nombre compuesto para cada especie además de otro compuesto para cada subespecie, mientras se busca simplificarlo, tiene el defecto de la rigidez, y el riesgo de no reconocer a un pez al desechar lo que sería un nombre perfecto y tradicionalmente utilizado. Dicha práctica es un intento para recrear—en los nombres comunes—la nomenclatura científica. Si una especie es transferida de un género a otro, o una subespecie es cambiada a nivel de especie en la literatura ictiológica y así se registra en la lista, el nombre común permanecerá sin cambio. Los nombres comunes no tienen el propósito prioritario de indicar tipos de relación. Este principio sigue siendo malentendido o rechazado por aquellos que abogan que los nombres comunes de todos los miembros de un género deberían incluir la(s) misma(s) palabra(s) raíz (e.g., que todos los *Oncorhynchus* deben ser llamados salmón, como "salmón arcoiris" en lugar de trucha arcoíris). La estabilidad de los nombres comunes sobrepasa cualquier ventaja que pueda ganarse en estricto apego a vincular los nombres comunes a los científicos. Cuando se establece que dos o más taxones (e.g., especies nominales) son idénticos (sinónimos), debe adoptarse un solo nombre grupal. Ver también el principio 13.

9. *Los nombres no deben violar las reglas del buen gusto (i.e., no deben contener palabras ofensivas).* Nuestros cambios a los nombres en inglés de squawfish a pikeminnow para especies de *Ptychocheilus*, y de jewfish a goliath grouper, fueron hechos en la lista de 2004, siguiendo este principio.

Los principios precedentes son meramente de procedimiento. Los siguientes descritos ayudan a la selección de nombres adecuados.

10. *Los nombres de coloración, románticos, elegantes, metafóricos y con cualquier otro elemento distintivo y original son particularmente adecuados.* Tal terminología agrega riqueza y amplía la nomenclatura, proveyendo satisfacción al usario. Algunos ejemplos de tales nombres en inglés incluyen Madtom, Dolly Varden, Midshipman, Chilipepper, Pumpkinseed, Flier, Angelfish, Moorish Idol y Hogchoker; en español encontramos bruja, guitarra, chucho y lacha; y en francés están tête-de-boule, ventre citron, y truite fardée.

11. *Los nombres comunes nativos norteamericanos o modificaciones de los mismos se aceptan como nombres comunes.* Algunos en uso vigente son Menhaden, Eulachon, Cisco, Chinook Salmon, Mummichog, Tautog, puyeki y totoaba.

12. *Independientemente del origen, los verdaderos nombres vernáculos utilizados ampliamente y en uso común por el público, deben retenerse hasta donde sea posible.* Muchos nombres bien conocidos de peces, utilizados al norte de México, incorporan (han acuñado) palabras en español o modificaciones de las mismas, e.g., barracuda, cero, mojarra, pompano (de pámpano) y sierra. Ejemplos en otros idiomas son capelin (francés), bocaccio (italiano) y mako (maorí). La mayoría de estos comprenden los principios 14 y 15 escritos más adelante.

13. *A los nombres comúnmente empleados y adoptados del inglés tradicional* (e.g., chub, minnow, trout, bass, perch, sole, flounder)*, español* (e.g., cazón, sardina, carpa, mojarra, perca, lenguado)*, o del francés* (e.g., méné y perche) *se les da mucha laxitud en cuanto a su posición taxonómica.* Se prefiere el apego al uso histórico, si éste no causa conflicto con el uso amplio y generalizado de otro nombre. Muchos nombres han sido asignados a peces de Norteamérica con apariencias semejantes, pero frecuentemente sin relaciones. Por ejemplo, encontramos "bass" y "lenguado" para representantes de varias familias de peces, y "perch" y "perca" para muchos más. "Chub" aparece en grupos sin relación como Cyprinidae y Kyphosidae, y "mojarra" en Cichlidae, Gerreidae y otras familias. El pez Ocean Whitefish o pierna, *Caulolatilus princeps*, algunas veces referido como "salmón" en el noroeste de México, no es un salmónido, y el Pacific Pompano (palometa plateado en español), *Peprilus simillimus*, no es un carángido (como otras especies llamadas pompanos), aun así cada uno es bien conocido por los pescadores en su área de distribución por el nombre indicado. Para especies ampliamente conocidas, es preferible aceptar el uso generalizado de un nombre. La práctica establecida del uso general de un nombre debería considerarse prioritario sobre los intentos de consistencia. Esto no es bien asimilado por algunos ictiólogos que sienten que "perch" no debería ser utilizado para un embiotócido, "trout" para un *Salvelinus*, "sardinita" para un carácido, o "ca-

zón" para un carcarínido. Algunos problemas se han evitado o minimizado al unir nombres en inglés para crear nuevas palabras (e.g., seatrout para sea trout, mudsucker para mud sucker, surfperch para surf perch); dichas combinaciones han tenido una gran aceptación desde su adopción en listas anteriores.

14. *Los atributos morfológicos, color y patrones de color, son elementos deseables para asignación de nombres y son comúnmente usados.* Sailfin, flathead, slippery, giant, mottled, copper, tripletail en inglés; chato, jorobado, bocón, gigante, jabonero, pinto, cobrizo en español; y citron, cuivré, fardé, y fossettes en francés, y una multitud de otras características descriptivas decoran los nombres de peces. Deben hacerse esfuerzos por seleccionar términos que describan con precisión y mantener al mínimo la repetición de aquellos que se emplean más frecuentemente: (e.g., white [blanco, blanc], black [negro, noir], spotted [manchado, tacheté], y banded [rayado/de cintas, barré]). Siguiendo la tradición para nombres en inglés en la ictiología y herpetología americana y canadiense, hemos intentado restringir el uso de "line" (línea) o "stripe" (raya) para indicar marcas longitudinales paralelas al eje corporal, y "bar" (barra) o "band" (banda) para indicar marcas transversales o verticales. Sin embargo, tal tradición no se aplica para nombres en español como se utilizan en México, donde el término "rayado/rayada" muy a menudo se adopta para indicar esas marcas.

15. *Características ecológicas son elementos deseables para la asignación de nombres.* Tales términos deben ser estrictamente descriptivos. Los sustantivos en inglés (español, francés) como reef (arrecifal, récif), coral (coralino, corail), sand (arenoso, sable), rock (piedrero, roche), lake (de lago, lac), fresh water (dulceacuícola, dulcicole), y mountain (montaña, montagne) son bien conocidos en nombres de peces.

16. *La distribución geográfica proporciona adjetivos calificativos adecuados.* Caracterizaciones geográficas pobres o engañosas deben ser corregidas, a menos de que

los nombres que las contengan estén sumamente enraizados en el uso popular (e.g., "Kentucky Bass" para una especie con una muy amplia distribución). En aras de que haya estabilidad, se han mantenido algunos de esos nombres (e.g., Alaska Blackfish, aún cuando la especie se encuentre también en Rusia; guatopote de Sonora, aún cuando se presenta fuera del estado de Sonora). Para hacerlos breves, generalmente es posible borrar palabras como lake (lago, lac), river (río, fleuve), gulf (golfo, golfe), o sea (mar, mer), en los nombres de especies (e.g., Colorado Pikeminnow, en lugar de "Colorado River Pikeminnow"; topote del Balsas en lugar de "topote del Río Balsas").

17. *Los nombres científicos para géneros pueden ser empleados directamente como nombres comunes* (e.g., gambusia, remora, anchoa, brótula, guavina) *o en formas modificadas* (e.g., molly, de *Mollienesia).* Una vez adoptados, dichos nombres deben mantenerse, aún si el nombre del género o el nombre científico de un nivel superior se cambia posteriormente. Esos nombres vernáculos se escriben en letra normal (i.e., no en cursiva, como se escribe el nombre científico del género).

18. *Si es posible, debe evitarse el duplicado de nombres comunes para peces y otros organismos, aunque los nombres con un uso generalizado no deben rechazarse sólo por esta razón.* Por ejemplo, "búfalo" ("buffalo") se emplea para varios mamíferos artiodáctilos y para matalotes catostómidos del género *Ictiobus,* "zorro" se usa para tiburones alópidos, y "mariposa" se usa para peces quetodóntidos (Chaetodontidae) y rayas del género *Gymnura.* Con fundamento en la dominancia de su uso, tales nombres son admisibles sin modificación como nombres para peces.

Relación de los Nombres Comunes y Científicos de las Especies

El objetivo de esta lista es para sugerir nombres comunes y para proporcionar los nombres científicos generalmente aceptados para todas las especies que inciden dentro de los límites geográficos considerados. Los nombres comunes pueden establecerse por acuerdo general. Por otro lado, los nombres científicos cambiarán según el avance en el conocimiento de las relaciones filogenéticas de las especies y de acuerdo con la visión de los taxónomos. La nomenclatura científica utilizada ha sido revisada cuidadosamente con relación a la ortografía, autoridad y año de descripción original. Enfatizamos que hay muchos grupos de peces para los cuales hay desacuerdos para su clasificación, o cuya clasificación es poco conocida. Así también, existen diferencias de opinión subjetivas entre los investigadores al asignar jerarquías para los taxones (ver discusiones en las secciones "Nombres de Familia", "Nombres Comunes", y particularmente el principio 8).

Formato de la Lista

La lista está ordenada en una secuencia filogenética de familias de peces Recientes, como es generalmente entendida. El arreglo de clases, órdenes y familias es generalmente con base a lo presentado por Nelson (2006), pero algunos cambios reflejan algunos resultados de estudios sistemáticos recientes. En la mayoría de los casos damos un nombre común individual para cada familia en inglés, español y francés. Sin embargo, ocasionalmente se dan dos nombres (y raramente tres) cuando el uso común así lo amerita. La ortografía de los autores de los nombres científicos siguen lo indicado por W. N. Eschmeyer (ed.), *Catálogo de Peces,* versión electrónica, http://research.calacademy. org/ichthyology/catalog/fishcatmain.asp.

Dentro de las familias, los géneros y especies se enlistan alfabéticamente. La parte I (que es la parte principal) de la lista consiste de cinco columnas: el nombre científico, los áreas de incidencia, el nombre común en inglés (independientemente del área de incidencia), el nombre común en español para las especies que inciden en México, y el nombre común en francés para las especies que inciden en Canadá.

Se siguió la última edición (cuarta) del Código Internacional de Nomenclatura Zoológica, 1999 (referido abajo como el "Código"; www. nhm.ac.uk/hosted-sites/iczn/code/) y se empleó la ortografía original de los nombres de las especies. En consecuencia, las terminaciones de algunos nombres patronímicos se cambiaron a *i* o *ii,* como correspondiera. En esta edición de la lista, continuamos poniendo después del nombre científico, el autor/los autores y el año de la publicación de la descripción original de la especie. Los autores y las fechas se necesitan a menudo, debido a que hay personas que no tienen un rápido acceso a la literatura original. Las determinaciones del autor y el año de publicación correctos pueden resultar complicadas, particularmente para aquellos nombres propuestos antes de 1900. La justificación para la ortografía en los nombres de Delaroche, Forsskål, Lacepède y Lesueur se explicó en las ediciones tercera (pág. 5) y cuarta (pág. 8) de la lista. La atribución de los nombres propuestos en M. E. Blochii Systema ichthyologiae, 1801, por J. G. Schneider se explicó en la cuarta edición (pág. 8).

La utilización del nombre de los autores refleja la interpretación actual del Código. En sintonía con estas reglas, el nombre de los autores sigue inmediatamente del nombre específico (escrito en cursiva). Si la especie, cuando fue descrita originalmente, fue asignada al mismo género que se asigna aquí, el nombre del (los) autor(es) no está entre paréntesis; si cuando se describió fue puesta en otro género, el nombre del (los) autor(es) está entre paréntesis. El año de publicación está separado del autor por una coma (y si se tiene paréntesis, el año está dentro de él). Por ejemplo, Mitchill originalmente nombró la trucha de arroyo, *Salmo fontinalis*, en un trabajo publicado en 1814; aquí aparece como *Salvelinus fontinalis* (Mitchill, 1814). Como se aprecia en la edición de 2004, no se anota el autor entre paréntesis en los casos donde el nombre grupal de la especie originalmente fue combinada con una ortografía incorrecta o una corrección injustificada del nombre genérico, aún cuando una corrección injustificada es un nombre disponible con su propia autoría y fecha (Artículo 51.3.1 del Código). Por lo tanto, al igual que en la edición de 2004, no se usan paréntesis para las especies descritas originalmente en los géneros *Rhinobatus* (hoy *Rhinobatos*), *Raia* (hoy *Raja*), *Lepidosteus* (hoy *Lepisosteus*), *Ophichthys* (hoy *Ophichthus*), *Nototropis* (hoy *Notropis*), *Amiurus* (hoy *Ameiurus*), *Hemirhamphus* (hoy *Hemiramphus*), *Opisthognathus* (hoy *Opistognathus*), y *Pomadasis* (hoy *Pomadasys*). Se debe ser cauteloso con la ortografía, porque la misma puede haber

aparecido como una corrección injustificada, o como una ortografía válida independiente.

Desde que se publicó la sexta edición en 2004, muchos usuarios han comunicado al comité sus sugerencias de cambios, y cada sugerencia fue considerada mientras se preparaba la presente edición. Se le dio la más alta prioridad a la estabilidad en los nombres comunes y los cambios realizados se hicieron sólo por razones sustanciales. El conocimiento científico sobre peces ha avanzado rápidamente desde la última edición, con la descripción de muchas especies nuevas, muchas especies adicionales registradas en Norteamérica y numerosas revisiones sistemáticas/taxonómicas publicadas. En la lista presente, todos los registros nuevos y todos los que se derivan en cualquier forma (nombre científico, autor(es), año de descripción, incidencia, y nombre común) de la edición 2004 están precedidas por un asterisco (*). La información que describe y explica un cambio para cada registro se encuentra en el Apéndice 1, identificado por el número de página en la que aparece el nombre en la lista principal. La información proporcionada anteriormente en el Apéndice 1 de las listas de 1970, 1980, 1991 y 2004 (págs. 65-87, 68-92, 71-96, y 187-253, respectivamente) que documentan los cambios realizados entre las ediciones 2 y 3; entre la 3 y la 4; entre la 4 y la 5; y entre la 5 y la 6, por lo general no se repite en esta edición.

Un signo de más (+) antes de un registro, indica que, no obstante que el registro no ha cambiado, se encontrará un comentario bajo ese nombre en el Apéndice 1. Esto incluye los taxones por arriba del nivel de especie (e.g., familia y orden) donde el nombre permanece sin cambio, pero la composición del taxón difiere del de la edición 2004 (por eliminación de taxones o transferencias de otros taxones superiores).

Aún cuando la mayoría de las decisiones del comité han sido unánimes, en diversas ocasiones se hicieron por voto mayoritario, por lo tanto no todos los miembros del comité se suscriben a las decisiones tomadas. Entendemos que no todas las decisiones serán aceptadas por todos los colegas, pero esperamos que todos los usuarios valoren nuestro esfuerzo. En muchos casos, la información accesible al comité excedió a lo que se encuentra disponible en la literatura y se debatió frecuentemente para tomar decisiones con relación a la inclusión de dicha información, por lo que ha sido muy cauteloso al efectuar cambios.

Índice

El Índice incluye nombres científicos y nombres comunes en los tres idiomas. Las páginas de referencia se dan para los nombres comunes aquí adoptados para familias y especies. Se proporciona un registro individual para cada especie; por ejemplo, Brook Trout se registra sólo como "Trout, Brook", y trucha de arroyo como "trucha, de arroyo".

Se proporcionan páginas de referencia para los nombres científicos de clases, órdenes, familias, géneros y especies. Cada especie está registrada sólo bajo su nombre científico específico. Por ejemplo, *Sciaenops ocellatus* puede ser localizado sólo como "*ocellatus, Sciaenops*", aunque el registro de *Sciaenops* llevará al lector a la página donde comienzan los registros del género. Los nombres científicos de las especies que no están aceptadas para la presente lista generalmente se excluyen del Índice, excepto por aquellos que aparecieron en la edición de 2004 (sexta edición) y que desde entonces se han colocado como sinónimos, como explicados para dichos casos en el Apéndice 1.

Agradecimientos

Esta lista es el resultado de más de siete décadas de aportes de los numerosos miembros pasados y presentes del Comité de Nombres de Peces. Por lo tanto se reconoce a los miembros pasados de este comité con quienes estamos en deuda. Muchas contribuciones fueron hechas también por muchos especialistas, que ayudaron en la segunda, tercera, cuarta, quinta y sexta ediciones en donde se agradeció su inapreciable ayuda.

En la preparación de la lista para esta edición, hemos recibido asistencia y asesoramiento con los nombres y literatura de muchas personas. Estamos en deuda especialmente con quienes participaron en las reuniones del comité, auspiciadas anualmente por la Sociedad Americana de Ictiólogos y Herpetólogos (American Society of Ichthyologists and Herpetologists), incluidos: William D. Anderson, Jr., George H. Burgess, Bruce B. Collette, Matthew T. Craig, William N. Eschmeyer, Karsten E. Hartel, John F. Morrissey, Robert H. Robins, Juan Jacobo Schmitter-Soto, Gerald R. Smith, W. Leo Smith, William F. Smith-Vaniz, Harold J. Walker, Jr. y James D. Williams.

Tantos individuos nos han asistido en nuestra tarea que es imposible nombrarlos a todos. Sin embargo, algunos nos han prestado una ayuda valiosa y merecen una mención especial: Arturo Acero P., Eduardo Balart, Carole Baldwin, Henry L. Bart, Jr., Richard J. Beamish, Hugues Benoit, D. A. Boguski, Brian W. Bowen, George H. Burgess, Mary Burridge, Brooks M. Burr, Gregor M. Cailliet, Kent E. Carpenter, Martin Castonguay, el recién fallecido José Luis Castro-Aguirre, David Catania, Don Clark, Brian Coad, Bruce B. Collette, el desaparecido Salvador Contreras-Balderas, Lara Cooper, Walter R. Courtenay, Matthew T. Craig, Margaret F. Docker, Jean-Denis Dutil, William N. Eschmeyer, Richard F. Feeney, Moretta Frederick, Jon D. Fong, Patricia Fuentes M., Anthony C. Gill, Graham Gillespie, R. Grant Gilmore, Adrián González A., D. H. Goodman, David W. Greenfield, Gavin Hanke, Karsten E. Hartel, Philip A. Hastings, Philip C. Heemstra, Dean A. Hendrickson, Mysi D. Hoang, Leticia Huidobro C., Tomio Iwamoto, Robert E. Jenkins, G. David Johnson, Cynthia Klepadlo, Jeffrey M. Leis, Andrew Lewin, María de Lourdes Lozano V., Milton Love, Zachary P. Martin, Katherine Maslenikov, John E. McCosker, Catherine W. Mecklenburg, Roberta Miller, Randy Mooi, James A. Morris, Jr., John F. Morrissey, David A. Neely, Leo G. Nico, James W. Orr, Mauricia Pérez-Tello, Frank L. Pezold, Edward J. Pfeiler, Theodore W. Pietsch, Héctor G. Plascencia, Kyle R. Piller, Dennis Polack, Zachary Randall, Stewart B. Reid, James D. Reist, Claude B. Renaud, D. Ross Robertson, Robert H. Robins, Luiz A. Rocha, Dawn M. Roje, Richard H. Rosenblatt, Ramón Ruíz-Carus, Kate Rutherford, Juan Jacobo Schmitter-Soto, Pamela J. Schofield, Jeffery A. Seigel, Randal A. Singer, Gerald R. Smith, W. Leo Smith, William F. Smith-Vaniz, Wayne C. Starnes, J. D. Stelfox, Duane E. Stevenson, Camm C. Swift, Michael S. Taylor, Christine E. Thacker, Alfred W. Thomson, Luke Tornabene, Xavier Valencia D., Albert M. van der Heiden, James Van Tassell, Lou Van Guelpen, Harold J. Walker, Jr., Edward O. Wiley, James D. Williams, y Mark V. H. Wilson.

El financiamiento para viajes de los miembros del comité, para atender a las tres sesiones maratónicas de trabajo, fueron proporcionados por la Sociedad Americana de Pesquerías (American Fisheries Society). En 2009, la reunión se realizó en el Instituto de Biología, de la Universidad Nacional Autónoma de México, en la ciudad de México, anfitrión H. S. Espinosa-Pérez, miembro del comité. Esta reunión fue apoyada por la Directora T. María Pérez y R. Cordero B., L. Huidobro C. y X. Valencia D. En 2007 y 2010, las reuniones se llevaron a cabo en el Museo de Historia Natural de Florida, de la Universidad de Florida, en Gainesville, donde los anfitriones fueron los miembros del comité Carter R. Gilbert y Larry M. Page, con la asistencia de otros ictiólogos locales.

También queremos agradecer a nuestras instituciones por apoyar nuestros esfuerzos en este proyecto, a menudo incluyendo fondos para los viajes, ayuda secretarial, servicios de fotocopiados y servicio postal, y concediendo espacios de trabajo para los miembros del comité.

Agradecemos al personal de la Sociedad Americana de Pesquerías, especialmente Aaron Lerner y Ghassan (Gus) Rassam, quienes nos ayudaron en muchas formas. Estamos especialmente agradecidos por la ayuda dedicada y afable de Deborah Lehman. A lo largo de los años, los diversos presidentes y otros funcionarios de la Sociedad Americana de Pesquerías y de la Sociedad Americana de Ictiólogos y Herpetólogos nos han alentado continuamente.

Las secciones nuevas y revisadas de la Introducción fueron traducidas al español por Gabriela Montemayor y editadas por los miembros del comité Héctor Espinosa-Pérez y Lloyd Findley con la ayuda de Juan Jacobo Schmitter-Soto. La traducción de la introducción al francés se hizo con el apoyo de Pesca y Océanos de Canadá (Fisheries and Oceans Canada) realizada por Jacqueline Lanteigne, Claude Renaud y Johannie Duhaime. Se recibió mucha ayuda de Claude Renaud y Pierre Dumont, proporcionando nombres comunes en francés. Jesse Grosso, del Museo de Historia Natural de Florida, ayudó a organizar el manuscrito final.

En la siguiente Parte I, la lista principal, los siguientes signos y abreviaturas claves significan:

[1] **A** = Atlántico; **AM** = Atlántico México pero no registrado en Estados Unidos o Canadá; **Ar** = Océano Ártico; **F:C** = Agua dulce Canadá; **F:M** = Agua dulce México; **F:U** = Agua dulce Estados Unidos (estados contiguos y/o Alaska); **P** = Pacífico; **PM** = Pacífico México pero no registrados en Estados Unidos o Canadá; **[I]** = No-nativos (introducidas o invasoras) y establecidos en nuestra área; **[X]** = extinta; **[XN]** = extincta en la naturaleza pero mantenida en cautiverio.

[2] Nombres comunes en inglés proporcionados para todas las especies en la lista (algunos son adaptaciones del nombre en español para especies que se encuentran en México), nombres en español indican especies de agua dulce y marinas en México, y nombres en francés indican especies de agua dulce y marinas de Canadá (la cobertura es nacional, no sólo en Quebec como en la lista de 2004). **En-, Sp-,** y **Fr-** indican nombres de familia en inglés, español y francés, respectivamente.

* Cambio de la lista de 2004 (sexta edición) de nombre científico o nombre común o de distribución (presencia) aparte de la adición de "Ar" que es nuevo para esta edición; ver Apéndice (Appendix) 1 para explicación del cambio.

^ Este superíndice denota un nombre común en inglés que contiene un nombre proprio (o una palabra tratada en la lista de 2004 como un sustantivo propio como "Gulf" [Golfo]); véase el principio 5.

+ Ver Apéndice (Appendix) 1 para comentario.

INTRODUCTION

Ce livre constitue une liste exhaustive de toutes les espèces de poissons retrouvées au Canada, au Mexique et dans la partie continentale des États-Unis. Toutes les espèces, allant des poissons de petite taille, discrets ou rares aux poissons de grande taille faisant l'objet d'une pêche sportive ou commerciale, sont importantes pour documenter et comprendre la biodiversité du continent. Nombre d'espèces de poissons sont utilisées comme animaux de laboratoire, sont exposées ou gardées dans des aquariums publics ou privés, servent d'appâts ou sont traitées comme des objets d'étude en histoire naturelle ou d'attrait esthétique. Certaines espèces autrefois méprisées comme étant des poissons de rebut font aujourd'hui l'objet d'une pêche commerciale et se vendent à gros prix. Une sensibilisation accrue à l'environnement a mis dans la mire les poissons indigènes à titre d'indicateurs de l'état des écosystèmes dulçaquatiques et marins, comme en témoigne la fréquence à laquelle les espèces en voie de disparition font l'objet d'exposés dans les médias. La structure de ce livre devrait en faciliter l'utilisation par ceux ayant des intérêts particuliers.

La grande nouveauté de cette septième édition de la liste des noms vernaculaires et scientifiques est l'inclusion du nom vernaculaire français pour chacune des espèces retrouvées au Canada et non seulement pour celles retrouvées au Québec. Bien que ce changement occasionne la perte d'une liste à jour des espèces présentes au Québec, nous obtenons une liste de contrôle pour toutes les espèces du Canada (nous donnons un nom vernaculaire français pour les espèces retrouvées au Canada, tout comme nous donnons un nom vernaculaire espagnol pour les espèces retrouvées au Mexique). En outre, nous mentionnons pour la première fois, à la rubrique « Occurrence », les espèces retrouvées dans l'océan Arctique, dans les eaux continentales de l'Amérique du Nord.

Comme dans le cas des éditions précédentes, nous adhérons au principe de stabilité des noms vernaculaires, ne les changeant que pour les raisons spécifiques documentées à l'annexe 1. Comme dans le cas de la liste de 2004, nous tentons soigneusement de suivre le consensus général de ce que les spécialistes ont publié.

Lorsque les opinions sont divergentes, nous exposons généralement le fondement de notre décision à l'annexe 1. De plus, comme en 2004, nous réglons les divergences d'opinion des membres du Comité en votant après débat libre.

Des listes de poissons ont déjà été publiées en 1948, 1960, 1970, 1980, 1991 et 2004 (respectivement en tant que Publications spéciales 1, 2, 6, 12, 20 et 29 de l'American Fisheries Society). Ces listes ont été largement utilisées, et elles ont nettement contribué à l'uniformisation de l'usage des noms vernaculaires tout en permettant d'éviter la confusion dans les noms scientifiques. La présente liste recommande les noms scientifiques à utiliser et reflète ce qui nous semble être l'opinion actuelle des spécialistes des différents taxons. Des 570 entrées de la liste abrégée de 1948 (qui comportait essentiellement les poissons les mieux connus de la pêche sportive et commerciale et les espèces-fourrages), la liste est passée à 1 892 espèces en 1960, 2 131 en 1970, 2 268 en 1980, puis 2 428 en 1991 (au Canada et dans la partie continentale des États-Unis). La sixième édition (2004), de par l'inclusion de la faune ichtyocole du Mexique, comprenait 3 700 espèces, dont 3 694 poissons et six céphalocordés ("amphioxes") nouvellement ajoutés. La présente édition comprend 3 875 espèces.

Pour cette liste, comme pour celle de 2004, le Comité conjoint American Fisheries Society/American Society of Ichthyologists and Herpetologists [AFS/ASIH] sur les noms de poissons a tenté de fournir des noms vernaculaires pour toutes les espèces indigènes et pour les espèces introduites et établies dans la région couverte, même si ces dernières ne sont présentes que dans des zones très limitées. Le nombre d'espèces introduites présentes dans les eaux nord américaines, par suite de lâchers intentionnels ou accidentels, est en hausse constante. S'il n'existe aucune preuve qu'une espèce non indigène a établi une population reproductrice (même si elle a été capturée), cette espèce n'apparaît pas dans la liste. De plus, quelques espèces introduites jadis considérées comme étant établies en Amérique du Nord mais qui ne le sont plus n'apparaissent plus dans la liste. De l'information sur les poissons non indigènes des États-Unis et du Mexique se trouve respectivement à http://nas.er.usgs.gov/taxgroup/fish/default.asp et www.conabio.gob.mx/invasoras/index.php/Especies_invasoras_-_Peces. Les noms vernaculaires des quelques poissons hybrides qui jouent un rôle important dans la gestion des pêches ou dans les pêches sportives ou commerciales apparaissent à l'annexe 2.

La plupart des ajouts de cette septième édition sont le résultat de la description de nouvelles espèces et de l'extension des aires de répartition découvertes au cours des relevés de nos eaux douces et marines. Les aires de répartition dans l'océan Arctique sont basées sur un échantillonnage limité et, par suite d'autres études et des changements climatiques en cours, nous nous attendons à ce que la liste s'allonge. De récentes études systématiques et la révision, par le Comité sur les noms de poissons (ci après le « Comité », de décisions antérieures ont mené à la reconnaissance de noms d'espèce jusque là considérés comme des synonymes plus récents et, inversement, ont mené à la conclusion que certains noms d'espèce figurant dans les listes antérieures sont en fait des synonymes plus récents; ces derniers ont été retirés de la liste. Il reste de nombreux cas d'incertitude quant au niveau auquel doit être assigné un taxon particulier (espèce ou sous-espèce), particulièrement chez les familles Cyprinidae, Catostomidae et Salmonidae. Des divergences d'opinion peuvent apparaître entre des utilisateurs faisant appel à différents concepts de l'espèce et à différents types de preuves (p. ex. données morphologiques, génétiques, écologiques ou comportementales). En acceptant comme valides les noms d'espèces tirés de divers travaux (portant sur la faune ou la systématique), nous ne portons pratiquement pas de jugement sur les différents concepts de l'espèce des divers auteurs. Les taxons dont le statut est incertain sont traités au cas par cas. Si des recherches sont en cours sur la question, nous préférons attendre que les preuves soient publiées avant de prendre une décision. Le lecteur trouvera ci dessous, sous diverses rubriques, une analyse complémentaire de notre démarche.

Nous avons tenté d'établir une liste exhaustive de toutes les espèces de la zone couverte en Amérique du Nord, avec quelques exceptions. De nombreuses espèces dont le stade adulte a été trouvé uniquement au-delà de nos limites bathymétriques (profondeur de 200 m) et géographiques manifestent à leurs premiers stades de vie des formes qui ont été signalées dans les eaux de notre plateau continental. Ces espèces à l'état d'œufs ou de larves sont toutefois exclues de la liste, tout comme de nombreuses espèces mésopélagiques au stade adulte qui peuvent se retrouver à la bordure du plateau continental aux endroits où le talus est très proche du littoral. D'autres restrictions sont précisées dans la section qui suit.

Zone couverte

La présente édition inclut, autant qu'on sache, toutes les espèces de poissons reconnues comme ayant ou ayant jadis eu des populations reproductrices dans les eaux douces de la partie continentale du Canada, des États-Unis et du Mexique, ainsi que les espèces marines qui occupent (au stade adulte) les eaux littorales du plateau continental jusqu'à une profondeur de 200 m (656 pi). Nous avons exclu les espèces qui vivent seulement aux endroits au-delà du plateau continental où la profondeur dépasse 200 m, même si elles se retrouvent en eaux mésopélagiques à moins de 200 m de la surface. Les espèces présentes dans l'océan Arctique sont incluses. La limite sud de l'océan Arctique en Amérique du Nord est définie comme suivant le 61o de latitude nord de la pointe nord du Labrador au Groenland, dans l'océan Atlantique, et de allant de la pointe ouest de la péninsule de Seward jusqu'à la frontière américano russe dans le détroit de Béring, dans l'océan Pacifique. La liste des espèces présentes dans l'océan Arctique a été essentiellement compilée à partir des travaux de Mecklenburg et al. (2002, 2011) et de Coad et Reist (2004). À mesure que l'exploration de l'océan Arctique prendra de l'ampleur, des espèces additionnelles seront certainement recensées. Dans le même ordre d'idées, de nombreuses espèces connues dans les eaux situées au sud du Mexique vont certainement être signalées dans les eaux mexicaines dans l'avenir. C'est particulièrement le cas sur la façade atlantique, où de nombreuses espèces des eaux du Bélize n'ont pas encore été signalées dans les eaux mexicaines. De plus, plusieurs espèces dulcicoles du Bélize n'ont pas été signalées au Mexique.

Dans l'Atlantique, nous recensons tous les poissons côtiers du Groenland, de l'est du Canada, des États-Unis et du Mexique, y compris ceux qui se retrouvent dans le golfe du Mexique et la mer des Caraïbes vers le sud jusqu'à la frontière Mexique-Bélize. Les espèces des eaux de l'Islande, des Bermudes, des Bahamas, de Cuba et des autres îles des Antilles (Caraïbes) sont exclues, à moins qu'elles ne se retrouvent aussi dans la région couverte. Dans le Pacifique, nous recensons les espèces présentes dans la partie du plateau continental allant du détroit de Béring à la frontière Mexique-Guatémala, y compris l'archipel océanique de Revillagigedo et l'île de Guadalupe, jusqu'à une profondeur de 200 m dans les eaux littorales contiguës. Il est particulièrement difficile de déterminer quelles sont les espèces à inclure pour les îles océaniques dépourvues de plateau continental, où des espèces océaniques peuvent être trouvées près de la côte en compagnie d'espèces néritiques. Dans de tels cas, nous n'avons inclus que les espèces généralement considérées comme étant des espèces des eaux continentales. Les eaux des îles Hawaï et de l'atoll de Clipperton, qui abritent des faunes hautement endémiques et en grande partie à caractère indo-pacifique, sont exclues. Les poissons des grands fonds, qu'ils soient benthiques ou mésopélagiques, y compris les espèces qui pénètrent temporairement dans la zone épipélagique lors de leur migration verticale, ainsi que les poissons strictement océaniques, sont exclus, sauf s'ils semblent être plus que des spécimens qui se sont aventurés dans les eaux du plateau nord-américain. Dans la pratique, ce distinguo est souvent difficile à appliquer et devient par conséquent arbitraire. Nous incluons les poissons pélagiques trouvés régulièrement dans les eaux du plateau continental, mais nous excluons les espèces qui, dans les eaux de l'Amérique du Nord, sont connues pour vivre seulement à des profondeurs de plus de 200 m, même si elles ont été capturées ailleurs dans des zones où le fond se trouve à moins de 200 m de la surface. Les utilisateurs devront être prudents lorsqu'ils veulent établir la plage de profondeur occupée par une espèce. Par exemple, *Enchelycore anatina*, espèce communément observée dans l'est de l'Atlantique nettement au-dessus de 200 m, n'a été signalée dans l'ouest de l'Atlantique qu'à des profondeurs dépassant 200 m, et *Ophichthus menezesi*, qui a été décrite comme étant présente à une profondeur de 169 à 209 m au large du Brésil, n'a été observée dans le golfe du Mexique, au large de la Floride, qu'à des profondeurs de 1 200 à 1 400 m.

Les abréviations utilisées dans la liste donnent une idée générale des eaux où se retrouve telle espèce. Un « **A** » signifie l'océan Atlantique et s'étend jusqu'à la limite de l'océan Arctique (définie ci dessus), tandis que « **AM** » signale la présence dans l'Atlantique, dans les eaux du Mexique, mais pas dans celles du Canada ni des États-Unis. Un « **Ar** » dénote la présence dans l'océan Arctique (ces espèces, à l'exception des nouveaux ajouts, ont été recensées dans les éditions précédentes comme étant présentes dans le Pacifique ou l'Atlantique suivant qu'elles étaient présentes à l'ouest ou à l'est, respectivement, de la péninsule de Boothia, au Canada). Le « **P** » désigne l'océan Pacifique et s'étend jusqu'à la limite de l'océan Arctique, tandis que « **PM** » signale la présence dans l'océan Pacifique, dans les eaux du Mexique mais pas dans celles du Canada ni des États-Unis. Un « **F:** » indique la présence en eau douce ou d'autres eaux intérieures qui sont salées (p. ex. la mer de Salton, en Californie). Certaines espèces sont parfois ainsi désignées à cause de mentions historiques, comme c'est le cas pour *Elops affinis* dans le cours inférieur du Colorado et la mer de Salton. Une désignation « **F:** » suivie par un « **C** » dénote les eaux douces du Canada, tandis que « **M** » dénote les eaux douces du Mexique, et « **U** » les eaux douces des États-Unis (états contigus et/ou Alaska). Il faut noter que (1) les espèces marines connues sur une côte à une profondeur de moins de 201 m, mais sur l'autre côte à des profondeurs de plus de 200 m, sont indiquées seulement comme présentes sur la côte moins profonde (p. ex. *Notacanthus chemnitzii* est désignée comme « **A** » seulement, mais sa présence est connue au large de la Californie à des profondeurs de plus de 200 m); (2) même si une espèce peut être désignée comme présente en eau de mer et en eau douce, elle peut être principalement marine ou principalement dulcicole et n'est que rarement trouvée dans l'autre milieu; et (3) de nombreuses espèces non désignées par « **F** » ont été capturées à l'occasion en estuaire ou en eau douce.

L'abréviation « **[I]** » entre crochets suit la lettre indiquant les eaux où est présente une espèce introduite (non indigène) établie dans la zone couverte par la liste, et peut être utilisée séparément ou conjointement aux abréviations « A », « P », « F », « C », « U » et « M » (il s'agit d'espèces introduites dans la zone désignée par suite de l'activité humaine). Ce symbole n'est pas utilisé pour les introductions d'une espèce qui est indigène dans une zone désignée (p. ex. le transfert de *Salvelinus fontinalis* de l'est à l'ouest du Canada), mais est employé pour une espèce qui, introduite dans un pays, se disperse par la suite dans un autre pays (p. ex. *Scardinius erythrophthalmus*). Comme dans l'édition de 2004, nous indiquons le succès de l'introduction d'une espèce d'un océan à l'autre; par exemple, *Alosa sapidissima* et *Morone saxatilis*, espèces de l'Atlantique, ont été introduites avec succès dans les eaux du Pacifique, et leur présence est donc indiquée par la désignation « A-P[I]-F:CU ». Le symbole « **[X]** » entre crochets indique que l'espèce est considérée comme disparue. Des espèces signalées dans l'édition de 2004 qui existent encore mais sont connues seulement par des mentions historiques dans une partie de leur ancienne aire de répartition, et ont probablement, à l'heure actuelle, disparu du Canada ou des États-Unis, sont encore inscrites dans la liste; par exemple, *Erimystax x-punctatus* n'existe plus au Canada, mais se retrouve aux États-Unis et est donc désignée comme « F:CU »; *Catostomus bernardini* n'existe plus à l'état indigène aux États-Unis, mais se retrouve au Mexique et est donc désignée comme « F:UM ». Le symbole « **[XN]** » entre crochets indique que l'espèce est considérée comme disparue du milieu naturel mais est maintenue en captivité. Les espèces désignées « A » ou « P » et portant un nom espagnol et/ou français se retrouvent dans les eaux des États-Unis, du Mexique et/ou du Canada.

La séquence de lettres codées dénotant la distribution des espèces présentes dans les habitats marins et d'eau douce peuvent différer, dans quelques cas, comparativement à celles affichées dans la liste de 2004. La différenciation des espèces d'eau douce canadiennes et américaines ainsi que l'addition d'espèces marines et d'eau douce du Mexique à la liste de 2004 a mené à l'utilisation de trois lettres correspondantes (C, U, M), qui sont souvent utilisées en combinaison et résultant ainsi en des codes de distribution complexes. Ceci c'est également compliqué au niveau de la présente liste par l'addition d'une catégorie arctique [Ar]. Afin de simplifier les codes de distribution, les occurrences sont maintenant codées selon la séquence suivante: A-P-Ar-F:CUM. Par exemple, *Oncorhynchus mykiss* était, selon la liste de 1991, codé en tant que A-F-P, codé en tant que A[I]-F:CUM-P au sein de la liste 2004 et maintenant codé en tant que A[I]-P-F:CUM dans la présente liste.

Noms de famille

Les noms des familles sont importants pour l'identification et la recherche d'information. Ils sont couramment employés dans la littérature scientifique, dans les ouvrages de vulgarisation sur les poissons, dans les dictionnaires et les encyclopédies. Bien que quelques noms de famille apparaissant dans des éditions précédentes de cette liste aient été mis en synonymie, la présente liste reflète une augmentation dans le nombre de familles reconnues par rapport à l'édition de 2004. Nous acceptons les changements dans la composition de certaines familles publiés depuis la parution de l'édition de 2004 lorsqu'ils semblaient clairement résulter en des taxons monophylétiques. Nous préférons toutefois ne pas apporter de changements arbitraires qui fractionnent une famille considérée comme étant monophylétique. Ainsi, par exemple, nous plaçons les corégones et ciscos, les ombres, les truites, les saumons et les ombles dans une seule famille (Salmonidae) plutôt que dans trois familles distinctes comme le font certains auteurs (en particulier en Europe). Les familles ajoutées à la liste sont annotées à l'annexe 1, et des notes y sont généralement incluses lorsque nous refusons d'apporter les changements proposés dans certaines publications.

Noms scientifiques

Les noms scientifiques des espèces et des taxons de rangs supérieurs sont les noms établis selon le Code international de nomenclature zoologique, un ensemble de règles permettant de nommer les animaux. Tout autre nom, qu'il soit publié ou non, n'est pas disponible.

Noms vernaculaires

Les noms vernaculaires des espèces existent depuis longtemps—beaucoup plus longtemps que les noms scientifiques—et, aussi longtemps que le grand public et les biologistes les emploient, il faut avoir en place un système efficace et normalisé pour ces noms. Le Comité a élaboré un corpus de noms vernaculaires (un seul nom vernaculaire anglais pour chaque espèce incluse dans la liste et un seul nom vernaculaire espagnol et/ou français pour chaque espèce présente au Mexique et/ou au Canada) qui correspond à l'usage le plus courant et vise à promouvoir la stabilité et l'universalité des noms assignés aux poissons de l'Amérique du Nord.

Les noms vernaculaires des poissons présentés dans cette liste s'appliquent à l'espèce. Ils sont parfois employés comme appellations commerciales. Toutefois, certaines appellations commerciales visent souvent plusieurs espèces. Dans l'intérêt de l'information du public, nous encourageons fortement les auteurs, commerçants et autres intervenants à adopter les noms vernaculaires proposés ici, même si un nom semble présenter peu d'attrait commercial (p. ex. nous désapprouvons l'emploi de l'appellation commerciale « mullet » en anglais pour les sucker ou meuniers, famille Catostomidae). Un résumé des appellations commerciales appliquées en anglais aux poissons (et aux invertébrés) commercialisés aux États-Unis se trouve dans le document *Guidance for Industry: The Seafood List—FDA's Guide to Acceptable Market Names for Seafood Sold in Interstate Commerce*, 1993, revu en 2009, United States Food and Drug Administration, (voir aussi le site www.fda.gov/Food/GuidanceCompliance-RegulatoryInformation/GuidanceDocuments/Seafood/ucm113260). Dans la présente liste, de nombreux noms diffèrent de ceux qui apparaissent dans les publications de l'Organisation des Nations Unies pour l'alimentation et l'agriculture. Nous espérons parvenir à davantage d'uniformité dans l'avenir.

Le nom vernaculaire, tel que nous l'entendons ici, est considéré comme une appellation officielle qui peut remplacer le nom scientifique d'une espèce. Nous soulignons que les noms vernaculaires ne visent pas à remplacer les noms scientifiques en signalant les relations phylogénétiques (voir le principe 8 ci-dessous). L'histoire confirme que les noms vernaculaires sont souvent plus stables que les noms scientifiques.

Les noms vernaculaires sont plus facilement adaptables aux usages courants que les noms scientifiques. Il est clairement nécessaire de normaliser et d'uniformiser les noms vernaculaires, pas seulement pour les poissons faisant l'objet d'une pêche sportive ou commerciale, mais pour la vente au consommateur, l'aquariophilie, la terminologie juridique, et pour remplacer les noms scientifiques dans les écrits populaires ou savants. Quelques noms vernaculaires espagnols nouvellement ajoutés à la liste en 2004 ont dû être modifiés pour refléter l'usage courant.

L'adoption d'un nom vernaculaire français pour toutes les espèces de poissons dulcicoles et marins retrouvées au Canada requiert une connaissance de la composition de l'ichtyofaune des eaux douces et des eaux canadiennes des océans Arctique, Atlantique et Pacifique. Comme une telle connaissance ne se trouve pas dans un seul ouvrage de référence, nous avons compilé des listes des espèces dulcicoles et marines. Nous avons compilé la liste des espèces dulcicoles à partir principalement de l'inventaire inédit du projet Espèces sauvages—La situation générale des espèces au Canada, achevé en 2005 (www.wildspecies.ca), et la liste des espèces présentes dans l'océan Arctique, à partir des travaux de Mecklenburg et al. (2002, 2011) et de Coad et Reist (2004). Pour les listes des espèces présentes dans les eaux canadiennes de l'Atlantique et du Pacifique, nous nous sommes appuyés sur l'inventaire inédit du projet Espèces sauvages—La situation générale des espèces au Canada, achevé en 2005 (www.wildspecies.ca), que nous avons complété par des données provenant du Centre Référence Atlantique, du Musée canadien de la nature, de Pêches et Océans Canada, du Royal British Columbia Museum et du Musée royal de l'Ontario. Les noms vernaculaires français des poissons dulcicoles sont tirés en grande partie de la liste de 2004, ainsi que des ouvrages de Scott et Crossman (1973) et de D.E. McAllister (1990, *A list of the fishes of Canada/Liste des poissons du Canada*, Syllogeus 64). Les noms vernaculaires français des espèces marines sont tirés du rapport de 2005 (liste inédite) de la série Espèces sauvages (www.wildspecies.ca), que nous avons complétés par les travaux de B.W. Coad (1995, *Encyclopedia of Canadian fishes*, Musée canadien de la nature et Canadian Sportfishing Productions, Ottawa) et des données tirées de FishBase (www.fishbase. org). Dans le cas des espèces pour lesquelles un nom vernaculaire français n'a pu être trouvé, le nom vernaculaire anglais a été traduit en français. Tous les noms vernaculaires français ont été évalués par C. B. Renaud et P. Dumont.

Plusieurs espèces portent un nom vernaculaire anglais dérivé directement du nom vernaculaire espagnol utilisé au Mexique et, le cas échéant, porte un accent. Le Comité était divisé sur la question du traitement de ces noms comme étant « automatiquement anglicisés » et donc ne portant pas d'accent ou des mots espagnols fixés en anglais. Nous avons conclu que certains noms géographiques, étant largement adoptés en anglais, peuvent être considérés comme étant déjà anglicisés (p. ex. Yucatan par opposition à Yucatán, Rio Grande par opposition à Río Grande), et certains autres, qui ne sont généralement pas utilisés en anglais, comme ne l'étant pas. Pour comprendre la signification des accents dans les mots espagnols (qui ont une signification différente dans les mots français), nous fournissons le guide suivant de prononciation correcte des noms vernaculaires anglais comprenant des mots dérivés de noms de lieux au Mexique. Dans la prononciation des mots espagnols sans accent qui se terminent par une voyelle, en général « n » ou « s », l'accent tombe sur l'avant-dernière syllabe (l'avant-dernière voyelle, p. ex. *bravo*), alors que dans le cas des mots qui se terminent par une consonne autre que « n » ou « s », l'accent tombe sur la dernière syllabe. Les mots qui ne suivent pas cette règle portent un accent (´) sur la voyelle de la syllabe accentuée (souvent la dernière, p. ex. Zirahuén, Michoacán). Comme il l'est indiqué ci dessus, les quelques noms vernaculaires anglais considérés comme étant des noms vernaculaires espagnols anglicisés ne portent pas d'accent, même s'ils en portent un en espagnol, parce qu'une telle ponctuation n'est pas un usage en anglais. La prononciation en anglais devrait s'appuyer sur l'orthographe en espagnol—ainsi, pour *Poeciliopsis scarlli*, la règle pour son nom vernaculaire en espagnol, qui est « guatopote michoacano » (cet adjectif ne porte pas d'accent),

serait de placer l'accent sur l'avant-dernière syllabe dans michoacano (sur la voyelle « a »). Le même accent devrait être mis dans le nom vernaculaire dérivé en anglais, mais maintenant, en raison de la différence dans l'orthographe, sur le dernier « a », il devrait être prononcé Michoacán Livebearer. Des exemples de l'endroit où l'accent serait placé sur la syllabe autre que l'avant-dernière suivent. Les espèces dont le nom vernaculaire en anglais, tel que dérivé d'un nom de lieu au Mexique (donc en espagnol), porte l'accent sur la dernière syllabe (accent sur la dernière voyelle) incluent Lacandón Sea Catfish, Tamesí Molly et Michoacán Livebearer, alors que celles dont le nom vernaculaire porte l'accent sur l'avant-avant-dernière syllabe (accent sur l'avant-avant-dernière voyelle) incluent San Jerónimo Livebearer et Cuatro Ciénegas Platyfish.

Pour de nombreux noms, il est facile d'arriver rapidement à une entente, mais d'autres suscitent des difficultés. C'est particulièrement le cas des poissons dont les appellations commerciales diffèrent des noms couramment utilisés par les pêcheurs sportifs, les biologistes et d'autres personnes (p. ex. le poisson souvent appelé « red snapper » sur la plus grande partie de la côte du Pacifique d'expression anglaise est généralement une espèce du genre *Sebastes* [sébastes], et non une espèce de vivaneau du genre *Lutjanus*). L'emploi de noms différents dans diverses parties de l'aire géographique d'une espèce crée des difficultés qui ne semblent pouvoir se résoudre que par l'arbitrage. Par contre, un nom donné peut être employé à plusieurs endroits pour des espèces différentes (comme dans l'exemple du red snapper ci-dessus). Si l'on ne peut s'attendre à ce que dans un tel cas l'intervention du Comité fasse changer rapidement l'usage local, il semble tout à fait incorrect de sanctionner l'usage d'un seul nom pour plusieurs espèces différentes. Nous soutenons que tous les utilisateurs des noms vernaculaires des poissons sont mal servis, et peut-être même induits en erreur, si ces noms sont employés de façon incohérente.

Après s'être acharné pendant de nombreuses années à établir des noms vernaculaires, un Comité antérieur sur les noms de poissons s'est rendu compte qu'il était important de formuler une série de principes directeurs pour choisir les noms. Une telle codification permet d'évaluer les mérites relatifs de plusieurs noms plus objectivement que si le choix était fondé avant tout sur l'expérience personnelle et sur les préférences. Lorsqu'on constate la multitude des noms vernaculaires de poissons, il apparaît qu'on ne peut guère établir de principes sans prévoir des exceptions. Il existe en fait de nombreuses exceptions, car au moment où le Comité a commencé à travailler, la majorité des espèces les plus grosses et les plus abondantes des États-Unis et du Canada possédaient des noms vernaculaires si fermement établis qu'il aurait été peu réaliste de les rejeter dans le seul but de respecter un principe nouvellement formulé. Pour s'entendre sur le nom d'une espèce, il faut souvent peser le pour et le contre de plusieurs choix possibles et retenir celui qui correspond le mieux à un ensemble de critères. Nous présentons ci-dessous les principes que le Comité juge appropriés pour le choix des noms vernaculaires des poissons; ils sont tirés des listes précédentes, avec quelques modifications.

Principes régissant le choix des noms vernaculaires

1. *Un seul nom vernaculaire, dans chaque langue retenue, sera accepté pour une espèce.* Dans l'édition de 1991, un seul poisson, *Coregonus artedi*, avait deux noms vernaculaires acceptés; dans la liste de 2004 et la présente liste, il n'y a plus d'exceptions.

2. *Le même nom vernaculaire ne peut être attribué à deux espèces de la liste.* Il faut autant que possible éviter de retenir pour des espèces de notre zone des noms couramment utilisés pour des espèces qui vivent en dehors de cette zone.

3. *Le qualificatif « commun » ou son équivalent anglais ou espagnol doit être évité dans la composition du nom d'un poisson.* Une exception est faite dans le cas des noms vernaculaires établis depuis longtemps, comme Common Carp/carpa común, Common Shiner, tiburón zorro común, cazón espinoso común et aiguillat commun.

4. *Il faut rechercher la simplicité.* En anglais et en espagnol, il faut omettre les traits d'union et les apostrophes (p. ex. Small-

mouth Bass), sauf lorsqu'ils sont essentiels au plan orthographique (p. ex. Three-eye Flounder), ont une signification spéciale (p. ex. C-O Sole), sont nécessaires pour éviter la possibilité d'erreur (p. ex. Cusk-eel), ou joignent deux noms de poissons, dont ni l'un ni l'autre représente le poisson en question, en un seul (p. ex. Trout-perch, qui n'est ni une truite ni une perche). Les déterminants composés, particulièrement appropriés en anglais, y compris les paires de structures telle une tache de chaque côté du pédoncule caudal, devraient habituellement être traités comme des noms singuliers apposés à un nom de groupe (p. ex. Spottail Shiner), mais un déterminant pluriel devrait habituellement être placé dans sa forme adjectivale (p. ex. Spotted Hake, Blackbanded Sunfish) à moins que sa nature plurielle soit évidente (p. ex. Fourspot Flounder). La préférence sera accordée aux noms courts et euphoniques. La fusion de mots courts et familiers en un seul nom, écrit sans trait d'union, peut dans certains cas promouvoir la clarté et la simplicité, en particulier en anglais (p. ex. Tomcod, Goldfish, Mudminnow), mais la pratique qu'est la combinaison de mots, en particulier de mots longs, peu élégants ou inconnus, doit être évitée.

5. *Les noms vernaculaires porteront une majuscule en anglais.* Il faut mettre une majuscule à la première lettre de chaque mot du nom vernaculaire en anglais, sauf après un trait d'union, à moins que la majuscule doit être mise à la première lettre de ce mot du fait qu'il est un nom propre (p. ex. Pit-Klamath Brook Lamprey, Ragged-tooth Shark, Atlantic Salmon, Dusky Cusk-eel, Tropical Two-wing Flyingfish, Northern Rock Sole). Ce changement s'écarte de ce qui a été établi dans les éditions précédentes. Les noms vernaculaires des taxons se situant au dessus du niveau de l'espèce (p. ex. Pacific salmons, temperate basses) ne sont pas touchés. Un lambda majuscule d'indice supérieur ($^\Lambda$) est placé après les noms vernaculaires qui, en anglais, contiennent un nom propre (ou un mot traité dans la liste de 2004 comme un nom, tel « Gulf », où un golfe particulier est désigné) qui doit

toujours porter une majuscule. Cette notation sera utile à certains utilisateurs car il
n'est parfois pas clair d'après les listes
précédentes quels noms contiennent un nom
propre (p. ex. Buffalo darter, Strawberry
darter et Warrior darter) et quels n'en contiennent pas (p. ex. colorado snapper et warsaw grouper).

6. *Les noms choisis pour honorer des personnes* (p. ex. les noms Allison's tuna, Julia's darter, Meek's halfbeak, blanquillo de
Hubbs autrefois utilisés) *sont à éviter car
ils n'ont aucune valeur descriptive.* Cependant, dans quelques cas, les patronymes
sont si largement utilisés qu'ils sont acceptés (p. ex. Guppy, Lane Snapper). Ce principe ne s'applique pas aux noms vernaculaires français (p. ex. le nom vernaculaire
de *Liparis coheni* est limace de Cohen).
Toutefois, lorsqu'un nom vernaculaire pat-
ronymique ou matronymique n'avait pas
de priorité établie, nous avons générale
ment choisi un autre nom vernaculaire.

7. *Un nom vernaculaire ne sera pas attribué aux
sous-espèces.* Comme dans l'édition de
2004, nous n'avons pas donné de nom vernaculaire ni de nom scientifique pour les
sous-espèces. Nous reconnaissons toutefois
que les sous-espèces, qui ont leur propre
histoire évolutionnaire sur le plan de
l'allopatrie, jouent un rôle important dans
les recherches sur l'évolution et peuvent
donc recevoir un statut de protection particulière et être reconnues dans les études
sur la biodiversité. Certaines sous-espèces
sont si différentes d'apparence (et pas seulement dans leur distribution géographique)
qu'il est facile de les distinguer; des noms
vernaculaires peuvent exister pour ces populations, ce qui contribue grandement à la
communication.

Les hybrides ne reçoivent générale
ment pas de nom vernaculaire, mais ceux
qui sont importants dans la gestion des
pêches et qui possèdent des noms vernaculaires bien établis sont traités à l'annexe 2.
Les variétés d'élevage, les phases et les
variantes morphologiques ne sont pas nom
mées même si elles peuvent être importantes
pour le commerce et l'élevage des poissons

d'aquarium (p. ex. les nombreuses varié
tés de carassin et de carpe; la phase ocel-
lée et la phase dorée de *Mycteroperca rosa
cea* et d'*Arothron meleagris*).

8. *Le nom vernaculaire ne doit pas nécessairement être étroitement lié au nom scientifique.* Les modifications périodiques et
nécessaires de la nomenclature scientifique
ne nécessitent pas forcément une adaptation
des noms vernaculaires. La pratique qui
consiste à établir un nom vernaculaire pour
chaque genre puis un qualificatif pour
chaque espèce, et un autre qualificatif
pour chaque sous-espèce, bien que
séduisante par sa simplicité, a le défaut
d'être dénuée de souplesse, de sorte qu'un
poisson risque de ne pas être reconnu
parce que l'on a rejeté ce qui pouvait être
un nom traditionnel parfaitement acceptable. Nous voyons dans cette pratique une
simple tentative de reprendre dans le nom
vernaculaire la nomenclature scientifique.
Si une espèce est transférée d'un genre
à un autre, ou une sous-espèce passe au statut d'espèce dans la littérature ichtyologique
et ainsi est inscrite à la liste, le nom vernaculaire ne devrait pas changer. Les noms
vernaculaires n'ont pas comme fonction
première d'indiquer la relation. Ce principe
reste toutefois incompris ou rejeté par ceux
qui soutiennent que les noms vernaculaires de tous les membres d'un genre devraient
comprendre le même mot racine (p. ex. que
tous les *Oncorhynchus* devraient s'appeler
saumon, comme dans « saumon arc-en-ciel »
et que tous les *Salvelinus* devraient s'appeler
omble, comme dans « omble touladi »). La
stabilité des noms vernaculaires contre
balance tout avantage que présente
l'adhésion rigoureuse à la liaison entre les
noms vernaculaires et les noms scientifiques. Lorsque deux taxons ou plus (p. ex.
des espèces ou des familles nominales) sont
jugés identiques (synonymes), un seul nom
sera adopté pour le groupe combiné. Voir
aussi le principe 13.

9. *Les noms respecteront les règles du bon
goût* (p. ex. *ils ne contiendront pas de
termes jugés offensants*). C'est par exemple
pour respecter ce principe que des noms

anglais ont été changés dans la liste de 2004 (squawfish et jewfish ont été remplacés respectivement par Pikeminnow et Goliath Grouper).

Les principes qui précèdent relèvent essentiellement des règles de procédure. Ceux qui suivent sont des critères qui pourront aider à choisir des noms appropriés.

10. *Des noms imagés, colorés, romantiques, fantaisistes, métaphoriques, ou intéressants par leur fraîcheur et leur originalité sont particulièrement appropriés.* Une telle terminologie ajoute à la richesse et à l'envergure de la nomenclature et procure une grande satisfaction à l'utilisateur. En voici quelques exemples: en français, tête-de-boule, ventre citron et truite fardée; en anglais, Madtom, Dolly Varden, Midshipman, Chilipepper, Garibaldi, Pumpkinseed, Flier, Angelfish, Moorish Idol et Hogchoker; en espagnol, bruja, guitarra, chucho et lacha.

11. *Les noms autochtones d'Amérique du Nord ou leurs modifications font d'excellents noms vernaculaires.* Des noms comme poulamon, achigan, ouitouche, maskinongé, ogac et touladi sont couramment utilisés en français; Menhaden, Eulachon, Cisco, Chinook Salmon, Mummichog, Tautog, en anglais; puyeki et totoaba, en espagnol.

12. *Quelle que soit leur origine, les noms réellement vernaculaires qui sont répandus et couramment utilisés dans le public doivent être retenus autant que possible.* De nombreux noms bien connus employés au nord du Mexique incluent des mots espagnols ou leurs modifications, p. ex. barracuda, cero, mojarra, pompano (de pámpano), et sierra. Voici des exemples tirés d'autres langues : capelin (de capelan, français), bo caccio (italien) et mako (maori). La plupart de ces noms se conforment aux principes 14 et 15 ci dessous.

13. *Des noms couramment employés dans l'usage traditionnel français* (p. ex. méné et perche)*, anglais* (p. ex. chub, minnow, trout, bass, perch, sole, flounder)*, espagnol* (p. ex. cazón, sardina, carpa, mojarra, perca, lenguado) *sont utilisés avec une latitude considérable en taxinomie.* Le respect des pratiques traditionnelles est préférable si cela n'entre pas en conflit avec l'usage généralisé d'un autre nom. Bien des noms ont été appliqués en Amérique du Nord à des poissons d'apparence similaire mais souvent peu apparentés. Par exemple, les termes « bass » et « lenguado » sont utilisés pour des représentants de plusieurs familles de poissons à rayons épineux, et les noms « perch » et « perca » pour un nombre encore plus grand de familles. Le nom « chub » est employé dans des groupes aussi éloignés que les Cyprinidae et les Kyphosidae, tandis que « mojarra » se retrouve dans les familles Cichlidae, Gerreidae et autres. *Caulolatilus princeps*, parfois appelé « salmón » dans le nord-ouest du Mexique, n'est pas un salmonidé, et *Peprilus simillimus* est appellé « pámpano » en espagnol mais ce n'est pas un carangidé, et pourtant c'est sous ces noms que les pêcheurs connaissent ces poissons dans toute leur aire. Pour les espèces bien connues, il est préférable de reconnaître l'usage général. L'utilisation bien établie d'un nom traditionnel devrait supplanter les efforts de cohérence. Ce principe n'est pas bien compris par certains ichtyologistes qui jugent que le nom de « perche » ne devrait pas être employé pour un embiotocidé, le nom de « truite » pour un *Salvelinus*, celui de « sardinita » pour un characidé, ni celui de « cazón » pour un carcharinidé. En anglais, on a pu éviter certains problèmes, ou les limiter, en créant des néologismes (p. ex. seatrout pour sea trout, mudsucker pour mud sucker, surfperch pour surf perch). Ces combinaisons sont maintenant largement acceptées depuis qu'elles ont été adoptées dans les listes antérieures.

14. *Les attributs morphologiques, la couleur et les motifs de la livrée sont de bonnes sources de noms, et sont souvent employés à cette fin.* Les noms de poissons s'agrémentent d'une multitude de descripteurs, par exemple citron, cuivré, fardé et à fossettes en français; sailfin, flathead, slippery, giant, mottled, copper, tripletail en anglais; chato,

jorobado, bocón, gigante, jabonero, pinto, cobrizo en espagnol. Il faut s'efforcer de choisir des termes qui sont exacts sur le plan descriptif, mais éviter la répétition de ceux qui sont le plus fréquemment employés (p. ex. blanc [white, blanco], noir [black, negro], tacheté [spotted, manchado], barré [banded, rayado/de cintas]). Selon la tradition canadienne et américaine de création des noms vernaculaires en ichtyologie et en herpétologie, nous avons tenté de restreindre l'usage des termes « ligne » ou « rayure» » aux marques longitudinales parallèles à l'axe du corps, et les termes « barre » ou « bande » aux marques verticales ou transversales. Cette tradition ne s'applique toutefois pas aux noms en espagnol utilisés au Mexique, où les termes « rayado/rayada » sont souvent appliqués à de telles marques.

15. *Les caractéristiques écologiques sont des sources désirables de noms.* Ces termes doivent avoir un caractère descriptif précis. Certains déterminants sont utilisés couramment dans les noms de poissons, en français (en anglais, en espagnol), comme de récif (reef, de arrecife), de corail (coral, coralino), de sable (sand, arenoso), de roche (rock, piedrero), de lac (lake, de lago), dulcicole (freshwater, dulciacuícola).

16. *La répartition géographique peut donner de bons déterminants adjectivaux.* Les caractères géographiques peu descriptifs ou trompeurs (p. ex. « Kentucky Bass » pour une espèce à très grande répartition) doivent être corrigés, sauf si l'usage est vraiment trop établi (à des fins de stabilité, nous avons gardé des noms comme Alaska Blackfish, bien que cet umbre soit aussi présent en Russie, et guatopote de Sonora même si cette poecilie se retrouve couramment hors des limites de l'État du même nom). Dans un souci de concision, il est généralement possible d'éliminer des mots comme lac (lake, lago), fleuve ou rivière (river, río), golfe (gulf, golfo) ou mer (sea, mar) dans le nom des espèces (p. ex. Colorado Pikeminnow, au lieu de « Colorado River Pikeminnow »; topote del Balsas, plutôt que « topote del Río Balsas »).

17. *Les noms scientifiques de genre peuvent servir de noms vernaculaires directement* (p. ex. gambusia, remora, anchoa, brótula, guavina) *ou sous une forme modifiée* (p. ex. alose à partir de *Alosa*). Une fois adoptés, ces noms doivent être maintenus même si le nom scientifique du genre ou du taxon supérieur est changé par la suite. Ces noms vernaculaires doivent être écrits en caractères romains (et non en italique comme le nom scientifique du genre).

18. *Le double emploi de noms vernaculaires pour des poissons et d'autres organismes doit être évité autant que possible, mais cet argument ne doit pas être invoqué seul pour rejeter certains noms couramment employés.* Par exemple, le mot « buffalo » est employé en anglais pour divers mammifères artiodactyles (le bison notamment) et pour les catostomidés du genre *Ictiobus* (buffalo en français); « renard » ou, en espagnol, « zorro » désignent des requins de la famille Alopiidae, tandis que le nom « mariposa » (papillon en espagnol) sert aussi bien pour les poissons-papillons de la famille Chaetodontidae que pour les raies-papillons de la famille Gymnuridae. Étant donné que leur usage est bien établi, ces noms peuvent être retenus comme noms vernaculaires sans modification.

Relation entre le nom vernaculaire et le nom scientifique d'une espèce

Les objectifs de cette liste sont de recommander le nom vernaculaire et de fournir le nom scientifique généralement accepté pour toutes les espèces de poissons retrouvées à l'intérieur des limites géographiques fixées. Les noms vernaculaires peuvent être établis par entente générale. Par contre, les noms scientifiques vont inévitablement changer avec le progrès des connaissances sur les relations phylogénétiques entre les espèces et selon les opinions des taxinomistes. Nous avons soigneusement vérifié la nomenclature scientifique utilisée en ce qui touche l'orthographe, les auteurs et la date de la description originale. Nous soulignons qu'il y a désaccord concernant la classification de nombreux groupes de poissons, ou encore que la classification présente des lacunes. Il se produit aussi souvent entre les chercheurs des divergences d'opinion à caractère subjectif pour la désignation du rang des taxons (voir l'analyse présentée ci dessus dans les sections Noms des familles et Noms vernaculaires, particulièrement le principe 8).

Plan de la liste

La liste se présente sous forme d'une série phylogénétique de familles de poissons récents établie d'après les connaissances actuelles. L'organisation des classes, des ordres et des familles suit globalement Nelson (2006), à part quelques changements reflétant des études systématiques récentes. Dans la plupart des cas, nous donnons un seul nom vernaculaire pour chaque famille en français, en anglais et en espagnol. Il arrive parfois que deux noms vernaculaires soient donnés à une famille lorsque l'usage le dicte. Pour l'orthographe des noms des auteurs des descriptions d'espèce, nous suivons le *Catalog of Fishes* de W. N. Eschmeyer (rédacteur en chef), http://research.calacademy.org/ichthyology/catalog/fishcatmain.asp (version électronique).

Au sein des familles, les genres et les espèces sont présentés par ordre alphabétique. La partie I comporte cinq colonnes, comme suit: le nom scientifique, la zone de présence, le nom vernaculaire anglais (quelle que soit la zone de présence), le nom vernaculaire espagnol pour les espèces du Mexique et le nom vernaculaire français pour les espèces du Canada.

Nous suivons la dernière édition (la quatrième) du Code International de Nomenclature Zoologique (ci après le « Code », http://www.nhm.ac.uk/hosted-sites/iczn/code/), publié en 1999, et nous retenons les orthographes originales des noms d'espèces. Par conséquent, les suffixes de certains noms patronymiques ont été changés, de -*i* ou -*ii*, le cas échéant. Dans cette édition de la liste, nous continuons d'ajouter, après le nom scientifique, l'auteur et la date de publication de la description originale de l'espèce. L'auteur et la date sont des renseignements souvent nécessaires pour les personnes qui n'ont pas forcément accès aux publications originales. Il est parfois compliqué de déterminer qui est l'auteur exact et quelle est l'année de publication, particulièrement pour les noms proposés avant 1900. Nos justifications de la graphie des noms Delaroche, Forsskål, Lacepède et Lesueur ont été présentées dans la

troisième édition (page 5) et la quatrième édition (page 8). L'attribution des noms proposés dans le M. E. Blochii Systema Ichthyologiae, 1801, par J. G. Schneider, a été expliquée dans la quatrième édition (page 8).

L'utilisation du nom de l'auteur correspond à l'interprétation actuelle du Code. Conformément à ces règles, le nom de l'auteur (ou des auteurs) suit directement le nom de l'espèce (écrit en italique). Si, dans sa description originale, l'espèce a été assignée au genre auquel elle est assignée ici, le nom de l'auteur est écrit sans parenthèses; si l'espèce a été décrite dans un autre genre, le nom de l'auteur apparaît entre parenthèses. L'année de publication est séparée du nom de l'auteur par une virgule et apparaît dans la parenthèse si présente. Par exemple, Mitchill a au départ nommé l'omble de fontaine *Salmo fontinalis* dans un ouvrage publié en 1814; ce poisson apparaît ici sous le nom de *Salvelinus fontinalis* (Mitchill, 1814). Dans l'édition de 2004, les parenthèses n'étaient pas placées autour du nom de l'auteur dans les cas où le nom du niveau espèce était au départ combiné à un nom de genre incorrectement orthographié ou faisant l'objet d'une émendation injustifiée, même si une émendation injustifiée est un nom disponible avec son propre auteur et sa propre date (article 51.3.1 du Code). C'est pourquoi, comme dans le cas de l'édition de 2004, nous n'utilisons pas de parenthèses pour des espèces décrites au départ dans des genres comme *Rhinobatus* (maintenant *Rhinobatos*), *Raia* (maintenant *Raja*), *Lepidosteus* (maintenant *Lepisosteus*), *Ophichthys* (maintenant *Ophichthus*), *Nototropis* (maintenant *Notropis*), *Amiurus* (maintenant *Ameiurus*), *Hemirhamphus* (maintenant *Hemiramphus*), *Opisthognathus* (maintenant *Opistognathus*) et *Pomadasis* (maintenant *Pomadasys*).

Depuis la publication de la sixième édition, en 2004, de nombreux utilisateurs ont fait part au Comité de propositions de changements, dont chacune a été considérée lors de la préparation de la présente édition. La stabilité des noms vernaculaires a été jugée prioritaire, et les modifications n'ont été apportées qu'avec une solide justification. Les connaissances scientifiques sur les poissons ont fait de rapides progrès depuis la publication de la dernière édition. De nombreuses espèces nouvelles ont été décrites, de nombreuses autres espèces ont été recensées dans les eaux nord-américaines, et une foule de révisions ont été apportées sur le plan de la taxinomie et de la systématique. Toutes les nouvelles entrées et toutes celles qui s'écartent de quelque manière que ce soit de l'édition de 2004 (nom scientifique, auteur ou auteurs, date de description, zone de présence ou nom vernaculaire) sont précédées d'un astérisque (*). Des renseignements décrivant et expliquant le changement sont fournis pour chacune de ces entrées, identifiées par le numéro de la page où apparaît le nom dans la liste, à l'annexe 1. L'information donnée autrefois à l'annexe 1 dans les listes de 1970, 1980, 1991 et 2004 (pages 65-87, 68-92, 71-96 et 187-253, respectivement), qui décrivait les changements apportés entre les éditions 2 et 3, 3 et 4, 4 et 5, puis 5 et 6, n'est généralement pas reprise dans la présente édition.

Le signe plus (+) placé avant une entrée indique que, même si cette entrée n'a pas été modifiée, un commentaire a été inséré à l'annexe 1 à son sujet. Il peut s'agir notamment d'un taxon situé au dessus du niveau de l'espèce (p. ex. famille et ordre) dont le nom n'a pas été modifié mais dont la composition diffère par rapport à l'édition de 2004 (suppression de taxons ou transfert d'autres taxons d'un niveau supérieur).

Si la plupart des décisions du Comité ont été unanimes, plusieurs d'entre elles ont été prises par vote majoritaire, de sorte qu'aucun membre du Comité ne souscrit nécessairement à toutes les décisions prises. Nous comprenons que toutes les décisions ne seront pas acceptées par tous nos collègues, mais nous espérons que tous les utilisateurs apprécieront nos efforts. Dans de nombreux cas, l'information dont disposait le Comité dépassait celle trouvée dans les travaux publiés. Le Comité a souvent dû débattre longuement pour arriver à une décision justifiant l'inclusion de ce genre d'information, et c'est avec prudence qu'il a adopté des changements de cet ordre.

Index

L'index intègre les noms scientifiques et les noms vernaculaires dans les trois langues. Le renvoi aux pages est indiqué pour les noms vernaculaires adoptés ici pour les familles et les espèces. L'index comporte une seule entrée pour chaque espèce; par exemple, l'omble de fontaine est inscrit seulement sous l'entrée « omble, de fontaine », et trucha de arroyo sous l'entrée « trucha, de arroyo ».

Le renvoi aux pages est indiqué pour les noms scientifiques des classes, des ordres, des familles, des genres et des espèces. Chaque espèce est inscrite seulement par son nom spécifique. Par exemple, *Sciaenops ocellatus* se trouve seulement à l'entrée « *ocellatus*, *Sciaenops* », bien qu'une entrée à « *Sciaenops* » renvoie le lecteur à la page où commencent les entrées correspondant aux espèces de ce genre. Les noms scientifiques des espèces qui n'ont pas été retenus pour cette liste n'apparaissent généralement pas, sauf ceux qui apparaissent dans la sixième édition (2004), et qui depuis ont été placés en synonymie, comme il l'est expliqué à l'annexe 1.

Remerciements

Cette liste constitue le résultat des contributions faites au cours de sept décennies par les multiples personnes étant ou ayant été membre du Comité sur les noms de poissons. Nous sommes très reconnaissants du travail des anciens membres. Des contributions durables ont aussi eu lieu avec plusieurs spécialistes ayant porté assistance dans la production de la deuxième, troisième, quatrième, cinquième et sixième édition et dans lesquelles leur aide a été remerciée.

Dans la préparation du matériel de la présente édition, plusieurs individus nous ont fourni de l'assistance et des conseils sur les noms et la littérature. Nous sommes particulièrement reconnaissants à ceux qui ont participés aux rencontres du comité, ainsi qu'aux rencontres tenues chaque année par la Société américaine des ichtyologistes et herpétologistes: William D. Anderson, Jr., George H. Burgess, Bruce B. Collette, Matthew T. Craig, William N. Eschmeyer, Karsten E. Hartel, John F. Morrissey, Robert H. Robins, Juan Jacobo Schmitter-Soto, Gerald R. Smith, W. Leo Smith, William F. Smith-Vaniz, Harold J. Walker, Jr., et James D. Williams.

Nous avons été assistés par un si grand nombre de gens qu'il nous est pratiquement impossible de tous les nommer. Certains d'entre eux ont cependant été particulièrement utiles et méritent une mention particulière: Arturo Acero P., Eduardo Balart, Carole Baldwin, Henry L. Bart, Jr., Richard J. Beamish, Hugues Benoit, D. A. Boguski, Brian W. Bowen, George H. Burgess, Mary Burridge, Brooks M. Burr, Gregor M Cailliet, Kent E. Carpenter, Martin Castonguay, le défunt José Luis Castro-Aguirre, David Catania, Don S. Clark, Brian Coad, Bruce B. Collette, le défunt Salvador Contreras-Balderas, Lara Cooper, Walter R. Courtenay, Matthew T. Craig, Margaret F. Docker, Jean-Denis Dutil, William N. Eschmeyer, Richard F. Feeney, Moretta Frederick, Jon D. Fong, Patricia Fuentes M., Anthony C. Gill, Graham Gillespie, R. Grant Gilmore, Adrián González A., D. H. Goodman, David W. Greenfield, Gavin Hanke, Karsten E. Hartel, Philip A. Hastings, Philip C. Heemstra, Dean A. Hendrickson, Mysi D. Hoang, Leticia Huidobro C., Tomio Iwamoto, Robert E. Jenkins, G. David Johnson, Cynthia Klepadlo, J. M. Leis, Andrew Lewin, María de Lourdes Lozano V., Milton Love, Zachary P. Martin, Katherine Maslenikov, John E. McCosker, Catherine W. Mecklenburg, Roberta Miller, Randy Mooi, James A. Morris, Jr., John F. Morrissey, David A. Neely, Leo G. Nico, James W. Orr, Mauricia Pérez-Tello, Frank L. Pezold, Edward J. Pfeiler, Theodore W. Pietsch, Héctor G. Plascencia, Kyle R. Piller, Dennis Polack, Zachary Randall, Stewart B. Reid, James D.Reist, Claude B. Renaud, D. Ross Robertson, Robert H. Robins, Luiz A. Rocha, Dawn M. Roje, Richard H. Rosenblatt, Ramón Ruíz-Carus, Kate Rutherford, Juan Jacobo Schmitter-Soto, Pamela J. Schofield, Jeffery A. Seigel, Randal A. Singer, Gerald R. Smith, W. Leo Smith, William F. Smith-Vaniz, Wayne C. Starnes, J. D. Stelfox, Duane E. Stevenson, Camm C. Swift, Michael S. Taylor, Christine E. Thacker, Alfred W. Thomson, Luke Tornabene, Xavier Valencia D., Albert M. van der Heiden, James Van Tassell, Lou Van Guelpen, Harold J. Walker, Jr., Edward O. Wiley, James D. Williams, et Mark V. H. Wilson.

La Société américaine des pêches a financé les déplacements des membres du Comité afin qu'ils assistent aux trois séances de travail marathon. En 2009, la rencontre a eu lieu à l'Instituto de Biología, Universidad Nacional Autónoma de México, dans la ville de Mexico, et était tenue par le membre du Comité H. S. Espinosa-Pérez. Une contribution fut apportée par les directeurs T. María Pérez et R. Cordero B., L. Huidobro et X. Valencia. En 2007 et 2010, les rencontres ont eu lieu au Musée de l'histoire naturelle de la Floride, Université de la Floride, Gainesville, et était tenues par Carter R. Gilbert et Larry M. Page, deux membres du Comité. Plusieurs ichtyologistes locaux y assistèrent.

Nous souhaitons également remercier nos institutions respectives pour la subdivision de nos efforts sur ce projet, incluant souvent du financement pour les voyages, de l'aide au niveau du secrétariat, la duplication des facilités et les services postaux, ainsi que pour avoir fourni un lieu de travail aux membres du Comité.

Les employés de la Société américaine des pêches, Aaron Lerner et Ghassan (Gus) Rassam particulièrement, nous ont aidés de plusieurs façons. Nous somme particulièrement reconnaissants de l'aide dévouée et agréable de Deborah Lehman. Au fil des ans, les divers présidents et autres officiers de la Société américaine des pêches et la Société américaine des ichtyologistes et des herpétologistes ont continuellement offert des encouragements au Comité.

Les sections nouvelles et révisées de l'introduction on été traduites en Espagnol par Gabriela Montemayor et éditées par Héctor Espinosa-Pérez et Lloyd Findley, membres du Comité. La traduction de l'introduction en Français a été accomplie avec l'aide de Pêches et Océans Canada par Jacqueline Lanteigne, Claude Renaud, and Johannie Duhaime. Une aide considérable dans la provision de noms communs français à été fournie par Claude Renaud et Pierre Dumont. Jesse Grosso, du Musée de l'histoire naturelle de la Floride, à porté assistance dans l'organisation du manuscrit final.

Note de la liste principale de la Partie I:

[1] **A** = Atlantique; **AM** = eaux atlantiques du Mexique, mais ne figure pas dans les registres des États-Unis ou du Canada; **Ar** = océan Arctique; **F:C** = eaux douces du Canada; **F:M** = eaux douces du Mexique; **F:U** = eaux douces des États-Unis (états contigus ou Alaska); **P** = Pacifique; **PM** = eaux pacifiques du Mexique, mais ne figure pas dans les registres des États-Unis ou du Canada; **[I]** = Non

indigène (introduction ou invasion) et établi dans nos eaux; **[X]** = disparu; **[XN]** = disparu dans la nature, mais entretenu en captivité.

2 Le nom commun anglais est indiqué pour toutes les espèces de la liste (plusieurs sont des adaptations de l'espagnol pour les espèces se trouvant au Mexique). Les noms en espagnol sont ceux des espèces marines et d'eau douce se trouvant au Mexique et les noms en français, ceux des espèces marines et d'eau douce se trouvant au Canada (dans tout le pays et non pas seulement au Québec comme dans la liste de 2004). **En-**, **Sp-**, et **Fr-** in-diquent les noms des familles en anglais, en espagnol et en français, respectivement.

* Modification par rapport à la liste de 2004 (6e édition) des noms scientifiques ou communs ou de la distribution (autre que l'ajout de **Ar** à cette édition); voir l'annexe 1 pour l'explication de ces changements.

^ Le lambda en exposant désigne un nom commun en anglais qui contient un nom propre (ou un mot traité comme un nom propre dans la liste de 2004, par exemple « Golfe »); voir le Principe 5

+ Voir les commentaires à l'annexe 1.

PART I

Scientific Name, Occurrence, and Accepted Common Name

SCIENTIFIC NAME	OCCURRENCE[1]	COMMON NAME (ENGLISH, SPANISH, FRENCH)[2]
SUBPHYLUM CEPHALOCHORDATA		
ORDER AMPHIOXIFORMES		
*Branchiostomatidae—En-lancelets, Sp-anfioxos, Fr-amphioxes		
Branchiostoma bennetti Boschung & Gunter, 1966	A	Mud Lancelet
Branchiostoma californiense Andrews, 1893	P	California Lancelet^ .... anfioxo californiano
Branchiostoma floridae Hubbs, 1922	A	Florida Lancelet^
Branchiostoma longirostrum Boschung, 1983	A	Shellhash Lancelet .... anfioxo conchalero
Branchiostoma virginiae Hubbs, 1922	A	Virginia Lancelet^
*Epigonichthyidae—En-lopsided lancelets, Sp-anfioxos chuecos, Fr- amphioxes asymétriques		
Epigonichthys lucayanus (Andrews, 1893)	A	Sharptail Lancelet
SUBPHYLUM CRANIATA		
CLASS MYXINI—HAGFISHES		
ORDER MYXINIFORMES		
Myxinidae—En-hagfishes, Sp-brujas, Fr-myxines		
Eptatretus deani (Evermann & Goldsborough, 1907)	P	Black Hagfish .... bruja pecosa .... myxine noire
Eptatretus fritzi Wisner & McMillan, 1990	PM	Guadalupe Hagfish^ .... bruja de Guadalupe

[1] **A** = Atlantic; **AM** = Atlantic Mexico but not recorded in United States or Canada; **Ar** = Arctic Ocean; **F:C** = Freshwater Canada; **F:M** = Freshwater Mexico; **F:U** = Freshwater United States (contiguous states and/or Alaska); **P** = Pacific; **PM** = Pacific Mexico but not recorded in United States or Canada; **[I]** = nonnative (introduced or invasive) and established in our waters; **[X]** = extinct; **[XN]** = extinct in nature but maintained in captivity.

[2] Common names in English are provided for all species in the list (several are adaptations of the name in Spanish for species occurring in Mexico), names in Spanish indicate freshwater and marine species occurring in Mexico, and names in French indicate freshwater and marine species in Canada (coverage is countrywide, not only in Quebec as in the 2004 list). **En-, Sp-,** and **Fr-** indicate family names in English, Spanish, and French, respectively.

* Change from 2004 list (sixth edition) in scientific or common name(s) or in distribution (other than addition of **Ar**—new in this edition); see Appendix 1 for explanation of change.

^ superscript caret denotes a common name in English that contains a proper noun (or a word treated in 2004 list as a proper noun, such as "Gulf"); see Principle 5.

+ See Appendix 1 for comment.

SCIENTIFIC NAME	OCCURRENCE[1]	COMMON NAME (ENGLISH, SPANISH, FRENCH)[2]
Eptatretus mcconnaugheyi Wisner & McMillan, 1990	P	Shorthead Hagfish .... bruja cabeza chica
Eptatretus sinus Wisner & McMillan, 1990	PM	Cortez Hagfish^ .... bruja de Cortés
Eptatretus stoutii (Lockington, 1878)	P	Pacific Hagfish^ .... bruja pintada .... myxine brune
Myxine glutinosa Linnaeus, 1758	A-Ar	Atlantic Hagfish^ .... myxine du nord

*CLASS PETROMYZONTIDA—LAMPREYS
ORDER PETROMYZONTIFORMES

+Petromyzontidae—En-lampreys, Sp-lampreas, Fr-lamproies

SCIENTIFIC NAME	OCCURRENCE[1]	COMMON NAME (ENGLISH, SPANISH, FRENCH)[2]
Entosphenus folletti Vladykov & Kott, 1976	F:U	Northern California Brook Lamprey^
Entosphenus lethophagus (Hubbs, 1971)	F:U	Pit-Klamath Brook Lamprey^
Entosphenus macrostomus (Beamish, 1982)	F:C	Vancouver Lamprey^ .... lamproie de Vancouver
Entosphenus minimus (Bond & Kan, 1973)	F:U	Miller Lake Lamprey^
Entosphenus similis Vladykov & Kott, 1979	F:U	Klamath Lamprey^
Entosphenus tridentatus (Gairdner, 1836)	P-F:CUM	Pacific Lamprey^ .... lamprea del Pacifico .... lamproie du Pacifique
Ichthyomyzon bdellium (Jordan, 1885)	F:U	Ohio Lamprey^
Ichthyomyzon castaneus Girard, 1858	F:CU	Chestnut Lamprey .... lamproie brune
Ichthyomyzon fossor Reighard & Cummins, 1916	F:CU	Northern Brook Lamprey .... lamproie du nord
Ichthyomyzon gagei Hubbs & Trautman, 1937	F:U	Southern Brook Lamprey
Ichthyomyzon greeleyi Hubbs & Trautman, 1937	F:U	Mountain Brook Lamprey
Ichthyomyzon unicuspis Hubbs & Trautman, 1937	F:CU	Silver Lamprey .... lamproie argentée
Lampetra aepyptera (Abbott, 1860)	F:U	Least Brook Lamprey
Lampetra ayresii (Günther, 1870)	P-F:CU	Western River Lamprey .... lamproie de rivière de l'ouest
+*Lampetra hubbsi* (Vladykov & Kott, 1976)	F:U	Kern Brook Lamprey^
Lampetra pacifica Vladykov, 1973	F:U	Pacific Brook Lamprey^
+*Lampetra richardsoni* Vladykov & Follett, 1965	F:CU	Western Brook Lamprey .... lamproie de ruisseau de l'ouest
Lethenteron alaskense Vladykov & Kott, 1978	F:CU	Alaskan Brook Lamprey^ .... lamproie d'Alaska
Lethenteron appendix (DeKay, 1842)	F:CU	American Brook Lamprey^ .... lamproie de l'est
Lethenteron camtschaticum (Tilesius, 1811)	P-Ar-F:CU	Arctic Lamprey^ .... lamproie arctique
Petromyzon marinus Linnaeus, 1758	A-F:CU	Sea Lamprey .... lamproie marine
Tetrapleurodon geminis Álvarez, 1964	F:M	Jacona Lamprey^ .... lamprea de Jacona
Tetrapleurodon spadiceus (Bean, 1887)	F:M	Chapala Lamprey^ .... lamprea de Chapala

SCIENTIFIC NAME	OCCURRENCE[1]	COMMON NAME (ENGLISH, SPANISH, FRENCH)[2]
		+CLASS CHONDRICHTHYES
		(SUBCLASSES HOLOCEPHALI and ELASMOBRANCHII)—CARTILAGINOUS FISHES
		ORDER CHIMAERIFORMES
		Chimaeridae—En-shortnose chimaeras, Sp-quimeras, Fr-chimères
Hydrolagus colliei (Lay & Bennett, 1839)	P	Spotted Ratfish......quimera manchada......chimère d'Amérique
Hydrolagus melanophasma James, Ebert, Long & Didier, 2009	PM	Eastern Pacific Black Ghostshark^......quimera negra......tiburón perro
		ORDER HETERODONTIFORMES
		Heterodontidae—En-bullhead sharks, Sp-tiburones cornudos, Fr-requins cornus
Heterodontus francisci (Girard, 1855)	P	Horn Shark......tiburón puerco
Heterodontus mexicanus Taylor & Castro-Aguirre, 1972	PM	Mexican Horn Shark^......tiburón perro
		ORDER ORECTOLOBIFORMES
		Ginglymostomatidae—En-nurse sharks, Sp-gatas, Fr-requins-nourrices
Ginglymostoma cirratum (Bonnaterre, 1788)	A-PM	Nurse Shark......tiburón gata
		Rhincodontidae—En-whale sharks, Sp-tiburones ballena, Fr-requins-baleines
Rhincodon typus Smith, 1828	A-P	Whale Shark......tiburón ballena......requin baleine
		ORDER LAMNIFORMES
		Odontaspididae—En-sand tigers, Sp-tiburones toro, Fr-requins-taureaux
Carcharias taurus Rafinesque, 1810	A-PM	Sand Tiger......tiburón arenero tigre......requin-taureau
Odontaspis ferox (Risso, 1810)	A-P	Ragged-tooth Shark......tiburón dientes de perro
Odontaspis noronhai (Maul, 1955)	A	Bigeye Sand Tiger
		Mitsukurinidae—En-goblin sharks, Sp-tiburones duende, Fr-requins-lutins
Mitsukurina owstoni Jordan, 1898	P	Goblin Shark

SCIENTIFIC NAME	OCCURRENCE[1]	COMMON NAME (ENGLISH, SPANISH, FRENCH)[2]
Pseudocarchariidae—En-crocodile sharks, Sp-tiburones cocodrilo, Fr-requins-crocodiles		
Pseudocarcharias kamoharai (Matsubara, 1936)	AM	Crocodile Shark ... tiburón cocodrilo
Megachasmidae—En-megamouth sharks, Sp-tiburones bocones, Fr-requins à grande gueule		
Megachasma pelagios Taylor, Compagno & Struhsaker, 1983	P	Megamouth Shark ... tiburón bocón
Alopiidae—En-thresher sharks, Sp-tiburones zorro, Fr-requins-renards		
Alopias pelagicus Nakamura, 1935	PM	Pelagic Thresher ... zorro pelágico
Alopias superciliosus (Lowe, 1841)	A-P	Bigeye Thresher ... tiburón zorro ojón
Alopias vulpinus (Bonnaterre, 1788)	A-P	Common Thresher Shark ... tiburón zorro común ... renard marin
Cetorhinidae—En-basking sharks, Sp-tiburones peregrino, Fr-pèlerins		
Cetorhinus maximus (Gunnerus, 1765)	A-P	Basking Shark ... tiburón peregrino ... pèlerin
Lamnidae—En-mackerel sharks, Sp-jaquetones, Fr-requins-taupes		
+*Carcharodon carcharias* (Linnaeus, 1758)	A-P	White Shark ... tiburón blanco ... requin blanc
Isurus oxyrinchus Rafinesque, 1810	A-P	Shortfin Mako ... mako ... requin-taupe bleu
Isurus paucus Guitart Manday, 1966	A-P	Longfin Mako ... mako aletón ... petit requin-taupe
Lamna ditropis Hubbs & Follett, 1947	P	Salmon Shark ... tiburón salmón ... taupe du Pacifique
Lamna nasus (Bonnaterre, 1788)	A	Porbeagle ... maraîche

ORDER CARCHARHINIFORMES

Scyliorhinidae—En-cat sharks, Sp-pejegatos, Fr-roussettes		
Apristurus brunneus (Gilbert, 1892)	P	Brown Cat Shark ... pejegato marrón ... holbiche brune
Cephaloscyllium ventriosum (Garman, 1880)	P	Swell Shark ... pejegato globo
Cephalurus cephalus (Gilbert, 1892)	PM	Lollipop Cat Shark ... pejegato renacuajo
Galeus arae (Nichols, 1927)	A	Marbled Cat Shark
Parmaturus xaniurus (Gilbert, 1892)	P	Filetail Cat Shark ... pejegato lima
Scyliorhinus retifer (Garman, 1881)	A	Chain Dogfish ... alitán mallero ... roussette maille

SCIENTIFIC NAME	OCCURRENCE[1]	COMMON NAME (ENGLISH, SPANISH, FRENCH)[2]
		Pseudotriakidae—En-false cat sharks, Sp-musolones, Fr-requins à longue dorsale
Pseudotriakis microdon de Brito Capello, 1868	A	False Cat Shark
		Triakidae—En-hound sharks, Sp-cazones, Fr-émissoles
Galeorhinus galeus (Linnaeus, 1758)	P	Tope ... tiburón aceitoso ... milandre
*Mustelus albipinnis Castro-Aguirre, Antuna-Mendiola, González-Acosta & De la Cruz-Agüero, 2005	PM	Whitemargin Smoothhound ... cazón hacat
Mustelus californicus Gill, 1864	P	Gray Smoothhound ... cazón mamón
Mustelus canis (Mitchill, 1815)	A	Smooth Dogfish ... cazón dientón ... émissole douce
Mustelus dorsalis Gill, 1864	PM	Sharptooth Smoothhound ... cazón tripa
Mustelus henlei (Gill, 1863)	P	Brown Smoothhound ... cazón hilacho
Mustelus lunulatus Jordan & Gilbert, 1882	P	Sicklefin Smoothhound ... cazón segador
Mustelus norrisi Springer, 1939	A	Florida Smoothhound^ ... cazón viuda
Mustelus sinusmexicanus Heemstra, 1997	A	Gulf Smoothhound^ ... cazón del Golfo
Triakis semifasciata Girard, 1855	P	Leopard Shark ... tiburón leopardo
		Carcharhinidae—En-requiem sharks, Sp-tiburones gambuso, Fr-mangeurs d'hommes
Carcharhinus acronotus (Poey, 1860)	A	Blacknose Shark ... tiburón cangüay
Carcharhinus albimarginatus (Rüppell, 1837)	PM	Silvertip Shark ... tiburón puntas blancas
Carcharhinus altimus (Springer, 1950)	A-PM	Bignose Shark ... tiburón narizón
Carcharhinus brachyurus (Günther, 1870)	P	Narrowtooth Shark ... tiburón cobrizo
Carcharhinus brevipinna (Müller & Henle, 1839)	A	Spinner Shark ... tiburón curro
*Carcharhinus cerdale Gilbert, 1898	PM	Pacific Smalltail Shark^ ... tiburón poroso del Pacífico
Carcharhinus falciformis (Müller & Henle, 1839)	A-PM	Silky Shark ... tiburón piloto
+Carcharhinus galapagensis (Snodgrass & Heller, 1905)	A-PM	Galapagos Shark^ ... tiburón de Galápagos
Carcharhinus isodon (Müller & Henle, 1839)	A	Finetooth Shark ... tiburón dentiliso
Carcharhinus leucas (Müller & Henle, 1839)	A-P-F:UM	Bull Shark ... tiburón toro
Carcharhinus limbatus (Müller & Henle, 1839)	A-PM	Blacktip Shark ... tiburón volador
Carcharhinus longimanus (Poey, 1861)	A-P	Oceanic Whitetip Shark ... tiburón oceánico ...requin à longues nageoires
Carcharhinus obscurus (Lesueur, 1818)	A-P	Dusky Shark ... tiburón gambuso ... requin obscur
+Carcharhinus perezii (Poey, 1876)	A	Reef Shark ... tiburón coralino

SCIENTIFIC NAME	OCCURRENCE[1]	COMMON NAME (ENGLISH, SPANISH, FRENCH)[2]
Carcharhinus plumbeus (Nardo, 1827)	A-PM	Sandbar Shark....tiburón aleta de cartón
**Carcharhinus porosus* (Ranzani, 1839)	A	Smalltail Shark....tiburón poroso
Carcharhinus signatus (Poey, 1868)	A	Night Shark....tiburón nocturno
Galeocerdo cuvier (Péron & Lesueur, 1822)	A-P	Tiger Shark....tintorera
Nasolamia velox (Gilbert, 1898)	PM	Whitenose Shark....tiburón coyotito
Negaprion brevirostris (Poey, 1868)	A-PM	Lemon Shark....tiburón limón
Prionace glauca (Linnaeus, 1758)	A-P	Blue Shark....tiburón azul....requin bleu
Rhizoprionodon longurio (Jordan & Gilbert, 1882)	P	Pacific Sharpnose Shark^....cazón bironche
Rhizoprionodon porosus (Poey, 1861)	AM	Caribbean Sharpnose Shark^..cazón antillano
Rhizoprionodon terraenovae (Richardson, 1836)	A	Atlantic Sharpnose Shark^....cazón de ley....requin à nez pointu
Triaenodon obesus (Rüppell, 1837)	PM	Whitetip Reef Shark....cazón coralero trompacorta

Sphyrnidae—En-hammerhead sharks, Sp-tiburones martillo, Fr-requins marteaux

Sphyrna corona Springer, 1940	PM	Scalloped Bonnethead....cornuda coronada
Sphyrna lewini (Griffith & Smith, 1834)	A-P	Scalloped Hammerhead....cornuda común
Sphyrna media Springer, 1940	PM	Scoophead....cornuda cuchara
Sphyrna mokarran (Rüppell, 1837)	A-PM	Great Hammerhead....cornuda gigante
Sphyrna tiburo (Linnaeus, 1758)	A-P	Bonnethead....cornuda cabeza de pala
Sphyrna zygaena (Linnaeus, 1758)	A-P	Smooth Hammerhead....cornuda prieta....requin-marteau commun

ORDER HEXANCHIFORMES

Chlamydoselachidae—En-frill sharks, Sp-tiburones anguila, Fr-requins-lézards

Chlamydoselachus anguineus Garman, 1884	P	Frill Shark....tiburón anguila

Hexanchidae—En-cow sharks, Sp-tiburones cañabota, Fr-grisets

Heptranchias perlo (Bonnaterre, 1788)	A	Sharpnose Sevengill Shark....tiburón de siete branquias
Hexanchus griseus (Bonnaterre, 1788)	A-P	Bluntnose Sixgill Shark....tiburón de seis branquias....requin griset
Hexanchus nakamurai Teng, 1962	A	Bigeye Sixgill Shark....cazón de seis branquias
Notorynchus cepedianus (Péron, 1807)	P	Broadnose Sevengill Shark....tiburón pinto....requin à sept branchies

SCIENTIFIC NAME	OCCURRENCE[1]	COMMON NAME (ENGLISH, SPANISH, FRENCH)[2]

*ORDER ECHINORHINIFORMES

Echinorhinidae—En-bramble sharks, Sp-tiburones espinosos, Fr-squales bouclés

+*Echinorhinus brucus* (Bonnaterre, 1788)	A	Bramble Shark
Echinorhinus cookei Pietschmann, 1928	P	Prickly Shark........tiburón espinoso negro

*ORDER SQUALIFORMES

Squalidae—En-dogfish sharks, Sp-cazones aguijones, Fr-chiens de mer

Cirrhigaleus asper (Merrett, 1973)	A	Roughskin Dogfish
**Squalus acanthias* Linnaeus, 1758	A	Spiny Dogfish........aiguillat commun
Squalus cubensis Howell Rivero, 1936	A	Cuban Dogfish^........cazón aguijón cubano
Squalus mitsukurii Jordan & Snyder, 1903	AM	Shortspine Dogfish........cazón aguijón galludo
*Squalus suckleyi (Girard, 1854)	P	Pacific Spiny Dogfish^........cazón espinoso común......aiguillat du Pacifique

*Etmopteridae—En-lantern sharks, Sp-tiburones luceros, Fr-requins-lanternes

Centroscyllium fabricii (Reinhardt, 1825)	A	Black Dogfish........aiguillat noir
Etmopterus bigelowi Shirai & Tachikawa, 1993	A	Blurred Lantern Shark
Etmopterus gracilispinis Krefft, 1968	A	Broadband Lantern Shark

Somniosidae—En-sleeper sharks, Sp-tiburones dormilones, Fr-somniosidés

Centroscymnus coelolepis Barbosa du Bocage & de Brito Capello, 1864	A	Portuguese Shark^
Somniosus microcephalus (Bloch & Schneider, 1801)	A-Ar.	Greenland Shark^........laimargue atlantique
Somniosus pacificus Bigelow & Schroeder, 1944	P	Pacific Sleeper Shark^........tiburón dormilón del......laimargue du Pacifique Pacífico

Dalatiidae—En-kitefin sharks, Sp-tiburones carochos, Fr-laimargues

Dalatias licha (Bonnaterre, 1788)	A	Kitefin Shark
**Euprotomicrus bispinatus* (Quoy & Gaimard, 1824)	PM	Pygmy Shark........tiburón pigmeo
Isistius brasiliensis (Quoy & Gaimard, 1824)	PM	Cookiecutter Shark........tiburón cigarro

SCIENTIFIC NAME	OCCURRENCE[1]	COMMON NAME (ENGLISH, SPANISH, FRENCH)[2]
ORDER SQUATINIFORMES		
Squatinidae—En-angel sharks, Sp-angelotes, Fr-anges de mer		
Squatina californica Ayres, 1859	P	Pacific Angel Shark^......angelote del Pacífico
Squatina dumeril Lesueur, 1818	A	Atlantic Angel Shark^......angelote del Atlántico
*Squatina heteroptera Castro-Aguirre, Espinosa-Pérez & Huidobro-Campos, 2007	AM	Disparate Angel Shark......angelote disparejo
*Squatina mexicana Castro-Aguirre, Espinosa-Pérez & Huidobro-Campos, 2007	AM	Mexican Angel Shark^......angelote mexicano
ORDER TORPEDINIFORMES		
Torpedinidae—En-torpedo electric rays, Sp-torpedos, Fr-torpilles		
Torpedo californica Ayres, 1855	P	Pacific Electric Ray^......torpedo del Pacífico......torpille du Pacifique
Torpedo nobiliana Bonaparte, 1835	A	Atlantic Torpedo^......torpedo del Atlántico......torpille noire
Narcinidae—En-electric rays, Sp-rayas eléctricas, Fr-narcinidés		
Diplobatis ommata (Jordan & Gilbert, 1890)	PM	Bullseye Electric Ray......raya eléctrica diana
Narcine bancroftii (Griffith & Smith, 1834)	A	Lesser Electric Ray......raya eléctrica torpedo
Narcine entemedor Jordan & Starks, 1895	PM	Giant Electric Ray......raya eléctrica gigante
Narcine vermiculatus Breder, 1928	PM	Vermiculate Electric Ray......raya eléctrica rayada
ORDER PRISTIFORMES		
Pristidae—En-sawfishes, Sp-peces sierra, Fr-poissons-scies		
Pristis pectinata Latham, 1794	A-PM-F:UM	Smalltooth Sawfish......pez sierra peine
Pristis pristis (Linnaeus, 1758)	A-PM-F:M	Largetooth Sawfish......pez sierra común
***ORDER RAJIFORMES**		
Rhinobatidae—En-guitarfishes, Sp-guitarras, Fr-guitares de mer		
Rhinobatos glaucostigma Jordan & Gilbert, 1883	PM	Speckled Guitarfish......guitarra punteada
Rhinobatos lentiginosus Garman, 1880	A	Atlantic Guitarfish^......guitarra diablito

SCIENTIFIC NAME	OCCURRENCE[1]	COMMON NAME (ENGLISH, SPANISH, FRENCH)[2]
Rhinobatos leucorhynchus Günther, 1867	PM	Whitesnout Guitarfish ... guitarra trompa blanca
**Rhinobatos percellens* (Walbaum, 1792)	AM	Chola Guitarfish^ ... guitarra chola
**Rhinobatos prahli* Acero & Franke, 1995	PM	Gorgona Guitarfish^ ... guitarra de Gorgona
Rhinobatos productus Ayres, 1854	P	Shovelnose Guitarfish ... guitarra viola
Rhinobatos spinosus Günther, 1870	PM	Spiny Guitarfish ... guitarra espinosa
Zapteryx exasperata (Jordan & Gilbert, 1880)	P	Banded Guitarfish ... guitarra rayada
*Zapteryx xyster Jordan & Evermann, 1896	PM	Witch Guitarfish ... guitarra bruja
		Rajidae—En-skates, Sp-rayas, Fr-raies
Amblyraja radiata (Donovan, 1808)	A-Ar	Thorny Skate ... raie épineuse
Bathyraja aleutica (Gilbert, 1896)	P	Aleutian Skate^ ... raie aléutienne
Bathyraja interrupta (Gill & Townsend, 1897)	P	Sandpaper Skate ... raie rugueuse
Bathyraja lindbergi Ishiyama & Ishihara, 1977	P	Commander Skate^ ... raie de Lindberg
Bathyraja maculata Ishiyama & Ishihara, 1977	P	Whiteblotched Skate
**Bathyraja mariposa* Stevenson, Orr, Hoff & McEachran, 2004	P	Butterfly Skate
**Bathyraja minispinosa* Ishiyama & Ishihara, 1977	P	Whitebrow Skate
Bathyraja parmifera (Bean, 1881)	P	Alaska Skate^ ... raie d'Alaska
Bathyraja spinicauda (Jensen, 1914)	A-Ar	Spinytail Skate ... raie à queue épineuse
Bathyraja taranetzi (Dolganov, 1983)	P	Mud Skate
Bathyraja violacea (Suvorov, 1935)	P	Okhotsk Skate^
Dipturus bullisi (Bigelow & Schroeder, 1962)	A	Lozenge Skate ... raya triangular
Dipturus laevis (Mitchill, 1818)	A	Barndoor Skate ... grande raie
Dipturus olseni (Bigelow & Schroeder, 1951)	A	Spreadfin Skate ... raya colona
Fenestraja sinusmexicanus (Bigelow & Schroeder, 1950)	AM	Gulf Skate^ ... raya pigmea
Leucoraja caribbaea (McEachran, 1977)	AM	Maya Skate^ ... raya maya
Leucoraja erinacea (Mitchill, 1825)	A	Little Skate ... raya maya
Leucoraja garmani (Whitley, 1939)	A	Rosette Skate
Leucoraja lentiginosa (Bigelow & Schroeder, 1951)	A	Freckled Skate ... raya pecosa
Leucoraja ocellata (Mitchill, 1815)	A	Winter Skate ... raie tachetée

SCIENTIFIC NAME	OCCURRENCE[1]	COMMON NAME (ENGLISH, SPANISH, FRENCH)[2]
Leucoraja virginica (McEachran, 1977)	A	Virginia Skate^ .... raie à queue de velours
Malacoraja senta (Garman, 1885)	A	Smooth Skate ....
Raja ackleyi Garman, 1881	A	Ocellate Skate...................... raya ocelada
Raja binoculata Girard, 1855	P	Big Skate...................... raya bruja gigante ....raie biocellée
Raja cortezensis McEachran & Miyake, 1988	PM	Cortez Skate^ .... raya de Cortés
Raja eglanteria Bosc, 1800	A	Clearnose Skate .... raya naricita ....raie blanc nez
Raja equatorialis Jordan & Bollman, 1890	PM	Equatorial Skate .... raya ecuatorial
Raja inornata Jordan & Gilbert, 1881	P	California Skate^ .... raya de California
Raja rhina Jordan & Gilbert, 1880	P	Longnose Skate .... raya narigona ....pocheteau long-nez
Raja stellulata Jordan & Gilbert, 1880	P	Starry Skate .... raya estrellada...................... raie du Pacifique
Raja texana Chandler, 1921	A	Roundel Skate .... raya tigre
Raja velezi Chirichigno, 1973	PM	Rasptail Skate .... raya chillona
*Rajella fyllae (Lütken, 1887)	A-Ar	Round Skate ....raie ronde

+ORDER MYLIOBATIFORMES

*Platyrhinidae—En-thornbacks, Sp-guitarras espinudas, Fr-guitares de mer épineuses

Platyrhinoidis triseriata (Jordan & Gilbert, 1880)	P	Thornback ....guitarra espinuda

*Urotrygonidae—En-American round stingrays, Sp-rayas redondas americanas, Fr-pastenagues arrondies américaines

Urobatis concentricus Osburn & Nichols, 1916	PM	Reef Stingray......................raya redonda de arrecife
Urobatis halleri (Cooper, 1863)	P	Round Stingray......................raya redonda común
Urobatis jamaicensis (Cuvier, 1816)	A	Yellow Stingray......................raya redonda de estero
Urobatis maculatus Garman, 1913	PM	Cortez Stingray^ ....raya redonda de Cortés
Urotrygon aspidura (Jordan & Gilbert, 1882)	PM	Panamic Stingray^ ....raya redonda panámica
Urotrygon chilensis (Günther, 1872)	PM	Blotched Stingray......................raya redonda moteada
Urotrygon munda Gill, 1863	PM	Spiny Stingray ....raya redonda áspera
Urotrygon nana Miyake & McEachran, 1988.	PM	Dwarf Stingray......................raya redonda enana
Urotrygon rogersi (Jordan & Starks, 1895)	PM	Thorny Stingray......................raya redonda de púas

Dasyatidae—En-whiptail stingrays, Sp-rayas látigo, Fr-pastenagues

Dasyatis americana Hildebrand & Schroeder, 1928	A	Southern Stingray......................raya látigo blanca
Dasyatis centroura (Mitchill, 1815)	A	Roughtail Stingray

SCIENTIFIC NAME	OCCURRENCE[1]	COMMON NAME (ENGLISH, SPANISH, FRENCH)[2]
Dasyatis dipterura (Jordan & Gilbert, 1880)	P	Diamond Stingray ...... raya látigo diamante
Dasyatis guttata (Bloch & Schneider, 1801)	AM	Longnose Stingray ...... raya látigo del Golfo
Dasyatis longa (Garman, 1880)	PM	Longtail Stingray ...... raya látigo largo
Dasyatis sabina (Lesueur, 1824)	A-F:UM	Atlantic Stingray^ ...... raya látigo de espina
Dasyatis say (Lesueur, 1817)	A	Bluntnose Stingray ...... raya látigo chata
Himantura pacifica (Beebe & Tee-Van, 1941)	PM	Pacific Whiptail Stingray^ ...... raya coluda del Pacífico
Himantura schmardae (Werner, 1904)	AM	Caribbean Whiptail Stingray^ . raya coluda caribeña
Pteroplatytrygon violacea (Bonaparte, 1832)	A-P	Pelagic Stingray ...... raya látigo obispo

Gymnuridae—En-butterfly rays, Sp-rayas mariposa, Fr-raies-papillons

Gymnura altavela (Linnaeus, 1758)	A	Spiny Butterfly Ray ...... raya de papel
Gymnura crebripunctata (Peters, 1869)	PM	Longsnout Butterfly Ray ...... raya mariposa picuda
Gymnura marmorata (Cooper, 1864)	P	California Butterfly Ray^ ...... raya mariposa californiana
Gymnura micrura (Bloch & Schneider, 1801)	A	Smooth Butterfly Ray ...... raya cola de rata

*Myliobatidae—En-eagle rays and mantas, Sp-mantas y águilas marinas, Fr-aigles de mer et mantes

Aetobatus narinari (Euphrasen, 1790)	A-PM	Spotted Eagle Ray ...... chucho pintado
Manta birostris (Walbaum, 1792)	A-P	Giant Manta ...... manta gigante ...... mante atlantique
Mobula hypostoma (Bancroft, 1831)	A	Devil Ray ...... manta del Golfo
Mobula japanica (Müller & Henle, 1841)	P	Spinetail Mobula ...... manta arpón
Mobula munkiana Notarbartolo di Sciara, 1987	PM	Pygmy Devil Ray ...... manta chica
Mobula tarapacana (Philippi, 1893)	A-PM	Sicklefin Devil Ray ...... manta cornuda
Mobula thurstoni (Lloyd, 1908)	PM	Smoothtail Mobula ...... manta doblada
Myliobatis californica Gill, 1865	P	Bat Ray ...... tecolote
Myliobatis freminvillei Lesueur, 1824	A	Bullnose Ray ...... águila nariz de vaca
Myliobatis goodei Garman, 1885	A	Southern Eagle Ray
Myliobatis longirostris Applegate & Fitch, 1964	PM	Longnose Eagle Ray ...... águila picuda
Pteromylaeus asperrimus (Gilbert, 1898)	PM	Rough Eagle Ray ...... águila cueruda
Rhinoptera bonasus (Mitchill, 1815)	A	Cownose Ray ...... gavilán cubanito
Rhinoptera brasiliensis Müller 1836	A	Brazilian Cownose Ray^ ...... manta hocico de vaca
Rhinoptera steindachneri Evermann & Jenkins, 1891	PM	Golden Cownose Ray ...... gavilán dorado

SCIENTIFIC NAME	OCCURRENCE[1]	COMMON NAME (ENGLISH, SPANISH, FRENCH)[2]
CLASS ACTINOPTERYGII— RAY-FINNED FISHES		
ORDER ACIPENSERIFORMES		
Acipenseridae—En-sturgeons, Sp-esturiones, Fr-esturgeons		
Acipenser brevirostrum Lesueur, 1818	A-F:CU	Shortnose Sturgeon ... esturgeon à museau court
Acipenser fulvescens Rafinesque, 1817	F:CU	Lake Sturgeon ... esturgeon jaune
Acipenser medirostris Ayres, 1854	P-F:CU	Green Sturgeon ... esturión verde ... esturgeon vert
Acipenser oxyrinchus Mitchill, 1815	A-F:CUM	Atlantic Sturgeon^ ... esturión del Atlántico ... esturgeon noir
Acipenser transmontanus Richardson, 1836	P-F:CU	White Sturgeon ... esturión blanco ... esturgeon blanc
Scaphirhynchus albus (Forbes & Richardson, 1905)	F:U	Pallid Sturgeon
Scaphirhynchus platorynchus (Rafinesque, 1820)	F:U	Shovelnose Sturgeon
Scaphirhynchus suttkusi Williams & Clemmer, 1991	F:U	Alabama Sturgeon^
Polyodontidae—En-paddlefishes, Sp-espátulas, Fr-spatules		
+Polyodon spathula (Walbaum, 1792)	F:CU	Paddlefish ... spatulaire
ORDER LEPISOSTEIFORMES		
Lepisosteidae—En-gars, Sp-pejelagartos, Fr-lépisostés		
*Atractosteus spatula (Lacepède, 1803)	A-F:UM	Alligator Gar ... catán
Atractosteus tropicus Gill, 1863	F:M	Tropical Gar ... pejelagarto
Lepisosteus oculatus Winchell, 1864	F:CUM	Spotted Gar ... catán pinto ... lépisosté tacheté
*Lepisosteus osseus (Linnaeus, 1758)	A-F:CUM	Longnose Gar ... catán aguja ... lépisosté osseux
*Lepisosteus platostomus Rafinesque, 1820	A-F:U	Shortnose Gar
Lepisosteus platyrhincus DeKay, 1842	F:U	Florida Gar^
ORDER AMIIFORMES		
Amiidae—En-bowfins, Sp-amias, Fr-poissons-castors		
Amia calva Linnaeus, 1766	F:CU	Bowfin ... poisson-castor

SCIENTIFIC NAME	OCCURRENCE[1]	COMMON NAME (ENGLISH, SPANISH, FRENCH)[2]

ORDER HIODONTIFORMES

Hiodontidae—En-mooneyes, Sp-ojos de luna, Fr-laquaiches

Hiodon alosoides (Rafinesque, 1819)	F:CU	Goldeye ....laquaiche aux yeux d'or
Hiodon tergisus Lesueur, 1818	F:CU	Mooneye.................................laquaiche argentée

ORDER OSTEOGLOSSIFORMES

Notopteridae—En-featherfin knifefishes, Sp-cuchillos de pluma, Fr-poissons-couteaux à nageoire plumeuse

Chitala ornata (Gray, 1831)	F[I]:U	Clown Knifefish

ORDER ELOPIFORMES

Elopidae—En-tenpounders, Sp-machetes, Fr-guinées

Elops affinis Regan, 1909	P-F:UM	Machete ....machete del Pacífico
Elops saurus Linnaeus, 1766	A-F:UM	Ladyfish ....machete del Atlántico
Elops smithi McBride, Rocha, Ruiz-Carus & Bowen, 2010	A-F:UM	Malacho ....machete malacho

Megalopidae—En-tarpons, Sp-sábalos, Fr-tarpons

Megalops atlanticus Valenciennes, 1847	A-F:CUM	Tarpon ....sábalo...................................tarpon

ORDER ALBULIFORMES

+Albulidae—En-bonefishes, Sp-macabíes, Fr-bananes de mer

Albula esuncula (Garman, 1899)	PM	Eastern Pacific Bonefish^.........macabí del Pacífico oriental
Albula gilberti Pfeiler & van der Heiden, 2011	P	Cortez Bonefish^.........macabí de Cortés
Albula pacifica (Beebe, 1942)	PM	Pacific Shafted Bonefish^.........macabí de hebra del Pacífico
+*Albula vulpes* (Linnaeus, 1758)	A	Bonefish.........macabí

*Notacanthidae—En-deep-sea spiny eels, Sp-anguilas espinosas de profundidad, Fr-poissons-tapirs à épines

Notacanthus chemnitzii Bloch, 1788	A-Ar.	Snubnosed Spiny Eel.................tapir à grandes écailles

SCIENTIFIC NAME	OCCURRENCE[1]	COMMON NAME (ENGLISH, SPANISH, FRENCH)[2]		

ORDER ANGUILLIFORMES

Anguillidae—En-freshwater eels, Sp-anguilas de río, Fr-anguilles d'eau douce

Scientific Name	Occurrence	English	Spanish	French
Anguilla rostrata (Lesueur, 1817)	A-F:CUM	American Eel^	anguila americana	anguille d'Amérique

Heterenchelyidae—En-mud eels, Sp-anguilas de fango, Fr-anguilles de vase

Pythonichthys asodes Rosenblatt & Rubinoff, 1972	PM	Pacific Mud Eel^	anguila de fango del Pacifico	

Moringuidae—En-spaghetti eels, Sp-anguilas fideo, Fr-anguilles-spaghettis

Moringua edwardsi (Jordan & Bollman, 1889)	A	Spaghetti Eel	morenita	
Neoconger mucronatus Girard, 1858	A	Ridged Eel	anguila fideo aquillada	
*Neoconger vermiformis Gilbert, 1890	PM	Smalleye Spaghetti Eel	anguila fideo macarrón	

Chlopsidae—En-false morays, Sp-morenas falsas, Fr-fausses murènes

Chilorhinus suensonii Lütken, 1852	A	Seagrass Eel	morena falsa bembona	
Chlopsis apterus (Beebe & Tee-Van, 1938)	PM	Stripesnout False Moray	morena falsa hocico rayado	
Chlopsis bicolor Rafinesque, 1810	A	Bicolor Eel		
Chlopsis dentatus (Seale, 1917)	AM	Mottled False Moray	morena falsa dientona	
*Chlopsis kazuko Lavenberg, 1988	PM	Mexican False Moray^	morena falsa mexicana	
Kaupichthys hyoproroides (Strömman, 1896)	A	False Moray	morena falsa de arrecife	
Kaupichthys nuchalis Böhlke, 1967	A	Collared Eel	morena falsa de collar	

Muraenidae—En-morays, Sp-morenas, Fr-murènes

Anarchias galapagensis (Seale, 1940)	PM	Hardtail Moray	morena cola dura	
Anarchias similis (Lea, 1913)	A	Pygmy Moray	morena enana	
Channomuraena vittata (Richardson, 1845)	AM	Broadbanded Moray	morena cinturones	
Echidna catenata (Bloch, 1795)	A	Chain Moray	morena cadena	
Echidna nebulosa (Ahl, 1789)	PM	Starry Moray	morena estrellada	
Echidna nocturna (Cope, 1872)	PM	Palenose Moray	morena pecosa	
Enchelycore carychroa Böhlke & Böhlke, 1976	A	Chestnut Moray	morena castaña	
Enchelycore nigricans (Bonnaterre, 1788)	A	Viper Moray	morena víbora	
Enchelycore octaviana (Myers & Wade, 1941)	PM	Slenderjaw Moray	morena octaviana	

SCIENTIFIC NAME	OCCURRENCE[1]	COMMON NAME (ENGLISH, SPANISH, FRENCH)[2]
Gymnomuraena zebra (Shaw, 1797)	PM	Zebra Moray	morena cebra
Gymnothorax castaneus (Jordan & Gilbert, 1883)	PM	Panamic Green Moray^	morena verde panámica
Gymnothorax conspersus Poey, 1867	A	Saddled Moray	
Gymnothorax dovii (Günther, 1870)	PM	Finespotted Moray	morena pintita
Gymnothorax equatorialis (Hildebrand, 1946)	PM	Spottail Moray	morena cola pintada
Gymnothorax flavimarginatus (Rüppell, 1830)	PM	Yellow-edged Moray	morena de borde amarillo
Gymnothorax funebris Ranzani, 1839	A	Green Moray	morena verde .... murène verte
Gymnothorax hubbsi Böhlke & Böhlke, 1977	A	Lichen Moray	
Gymnothorax kolpos Böhlke & Böhlke, 1980	A	Blacktail Moray	morena cola negra
Gymnothorax maderensis (Johnson, 1862)	A	Sharktooth Moray	
Gymnothorax miliaris (Kaup, 1856)	A	Goldentail Moray	morena cola dorada
Gymnothorax mordax (Ayres, 1859)	P	California Moray^	morena de California
Gymnothorax moringa (Cuvier, 1829)	A	Spotted Moray	morena manchada
Gymnothorax nigromarginatus (Girard, 1858)	A	Blackedge Moray	morena de margen negro
Gymnothorax ocellatus Agassiz, 1831	AM	Ocellated Moray	morena ocelada
Gymnothorax panamensis (Steindachner, 1876)	PM	Masked Moray	morena mapache
Gymnothorax pictus Ahl, 1789	PM	Paintspotted Moray	morena pecas pintura
Gymnothorax polygonius Poey, 1875	A	Polygon Moray	morena poligona
Gymnothorax saxicola Jordan & Davis, 1891	A	Honeycomb Moray	morena panal
Gymnothorax undulatus (Lacepède, 1803)	PM	Undulated Moray	morena ondulada
Gymnothorax verrilli (Jordan & Gilbert, 1883)	PM	White-edged Moray	morena de borde blanco
Gymnothorax vicinus (Castelnau, 1855)	A	Purplemouth Moray	morena amarilla
Monopenchelys acuta (Parr, 1930)	AM	Redface Moray	morena rubicunda
Muraena argus (Steindachner, 1870)	P	Argus Moray^	morena Argos
Muraena clepsydra Gilbert, 1898	PM	Hourglass Moray	morena clepsidra
Muraena lentiginosa Jenyns, 1842	PM	Jewel Moray	morena pinta
Muraena retifera Goode & Bean, 1882	A	Reticulate Moray	morena reticulada
Muraena robusta Osório, 1911	A	Stout Moray	
Scuticaria tigrina (Lesson, 1828)	PM	Tiger Reef Eel	morena atigrada
Uropterygius macrocephalus (Bleeker, 1865)	PM	Largehead Moray	morena cabezona
Uropterygius macularius (Lesueur, 1825)	A	Marbled Moray	morena jaspeada
Uropterygius polystictus Myers & Wade, 1941	PM	Peppered Moray	morena pintada
Uropterygius versutus Bussing, 1991	PM	Crafty Moray	morena lista

SCIENTIFIC NAME	OCCURRENCE[1]	COMMON NAME (ENGLISH, SPANISH, FRENCH)[2]
Synaphobranchidae—En-cutthroat eels, Sp-anguilas branquias bajas, Fr-anguilles égorgées		
Dysomma anguillare Barnard, 1923	A	Shortbelly Eel...anguila panzacorta
Synaphobranchus kaupii Johnson, 1862	A-Ar	Northern Cutthroat Eel...anguille égorgée bécue
+Ophichthidae—En-snake eels, Sp-tiesos, Fr-serpents de mer		
Ahlia egmontis (Jordan, 1884)	A	Key Worm Eel...tieso de cayo
Aplatophis chauliodus Böhlke, 1956	A	Tusky Eel
Aprognathodon platyventris Böhlke, 1967	A	Stripe Eel
Apterichtus ansp (Böhlke, 1968)	A	Academy Eel^
Apterichtus equatorialis (Myers & Wade, 1941)	PM	Equatorial Eel...tieso ecuatorial
Apterichtus kendalli (Gilbert, 1891)	A	Finless Eel
Bascanichthys bascanium (Jordan, 1884)	A	Sooty Eel...tieso tiznado
Bascanichthys bascanoides Osburn & Nichols, 1916	PM	Sooty Sand Eel...tieso manchitas
Bascanichthys panamensis Meek & Hildebrand, 1923	PM	Panamic Sand Eel^...tieso panámico
Bascanichthys scuticaris (Goode & Bean, 1880)	A	Whip Eel
Callechelys bilinearis Kanazawa, 1952	AM	Twostripe Snake Eel...tieso dos rayas
Callechelys cliffi Böhlke & Briggs, 1954	PM	Sandy Ridgefin Eel...tieso aquillado arenero
Callechelys eristigma McCosker & Rosenblatt, 1972	PM	Spotted Ridgefin Eel...tieso aquillado manchado
Callechelys guineensis (Osório, 1893)	A	Shorttail Snake Eel...tieso colicorta
Callechelys muraena Jordan & Evermann, 1887	A	Blotched Snake Eel...tieso moteado
Callechelys springeri (Ginsburg, 1951)	A	Ridgefin Eel
Caralophia loxochila Böhlke, 1955	A	Slantlip Eel
Echiophis brunneus (Castro-Aguirre & Suárez de los Cobos, 1983)	PM	Fangjaw Eel...tieso colmillón
Echiophis intertinctus (Richardson, 1848)	A	Spotted Spoon-nose Eel...tieso cucharón manchado
Echiophis punctifer (Kaup, 1860)	A	Snapper Eel...tieso pecoso
Ethadophis akkistikos McCosker & Böhlke, 1984	A	Indifferent Eel
Ethadophis byrnei Rosenblatt & McCosker, 1970	PM	Ordinary Eel...tieso de Cortés
Ethadophis merenda Rosenblatt & McCosker, 1970	PM	Snack Eel...tieso merienda
Gordiichthys ergodes McCosker, Böhlke & Böhlke, 1989	A	Irksome Eel...tieso fastidioso
Gordiichthys irretitus Jordan & Davis, 1891	A	Horsehair Eel...tieso pelo de burro

SCIENTIFIC NAME	OCCURRENCE[1]	COMMON NAME (ENGLISH, SPANISH, FRENCH)[2]
Gordiichthys leibyi McCosker & Böhlke, 1984	A	String Eel......tieso bobo
Herpetoichthys fossatus (Myers & Wade, 1941)	PM	Mustachioed Snake Eel......tieso bigotón
Ichthyapus ophioneus (Evermann & Marsh, 1900)	A	Surf Eel......tieso alacrán
Ichthyapus selachops (Jordan & Gilbert, 1882)	PM	Smiling Sand Eel......tieso sonriente
Letharchus rosenblatti McCosker, 1974	PM	Black Sailfin Eel......tieso vela negro
Letharchus velifer Goode & Bean, 1882	A	Sailfin Eel
Lethogoleos andersoni McCosker & Böhlke, 1982	A	Forgetful Snake Eel
Leuropharus lasiops Rosenblatt & McCosker, 1970	PM	Acned Snake Eel......tieso pustuloso
Myrichthys aspetocheiros McCosker & Rosenblatt, 1993	PM	Longfin Spotted Snake Eel......tieso aletón
Myrichthys breviceps (Richardson, 1848)	A	Sharptail Eel......tieso afilado
Myrichthys ocellatus (Lesueur, 1825)	A	Goldspotted Eel......tieso manchas doradas
Myrichthys pantostigmius Jordan & McGregor, 1898	PM	Clarion Snake Eel^......tieso manchado de Clarión
Myrichthys tigrinus Girard, 1859	P	Tiger Snake Eel......tieso tigre
Myrophis platyrhynchus Breder, 1927	AM	Broadnose Worm Eel......tieso chato
Myrophis punctatus Lütken, 1852	A	Speckled Worm Eel......tieso gusano
Myrophis vafer Jordan & Gilbert, 1883	P	Pacific Worm Eel^......tieso lombriz
Ophichthus apachus McCosker & Rosenblatt, 1998	PM	Thin Snake Eel......tieso delgado
Ophichthus cruentifer (Goode & Bean, 1896)	A	Margined Snake Eel
Ophichthus frontalis Garman, 1899	PM	Deathbanded Snake Eel......tieso funebre
Ophichthus gomesii (Castelnau, 1855)	A	Shrimp Eel......tieso camaronero
Ophichthus hyposagmatus McCosker & Böhlke, 1984	A	Faintsaddled Snake Eel
Ophichthus longipenis McCosker & Rosenblatt, 1998	PM	Slender Snake Eel......tieso fino
Ophichthus mecopterus McCosker & Rosenblatt, 1998	PM	Longarmed Snake Eel......tieso brazo largo
Ophichthus melanoporus Kanazawa, 1963	A	Blackpored Eel
Ophichthus omorgmus McCosker & Böhlke, 1984	A	Dottedline Snake Eel
Ophichthus ophis (Linnaeus, 1758)	A	Spotted Snake Eel
Ophichthus puncticeps (Kaup, 1860)	A	Palespotted Eel
Ophichthus rex Böhlke & Caruso, 1980	A	King Snake Eel......lairón
Ophichthus triserialis (Kaup, 1856)	P	Pacific Snake Eel^......tieso del Pacifico
Ophichthus zophochir Jordan & Gilbert, 1882	P	Yellow Snake Eel......tieso amarillo
Paraletharchus opercularis (Myers & Wade, 1941)	PM	Pouch Snake Eel......tieso bolsa

SCIENTIFIC NAME	OCCURRENCE[1]	COMMON NAME (ENGLISH, SPANISH, FRENCH)[2]
Paraletharchus pacificus (Osburn & Nichols, 1916)	PM	Pacific Sailfin Eel^ .... tieso vela del Pacífico
Phaenomonas pinnata Myers & Wade, 1941	PM	Elastic Eel .... tieso elástico
Pisodonophis daspilotus Gilbert, 1898	PM	Blunt-toothed Snake Eel .... tieso dientes romos
Pseudomyrophis fugesae McCosker, Böhlke & Böhlke, 1989	A	Diminutive Worm Eel
Pseudomyrophis micropinna Wade, 1946	PM	Plain Worm Eel .... tieso enano
Quassiremus nothochir (Gilbert, 1890)	PM	Redsaddled Snake Eel .... tieso bisagra
Scytalichthys miurus (Jordan & Gilbert, 1882)	PM	Shorttail Viper Eel .... tieso víbora
Muraenesocidae—En-pike congers, Sp-congrios picudos, Fr-congres-brochets		
Cynoponticus coniceps (Jordan & Gilbert, 1882)	PM	Conehead Eel .... congrio espantoso
Nemichthyidae—En-snipe eels, Sp-anguilas tijera, Fr-poissons-avocettes		
Nemichthys scolopaceus Richardson, 1848	A-P-Ar	Slender Snipe Eel .... tijera esbelta .... avocette ruban
Congridae—En-conger eels, Sp-congrios, Fr-congres		
Ariosoma anale (Poey, 1860)	A	Longtrunk Conger
Ariosoma balearicum (Delaroche, 1809)	A	Bandtooth Conger .... congrio balear
Ariosoma gilberti (Ogilby, 1898)	PM	Sharpnose Conger .... congrio narigón
Bathycongrus bullisi (Smith & Kanazawa, 1977)	AM	Bullish Conger .... congrio disparatado
Bathycongrus dubius (Breder, 1927)	A	Dubious Conger
Bathycongrus macrurus (Gilbert, 1891)	PM	Shorthead Conger .... congrio cabeza corta
Bathycongrus varidens (Garman, 1899)	PM	Largehead Conger .... congrio cabezón
Bathycongrus vicinalis (Garman, 1899)	AM	Neighbor Conger .... congrio vecino
Chiloconger dentatus (Garman, 1899)	PM	Thicklip Conger .... congrio labioso
Conger oceanicus (Mitchill, 1818)	A	Conger Eel .... congre à museau aigu
Conger triporiceps Kanazawa, 1958	A	Manytooth Conger .... congrio dentudo
Gnathophis bathytopos Smith & Kanazawa, 1977	A	Blackgut Conger
Gnathophis bracheatopos Smith & Kanazawa, 1977	A	Longeye Conger
Gnathophis cinctus (Garman, 1899)	P	Hardtail Conger .... congrio cola tiesa

SCIENTIFIC NAME	OCCURRENCE[1]	COMMON NAME (ENGLISH, SPANISH, FRENCH)[2]
Gorgasia punctata Meek & Hildebrand, 1923	PM	Peppered Garden Eel............congrio punteado
Heteroconger canabus (Cowan & Rosenblatt, 1974)	PM	Cape Garden Eel^............congrio del Cabo
Heteroconger digueti (Pellegrin, 1923)	PM	Cortez Garden Eel^............congrio de Cortés
Heteroconger longissimus Günther, 1870	A	Brown Garden Eel
Heteroconger luteolus Smith, 1989	A	Yellow Garden Eel
Heteroconger pellegrini Castle, 1999	PM	Speckled Garden Eel............congrio pecoso
Parabathymyrus oregoni Smith & Kanazawa, 1977	AM	Flapnose Conger............congrio nariz colgada
Paraconger californiensis Kanazawa, 1961	PM	Ringeye Conger............congrio anteojos
Paraconger caudilimbatus (Poey, 1867)	A	Margintail Conger............congrio cola de bordes
Paraconger similis (Wade, 1946)	PM	Shorttail Conger............congrio colicorta
Rhynchoconger flavus (Goode & Bean, 1896)	A	Yellow Conger............congrio amarillo
Rhynchoconger gracilior (Ginsburg, 1951)	A	Whiptail Conger............congrio grácil
Rhynchoconger nitens (Jordan & Bollman, 1890)	PM	Needletail Conger............congrio estilete
Uroconger syringinus Ginsburg, 1954	A	Threadtail Conger............congrio plumilla
Xenomystax congroides Smith & Kanazawa, 1989	A	Bristletooth Conger

Nettastomatidae—En-duckbill eels, Sp-serpentinas, Fr-anguilles à bec de canard

Facciolella equatorialis (Gilbert, 1891)	P	Dogface Witch Eel............serpentina bruja
Hoplunnis diomediana Goode & Bean, 1896	A	Blacktail Pikeconger............serpentina albatros
Hoplunnis macrura Ginsburg, 1951	A	Freckled Pikeconger............serpentina cola grande
Hoplunnis pacifica Lane & Stewart, 1968	PM	Silver Pikeconger............serpentina plateada
Hoplunnis tenuis Ginsburg, 1951	A	Spotted Pikeconger............serpentina dientona
Nettenchelys pygmaea Smith & Böhlke, 1981	A	Pygmy Pikeconger............serpentina enana
Saurenchelys cognita Smith, 1989	A	Longface Eel............serpentina noble

*Serrivomeridae—En-sawtooth eels, Sp-anguilas dientes aserrados, Fr- anguilles dents-de-scie

Serrivomer beanii Gill & Ryder, 1883	A	Stout Sawpalate............serrivomer trapu

+ORDER CLUPEIFORMES

Pristigasteridae—En-longfin herrings, Sp-sardinas machete, Fr-pristigastéridés

Ilisha fuerthii (Steindachner, 1875)	PM	Hatchet Herring............sardina hacha

SCIENTIFIC NAME	OCCURRENCE[1]	COMMON NAME (ENGLISH, SPANISH, FRENCH)[2]
Neoopisthopterus tropicus (Hildebrand, 1946)	PM	Tropical Longfin Herring .... sardinela pelada
Odontognathus panamensis (Steindachner, 1876)	PM	Panama Longfin Herring^ .... sardina machete panameña
Opisthopterus dovii (Günther, 1868)	PM	Pacific Longfin Herring^ .... sardina machete chata
Pliosteostoma lutipinnis (Jordan & Gilbert, 1882)	PM	Yellowfin Herring .... arenquilla aleta amarilla

Engraulidae—En-anchovies, Sp-anchoas, Fr-anchois

SCIENTIFIC NAME	OCCURRENCE[1]	COMMON NAME (ENGLISH, SPANISH, FRENCH)[2]
*Anchoa analis (Miller, 1945)	PM	Longfin Pacific Anchovy^ .... anchoa aletona del Pacifico
Anchoa argentivittata (Regan, 1904)	PM	Silverstripe Anchovy .... anchoa plateada
Anchoa belizensis (Thomerson & Greenfield, 1975)	F:M	Belize Anchovy^ .... anchoa beliceña
Anchoa cayorum (Fowler, 1906)	A	Key Anchovy .... anchoa de cayo
Anchoa colonensis Hildebrand, 1943	AM	Narrowstriped Anchovy .... anchoa rayita
Anchoa compressa (Girard, 1858)	P	Deepbody Anchovy .... anchoa alta
Anchoa cubana (Poey, 1868)	A	Cuban Anchovy^ .... anchoa cubana
Anchoa curta (Jordan & Gilbert, 1882)	PM	Short Anchovy .... anchoa chaparra
Anchoa delicatissima (Girard, 1854)	P	Slough Anchovy .... anchoa delicada
*Anchoa exigua (Jordan & Gilbert, 1882)	PM	Slender Anchovy .... anchoa fina
Anchoa helleri (Hubbs, 1921)	PM	Gulf Anchovy^ .... anchoa del Golfo
Anchoa hepsetus (Linnaeus, 1758)	A-F:M	Striped Anchovy .... anchoa legitima....... piquitinga
Anchoa ischana (Jordan & Gilbert, 1882)	PM	Sharpnose Anchovy .... anchoa chicotera
Anchoa lamprotaenia Hildebrand, 1943	A	Bigeye Anchovy .... anchoa ojuda
Anchoa lucida (Jordan & Gilbert, 1882)	PM	Bright Anchovy .... anchoa ojitos
Anchoa lyolepis (Evermann & Marsh, 1900)	A	Dusky Anchovy .... anchoa mulata
Anchoa mitchilli (Valenciennes, 1848)	A-F:UM	Bay Anchovy .... anchoa de caleta
Anchoa mundeola (Gilbert & Pierson, 1898)	PM	False Panama Anchovy^ .... anchoa panameña falsa
Anchoa mundeoloides (Breder, 1928)	PM	Northern Gulf Anchovy^ .... anchoa golfina
Anchoa nasus (Kner & Steindachner, 1867)	PM	Bignose Anchovy .... anchoa trompuda
Anchoa parva (Meek & Hildebrand, 1923)	AM-F:M	Little Anchovy .... anchoa parva
Anchoa scofieldi (Jordan & Culver, 1895)	PM	Yellow Anchovy .... anchoa amarilla
*Anchoa walkeri Baldwin & Chang, 1970	PM-F:M	Persistent Anchovy .... anchoa persistente
Anchovia clupeoides (Swainson, 1839)	AM	Zabaleta Anchovy .... anchoveta sardina
*Anchovia macrolepidota (Kner, 1863)	PM-F:M	Bigscale Anchovy .... anchoveta escamuda
Anchoviella perfasciata (Poey, 1860)	A	Flat Anchovy .... anchoa chata

SCIENTIFIC NAME	OCCURRENCE[1]	COMMON NAME (ENGLISH, SPANISH, FRENCH)[2]		
Cetengraulis edentulus (Cuvier, 1829)	AM	Atlantic Anchoveta^	anchoveta rabo amarillo	
Cetengraulis mysticetus (Günther, 1867)	P	Anchoveta	anchoveta bocona	
Engraulis eurystole (Swain & Meek, 1884)	A	Silver Anchovy		anchois argenté
Engraulis mordax Girard, 1854	P	Northern Anchovy	anchoveta norteña	anchois du Pacifique
Clupeidae—En-herrings, Sp-sardinas, Fr-harengs				
Alosa aestivalis (Mitchill, 1814)	A-F:CU	Blueback Herring		alose d'été
Alosa alabamae Jordan & Evermann, 1896	A-F:U	Alabama Shad^		
Alosa chrysochloris (Rafinesque, 1820)	A-F:U	Skipjack Herring		
Alosa mediocris (Mitchill, 1814)	A-F:U	Hickory Shad		
Alosa pseudoharengus (Wilson, 1811)	A-F:CU	Alewife		gaspareau
Alosa sapidissima (Wilson, 1811)	A-P[I]-F:CU	American Shad^	sábalo americano	alose savoureuse
Brevoortia gunteri Hildebrand, 1948	A	Finescale Menhaden	sardina escamitas	
Brevoortia patronus Goode, 1878	A	Gulf Menhaden^	sardina lacha	
Brevoortia smithi Hildebrand, 1941	A	Yellowfin Menhaden		
Brevoortia tyrannus (Latrobe, 1802)	A	Atlantic Menhaden^		alose tyran
Clupea harengus Linnaeus, 1758	A-Ar	Atlantic Herring^		hareng atlantique
Clupea pallasii Valenciennes, 1847	P-Ar	Pacific Herring^	arenque del Pacifico	hareng du Pacifique
Dorosoma anale Meek, 1904	F:M	Longfin Gizzard Shad	sardina del Papaloapan	
Dorosoma cepedianum (Lesueur, 1818)	A-F:CUM	Gizzard Shad	sardina molleja	alose à gésier
Dorosoma petenense (Günther, 1867)	A-P[I]-F:UM	Threadfin Shad	sardina maya	
Dorosoma smithi Hubbs & Miller, 1941	F:M	Pacific Gizzard Shad^	sardina norteña	
Etrumeus teres (DeKay, 1842)	A-P	Round Herring	sardina japonesa	shadine
Harengula clupeola (Cuvier, 1829)	A	False Pilchard	sardinita carapachona	
Harengula humeralis (Cuvier, 1829)	A	Redear Sardine	sardinita de ley	
Harengula jaguana Poey, 1865	A-F:UM	Scaled Sardine	sardinita vivita escamuda	
Harengula thrissina (Jordan & Gilbert, 1882)	P	Flatiron Herring	sardinita plumilla	
Jenkinsia lamprotaenia (Gosse, 1851)	A	Dwarf Herring	sardinita flaca	
Jenkinsia majua Whitehead, 1963	A	Little-eye Herring	sardinita ojito	
Jenkinsia stolifera (Jordan & Gilbert, 1884)	A	Shortband Herring	sardinita de cayo	
Lile gracilis Castro-Aguirre & Vivero, 1990	PM-F:M	Graceful Herring	sardinita agua dulce	

SCIENTIFIC NAME	OCCURRENCE[1]	COMMON NAME (ENGLISH, SPANISH, FRENCH)[2]
Lile nigrofasciata Castro-Aguirre, Ruiz-Campos & Balart, 2002	PM	Blackstripe Herring............sardinita raya negra
Lile stolifera (Jordan & Gilbert, 1882)	PM-F:M	Striped Herring............sardinita rayada
Opisthonema bulleri (Regan, 1904)	PM	Slender Thread Herring........sardina crinuda azul
Opisthonema libertate (Günther, 1867)	P	Deepbody Thread Herring......sardina crinuda
Opisthonema medirastre Berry & Barrett, 1963	P	Middling Thread Herring.......sardina crinuda machete
Opisthonema oglinum (Lesueur, 1818)	A-F:U	Atlantic Thread Herring^............sardina vivita de hebra
Sardinella aurita Valenciennes, 1847	A	Spanish Sardine^............sardina española
Sardinops sagax (Jenyns, 1842)	P	Pacific Sardine^............sardina monterrey............sardine du Pacifique

ORDER GONORYNCHIFORMES

Chanidae—En-milkfishes, Sp-sabalotes, Fr-chanos

Chanos chanos (Forsskål, 1775)	P	Milkfish............sabalote

ORDER CYPRINIFORMES

+Cyprinidae—En-carps and minnows, Sp-carpas y carpitas, Fr-carpes et ménés

Acrocheilus alutaceus Agassiz & Pickering, 1855	F:CU	Chiselmouth............bouche coupante
Agosia chrysogaster Girard, 1856	F:UM	Longfin Dace............pupo panzaverde
Algansea amecae Pérez-Rodríguez, Pérez-Ponce de León, Domínguez-Domínguez & Doadrio, 2009	F:M	Ameca Chub^............pupo del Ameca
Algansea aphanea Barbour & Miller, 1978	F:M	Riffle Chub............pupo del Ayutla
Algansea avia Barbour & Miller, 1978	F:M	Remote Chub............pupo de Tepic
Algansea barbata Álvarez & Cortés, 1964	F:M	Lerma Chub^............pupo del Lerma
Algansea lacustris Steindachner, 1895	F:M	Pátzcuaro Chub^............acúmara
Algansea monticola Barbour & Contreras-Balderas, 1968	F:M	Mountain Chub............pupo del Juchipila
Algansea popoche (Jordan & Snyder, 1899)	F:M	Popoche Chub............popocha
+*Algansea tincella* (Valenciennes, 1844)	F:M	Spottail Chub............pupo del Valle
+*Campostoma anomalum* (Rafinesque, 1820)	F:CUM	Central Stoneroller............rodapiedras del centro............roule-caillou
Campostoma oligolepis Hubbs & Greene, 1935	F:U	Largescale Stoneroller

SCIENTIFIC NAME	OCCURRENCE[1]	COMMON NAME (ENGLISH, SPANISH, FRENCH)[2]
Campostoma ornatum Girard, 1856	F:UM	Mexican Stoneroller^ ......rodapiedras mexicano
Campostoma pauciradii Burr & Cashner, 1983	F:U	Bluefin Stoneroller
Campostoma spadiceum (Girard, 1856)	F:U	Highland Stoneroller
Carassius auratus (Linnaeus, 1758)	F[I]:CUM	Goldfish......carpa dorada......carassin
Chrosomus cumberlandensis (Starnes & Starnes, 1978)	F:U	Blackside Dace
Chrosomus eos Cope, 1862	F:CU	Northern Redbelly Dace......ventre rouge du nord
Chrosomus erythrogaster (Rafinesque, 1820)	F:U	Southern Redbelly Dace
Chrosomus neogaeus (Cope, 1867)	F:CU	Finescale Dace ......ventre citron
Chrosomus oreas Cope, 1868	F:U	Mountain Redbelly Dace
Chrosomus saylori (Skelton, 2001)	F:U	Laurel Dace
Chrosomus tennesseensis (Starnes & Jenkins, 1988)	F:U	Tennessee Dace^
Clinostomus elongatus (Kirtland, 1841)	F:CU	Redside Dace......méné long
Clinostomus funduloides Girard, 1856	F:U	Rosyside Dace
Codoma ornata Girard, 1856	F:M	Ornate Shiner ......carpita adornada
Couesius plumbeus (Agassiz, 1850)	F:CU	Lake Chub ......méné de lac
Ctenopharyngodon idella (Valenciennes, 1844)	F[I]:UM	Grass Carp......carpa herbívora......carpe de roseau
Cyprinella alvarezdelvillari Contreras-Balderas & Lozano-Vilano, 1994	F:M	Tepehuan Shiner^ ......carpita tepehuana
Cyprinella analostana Girard, 1859	F:U	Satinfin Shiner
Cyprinella bocagrande (Chernoff & Miller, 1982)	F:M	Largemouth Shiner......carpita bocagrande
Cyprinella caerulea (Jordan, 1877)	F:U	Blue Shiner
Cyprinella callisema (Jordan, 1877)	F:U	Ocmulgee Shiner^
Cyprinella callistia (Jordan, 1877)	F:U	Alabama Shiner^
Cyprinella callitaenia (Bailey & Gibbs, 1956)	F:U	Bluestripe Shiner
Cyprinella camura (Jordan & Meek, 1884)	F:U	Bluntface Shiner
Cyprinella chloristia (Jordan & Brayton, 1878)	F:U	Greenfin Shiner
Cyprinella formosa (Girard, 1856)	F:UM	Beautiful Shiner ......carpita yaqui
Cyprinella galactura (Cope, 1868)	F:U	Whitetail Shiner
Cyprinella garmani (Jordan, 1885)	F:M	Gibbous Shiner......carpita jorobada
Cyprinella gibbsi (Howell & Williams, 1971)	F:U	Tallapoosa Shiner^
Cyprinella labrosa (Cope, 1870)	F:U	Thicklip Chub
Cyprinella leedsi (Fowler, 1942)	F:U	Bannerfin Shiner

SCIENTIFIC NAME	OCCURRENCE[1]	COMMON NAME (ENGLISH, SPANISH, FRENCH)[2]
Cyprinella lepida Girard, 1856	F:U	Plateau Shiner
+Cyprinella lutrensis (Baird & Girard, 1853)	F:UM	Red Shiner....carpita roja
Cyprinella nivea (Cope, 1870)	F:U	Whitefin Shiner
Cyprinella panarcys (Hubbs & Miller, 1978)	F:M	Conchos Shiner^....carpita del Conchos
Cyprinella proserpina (Girard, 1856)	F:UM	Proserpine Shiner....carpita del Norte
Cyprinella pyrrhomelas (Cope, 1870)	F:U	Fieryblack Shiner
Cyprinella rutila (Girard, 1856)	F:M	Mexican Red Shiner^....carpita regiomontana
Cyprinella spiloptera (Cope, 1867)	F:CU	Spotfin Shiner....méné bleu
Cyprinella trichroistia (Jordan & Gilbert, 1878)	F:U	Tricolor Shiner
Cyprinella venusta Girard, 1856	F:UM	Blacktail Shiner....carpita colinegra
Cyprinella whipplei Girard, 1856	F:U	Steelcolor Shiner
Cyprinella xaenura (Jordan, 1877)	F:U	Altamaha Shiner^
Cyprinella xanthicara (Minckley & Lytle, 1969)	F:M	Cuatro Ciénegas Shiner^....carpita de Cuatro Ciénegas
Cyprinella zanema (Jordan & Brayton, 1878)	F:U	Santee Chub^
Cyprinus carpio Linnaeus, 1758	F:[I]:CUM	Common Carp....carpa común....carpe
Dionda argentosa Girard, 1856	F:UM	Manantial Roundnose Minnow^ carpa de manantial
Dionda diaboli Hubbs & Brown, 1957	F:UM	Devils River Minnow^....carpa diabla
Dionda episcopa Girard, 1856	F:UM	Roundnose Minnow....carpa obispa
Dionda melanops Girard, 1856	F:M	Spotted Minnow....carpa manchada
Dionda nigrotaeniata (Cope, 1880)	F:U	Guadalupe Roundnose Minnow^
Dionda serena Girard, 1856	F:U	Nueces Roundnose Minnow^
Eremichthys acros Hubbs & Miller, 1948	F:U	Desert Dace
Erimonax monachus (Cope, 1868)	F:U	Spotfin Chub
Erimystax cahni (Hubbs & Crowe, 1956)	F:U	Slender Chub
Erimystax dissimilis (Kirtland, 1841)	F:U	Streamline Chub
Erimystax harryi (Hubbs & Crowe, 1956)	F:U	Ozark Chub^
Erimystax insignis (Hubbs & Crowe, 1956)	F:U	Blotched Chub
+Erimystax x-punctatus (Hubbs & Crowe, 1956)	F:CU	Gravel Chub....gravelier
Evarra bustamantei Navarro, 1955	F[X]:M	Mexican Chub^....carpa xochimilca
Evarra eigenmanni Woolman, 1894	F[X]:M	Plateau Chub^....carpa verde
Evarra tlahuacensis Meek, 1902	F[X]:M	Endorheic Chub....carpa de Tláhuac
Exoglossum laurae (Hubbs, 1931)	F:U	Tonguetied Minnow
Exoglossum maxillingua (Lesueur, 1817)	F:CU	Cutlip Minnow....bec-de-lièvre

SCIENTIFIC NAME	OCCURRENCE[1]	COMMON NAME (ENGLISH, SPANISH, FRENCH)[2]
Gila atraria (Girard, 1856)	F:U	Utah Chub^
Gila brevicauda Norris, Fischer & Minckley, 2003	F:M	Shorttail Chub............carpa colicorta
Gila coerulea (Girard, 1856)	F:U	Blue Chub
*Gila conspersa Garman, 1881	F:M	Nazas Chub^...........carpa de Mayrán
Gila crassicauda (Baird & Girard, 1854)	F[X]:U	Thicktail Chub
Gila cypha Miller, 1946	F:U	Humpback Chub
Gila ditaenia Miller, 1945	F:UM	Sonora Chub^...........carpa sonorense
Gila elegans Baird & Girard, 1853	F:UM	Bonytail..........carpa elegante
Gila eremica DeMarais, 1991	F:M	Desert Chub...........carpa del desierto
Gila intermedia (Girard, 1856)	F:UM	Gila Chub^..........carpa del Gila
*Gila jordani Tanner, 1950	F:U	White River Chub^
Gila minacae Meek, 1902	F:M	Mexican Roundtail Chub^.......carpa cola redonda mexicana
Gila modesta (Garman, 1881)	F:M	Saltillo Chub^...........carpa de Saltillo
Gila nigra Cope, 1875	F:U	Headwater Chub
Gila nigrescens (Girard, 1856)	F:UM	Chihuahua Chub^..........carpa de Chihuahua
Gila orcuttii (Eigenmann & Eigenmann, 1890)	F:U	Arroyo Chub
Gila pandora (Cope, 1872)	F:U	Rio Grande Chub^
Gila pulchra (Girard, 1856)	F:M	Conchos Chub^............carpa del Conchos
Gila purpurea (Girard, 1856)	F:UM	Yaqui Chub^.........carpa púrpura
*Gila robusta Baird & Girard, 1853	F:UM	Roundtail Chub.........carpa cola redonda
Gila seminuda Cope & Yarrow, 1875	F:U	Virgin Chub^
Hemitremia flammea (Jordan & Gilbert, 1878)	F:U	Flame Chub
+*Hesperoleucus symmetricus* (Baird & Girard, 1854)	F:U	California Roach^
+*Hybognathus amarus* (Girard, 1856)	F:UM	Rio Grande Silvery Minnow^ . carpa Chamizal
Hybognathus argyritis Girard, 1856	F:CU	Western Silvery Minnow........méné d'argent de l'ouest
Hybognathus hankinsoni Hubbs, 1929	F:CU	Brassy Minnow ....méné laiton
Hybognathus hayi Jordan, 1885	F:U	Cypress Minnow
Hybognathus nuchalis Agassiz, 1855	F:U	Mississippi Silvery Minnow^
**Hybognathus placitus* Girard, 1856	F:CU	Plains Minnow...........méné des plaines
**Hybognathus regius* Girard, 1856	F:CU	Eastern Silvery Minnow..........méné d'argent de l'est
Hybopsis amblops (Rafinesque, 1820)	F:U	Bigeye Chub
Hybopsis amnis (Hubbs & Greene, 1951)	F:U	Pallid Shiner
Hybopsis hypsinotus (Cope, 1870)	F:U	Highback Chub

SCIENTIFIC NAME	OCCURRENCE[1]	COMMON NAME (ENGLISH, SPANISH, FRENCH)[2]
Hybopsis lineapunctata Clemmer & Suttkus, 1971	F:U	Lined Chub
Hybopsis rubrifrons (Jordan, 1877)	F:U	Rosyface Chub
Hybopsis winchelli Girard, 1856	F:U	Clear Chub
Hypophthalmichthys molitrix (Valenciennes, 1844)	F[I]:UM	Silver Carp .... carpa plateada
+*Hypophthalmichthys nobilis* (Richardson, 1845)	F[I]:UM	Bighead Carp .... carpa cabezona
Iotichthys phlegethontis (Cope, 1874)	F:U	Least Chub
Lavinia exilicauda Baird & Girard, 1854	F:U	Hitch
Lepidomeda albivallis Miller & Hubbs, 1960	F:U	White River Spinedace^
*Lepidomeda aliciae (Jouy, 1881)	F:U	Southern Leatherside Chub
Lepidomeda altivelis Miller & Hubbs, 1960	F[X]:U	Pahranagat Spinedace^
*Lepidomeda copei (Jordan & Gilbert, 1881)	F:U	Northern Leatherside Chub
Lepidomeda mollispinis Miller & Hubbs, 1960	F:U	Virgin Spinedace^
Lepidomeda vittata Cope, 1874	F:U	Little Colorado Spinedace^
Leuciscus idus (Linnaeus, 1758)	F[I]:U	Ide
Luxilus albeolus (Jordan, 1889)	F:U	White Shiner
Luxilus cardinalis (Mayden, 1988)	F:U	Cardinal Shiner
Luxilus cerasinus (Cope, 1868)	F:U	Crescent Shiner
Luxilus chrysocephalus Rafinesque, 1820	F:CU	Striped Shiner .... méné rayé
Luxilus coccogenis (Cope, 1868)	F:U	Warpaint Shiner
Luxilus cornutus (Mitchill, 1817)	F:CU	Common Shiner .... méné à nageoires rouges
Luxilus pilsbryi (Fowler, 1904)	F:U	Duskystripe Shiner
+*Luxilus zonatus* (Agassiz, 1863)	F:U	Bleeding Shiner
Luxilus zonistius Jordan, 1880	F:U	Bandfin Shiner
Lythrurus alegnotus (Snelson, 1972)	F:U	Warrior Shiner^
Lythrurus ardens (Cope, 1868)	F:U	Rosefin Shiner
Lythrurus atrapiculus (Snelson, 1972)	F:UM	Blacktip Shiner
Lythrurus bellus (Hay, 1881)	F:U	Pretty Shiner
Lythrurus fasciolaris (Gilbert, 1891)	F:U	Scarlet Shiner
Lythrurus fumeus (Evermann, 1892)	F:U	Ribbon Shiner
Lythrurus lirus (Jordan, 1877)	F:U	Mountain Shiner
Lythrurus matutinus (Cope, 1870)	F:U	Pinewoods Shiner
Lythrurus roseipinnis (Hay, 1885)	F:U	Cherryfin Shiner
Lythrurus snelsoni (Robison, 1985)	F:U	Ouachita Shiner^

SCIENTIFIC NAME	OCCURRENCE[1]	COMMON NAME (ENGLISH, SPANISH, FRENCH)[2]
Lythrurus umbratilis (Girard, 1856)	F:CU	Redfin Shiner................méné d'ombre
Macrhybopsis aestivalis (Girard, 1856)	F:UM	Speckled Chub.........carpa pecosa
Macrhybopsis australis (Hubbs & Ortenburger, 1929)	F:U	Prairie Chub
Macrhybopsis gelida (Girard, 1856)	F:U	Sturgeon Chub
Macrhybopsis hyostoma (Gilbert, 1884)	F:U	Shoal Chub
Macrhybopsis marconis (Jordan & Gilbert, 1886)	F:U	Burrhead Chub
Macrhybopsis meeki (Jordan & Evermann, 1896)	F:U	Sicklefin Chub
Macrhybopsis storeriana (Kirtland, 1845)	F:CU	Silver Chub........méné à grandes écailles
Macrhybopsis tetranema (Gilbert, 1886)	F:U	Peppered Chub
*Margariscus margarita (Cope, 1867)	F:U	Allegheny Pearl Dace^
*Margariscus nachtriebi (Cox, 1896)	F:CU	Northern Pearl Dace........mulet perlé du nord
+Meda fulgida Girard, 1856	F:UM	Spikedace........carpita aguda
Moapa coriacea Hubbs & Miller, 1948	F:U	Moapa Dace^
Mylocheilus caurinus (Richardson, 1836)	F:CU	Peamouth........méné deux-barres
Mylopharodon conocephalus (Baird & Girard, 1854)	F:U	Hardhead
*Mylopharyngodon piceus (Richardson, 1846)	F[I]:U	Black Carp
Nocomis asper Lachner & Jenkins, 1971	F:U	Redspot Chub
Nocomis biguttatus (Kirtland, 1841)	F:CU	Hornyhead Chub........tête à taches rouges
Nocomis effusus Lachner & Jenkins, 1967	F:U	Redtail Chub
Nocomis leptocephalus (Girard, 1856)	F:U	Bluehead Chub
Nocomis micropogon (Cope, 1865)	F:CU	River Chub........méné baton
Nocomis platyrhynchus Lachner & Jenkins, 1971	F:U	Bigmouth Chub
Nocomis raneyi Lachner & Jenkins, 1971	F:U	Bull Chub
Notemigonus crysoleucas (Mitchill, 1814)	F:CU	Golden Shiner........méné jaune
Notropis aguirrepequenoi Contreras-Balderas & Rivera-Teillery, 1973	F:M	Soto la Marina Shiner^........carpita del Pilón
Notropis albizonatus Warren & Burr, 1994	F:U	Palezone Shiner
Notropis alborus Hubbs & Raney, 1947	F:U	Whitemouth Shiner
Notropis altipinnis (Cope, 1870)	F:U	Highfin Shiner
Notropis amabilis (Girard, 1856)	F:UM	Texas Shiner^........carpita texana
*Notropis amecae Chernoff & Miller, 1986	F:M	Ameca Shiner^........carpita del Ameca
Notropis ammophilus Suttkus & Boschung, 1990	F:U	Orangefin Shiner

SCIENTIFIC NAME	OCCURRENCE[1]	COMMON NAME (ENGLISH, SPANISH, FRENCH)[2]
Notropis amoenus (Abbott, 1874)	F:U	Comely Shiner
**Notropis amplamala* Pera & Armbruster, 2006	F:U	Longjaw Minnow
Notropis anogenus Forbes, 1885	F:CU	Pugnose Shiner................................ méné camus
Notropis ariommus (Cope, 1867)	F:U	Popeye Shiner
Notropis asperifrons Suttkus & Raney, 1955	F:U	Burrhead Shiner
Notropis atherinoides Rafinesque, 1818	F:CU	Emerald Shiner.............................. méné émeraude
Notropis atrocaudalis Evermann, 1892	F:U	Blackspot Shiner
Notropis aulidion Chernoff & Miller, 1986	F[X]:M	Durango Shiner^.........................carpita de Durango
Notropis baileyi Suttkus & Raney, 1955	F:U	Rough Shiner
Notropis bairdi Hubbs & Ortenburger, 1929	F:U	Red River Shiner^............................... méné d'herbe
Notropis bifrenatus (Cope, 1867)	F:CU	Bridle Shiner............................... méné de rivière
Notropis blennius (Girard, 1856)	F:CU	River Shiner
Notropis boops Gilbert, 1884	F:U	Bigeye Shiner
Notropis boucardi (Günther, 1868)	F:M	Balsas Shiner^.............................carpita del Balsas
Notropis braytoni Jordan & Evermann, 1896	F:UM	Tamaulipas Shiner^.....................carpita tamaulipeca
+*Notropis buccatus* (Cope, 1865)	F:U	Silverjaw Minnow
Notropis buccula Cross, 1953	F:U	Smalleye Shiner
Notropis buchanani Meek, 1896	F:CUM	Ghost Shiner^..............................carpita fantasma................ méné fantôme
Notropis cahabae Mayden & Kuhajda, 1989	F:U	Cahaba Shiner^
**Notropis calabazas* Lyons & Mercado-Silva, 2004	F:M	Calabazas Shiner^.....................carpita del Calabazas
+*Notropis calientis* Jordan & Snyder, 1899	F:M	Yellow Shiner^..............................carpita amarilla
Notropis candidus Suttkus, 1980	F:U	Silverside Shiner
Notropis chalybaeus (Cope, 1867)	F:U	Ironcolor Shiner
Notropis chihuahua Woolman, 1892	F:UM	Chihuahua Shiner^.....................carpita chihuahuense
Notropis chiliticus (Cope, 1870)	F:U	Redlip Shiner
Notropis chlorocephalus (Cope, 1870)	F:U	Greenhead Shiner
Notropis chrosomus (Jordan, 1877)	F:U	Rainbow Shiner
+*Notropis cumingii* (Günther, 1868)	F:M	Atoyac Chub^..............................carpita del Atoyac
Notropis cummingsae Myers, 1925	F:U	Dusky Shiner
Notropis dorsalis (Agassiz, 1854)	F:CU	Bigmouth Shiner..................... méné à grande bouche
Notropis edwardraneyi Suttkus & Clemmer, 1968	F:U	Fluvial Shiner

SCIENTIFIC NAME	OCCURRENCE[1]	COMMON NAME (ENGLISH, SPANISH, FRENCH)[2]
Notropis girardi Hubbs & Ortenburger, 1929	F:U	Arkansas River Shiner^
*Notropis grandis Domínguez-Domínguez, Pérez-Rodríguez, Escalera-Vázquez & Doadrio, 2009	F:M	Zacapu Shiner^ .... carpita de Zacapu
Notropis greenei Hubbs & Ortenburger, 1929	F:U	Wedgespot Shiner
Notropis harperi Fowler, 1941	F:U	Redeye Chub
Notropis heterodon (Cope, 1865)	F:CU	Blackchin Shiner .... menton noir
Notropis heterolepis Eigenmann & Eigenmann, 1893	F:CU	Blacknose Shiner .... museau noir
Notropis hudsonius (Clinton, 1824)	F:CU	Spottail Shiner .... queue à tache noire
Notropis hypsilepis Suttkus & Raney, 1955	F:U	Highscale Shiner
Notropis jemezanus (Cope, 1875)	F:UM	Rio Grande Shiner^ .... carpita del Bravo
Notropis leuciodus (Cope, 1868)	F:U	Tennessee Shiner^
Notropis longirostris (Hay, 1881)	F:U	Longnose Shiner
Notropis lutipinnis (Jordan & Brayton, 1878)	F:U	Yellowfin Shiner
Notropis maculatus (Hay, 1881)	F:U	Taillight Shiner
**Notropis marhabatiensis* Domínguez-Domínguez, Pérez-Rodríguez, Escalera-Vázquez & Doadrio, 2009	F:M	Maravatío Shiner^ .... carpita de Maravatío
Notropis mekistocholas Snelson, 1971	F:U	Cape Fear Shiner^
Notropis melanostomus Bortone, 1989	F:U	Blackmouth Shiner
Notropis micropteryx (Cope, 1868)	F:U	Highland Shiner
**Notropis moralesi* de Buen, 1955	F:M	Papaloapan Chub^ .... carpita del Tepelmeme
Notropis nazas Meek, 1904	F:M	Nazas Shiner^ .... carpita del Nazas
Notropis nubilus (Forbes, 1878)	F:U	Ozark Minnow^
Notropis orca Woolman, 1894	F[X]:UM	Phantom Shiner .... carpita de El Paso
Notropis ortenburgeri Hubbs, 1927	F:U	Kiamichi Shiner^
Notropis oxyrhynchus Hubbs & Bonham, 1951	F:U	Sharpnose Shiner
Notropis ozarcanus Meek, 1891	F:U	Ozark Shiner^
Notropis percobromus (Cope, 1871)	F:CU	Carmine Shiner .... tête carminée
Notropis perpallidus Hubbs & Black, 1940	F:U	Peppered Shiner
Notropis petersoni Fowler, 1942	F:U	Coastal Shiner
Notropis photogenis (Cope, 1865)	F:CU	Silver Shiner .... méné-miroir
Notropis potteri Hubbs & Bonham, 1951	F:U	Chub Shiner

SCIENTIFIC NAME	OCCURRENCE[1]	COMMON NAME (ENGLISH, SPANISH, FRENCH)[2]
Notropis procne (Cope, 1865)	F:U	Swallowtail Shiner
Notropis rafinesquei Suttkus, 1991	F:U	Yazoo Shiner^
Notropis rubellus (Agassiz, 1850)	F:CU	Rosyface Shiner ... tête rose
Notropis rubricroceus (Cope, 1868)	F:U	Saffron Shiner
Notropis rupestris Page, 1987	F:U	Bedrock Shiner
Notropis sabinae Jordan & Gilbert, 1886	F:U	Sabine Shiner^
Notropis saladonis Hubbs & Hubbs, 1958	F[X]:M	Salado Shiner^ ... carpita del Salado
*Notropis sallaei (Günther, 1868)	F:M	Aztec Chub^ ... carpita azteca
Notropis scabriceps (Cope, 1868)	F:U	New River Shiner^
Notropis scepticus (Jordan & Gilbert, 1883)	F:U	Sandbar Shiner
Notropis semperasper Gilbert, 1961	F:U	Roughhead Shiner
Notropis shumardi (Girard, 1856)	F:U	Silverband Shiner
Notropis simus (Cope, 1875)	F:UM	Bluntnose Shiner ... carpita chata
Notropis spectrunculus (Cope, 1868)	F:U	Mirror Shiner
Notropis stilbius Jordan, 1877	F:U	Silverstripe Shiner
Notropis stramineus (Cope, 1865)	F:CUM	Sand Shiner ... carpita arenera ... méné paille
Notropis suttkusi Humphries & Cashner, 1994	F:U	Rocky Shiner
Notropis telescopus (Cope, 1868)	F:U	Telescope Shiner
Notropis texanus (Girard, 1856)	F:CU	Weed Shiner ... méné diamant
Notropis topeka (Gilbert, 1884)	F:U	Topeka Shiner^
Notropis tropicus Hubbs & Miller, 1975	F:M	Pygmy Shiner^ ... carpita tropical
Notropis uranoscopus Suttkus, 1959	F:U	Skygazer Shiner
Notropis volucellus (Cope, 1865)	F:CU	Mimic Shiner ... méné pâle
Notropis wickliffi Trautman, 1931	F:U	Channel Shiner
Notropis xaenocephalus (Jordan, 1877)	F:U	Coosa Shiner^
Opsopoeodus emiliae Hay, 1881	F:CU	Pugnose Minnow ... petit-bec
Oregonichthys crameri (Snyder, 1908)	F:U	Oregon Chub^
Oregonichthys kalawatseti Markle, Pearsons & Bills, 1991	F:U	Umpqua Chub^
Orthodon microlepidotus (Ayres, 1854)	F:U	Sacramento Blackfish^
Phenacobius catostomus Jordan, 1877	F:U	Riffle Minnow
Phenacobius crassilabrum Minckley & Craddock, 1962	F:U	Fatlips Minnow

SCIENTIFIC NAME	OCCURRENCE[1]	COMMON NAME (ENGLISH, SPANISH, FRENCH)[2]
Phenacobius mirabilis (Girard, 1856)	F:U	Suckermouth Minnow
Phenacobius teretulus Cope, 1867	F:U	Kanawha Minnow^
Phenacobius uranops Cope, 1867	F:U	Stargazing Minnow
Pimephales notatus (Rafinesque, 1820)	F:CU	Bluntnose Minnow ... ventre-pourri
Pimephales promelas Rafinesque, 1820	F:CUM	Fathead Minnow ... carpita cabezona ... tête-de-boule
Pimephales tenellus (Girard, 1856)	F:U	Slim Minnow
Pimephales vigilax (Baird & Girard, 1853)	F:UM	Bullhead Minnow ... carpita cabeza de toro
+Plagopterus argentissimus Cope, 1874	F:UM	Woundfin ... carpita afilada
Platygobio gracilis (Richardson, 1836)	F:CU	Flathead Chub ... méné à tête plate
Pogonichthys ciscoides Hopkirk, 1974	F[X]:U	Clear Lake Splittail^
Pogonichthys macrolepidotus (Ayres, 1854)	F:U	Splittail
Pteronotropis euryzonus (Suttkus, 1955)	F:U	Broadstripe Shiner
Pteronotropis grandipinnis (Jordan, 1877)	F:U	Apalachee Shiner^
Pteronotropis hubbsi (Bailey & Robison, 1978)	F:U	Bluehead Shiner
+Pteronotropis hypselopterus (Günther, 1868)	F:U	Sailfin Shiner
Pteronotropis merlini (Suttkus & Mettee, 2001)	F:U	Orangetail Shiner
*Pteronotropis metallicus (Jordan & Meek, 1884)	F:U	Metallic Shiner
Pteronotropis signipinnis (Bailey & Suttkus, 1952)	F:U	Flagfin Shiner
*Pteronotropis stonei (Fowler, 1921)	F:U	Lowland Shiner
Pteronotropis welaka (Evermann & Kendall, 1898)	F:U	Bluenose Shiner
Ptychocheilus grandis (Ayres, 1854)	F:U	Sacramento Pikeminnow^
Ptychocheilus lucius Girard, 1856	F:UM	Colorado Pikeminnow^ ... carpa gigante del Colorado
Ptychocheilus oregonensis (Richardson, 1836)	F:CU	Northern Pikeminnow ... méné-brochet du nord
Ptychocheilus umpquae Snyder, 1908	F:U	Umpqua Pikeminnow^
Relictus solitarius Hubbs & Miller, 1972	F:U	Relict Dace
*Rhinichthys atratulus (Hermann, 1804)	F:CU	Blacknose Dace
Rhinichthys cataractae (Valenciennes, 1842)	F:CUM	Longnose Dace ... carpita rinconera ... naseux des rapides
Rhinichthys cobitis (Girard, 1856)	F:UM	Loach Minnow ... carpita locha
Rhinichthys deaconi Miller, 1984	F[X]:U	Las Vegas Dace^
Rhinichthys evermanni Snyder, 1908	F:U	Umpqua Dace^
Rhinichthys falcatus (Eigenmann & Eigenmann, 1893)	F:CU	Leopard Dace ... naseux léopard
+Rhinichthys osculus (Girard, 1856)	F:CUM	Speckled Dace ... carpita pinta ... naseux moucheté
*Rhinichthys atratulus (Hermann, 1804)	F:CU	Blacknose Dace ... naseux noir

SCIENTIFIC NAME	OCCURRENCE[1]	COMMON NAME (ENGLISH, SPANISH, FRENCH)[2]
Rhinichthys umatilla (Gilbert & Evermann, 1894)	F:CU	Umatilla Dace^ ....naseux d'Umatilla
+*Rhodeus sericeus* (Pallas, 1776)	F[I]:U.	Bitterling
Richardsonius balteatus (Richardson, 1836)	F:CU	Redside Shiner ....méné rose
Richardsonius egregius (Girard, 1858)	F:U.	Lahontan Redside^
Scardinius erythrophthalmus (Linnaeus, 1758)	F[I]:CU	Rudd ....gardon rouge
Semotilus atromaculatus (Mitchill, 1818)	F:CU	Creek Chub ....mulet à cornes
Semotilus corporalis (Mitchill, 1817)	F:CU	Fallfish ....outouche
Semotilus lumbee Snelson & Suttkus, 1978	F:U.	Sandhills Chub
Semotilus thoreauianus Jordan, 1877	F:U.	Dixie Chub^
**Siphateles alvordensis* (Hubbs & Miller, 1972)	F:U.	Alvord Chub^
**Siphateles bicolor* (Girard, 1856)	F:U.	Tui Chub
**Siphateles boraxobius* (Williams & Bond, 1980)	F:U.	Borax Lake Chub^
Stypodon signifer Garman, 1881	F[X]:M	Stumptooth Minnow ....carpa de Parras
**Tampichthys catostomops* (Hubbs & Miller, 1977)	F:M	Pánuco Minnow^ ....carpa de Tamasopo
**Tampichthys dichroma* (Hubbs & Miller, 1977)	F:M	Bicolor Minnow ....carpa bicolor
**Tampichthys erimyzonops* (Hubbs & Miller, 1974)	F:M	Chubsucker Minnow ....carpa del Mante
**Tampichthys ipni* (Álvarez & Navarro, 1953)	F:M	Lantern Minnow ....carpa veracruzana
**Tampichthys mandibularis* (Contreras-Balderas & Verduzco-Martínez, 1977)	F:M	Flatjaw Minnow ....carpa quijarona
**Tampichthys rasconis* (Jordan & Snyder, 1899)	F:M	Blackstripe Minnow ....carpa potosina
Tinca tinca (Linnaeus, 1758)	F[I]:CU	Tench ....tanche
+*Yuriria alta* (Jordan, 1880)	F:M	Jalisco Chub^ ....carpa blanca
**Yuriria amatlana* Domínguez-Domínguez, Pompa-Domínguez & Doadrio, 2007	F:M	Amatlán Chub^ ....carpa amatlana
Yuriria chapalae (Jordan & Snyder, 1899)	F:M	Chapala Chub^ ....carpa de Chapala

Catostomidae—En-suckers, Sp-matalotes, Fr-catostomes

SCIENTIFIC NAME	OCCURRENCE[1]	COMMON NAME (ENGLISH, SPANISH, FRENCH)[2]
Carpiodes carpio (Rafinesque, 1820)	F:UM.	River Carpsucker ....matalote chato
Carpiodes cyprinus (Lesueur, 1817)	F:CU	Quillback ....couette
Carpiodes velifer (Rafinesque, 1820)	F:U.	Highfin Carpsucker
+*Catostomus ardens* Jordan & Gilbert, 1881	F:U.	Utah Sucker^
Catostomus bernardini Girard, 1856	F:UM.	Yaqui Sucker^ ....matalote yaqui

SCIENTIFIC NAME	OCCURRENCE[1]	COMMON NAME (ENGLISH, SPANISH, FRENCH)[2]
Catostomus cahita Siebert & Minckley, 1986	F:M	Cahita Sucker^ ... matalote cahita
Catostomus catostomus (Forster, 1773)	F:CU	Longnose Sucker ... meunier rouge
+Catostomus clarkii Baird & Girard, 1854	F:UM	Desert Sucker ... matalote del desierto
+Catostomus columbianus (Eigenmann & Eigenmann, 1893)	F:CU	Bridgelip Sucker ... meunier de l'ouest
+Catostomus commersonii (Lacepède, 1803)	F:CU	White Sucker ... meunier noir
Catostomus discobolus Cope, 1871	F:U	Bluehead Sucker
Catostomus fumeiventris Miller, 1973	F:U	Owens Sucker^
Catostomus insignis Baird & Girard, 1854	F:UM	Sonora Sucker^ ... matalote de Sonora
+Catostomus latipinnis Baird & Girard, 1853	F:UM	Flannelmouth Sucker ... matalote boca de franela
Catostomus leopoldi Siebert & Minckley, 1986	F:M	Fleshylip Sucker ... matalote del Bavispe
+Catostomus macrocheilus Girard, 1856	F:CU	Largescale Sucker ... meunier à grandes écailles
Catostomus microps Rutter, 1908	F:U	Modoc Sucker^
Catostomus nebuliferus Garman, 1881	F:M	Nazas Sucker^ ... matalote del Nazas
Catostomus occidentalis Ayres, 1854	F:U	Sacramento Sucker^
Catostomus platyrhynchus (Cope, 1874)	F:CU	Mountain Sucker ... meunier des montagnes
Catostomus plebeius Baird & Girard, 1854	F:UM	Rio Grande Sucker^ ... matalote del Bravo
Catostomus rimiculus Gilbert & Snyder, 1898	F:U	Klamath Smallscale Sucker^
Catostomus santaanae (Snyder, 1908)	F:U	Santa Ana Sucker^
Catostomus snyderi Gilbert, 1898	F:U	Klamath Largescale Sucker^
Catostomus tahoensis Gill & Jordan, 1878	F:U	Tahoe Sucker^
*Catostomus tsiltcoosensis Evermann & Meek, 1898	F:U	Tyee Sucker
*Catostomus utawana Mather, 1886	F:U	Summer Sucker
Catostomus warnerensis Snyder, 1908	F:U	Warner Sucker^
*Catostomus wigginsi Herre & Brock, 1936	F:M	Ópata Sucker^ ... matalote ópata
Chasmistes brevirostris Cope, 1879	F:U	Shortnose Sucker
+Chasmistes cujus Cope, 1883	F:U	Cui-ui
+Chasmistes liorus Jordan, 1878	F:U	June Sucker^
Chasmistes muriei Miller & Smith, 1981	F[X]:U	Snake River Sucker^
Cycleptus elongatus (Lesueur, 1817)	F:UM	Blue Sucker ... matalote azul
Cycleptus meridionalis Burr & Mayden, 1999	F:U	Southeastern Blue Sucker
Deltistes luxatus (Cope, 1879)	F:U	Lost River Sucker^
*Erimyzon claviformis (Girard, 1856)	F:U	Western Creek Chubsucker

SCIENTIFIC NAME	OCCURRENCE[1]	COMMON NAME (ENGLISH, SPANISH, FRENCH)[2]
*Erimyzon oblongus (Mitchill, 1814)	F:U	Eastern Creek Chubsucker
Erimyzon sucetta (Lacepède, 1803)	F:CU	Lake Chubsucker……………………………………sucet de lac
Erimyzon tenuis (Agassiz, 1855)	F:U	Sharpfin Chubsucker
Hypentelium etowanum (Jordan, 1877)	F:U	Alabama Hog Sucker^
Hypentelium nigricans (Lesueur, 1817)	F:CU	Northern Hog Sucker………………………meunier à tête carrée
Hypentelium roanokense Raney & Lachner, 1947	F:U	Roanoke Hog Sucker^
*Ictiobus bubalus (Rafinesque, 1818)	F:CUM	Smallmouth Buffalo…………matalote boquín………buffalo à petite bouche
Ictiobus cyprinellus (Valenciennes, 1844)	F:CU	Bigmouth Buffalo………………………………buffalo à grande bouche
Ictiobus labiosus (Meek, 1904)	F:M	Fleshylip Buffalo……………………matalote bocón
Ictiobus meridionalis (Günther, 1868)	F:M	Southern Buffalo……………………matalote meridional
*Ictiobus niger (Rafinesque, 1819)	F:CUM	Black Buffalo………………………matalote negro……………buffalo noir
Minytrema melanops (Rafinesque, 1820)	F:CU	Spotted Sucker……………………………………………meunier tacheté
Moxostoma albidum (Girard, 1856)	F:M	Longlip Jumprock…………………matalote blanco
Moxostoma anisurum (Rafinesque, 1820)	F:CU	Silver Redhorse……………………………………chevalier blanc
Moxostoma ariommum Robins & Raney, 1956	F:U	Bigeye Jumprock
Moxostoma austrinum Bean, 1880	F:UM	Mexican Redhorse^………………matalote chuime
Moxostoma breviceps (Cope, 1870)	F:U	Smallmouth Redhorse
Moxostoma carinatum (Cope, 1870)	F:CU	River Redhorse……………………………………chevalier de rivière
Moxostoma cervinum (Cope, 1868)	F:U	Blacktip Jumprock
Moxostoma collapsum (Cope, 1870)	F:U	Notchlip Redhorse
Moxostoma congestum (Baird & Girard, 1854)	F:U	Gray Redhorse
Moxostoma duquesnei (Lesueur, 1817)	F:CU	Black Redhorse…………………………………………chevalier noir
Moxostoma erythrurum (Rafinesque, 1818)	F:CU	Golden Redhorse………………………………………chevalier doré
Moxostoma hubbsi Legendre, 1952	F:C	Copper Redhorse……………………………………chevalier cuivré
Moxostoma lacerum (Jordan & Brayton, 1877)	F[X]:U	Harelip Sucker
Moxostoma lachneri Robins & Raney, 1956	F:U	Greater Jumprock
Moxostoma macrolepidotum (Lesueur, 1817)	F:CU	Shorthead Redhorse………………………………chevalier rouge
Moxostoma mascotae Regan, 1907	F:M	Mascota Jumprock^…………matalote de Mascota
Moxostoma pappillosum (Cope, 1870)	F:U	V-lip Redhorse
Moxostoma pisolabrum Trautman & Martin, 1951	F:U	Pealip Redhorse
Moxostoma poecilurum Jordan, 1877	F:U	Blacktail Redhorse
Moxostoma robustum (Cope, 1870)	F:U	Robust Redhorse

SCIENTIFIC NAME	OCCURRENCE[1]	COMMON NAME (ENGLISH, SPANISH, FRENCH)[2]
Moxostoma rupiscartes Jordan & Jenkins, 1889	F:U	Striped Jumprock
Moxostoma valenciennesi Jordan, 1885	F:CU	Greater Redhorse........chevalier jaune
Thoburnia atripinnis (Bailey, 1959)	F:U	Blackfin Sucker
Thoburnia hamiltoni Raney & Lachner, 1946	F:U	Rustyside Sucker
Thoburnia rhothoeca (Thoburn, 1896)	F:U	Torrent Sucker
Xyrauchen texanus (Abbott, 1860)	F:UM	Razorback Sucker......matalote jorobado
		Cobitidae—En-loaches, Sp-lochas, Fr-loches
*Misgurnus anguillicaudatus (Cantor, 1842)	F[I]:CU	Oriental Weatherfish........ loche asiatique

ORDER CHARACIFORMES

*Characidae—En-tetras, Sp- pepescas y sardinitas, Fr-characins

SCIENTIFIC NAME	OCCURRENCE[1]	COMMON NAME (ENGLISH, SPANISH, FRENCH)[2]
+*Astyanax aeneus* (Günther, 1860)	F:M	Banded Tetra ....pepesca
Astyanax altior Hubbs, 1936	F:M	Yucatan Tetra^ .... sardinita yucateca
+*Astyanax mexicanus* (De Filippi, 1853)	F:UM	Mexican Tetra^ .... sardinita mexicana
Bramocharax caballeroi Contreras-Balderas & Rivera-Teillery, 1985	F:M	Catemaco Characin ^ ......pepesca de Catemaco
Brycon guatemalensis Regan, 1908	F:M	Macabi Tetra........... sardinita macabí
Hyphessobrycon compressus (Meek, 1904)	F:M	Maya Tetra^ .... sardinita plateada
Roeboides bouchellei Fowler, 1923	F:M	Crystal Tetra........ sardinita cristal

*ORDER SILURIFORMES

Callichthyidae—En-callichthyid armored catfishes, Sp-coridoras, Fr-poissons-chats cuirassés

SCIENTIFIC NAME	OCCURRENCE[1]	COMMON NAME (ENGLISH, SPANISH, FRENCH)[2]
Hoplosternum littorale (Hancock, 1828)	F[I]:U	Brown Hoplo

Loricariidae—En-suckermouth armored catfishes, Sp-plecóstomas, Fr-loricariidés

SCIENTIFIC NAME	OCCURRENCE[1]	COMMON NAME (ENGLISH, SPANISH, FRENCH)[2]
+*Hypostomus plecostomus* (Linnaeus, 1758)	F[I]:U	Suckermouth Catfish
*Pterygoplichthys anisitsi Eigenmann & Kennedy, 1903	F[I]:UM	Paraná Sailfin Catfish^ .... plecóstoma del Paraná
*Pterygoplichthys disjunctivus (Weber, 1991)	F[I]:UM	Vermiculated Sailfin Catfish ..plecóstoma rayado

SCIENTIFIC NAME	OCCURRENCE[1]	COMMON NAME (ENGLISH, SPANISH, FRENCH)[2]
+*Pterygoplichthys multiradiatus* (Hancock, 1828)	F[I]:UM	Orinoco Sailfin Catfish^, Sp-bagre sierra, Fr-poissons-chats épineux
Pterygoplichthys pardalis (Castelnau, 1855)	F[I]:UM	Amazon Sailfin Catfish^, plecóstoma del Amazonas
Doradidae—En-thorny catfishes, Sp-bagres sierra, Fr-poissons-chats épineux		
Platydoras armatulus (Valenciennes, 1840)	F[I]:U	Southern Striped Raphael^
+Clariidae—En-labyrinth catfishes, Sp-bagres laberintos, Fr-poissons-chats à labyrinthes		
+*Clarias batrachus* (Linnaeus, 1758)	F[I]:U	Walking Catfish
*Ariidae—En-sea catfishes, Sp-bagres marinos, Fr-poissons-chats marins		
Ariopsis assimilis (Günther, 1864)	AM	Maya Sea Catfish^, bagre maya
Ariopsis felis (Linnaeus, 1766)	A-F:UM	Hardhead Catfish, bagre boca chica
Ariopsis guatemalensis (Günther, 1864)	PM	Widehead Sea Catfish, bagre cuatete
Ariopsis seemanni (Günther, 1864)	PM	Tete Sea Catfish, bagre tete
Bagre marinus (Mitchill, 1815)	A	Gafftopsail Catfish, bagre bandera
Bagre panamensis (Gill, 1863)	P	Chihuil, bagre chihuil
Bagre pinnimaculatus (Steindachner, 1877)	PM	Long-barbeled Sea Catfish, bagre barbón
Cathorops aguadulce (Meek, 1904)	AM-F:M	Estuarine Sea Catfish, bagre aguadulce
*Cathorops belizensis Marceniuk & Betancur-R., 2008	AM	Belize Sea Catfish^, bagre de Belice
*Cathorops dasycephalus (Günther, 1864)	PM	Bigbelly Sea Catfish, bagre barrigón
*Cathorops kailolae Marceniuk & Betancur-R., 2008	F:M	Papillate Sea Catfish, bagre papilosa
*Cathorops liropus (Bristol, 1897)	PM	Conguito Sea Catfish, bagre conguito
*Cathorops raredonae Marceniuk, Betancur-R. & Acero P., 2009	PM	Curator Sea Catfish, bagre curadora
*Notarius kessleri (Steindachner, 1877)	PM	Sculptured Sea Catfish, bagre esculpido
*Notarius planiceps (Steindachner, 1877)	PM	Flathead Sea Catfish, bagre cabeza chata
*Notarius troschelii (Gill, 1863)	PM	Chili Sea Catfish, bagre chili
*Occidentarius platypogon (Günther, 1864)	PM	Cominate Sea Catfish, bagre cominate
*Potamarius nelsoni (Evermann & Goldsborough, 1902)	F:M	Lacandón Sea Catfish^, bagre lacandón
*Potamarius usumacintae Betancur-R. & Willink, 2007	F:M	Usumacinta Sea Catfish^, bagre del Usumacinta

SCIENTIFIC NAME	OCCURRENCE[1]	COMMON NAME (ENGLISH, SPANISH, FRENCH)[2]
*Sciades dowii (Gill, 1863)	PM	Flapnose Sea Catfish....bagre moreno
		*Heptapteridae—En-seven-finned catfishes, Sp-juiles, Fr-poissons-chats à sept nageoires
Rhamdia guatemalensis (Günther, 1864)	F:M	Pale Catfish....juil descolorido
*Rhamdia laluchensis Weber, Allegrucci & Sbordoni, 2003	F:M	La Lucha Blind Catfish^....juil ciego de La Lucha
Rhamdia laticauda (Kner, 1858)	F:M	Rock Catfish....juil de Jamapa
Rhamdia macuspanensis Weber & Wilkens, 1998	F:M	Olmec Blind Catfish^....juil ciego olmeca
*Rhamdia parryi Eigenmann & Eigenmann, 1888	F:M	Tonalá Catfish^....juil de Tonalá
*Rhamdia reddelli Miller, 1984	F:M	Blind Whiskered Catfish....juil ciego oaxaqueño
*Rhamdia zongolicensis Wilkens, 1993	F:M	Zongolica Catfish^....juil ciego de Zongolica
		*Lacantuniidae—En-Lacantún catfishes, Sp-bagres del Lacantún, Fr-poissons-chats de Lacantún
*Lacantunia enigmatica Rodiles-Hernández, Hendrickson & Lundberg, 2005	F:M	Chiapas Catfish^....bagre de Chiapas
		Ictaluridae—En-North American catfishes, Sp-bagres de agua dulce, Fr-barbottes et barbues
Ameiurus brunneus Jordan, 1877	F:U	Snail Bullhead
Ameiurus catus (Linnaeus, 1758)	F:U	White Catfish
Ameiurus melas (Rafinesque, 1820)	F:CUM[I]	Black Bullhead....bagre torito negro....barbotte noire
Ameiurus natalis (Lesueur, 1819)	F:CUM[I]	Yellow Bullhead....bagre torito amarillo....barbotte jaune
Ameiurus nebulosus (Lesueur, 1819)	F:CU	Brown Bullhead....barbotte brune
Ameiurus platycephalus (Girard, 1859)	F:U	Flat Bullhead
Ameiurus serracanthus (Yerger & Relyea, 1968)	F:U	Spotted Bullhead
*Ictalurus australis (Meek, 1904)	F:M	Pánuco Catfish^....bagre del Pánuco
Ictalurus balsanus (Jordan & Snyder, 1899)	F:M	Balsas Catfish^....bagre del Balsas
Ictalurus dugesii (Bean, 1880)	F:M	Lerma Catfish^....bagre del Lerma
+Ictalurus furcatus (Lesueur, 1840)	F:UM	Blue Catfish....bagre azul
Ictalurus lupus (Girard, 1858)	F:UM	Headwater Catfish....bagre lobo
*Ictalurus meridionalis (Günther, 1864)	F:M	Southern Blue Catfish....bagre azul del sureste
Ictalurus mexicanus (Meek, 1904)	F:M	Río Verde Catfish^....bagre del Verde
Ictalurus ochoterenai (de Buen, 1946)	F:M	Chapala Catfish^....bagre de Chapala

SCIENTIFIC NAME	OCCURRENCE[1]	COMMON NAME (ENGLISH, SPANISH, FRENCH)[2]
Ictalurus pricei (Rutter, 1896)	F:UM	Yaqui Catfish^ ... bagre yaqui
Ictalurus punctatus (Rafinesque, 1818)	F:CUM	Channel Catfish ... bagre de canal ... barbue de rivière
+Noturus albater Taylor, 1969	F:U	Ozark Madtom^
+Noturus baileyi Taylor, 1969	F:U	Smoky Madtom^
*Noturus crypticus Burr, Eisenhour & Grady, 2005	F:U	Chucky Madtom^
+Noturus elegans Taylor, 1969	F:U	Elegant Madtom
Noturus eleutherus Jordan, 1877	F:U	Mountain Madtom
Noturus exilis Nelson, 1876	F:U	Slender Madtom
*Noturus fasciatus Burr, Eisenhour & Grady, 2005	F:U	Saddled Madtom
Noturus flavater Taylor, 1969	F:U	Checkered Madtom
Noturus flavipinnis Taylor, 1969	F:U	Yellowfin Madtom
Noturus flavus Rafinesque, 1818	F:CU	Stonecat ... barbotte des rapides
Noturus funebris Gilbert & Swain, 1891	F:U	Black Madtom
Noturus furiosus Jordan & Meek, 1889	F:U	Carolina Madtom^
Noturus gilberti Jordan & Evermann, 1889	F:U	Orangefin Madtom
*Noturus gladiator Thomas & Burr, 2004	F:U	Piebald Madtom
Noturus gyrinus (Mitchill, 1817)	F:CU	Tadpole Madtom ... chat-fou brun
Noturus hildebrandi (Bailey & Taylor, 1950)	F:U	Least Madtom
Noturus insignis (Richardson, 1836)	F:C[I]U	Margined Madtom ... chat-fou liséré
Noturus lachneri Taylor, 1969	F:U	Ouachita Madtom^
Noturus leptacanthus Jordan, 1877	F:U	Speckled Madtom
*Noturus maydeni Egge, 2006	F:U	Black River Madtom^
Noturus miurus Jordan, 1877	F:CU	Brindled Madtom ... chat-fou tacheté
Noturus munitus Suttkus & Taylor, 1965	F:U	Frecklebelly Madtom
Noturus nocturnus Jordan & Gilbert, 1886	F:U	Freckled Madtom
Noturus phaeus Taylor, 1969	F:U	Brown Madtom
Noturus placidus Taylor, 1969	F:U	Neosho Madtom^
Noturus stanauli Etnier & Jenkins, 1980	F:U	Pygmy Madtom
+Noturus stigmosus Taylor, 1969	F:CU	Northern Madtom ... chat-fou du nord
Noturus taylori Douglas, 1972	F:U	Caddo Madtom^
Noturus trautmani Taylor, 1969	F[X]:U	Scioto Madtom^
Prietella lundbergi Walsh & Gilbert, 1995	F:M	Phantom Blindcat ... bagre ciego duende
Prietella phreatophila Carranza, 1954	F:M	Mexican Blindcat^ ... bagre ciego de Múzquiz

SCIENTIFIC NAME	OCCURRENCE[1]	COMMON NAME (ENGLISH, SPANISH, FRENCH)[2]
Pylodictis olivaris (Rafinesque, 1818)	F:C[I]UM	Flathead Catfish........bagre piltontle........barbue à tête plate
Satan eurystomus Hubbs & Bailey, 1947	F:U	Widemouth Blindcat
Trogloglanis pattersoni Eigenmann, 1919	F:U	Toothless Blindcat
ORDER GYMNOTIFORMES		
Gymnotidae—En-nakedback knifefishes, Sp-cuchillos, Fr-poissons-couteaux		
Gymnotus maculosus Albert & Miller, 1995	F:M	Spotted Knifefish........cuchillo
+ORDER ARGENTINIFORMES		
Argentinidae—En-argentines, Sp-argentinas, Fr-argentines		
Argentina georgei Cohen & Atsaides, 1969	A	Blackbelly Argentine
Argentina sialis Gilbert, 1890	P	Pacific Argentine^........argentina del Pacífico
Argentina silus (Ascanius, 1775)	A-Ar	Atlantic Argentine^........grande argentine
Argentina striata Goode & Bean, 1896	A	Striated Argentine........argentina estriada........argentine striée
Glossanodon pygmaeus Cohen, 1958	A	Pygmy Argentine
*Microstomatidae—En-pencilsmelts, Sp-peces boquita, Fr-microbecs		
Leuroglossus schmidti Rass, 1955	P	Northern Smoothtongue........leuroglosse luisant
Leuroglossus stilbius Gilbert, 1890	P	California Smoothtongue^........lengualisa californiana
Opisthoproctidae—En-spookfishes, Sp-peces duende, Fr-revenants		
Macropinna microstoma Chapman, 1939	P	Barreleye........vise-en-l'air
*ORDER OSMERIFORMES		
Osmeridae—En-smelts, Sp-capellanes, Fr-éperlans		
Allosmerus elongatus (Ayres, 1854)	P	Whitebait Smelt
Hypomesus nipponensis McAllister, 1963	F[I]:U	Wakasagi
Hypomesus olidus (Pallas, 1814)	Ar-F:CU	Pond Smelt........éperlan à petite bouche
Hypomesus pretiosus (Girard, 1854)	P-F:CU	Surf Smelt........éperlan argenté

SCIENTIFIC NAME	OCCURRENCE[1]	COMMON NAME (ENGLISH, SPANISH, FRENCH)[2]
Hypomesus transpacificus McAllister, 1963	P-F:U	Delta Smelt^
Mallotus villosus (Müller, 1776)	A-P-Ar-F:C	Capelin ... capelan
Osmerus dentex Steindachner & Kner, 1870	P-Ar-F:CU	Pacific Rainbow Smelt^ ... éperlan du Pacifique
Osmerus mordax (Mitchill, 1814)	A-Ar-F:CU	Rainbow Smelt ... éperlan arc-en-ciel
Spirinchus starksi (Fisk, 1913)	P	Night Smelt ... éperlan nocturne
Spirinchus thaleichthys (Ayres, 1860)	P-F:CU	Longfin Smelt ... éperlan d'hiver
Thaleichthys pacificus (Richardson, 1836)	P-F:CU	Eulachon ... eulakane

*ORDER SALMONIFORMES

Salmonidae—En-trouts and salmons, Sp-truchas y salmones, Fr-truites et saumons

SCIENTIFIC NAME	OCCURRENCE	COMMON NAME
+*Coregonus artedi* Lesueur, 1818	F:CU	Cisco ... cisco de lac
Coregonus autumnalis (Pallas, 1776)	Ar-F:CU	Arctic Cisco^ ... cisco arctique
+*Coregonus clupeaformis* (Mitchill, 1818)	A-Ar-F:CU	Lake Whitefish ... grand corégone
Coregonus hoyi (Milner, 1874)	F:CU	Bloater ... cisco de fumage
Coregonus huntsmani Scott, 1987	A-F:C	Atlantic Whitefish^ ... corégone atlantique
Coregonus johannae (Wagner, 1910)	F[X]:CU	Deepwater Cisco ... cisco de profondeur
Coregonus kiyi (Koelz, 1921)	F:CU	Kiyi ... cisco kiyi
Coregonus laurettae Bean, 1881	Ar-F:CU	Bering Cisco^ ... cisco de Béring
Coregonus nasus (Pallas, 1776)	Ar-F:CU	Broad Whitefish ... corégone tschir
Coregonus nigripinnis (Milner, 1874)	F:CU	Blackfin Cisco ... cisco à nageoires noires
+*Coregonus pidschian* (Gmelin, 1789)	F:U	Humpback Whitefish
Coregonus reighardi (Koelz, 1924)	F[X]:CU	Shortnose Cisco
Coregonus sardinella Valenciennes, 1848	Ar-F:CU	Least Cisco ... cisco sardinelle
Coregonus zenithicus (Jordan & Evermann, 1909)	F:CU	Shortjaw Cisco ... cisco à mâchoires égales
Oncorhynchus aguabonita (Jordan, 1892)	F:C[I]U	Golden Trout ... truite dorée
Oncorhynchus apache (Miller, 1972)	F:U	Apache Trout^
Oncorhynchus chrysogaster (Needham & Gard, 1964)	F:M	Mexican Golden Trout^ ... trucha dorada mexicana
Oncorhynchus clarkii (Richardson, 1836)	P-F:CUM	Cutthroat Trout ... trucha degollada ... truite fardée
+*Oncorhynchus gilae* (Miller, 1950)	F:U	Gila Trout^
Oncorhynchus gorbuscha (Walbaum, 1792)	P-Ar-F:CU	Pink Salmon ... saumon rose
Oncorhynchus keta (Walbaum, 1792)	P-Ar-F:CU	Chum Salmon ... saumon kéta

SCIENTIFIC NAME	OCCURRENCE[1]	COMMON NAME (ENGLISH, SPANISH, FRENCH)[2]
Oncorhynchus kisutch (Walbaum, 1792)	P-Ar-F:CU	Coho Salmon......salmón plateado......saumon coho
+*Oncorhynchus mykiss* (Walbaum, 1792)	A[I]-P-F:CUM	Rainbow Trout......trucha arcoiris......truite arc-en-ciel
+*Oncorhynchus nerka* (Walbaum, 1792)	P-Ar-F:CU	Sockeye Salmon......saumon rouge
Oncorhynchus tshawytscha (Walbaum, 1792)	P-Ar-F:CU	Chinook Salmon^......salmón boquinegra......saumon chinook
Prosopium abyssicola (Snyder, 1919)	F:U	Bear Lake Whitefish^
Prosopium coulterii (Eigenmann & Eigenmann, 1892)	F:CU	Pygmy Whitefish......ménomini pygmée
Prosopium cylindraceum (Pennant, 1784)	Ar-F:CU	Round Whitefish......ménomini rond
Prosopium gemmifer (Snyder, 1919)	F:U	Bonneville Cisco^
Prosopium spilonotus (Snyder, 1919)	F:U	Bonneville Whitefish^
Prosopium williamsoni (Girard, 1856)	F:CU	Mountain Whitefish......ménomini de montagne
Salmo salar Linnaeus, 1758	A-P[I]-Ar-F:CU	Atlantic Salmon^......saumon atlantique
Salmo trutta Linnaeus, 1758	A[I]-F[I]:CU	Brown Trout......truite brune
Salvelinus alpinus (Linnaeus, 1758)	A-P-Ar-F:CU	Arctic Char^......omble chevalier
Salvelinus confluentus (Suckley, 1859)	P-F:CU	Bull Trout......omble à tête plate
Salvelinus fontinalis (Mitchill, 1814)	A-Ar-F:CUM[I]	Brook Trout......omble de fontaine
Salvelinus malma (Walbaum, 1792)	P-Ar-F:CU	Dolly Varden^......trucha de arroyo
Salvelinus namaycush (Walbaum, 1792)	Ar-F:CU	Lake Trout......omble malma
+*Stenodus leucichthys* (Güldenstädt, 1772)	Ar-F:CU	Inconnu......touladi
Thymallus arcticus (Pallas, 1776)	Ar-F:CU	Arctic Grayling^......inconnu
		......ombre arctique

ORDER ESOCIFORMES

*Esocidae—En-pikes and mudminnows, Sp-lucios y peces del fango, Fr-brochets et umbres

Dallia pectoralis Bean, 1880	F:U	Alaska Blackfish^
+*Esox americanus* Gmelin, 1789	F:CU	Redfin Pickerel......brochet d'Amérique
Esox lucius Linnaeus, 1758	F:CU	Northern Pike......grand brochet
Esox masquinongy Mitchill, 1824	F:CU	Muskellunge......maskinongé
Esox niger Lesueur, 1818	F:CU	Chain Pickerel......brochet maillé
Novumbra hubbsi Schultz, 1929	F:U	Olympic Mudminnow^
Umbra limi (Kirtland, 1840)	F:CU	Central Mudminnow......umbre de vase
Umbra pygmaea (DeKay, 1842)	F:U	Eastern Mudminnow

SCIENTIFIC NAME	OCCURRENCE[1]	COMMON NAME (ENGLISH, SPANISH, FRENCH)[2]

ORDER STOMIIFORMES

Sternoptychidae—En-marine hatchetfishes, Sp-peces hacha, Fr-haches d'argent

Maurolicus muelleri (Gmelin, 1789)	A	Daisy Pearlside..........marguerite perlée
Maurolicus weitzmani Parin & Kobyliansky, 1993	A	Atlantic Pearlside^..........marguerite perlée de Weitzman
Polyipnus clarus Harold, 1994	A	Slope Hatchetfish..........dix-bards à épines courtes

Phosichthyidae—En-lightfishes, Sp-peces luminosos, Fr-poissons étoilés

Pollichthys mauli (Poll, 1953)	A	Stareye Lightfish..........cyclothone étoilé

+Stomiidae—En-dragonfishes, Sp-peces demonios, Fr-dragons à écailles

Chauliodus macouni Bean, 1890	P	Pacific Viperfish^..........vibora del Pacifico..........chauliode féroce
Stomias boa (Risso, 1810)	A-Ar	Boa Dragonfish..........dragon-boa
Tactostoma macropus Bolin, 1939	P	Longfin Dragonfish..........dragon à longues nageoires

+ORDER AULOPIFORMES

Aulopidae—En-flagfins, Sp-aulópidos, Fr-limberts

Aulopus bajacali Parin & Kotlyar, 1984	PM	Eastern Pacific Flagfin^..........lagarto del Pacifico oriental
Aulopus filamentosus (Bloch, 1792)	A	Yellowfin Aulopus

Synodontidae—En-lizardfishes, Sp-chiles, Fr-poissons-lézards

Saurida brasiliensis Norman, 1935	A	Largescale Lizardfish..........chile brasileño
Saurida caribbaea Breder, 1927	A	Smallscale Lizardfish..........chile caribeño
Saurida normani Longley, 1935	A	Shortjaw Lizardfish..........chile espinoso
Synodus evermanni Jordan & Bollman, 1890	PM	Spotted Lizardfish..........chile cadena
Synodus foetens (Linnaeus, 1766)	A	Inshore Lizardfish..........chile apestoso
Synodus intermedius (Spix & Agassiz, 1829)	A	Sand Diver..........chile manchado
Synodus lacertinus Gilbert, 1890	PM	Calico Lizardfish..........chile lagarto
Synodus lucioceps (Ayres, 1855)	P	California Lizardfish^..........chile lucio
Synodus poeyi Jordan, 1887	A	Offshore Lizardfish..........chile barbado
Synodus saurus (Linnaeus, 1758)	A	Bluestripe Lizardfish

SCIENTIFIC NAME	OCCURRENCE[1]	COMMON NAME (ENGLISH, SPANISH, FRENCH)[2]
Synodus scituliceps Jordan & Gilbert, 1882	PM	Lance Lizardfish...........chile arpón
Synodus sechurae Hildebrand, 1946	PM	Iguana Lizardfish.............chile iguana
Synodus synodus (Linnaeus, 1758)	A	Red Lizardfish.............chile rojo
Trachinocephalus myops (Forster, 1801)	A	Snakefish.............chile chato.............poisson-lézard paille
Chlorophthalmidae—En-greeneyes, Sp-ojiverdes, Fr-yeux-verts		
Chlorophthalmus agassizi Bonaparte, 1840	A	Shortnose Greeneye ....ojiverde chato ....oeil-vert camus
Parasudis truculenta (Goode & Bean, 1896)	A	Longnose Greeneye.............ojiverde truculento.............oeil-vert à long nez
Scopelarchidae—En-pearleyes, Sp-ojos de perla, Fr-yeux-perlés		
Benthalbella dentata (Chapman, 1939)	P	Northern Pearleye.............perlado norteño.............oeil-perlé du nord
Alepisauridae—En-lancetfishes, Sp-lanzones, Fr-cavalos		
Alepisaurus brevirostris Gibbs, 1960	A	Shortnose Lancetfish.............lanzón picudo.............cavalo ocellé
Alepisaurus ferox Lowe, 1833	A-P	Longnose Lancetfish ....lanzón picudo.............cavalo féroce
*Paralepididae—En-barracudinas and daggertooths, Sp-barracudinas y dagas, Fr-lussions et pharaons		
+*Anotopterus nikparini* Kukuev, 1998	P	North Pacific Daggertooth^.....daga
+*Anotopterus pharao* Zugmayer, 1911	A-Ar	Daggertooth.............pharaon
Arctozenus risso (Bonaparte, 1840)	A-Ar	White Barracudina ....lussion blanc
Macroparalepis johnfitchi (Rofen, 1960)	P	Black Barracudina
Magnisudis atlantica (Krøyer, 1868)	A-P-Ar	Duckbill Barracudina.............barracudina pico de pato.. lussion à bec de canard

ORDER MYCTOPHIFORMES

+Myctophidae—En-lanternfishes, Sp-linternillas, Fr-poissons-lanternes

Benthosema glaciale (Reinhardt, 1837)	A-Ar	Glacier Lanternfish.............lanterne glaciaire
Benthosema panamense (Táning, 1932)	PM	Panama Lanternfish^ ....linternilla panameña
Ceratoscopelus maderensis (Lowe, 1839)	A	Horned Lanternfish.............lampe cornée
Ceratoscopelus townsendi (Eigenmann & Eigenmann, 1889)	P	Dogtooth Lampfish ....diente de perro ....lampe à sourcils lumineux

SCIENTIFIC NAME	OCCURRENCE[1]	COMMON NAME (ENGLISH, SPANISH, FRENCH)[2]
Diaphus theta Eigenmann & Eigenmann, 1890	P	California Headlightfish^ ...... linternilla californiana .... lampe-de-tête à taches blanches
Diogenichthys laternatus (Garman, 1899)	P	Diogenes Lanternfish^ .... linternilla de Diogenes
Gonichthys cocco (Cocco, 1829)	A	Linestop Lanternfish .... lanterne boute-ligne
Hygophum hygomii (Lütken, 1892)	A	Bermuda Lanternfish^ .... lanterne des Bermudes
Lampadena speculigera Goode & Bean, 1896	A	Mirror Lanternfish .... lampe à nez denté
Lampanyctus crocodilus (Risso, 1810)	A-Ar	Jewel Lanternfish .... lanterne-joyau
Lobianchia dofleini (Zugmayer, 1911)	A	Mediterranean Divinglamp^ .... lampe-de-plongée de la Méditerranée
Myctophum affine (Lütken, 1892)	A	Metallic Lanternfish .... lanterne rude du nord
Myctophum punctatum Rafinesque, 1810	A	Spotted Lanternfish .... lanterne ponctuée
Nannobrachium regale (Gilbert, 1892)	P	Pinpoint Lampfish .... linternilla puntita
Notoscopelus resplendens (Richardson, 1845)	A-P	Patchwork Lampfish .... linternilla brillante ... lampe-voilière sao-en-coin
Protomyctophum crockeri (Bolin, 1939)	P	California Flashlightfish^ .... linternilla luciérnaga
Stenobrachius leucopsarus (Eigenmann & Eigenmann, 1890)	P	Northern Lampfish .... linternilla norteña .... lanterne du nord
Tarletonbeania crenularis (Jordan & Gilbert, 1880)	P	Blue Lanternfish .... linternilla azul .... lanterne bleue
Triphoturus mexicanus (Gilbert, 1890)	P	Mexican Lampfish^ .... linternilla mexicana

*ORDER LAMPRIFORMES

*Lampridae—En-opahs, Sp-opahs, Fr-opahs

Lampris guttatus (Brünnich, 1788)	A-P	Opah .... opah ....opah

Stylephoridae—En-tube-eyes, Sp-ojilargos, Fr-stylephoridés

+*Stylephorus chordatus* Shaw, 1791	A	Tube-eye

Lophotidae—En-crestfishes, Sp-peces flecos, Fr-poissons crêtés

Eumecichthys fiski (Günther, 1890)	A	Unicornfish
Lophotus capellei Temminck & Schlegel, 1845	P	North Pacific Crestfish^
Lophotus lacepede Giorna, 1809	A	Crestfish ....fleco de gallo

SCIENTIFIC NAME	OCCURRENCE[1]	COMMON NAME (ENGLISH, SPANISH, FRENCH)[2]
		Trachipteridae—En-ribbonfishes, Sp-listoncillos, Fr-trachiptères
Desmodema lorum Rosenblatt & Butler, 1977	P	Whiptail Ribbonfish............listoncillo látigo
Desmodema polystictum (Ogilby, 1898)	A	Polka-dot Ribbonfish
Trachipterus altivelis Kner, 1859	P	King-of-the-salmon.........rey de los salmones ....roi-des-saumons
Trachipterus arcticus (Brünnich, 1788)	A	Dealfish
Trachipterus fukuzakii Fitch, 1964	P	Tapertail Ribbonfish............listoncillo pabilo
Trachipterus jacksonensis (Ramsey, 1881)	PM	Blackflash Ribbonfish.........listoncillo negro
Zu cristatus (Bonelli, 1819)	A-P	Scalloped Ribbonfish.........listoncillo festón
		Regalecidae—En-oarfishes, Sp-peces remo, Fr-régalées
Regalecus glesne Ascanius, 1772	A-P	Oarfish..................rey de los arenques ....roi des harengs

ORDER POLYMIXIIFORMES

SCIENTIFIC NAME	OCCURRENCE[1]	COMMON NAME (ENGLISH, SPANISH, FRENCH)[2]
		Polymixiidae—En-beardfishes, Sp-colas de maguey, Fr-poissons à barbe
Polymixia lowei Günther, 1859	A	Beardfish..................cola de maguey

ORDER PERCOPSIFORMES

SCIENTIFIC NAME	OCCURRENCE[1]	COMMON NAME (ENGLISH, SPANISH, FRENCH)[2]
		Percopsidae—En-trout-perches, Sp-percas falsas, Fr-omiscos
Percopsis omiscomaycus (Walbaum, 1792)	F:CU	Trout-perch.........................omisco
Percopsis transmontana (Eigenmann & Eigenmann, 1892)	F:U	Sand Roller
		Aphredoderidae—En-pirate perches, Sp-percas pirata, Fr-perches-pirates
Aphredoderus sayanus (Gilliams, 1824)	F:U	Pirate Perch
		Amblyopsidae—En-cavefishes, Sp-peces cavernicolas, Fr-amblyopes
Amblyopsis rosae (Eigenmann, 1898)	F:U	Ozark Cavefish^
Amblyopsis spelaea DeKay, 1842	F:U	Northern Cavefish

SCIENTIFIC NAME	OCCURRENCE[1]	COMMON NAME (ENGLISH, SPANISH, FRENCH)[2]
Chologaster cornuta Agassiz, 1853	F:U	Swampfish
Forbesichthys agassizii (Putnam, 1872)	F:U	Spring Cavefish
Speoplatyrhinus poulsoni Cooper & Kuehne, 1974	F:U	Alabama Cavefish^
Typhlichthys subterraneus Girard, 1859	F:U	Southern Cavefish

+ORDER GADIFORMES

Bregmacerotidae—En-codlets, Sp-bacaletes, Fr-varlets

Bregmaceros atlanticus Goode & Bean, 1886	A	Antenna Codlet	bacalete antena
Bregmaceros bathymaster Jordan & Bollman, 1890	PM	East Pacific Codlet^	bacalete del Pacífico oriental
Bregmaceros cantori Milliken & Houde, 1984	A	Striped Codlet	bacalete rayado
Bregmaceros houdei Saksena & Richards, 1986	A	Stellate Codlet	

Macrouridae—En-grenadiers, Sp-granaderos, Fr-grenadiers

Coelorinchus caelorinchus (Risso, 1810)	A	Saddled Grenadier	granadero tristón
Coelorinchus caribbaeus (Goode & Bean, 1885)	A	Blackfin Grenadier	granadero caribeño
Coelorinchus scaphopsis (Gilbert, 1890)	P	Shoulderspot Grenadier	granadero carepala
Coryphaenoides pectoralis (Gilbert, 1892)	P	Giant Grenadier	
Macrourus berglax Lacepède, 1801	A	Roughhead Grenadier	grenadier berglax
Malacocephalus occidentalis Goode & Bean, 1885	A	Western Softhead Grenadier	granadero carapacho	queue-de-rat d'Amérique
Nezumia bairdii (Goode & Bean, 1877)	A-Ar	Marlin-spike	
Nezumia sclerorhynchus (Valenciennes, 1838)	A	Bluntsnout Grenadier	
Nezumia stelgidolepis (Gilbert, 1890)	P	California Grenadier^	grenadier du Grand Banc

Moridae—En-codlings, Sp-moras y carboneros, Fr-moras

Antimora microlepis Bean, 1890	P	Pacific Flatnose^	mora viola	antimore à petites écailles
Laemonema barbatulum Goode & Bean, 1883	A	Shortbeard Codling	
Physiculus fulvus Bean, 1884	A	Metallic Codling	carbonero metálico	physicule fauve
Physiculus nematopus Gilbert, 1890	PM	Charcoal Codling	carbonero de fango
Physiculus rastrelliger Gilbert, 1890	P	Hundred-fathom Codling	carbonero negro
Physiculus talarae Hildebrand & Barton, 1949	PM	Peruvian Codling^	carbonero peruano

SCIENTIFIC NAME	OCCURRENCE[1]	COMMON NAME (ENGLISH, SPANISH, FRENCH)[2]		

*Merlucciidae—En-merlucciid hakes, Sp-merluzas, Fr-merlus

Scientific name	Occ.	English	Spanish	French
Merluccius albidus (Mitchill, 1818)	A	Offshore Hake		merlu du large
Merluccius bilinearis (Mitchill, 1814)	A	Silver Hake		merlu argenté
+*Merluccius productus* (Ayres, 1855)	P	Pacific Hake^	merluza norteña	merlu du Pacifique
+*Steindachneria argentea* Goode & Bean, 1896	A	Luminous Hake	mollera luminosa	

Phycidae—En-phycid hakes, Sp-merluzas barbonas, Fr-phycidés

Scientific name	Occ.	English	Spanish	French
Ciliata septentrionalis (Collett, 1875)	A	Northern Rockling		
Enchelyopus cimbrius (Linnaeus, 1766)	A	Fourbeard Rockling		motelle à quatre barbillons
Phycis chesteri (Goode & Bean, 1878)	A-Ar	Longfin Hake		merluche à longues nageoires
Urophycis chuss (Walbaum, 1792)	A	Red Hake		merluche-écureuil
Urophycis cirrata (Goode & Bean, 1896)	A	Gulf Hake^	merluza barbona del Golfo	
Urophycis earllii (Bean, 1880)	A	Carolina Hake^		
Urophycis floridana (Bean & Dresel, 1884)	A	Southern Hake	merluza barbona floridana	
Urophycis regia (Walbaum, 1792)	A	Spotted Hake	merluza barbona reina	merluche tachetée
Urophycis tenuis (Mitchill, 1814)	A	White Hake		merluche blanche

Gadidae—En-cods, Sp-bacalaos, Fr-morues

Scientific name	Occ.	English	Spanish	French
+*Arctogadus glacialis* (Peters, 1872)	A-P-Ar	Polar Cod		saïda imberbe
Boreogadus saida (Lepechin, 1774)	A-P-Ar	Arctic Cod^		saïda franc
Brosme brosme (Ascanius, 1772)	A	Cusk		brosme
Eleginus gracilis (Tilesius, 1810)	P-Ar	Saffron Cod		navaga jaune
Gadus chalcogrammus Pallas, 1814	P-Ar	Walleye Pollock		goberge de l'Alaska
+*Gadus macrocephalus* Tilesius, 1810	A-P-Ar	Pacific Cod^		ogac
Gadus morhua Linnaeus, 1758	A-Ar	Atlantic Cod^		morue franche
Gaidropsarus argentatus (Reinhardt, 1837)	A-Ar	Silver Rockling		mustèle argentée
Gaidropsarus ensis (Reinhardt, 1837)	A	Threebeard Rockling		mustèle arctique à trois barbillons
+*Lota lota* (Linnaeus, 1758)	Ar-F:CU	Burbot		lotte
Melanogrammus aeglefinus (Linnaeus, 1758)	A	Haddock		aiglefin
Merlangius merlangus (Linnaeus, 1758)	A	Whiting		
Microgadus proximus (Girard, 1854)	P	Pacific Tomcod^		poulamon du Pacifique

SCIENTIFIC NAME	OCCURRENCE[1]	COMMON NAME (ENGLISH, SPANISH, FRENCH)[2]		
Microgadus tomcod (Walbaum, 1792)	A-F:CU	Atlantic Tomcod^		poulamon atlantique
Micromesistius poutassou (Risso, 1827)	A	Blue Whiting		merlan bleu
Molva molva (Linnaeus, 1758)	A	European Ling^		lingue
Pollachius virens (Linnaeus, 1758)	A	Pollock		goberge

+ORDER OPHIDIIFORMES

Carapidae—En-pearlfishes, Sp-perleros, Fr-aurins

Carapus bermudensis (Jones, 1874)	A	Pearlfish		perlero del Atlántico
Echiodon dawsoni Williams & Shipp, 1982	A	Chain Pearlfish		
Echiodon exsilium Rosenblatt, 1961	PM	Nocturnal Pearlfish		perlero nocturno
Encheliophis dubius (Putnam, 1874)	PM	Pacific Pearlfish^		perlero del Pacífico
Encheliophis vermicularis Müller, 1842	PM	Finless Pearlfish		perlero mocho

Ophidiidae—En-cusk-eels, Sp-brótulas y congriperlas, Fr-donzelles

Brotula barbata (Bloch & Schneider, 1801)	A	Atlantic Bearded Brotula^		brótula barbona
Brotula clarkae Hubbs, 1944	P	Pacific Bearded Brotula^		lengua rosada
Brotula ordwayi Hildebrand & Barton, 1949	PM	Fore-spotted Brotula		lengua pintada
Chilara taylori (Girard, 1858)	P	Spotted Cusk-eel		congriperla moteada
Lepophidium brevibarbe (Cuvier, 1829)	A	Blackedge Cusk-eel		congriperla clarín
Lepophidium jeannae Fowler, 1941	A	Mottled Cusk-eel		congriperla jaspeada
Lepophidium marmoratum (Goode & Bean, 1885)	AM	Marbled Cusk-eel		congriperla marmoleada
Lepophidium microlepis (Gilbert, 1890)	PM	Finescale Cusk-eel		congriperla plateada
Lepophidium negropinna Hildebrand & Barton, 1949	PM	Specklefin Cusk-eel		congriperla pinta
Lepophidium pardale (Gilbert, 1890)	PM	Leopard Cusk-eel		congriperla leopardo
Lepophidium pheromystax Robins, 1960	AM	Upsilon Cusk-eel		congriperla bigotona
Lepophidium profundorum (Gill, 1863)	A	Fawn Cusk-eel		congriperla amarilla
Lepophidium prorates (Jordan & Bollman, 1890)	PM	Prowspine Cusk-eel		congriperla cornuda
Lepophidium staurophor Robins, 1959	A	Barred Cusk-eel		congriperla rayada
Lepophidium stigmatistium (Gilbert, 1890)	PM	Mexican Cusk-eel^		congriperla mexicana
Neobythites gilli Goode & Bean, 1885	A	Twospot Brotula		brótula amarillenta

SCIENTIFIC NAME	OCCURRENCE[1]	COMMON NAME (ENGLISH, SPANISH, FRENCH)[2]
Neobythites marginatus Goode & Bean, 1886	A	Stripefin Brotula
Neobythites stelliferoides Gilbert, 1890	PM	Thread Brotula .... brótula de hebra
Ophidion antipholus Lea & Robins, 2003	A	Longnose Cusk-eel .... congriperla narizón
Ophidion dromio Lea & Robins, 2003	A	Shorthead Cusk-eel
Ophidion galeoides (Gilbert, 1890)	PM	Spotfin Cusk-eel .... congriperla adornada
Ophidion grayi (Fowler, 1948)	A	Blotched Cusk-eel
Ophidion holbrookii Putnam, 1874	A	Bank Cusk-eel .... congriperla de bajos
Ophidion imitator Lea, 1997	PM	Mimic Cusk-eel .... congriperla mimética
Ophidion iris Breder, 1936	PM	Brighteye Cusk-eel .... congriperla arcoiris
Ophidion josephi Girard, 1858	A	Crested Cusk-eel .... congriperla crestada
* *Ophidion lagochila* (Böhlke & Robins, 1959)	AM	Harelip Cusk-eel .... congriperla labio leporino
Ophidion marginatum (DeKay, 1842)	A	Striped Cusk-eel
Ophidion nocomis Robins & Böhlke, 1959	AM	Letter Opener .... congriperla nacarada
Ophidion robinsi Fahay, 1992	A	Colonial Cusk-eel
Ophidion scrippsae (Hubbs, 1916)	P	Basketweave Cusk-eel .... congriperla canastera
Ophidion selenops Robins & Böhlke, 1959	A	Mooneye Cusk-eel
Otophidium chickcharney Böhlke & Robins, 1959	AM	Ghost Cusk-eel .... congriperla fantasma
Otophidium dormitator Böhlke & Robins, 1959	A	Sleeper Cusk-eel
Otophidium indefatigabile Jordan & Bollman, 1890	PM	Panamic Cusk-eel^ .... congriperla cabezona
Otophidium omostigma (Jordan & Gilbert, 1882)	A	Polka-dot Cusk-eel .... congriperla lunareja
Parophidion schmidti (Woods & Kanazawa, 1951)	A	Dusky Cusk-eel .... congriperla parda
Petrotyx hopkinsi Heller & Snodgrass, 1903	PM	Velvetnose Brotula .... brótula hocico terciopelado
Petrotyx sanguineus (Meek & Hildebrand, 1928)	A	Redfin Brotula .... brótula aletirroja

Bythitidae—En-viviparous brotulas, Sp-brótulas vivíparas, Fr-donzelles vivipares

Brosmophycis marginata (Ayres, 1854)	P	Red Brotula .... brótula roja .... donzelle rouge
Calamopteryx goslinei Böhlke & Cohen, 1966	AM	Longarm Brotula .... brótula aletona
+ *Calamopteryx robinsorum* Cohen, 1973	AM	Teacher Brotula .... brótula del maestro
Grammonus claudei (de la Torre y Huerta, 1930)	A	Reef-cave Brotula
Grammonus diagrammus (Heller & Snodgrass, 1903)	P	Purple Brotula .... brótula púrpura
Gunterichthys longipenis Dawson, 1966	A	Gold Brotula

SCIENTIFIC NAME	OCCURRENCE[1]	COMMON NAME (ENGLISH, SPANISH, FRENCH)[2]
*Ogilbia boydwalkeri Møller, Schwarzhans & Nielsen, 2005	PM	Professor Brotula......brótula del profesor
*Ogilbia cayorum Evermann & Kendall, 1898	A	Key Brotula
*Ogilbia davidsmithi Møller, Schwarzhans & Nielsen, 2005	PM	Cortez Brotula^......brótula de Cortés
*Ogilbia nigromarginata Møller, Schwarzhans & Nielsen, 2005	PM	Blackmargin Brotula......brótula de margen negro
*Ogilbia nudiceps Møller, Schwarzhans & Nielsen, 2005	PM	Slickhead Brotula......brótula pelona
*Ogilbia robertsoni Møller, Schwarzhans & Nielsen, 2005	PM	Brown Brotula......brótula café
*Ogilbia sabaji Møller, Schwarzhans & Nielsen, 2005	A	Curator Brotula
*Ogilbia sedorae Møller, Schwarzhans & Nielsen, 2005	PM	Notchspine Brotula......brótula espina partida
*Ogilbia suarezae Møller, Schwarzhans & Nielsen, 2005	A	Shy Brotula......brótula tímida
*Ogilbia ventralis (Gill, 1863)	PM	Gulf Brotula^......brótula del Golfo
Stygnobrotula latebricola Böhlke, 1957	A	Black Brotula
*Typhliasina pearsei (Hubbs, 1938)	F:M	Mexican Blind Brotula^......dama blanca ciega

ORDER BATRACHOIDIFORMES

Batrachoididae—En-toadfishes, Sp-peces sapo, Fr-poissons-crapauds

Batrachoides gilberti Meek & Hildebrand, 1928	AM	Large-eye Toadfish......sapo ojón
Batrachoides goldmani Evermann & Goldsborough, 1902	F:M	Mexican Freshwater Toadfish^......sapo mexicano
Batrachoides waltersi Collette & Russo, 1981	PM	Multipored Toadfish......sapo peludo
Opsanus beta (Goode & Bean, 1880)	A	Gulf Toadfish^......sapo boquiblanco
Opsanus dichrostomus Collette, 2001	AM	Bicolor Toadfish......sapo bicolor
Opsanus pardus (Goode & Bean, 1880)	A	Leopard Toadfish......sapo leopardo
Opsanus tau (Linnaeus, 1766)	A	Oyster Toadfish
Porichthys analis Hubbs & Schultz, 1939	PM	Darkedge Midshipman......sapo de luto
Porichthys ephippiatus Walker & Rosenblatt, 1988	PM	Saddle Midshipman......sapo ensillado

SCIENTIFIC NAME	OCCURRENCE[1]	COMMON NAME (ENGLISH, SPANISH, FRENCH)[2]
Porichthys greenei Gilbert & Starks, 1904	PM	Shorthead Midshipman...sapo cabeza corta
Porichthys margaritatus (Richardson, 1844)	PM	Pearlspot Midshipman...sapo luminoso
Porichthys mimeticus Walker & Rosenblatt, 1988	PM	Mimetic Midshipman...sapo mimético
Porichthys myriaster Hubbs & Schultz, 1939	P	Specklefin Midshipman...sapo aleta pintada
Porichthys notatus Girard, 1854	P	Plainfin Midshipman...sapo aleta lucia...pilotin tacheté
Porichthys plectrodon Jordan & Gilbert, 1882	A	Atlantic Midshipman^...doradilla
Sanopus johnsoni Collette & Starck, 1974	AM	Cozumel Toadfish^...sapo de Cozumel
Sanopus reticulatus Collette, 1983	AM	Reticulate Toadfish...sapo reticulado
Sanopus splendidus Collette, Starck & Phillips, 1974	AM	Splendid Toadfish...sapo magnífico

ORDER LOPHIIFORMES

Lophiidae—En-goosefishes, Sp-rapes pescadores, Fr-baudroies

Lophiodes caulinaris (Garman, 1899)	P	Spottedtail Goosefish...rape rabo manchado
Lophiodes reticulatus Caruso & Suttkus, 1979	A	Reticulate Goosefish...rape hocicón
Lophiodes spilurus (Garman, 1899)	P	Threadfin Goosefish...rape de hebra
+*Lophius americanus* Valenciennes, 1837	A	Goosefish...baudroie d'Amérique
Lophius gastrophysus Miranda-Ribeiro, 1915	A	Blackfin Goosefish...rape pescador

Antennariidae—En-frogfishes, Sp-ranisapos, Fr-antennaires

Antennarius commerson (Lacepède, 1798)	PM	Giant Frogfish...ranisapo gigante
Antennarius multiocellatus (Valenciennes, 1837)	A	Longlure Frogfish...ranisapo ceboso
Antennarius pauciradiatus Schultz, 1957	A	Dwarf Frogfish...ranisapo enano
Antennarius striatus (Shaw, 1794)	A	Striated Frogfish...ranisapo estriado
Antennatus coccineus (Lesson, 1831)	PM	Scarlet Frogfish...ranisapo escarlata
Antennatus sanguineus (Gill, 1863)	PM	Sanguine Frogfish...ranisapo sangrón
Antennatus strigatus (Gill, 1863)	PM	Bandtail Frogfish...ranisapo rabo listado
Fowlerichthys avalonis (Jordan & Starks, 1907)	P	Roughjaw Frogfish...ranisapo antenado
Fowlerichthys ocellatus (Bloch & Schneider, 1801)	A	Ocellated Frogfish...ranisapo pescador
Fowlerichthys radiosus (Garman, 1896)	A	Singlespot Frogfish...ranisapo uniocelado
Histrio histrio (Linnaeus, 1758)	A	Sargassumfish...pez sargazo...sargassier

SCIENTIFIC NAME	OCCURRENCE[1]	COMMON NAME (ENGLISH, SPANISH, FRENCH)[2]		
Chaunacidae—En-gapers, Sp-gómitas Fr-crapauds de mer				
Chaunax stigmaeus Fowler, 1946	A	Redeye Gaper		
Ogcocephalidae—En-batfishes, Sp-murciélagos, Fr-chauves-souris de mer				
Dibranchus atlanticus Peters, 1876	A	Atlantic Batfish^		malthe atlantique
+*Halieutichthys aculeatus* (Mitchill, 1818)	A	Pancake Batfish	murciélago picudo	
*Halieutichthys bispinosus Ho, Chakrabarty & Sparks, 2010	A	Spiny Batfish	murciélago tubos	
*Halieutichthys intermedius Ho, Chakrabarty & Sparks, 2010	A	Gulf Batfish^		
Ogcocephalus corniger Bradbury, 1980	A	Longnose Batfish		
Ogcocephalus cubifrons (Richardson, 1836)	A	Polka-dot Batfish	murciélago diablo	
Ogcocephalus declivirostris Bradbury, 1980	A	Slantbrow Batfish	murciélago inclinado	
Ogcocephalus nasutus (Cuvier, 1829)	A	Shortnose Batfish	murciélago tapacaminos	
Ogcocephalus pantostictus Bradbury, 1980	A	Spotted Batfish	murciélago manchado	
Ogcocephalus parvus Longley & Hildebrand, 1940	A	Roughback Batfish	murciélago lomo áspero	
Ogcocephalus rostellum Bradbury, 1980	A	Palefin Batfish		
Zalieutes elater (Jordan & Gilbert, 1882)	P	Roundel Batfish	murciélago biocelado	
Zalieutes mcgintyi (Fowler, 1952)	A	Tricorn Batfish	murciélago tres cuernos	
Himantolophidae—En-footballfishes, Sp-peces balón, Fr-poissons-football				
Himantolophus groenlandicus Reinhardt, 1837	A	Atlantic Footballfish^		football fine-lampe
Himantolophus sagamius (Tanaka, 1918)	P	Pacific Footballfish^		
Ceratiidae—En-seadevils, Sp-peces anzuelo, Fr-poissons-pêcheurs				
*Ceratias holboelli Krøyer, 1845	A	Northern Giant Seadevil		pêcheur à deux massettes
Cryptopsaras couesii Gill, 1883	A-P	Triplewart Seadevil	anzuelo diablo	pêcheur à trèfle

ORDER MUGILIFORMES

Mugilidae—En-mullets, Sp-lisas, Fr-muges				
Agonostomus monticola (Bancroft, 1834)	A-PM-F:UM	Mountain Mullet		trucha de tierra caliente

SCIENTIFIC NAME	OCCURRENCE[1]	COMMON NAME (ENGLISH, SPANISH, FRENCH)[2]
Chaenomugil proboscideus (Günther, 1861)	PM	Snouted Mullet......lisa hocicona
Joturus pichardi Poey, 1860	AM	Bobo Mullet......bobo
Mugil cephalus Linnaeus, 1758	A-P-F:UM	Striped Mullet......lisa rayada
Mugil curema Valenciennes, 1836	A-P-F:UM	White Mullet......lisa blanca......muge curema
+*Mugil hospes* Jordan & Culver, 1895	PM	Hospe Mullet......lisa hospe
Mugil liza Valenciennes, 1836	A	Liza
Mugil setosus Gilbert, 1892	PM	Liseta Mullet......lisa liseta
*Mugil rubrioculus Harrison, Nirchio, Oliveira, Ron & Gaviria, 2007	A	Redeye Mullet
+*Mugil trichodon* Poey, 1875	A	Fantail Mullet......lisa amarilla
Xenomugil thoburni (Jordan & Starks, 1896)	PM	Orange-eye Mullet......lisa agugú

ORDER ATHERINIFORMES

Atherinopsidae—En-New World silversides, Sp-charales y pejerreyes, Fr-poissons d'argent

SCIENTIFIC NAME	OCCURRENCE[1]	COMMON NAME (ENGLISH, SPANISH, FRENCH)[2]
Atherinella alvarezi (Diaz-Pardo, 1972)	F:M	Gulf Silverside^......plateadito de Tacotalpa
Atherinella ammophila Chernoff & Miller, 1984	F:M	La Palma Silverside^......plateadito de La Palma
Atherinella balsana (Meek, 1902)	F:M	Balsas Silverside^......plateadito del Balsas
*Atherinella callida Chernoff, 1986	F[X]:M	Cunning Silverside......plateadito del Refugio
Atherinella crystallina (Jordan & Culver, 1895)	F:M	Blackfin Silverside......plateadito del Presidio
Atherinella elegans Chernoff, 1986	F:M	Fuerte Silverside^......plateadito del Fuerte
Atherinella eriarcha Jordan & Gilbert, 1882	PM	Longfin Silverside......plateadito plateado
Atherinella guatemalensis (Günther, 1864)	F:M	Peppered Silverside......plateadito de Huamuchal
Atherinella lisa (Meek, 1904)	F:M	Naked Silverside......plateadito de El Hule
Atherinella marvelae (Chernoff & Miller, 1982)	F:M	Eyipantla Silverside^......plateadito de Eyipantla
Atherinella nepenthe (Myers & Wade, 1942)	PM	Pitcher Silverside......plateadito marino
Atherinella pellosemion Chernoff, 1986	F:M	Mancuernas Silverside^......plateadito del Mancuernas
Atherinella sallei (Regan, 1903)	F:M	Large-eye Silverside......plateadito del Papaloapan
*Atherinella schultzi (Álvarez & Carranza, 1952)	F:M	Chimalapa Silverside^......plateadito de Chimalapa
Atherinops affinis (Ayres, 1860)	P	Topsmelt......pejerrey pescadillo
Atherinopsis californiensis Girard, 1854	P	Jacksmelt......pejerrey mocho
Chirostoma aculeatum Barbour, 1973	F:M	Scowling Silverside......charal cuchillo
Chirostoma arge (Jordan & Snyder, 1899)	F:M	Largetooth Silverside......charal del Verde

SCIENTIFIC NAME	OCCURRENCE[1]	COMMON NAME (ENGLISH, SPANISH, FRENCH)[2]
Chirostoma attenuatum Meek, 1902	F:M	Slender Silverside.....charal prieto
Chirostoma bartoni Jordan & Evermann, 1896	F:M	Alberca Silverside^.....charal de La Caldera
Chirostoma chapalae Jordan & Snyder, 1899	F:M	Smallmouth Silverside .....charal de Chapala
Chirostoma charari (de Buen, 1945)	F:M	Least Silverside .....charal tarasco
Chirostoma consocium Jordan & Hubbs, 1919	F:M	Ranch Silverside.....charal de rancho
Chirostoma contrerasi Barbour, 2002	F:M	Ajijic Silverside^.....charal de Ajijic
Chirostoma estor Jordan, 1880	F:M	Pike Silverside.....pescado blanco
Chirostoma grandocule (Steindachner, 1894)	F:M	Bigeye Silverside.....charal del lago
Chirostoma humboldtianum (Valenciennes, 1835)	F:M	Shortfin Silverside.....charal de Xochimilco
Chirostoma jordani Woolman, 1894.	F:M	Mesa Silverside.....charale
Chirostoma labarcae Meek, 1902	F:M	Sharpnose Silverside.....charal de La Barca
Chirostoma lucius Boulenger, 1900.	F:M	Longjaw Silverside.....charal de la laguna
*Chirostoma melanoccus Álvarez, 1963	F:M	Blunthead Silverside.....charal de San Juanico
Chirostoma mezquital Meek, 1904	F:M	Mezquital Silverside^.....charal del Mezquital
*Chirostoma patzcuaro Meek, 1902	F:M	Pátzcuaro Silverside^.....charal pinto
Chirostoma promelas Jordan & Snyder, 1899	F:M	Blacknose Silverside.....charal boca negra
Chirostoma riojai Solórzano & López, 1966	F:M	Toluca Silverside^.....charal de Santiago
Chirostoma sphyraena Boulenger, 1900	F:M	Bigmouth Silverside.....charal barracuda
Colpichthys hubbsi Crabtree, 1989	PM	Delta Silverside^.....pejerrey delta
Colpichthys regis (Jenkins & Evermann, 1889)	PM	False Grunion .....pejerrey charal
Labidesthes sicculus (Cope, 1865)	F:CU	Brook Silverside.....crayon d'argent
Leuresthes sardina (Jenkins & Evermann, 1889)	PM	Gulf Grunion^.....pejerrey sardina
Leuresthes tenuis (Ayres, 1860)	P	California Grunion^.....pejerrey californiano
Melanorhinus cyanellus (Meek & Hildebrand, 1923)	PM	Blackback Silverside.....pejerrey azulado
Membras gilberti (Jordan & Bollman, 1890)	PM	Landia Silverside.....pejerrey landia
Membras martinica (Valenciennes, 1835)	A-F:UM	Rough Silverside.....pejerrey rasposo
+Menidia audens Hay, 1882	F:U	Mississippi Silverside^
Menidia beryllina (Cope, 1867)	A-F:UM	Inland Silverside.....plateadito salado
Menidia clarkhubbsi Echelle & Mosier, 1982	A	Texas Silverside^
Menidia colei Hubbs, 1936	F:M	Golden Silverside.....plateadito de Progreso
+Menidia conchorum Hildebrand & Ginsburg, 1927	A	Key Silverside
Menidia extensa Hubbs & Raney, 1946	F:U	Waccamaw Silverside^
Menidia menidia (Linnaeus, 1766)	A	Atlantic Silverside^.....capucette

SCIENTIFIC NAME	OCCURRENCE[1]	COMMON NAME (ENGLISH, SPANISH, FRENCH)[2]
Menidia peninsulae (Goode & Bean, 1879)	A	Tidewater Silverside....plateadito playero
Poblana alchichica de Buen, 1945	F:M	Alchichica Silverside^....charal de Alchichica
Poblana ferdebueni Solórzano & López, 1965	F:M	Chignahuapan Silverside^....charal de Almoloya
Poblana letholepis Álvarez, 1950	F:M	La Preciosa Silverside^....charal de La Preciosa
Poblana squamata Álvarez, 1950	F:M	Quechulac Silverside^....charal de Quechulac
		Atherinidae—En-Old World silversides, Sp-tinícalos Fr-athérines
Atherinomorus stipes (Müller & Troschel, 1848)	A	Hardhead Silverside....tinícalo cabezón
Hypoatherina harringtonensis (Goode, 1877)	A	Reef Silverside....tinícalo de arrecife

+ORDER BELONIFORMES

Exocoetidae— En-flyingfishes, Sp-voladores, Fr-exocets

SCIENTIFIC NAME	OCCURRENCE[1]	COMMON NAME (ENGLISH, SPANISH, FRENCH)[2]
Cheilopogon atrisignis (Jenkins, 1903)	PM	Glider Flyingfish....volador planeador
Cheilopogon cyanopterus (Valenciennes, 1847)	A	Margined Flyingfish....volador azul
Cheilopogon dorsomacula (Fowler, 1944)	PM	Blackspot Flyingfish....volador lomo manchado
Cheilopogon exsiliens (Linnaeus, 1771)	A	Bandwing Flyingfish....volador campechano
Cheilopogon furcatus (Mitchill, 1815)	A-PM	Spotfin Flyingfish....volador ala manchada....exocet à nageoires tachetées
Cheilopogon heterurus (Rafinesque, 1810)	P	Blotchwing Flyingfish....volador ala lunada
Cheilopogon melanurus (Valenciennes, 1847)	A	Atlantic Flyingfish^....volador blanquito
Cheilopogon papilio (Clark, 1936)	PM	Butterfly Flyingfish....volador mariposa
Cheilopogon pinnatibarbatus (Bennett, 1831)	P	Smallhead Flyingfish....volador cabecita
Cheilopogon spilonotopterus (Bleeker, 1866)	PM	Stained Flyingfish....volador jaspeado
Cheilopogon xenopterus (Gilbert, 1890)	PM	Whitetip Flyingfish....volador puntas blancas
Cypselurus angusticeps Nichols & Breder, 1935	PM	Narrowhead Flyingfish....volador isleño
Cypselurus callopterus (Günther, 1866)	PM	Beautyfin Flyingfish....volador bonito
Cypselurus comatus (Mitchill, 1815)	A	Clearwing Flyingfish
Exocoetus monocirrhus Richardson, 1846	PM	Barbel Flyingfish....volador barbudo
Exocoetus obtusirostris Günther, 1866	A	Oceanic Two-wing Flyingfish....volador flecha
Exocoetus volitans Linnaeus, 1758	A-PM	Tropical Two-wing Flyingfish....volador tropical
Fodiator acutus (Valenciennes, 1847)	P	Sharpchin Flyingfish....volador picudo

SCIENTIFIC NAME	OCCURRENCE[1]	COMMON NAME (ENGLISH, SPANISH, FRENCH)[2]
Hirundichthys affinis (Günther, 1866)	A	Fourwing Flyingfish......volador golondrina......exocet à frange blanche
Hirundichthys marginatus (Nichols & Breder, 1928)	PM	Bladewing Flyingfish......volador ala navaja
Hirundichthys rondeletii (Valenciennes, 1847)	A-P	Blackwing Flyingfish......volador ala negra
Hirundichthys speculiger (Valenciennes, 1847)	PM	Mirrorwing Flyingfish......volador espejo
Parexocoetus brachypterus (Richardson, 1846)	A	Sailfin Flyingfish......volador aletón
Prognichthys occidentalis Parin, 1999	A	Bluntnose Flyingfish......volador chato
Prognichthys sealei Abe, 1955	PM	Sailor Flyingfish......volador marinero
Prognichthys tringa Breder, 1928	PM	Panamic Flyingfish^......volador panámico
Hemiramphidae—En-halfbeaks, Sp-pajaritos, Fr-demi-becs		
Chriodorus atherinoides Goode & Bean, 1882	A	Hardhead Halfbeak......pajarito cabeciduro
Euleptorhamphus velox Poey, 1868	A	Flying Halfbeak......agujeta voladora
Euleptorhamphus viridis (van Hasselt, 1823)	P	Ribbon Halfbeak......agujeta alargada
Hemiramphus balao Lesueur, 1821	A	Balao......agujeta balao
Hemiramphus brasiliensis (Linnaeus, 1758)	A	Ballyhoo......agujeta brasileña......demi-bec brésilien
Hemiramphus saltator Gilbert & Starks, 1904	P	Longfin Halfbeak......pajarito saltador
Hyporhamphus gilli Meek & Hildebrand, 1923	PM	Choelo Halfbeak......pajarito cholo
Hyporhamphus meeki Banford & Collette, 1993	A	False Silverstripe Halfbeak......agujeta flaca
Hyporhamphus mexicanus Álvarez, 1959	F:M	Mexican Halfbeak^......pajarito mexicano
Hyporhamphus naos Banford & Collette, 2001	P	Pacific Silverstripe Halfbeak^......pajarito blanco del Pacífico
Hyporhamphus roberti (Valenciennes, 1837)	AM	Slender Halfbeak......agujeta larga
Hyporhamphus rosae (Jordan & Gilbert, 1880)	P	California Halfbeak^......pajarito californiano
Hyporhamphus snyderi Meek & Hildebrand, 1923	PM	Skipper Halfbeak......pajarito choca
Hyporhamphus unifasciatus (Ranzani, 1841)	A	Atlantic Silverstripe Halfbeak^......pajarito blanco del Atlántico
Oxyporhamphus micropterus (Valenciennes, 1847)	A-PM	Smallwing Flyingfish......volador alita
Belonidae—En-needlefishes, Sp-agujones, Fr-aiguillettes		
Ablennes hians (Valenciennes, 1846)	A-PM	Flat Needlefish......agujón sable
Platybelone argalus (Lesueur, 1821)	A-PM	Keeltail Needlefish......agujón de quilla
Strongylura exilis (Girard, 1854)	P	California Needlefish^......agujón californiano
Strongylura hubbsi Collette, 1974	F:M	Maya Needlefish^......agujón maya
Strongylura marina (Walbaum, 1792)	A-F:UM	Atlantic Needlefish^......agujón verde

SCIENTIFIC NAME	OCCURRENCE[1]	COMMON NAME (ENGLISH, SPANISH, FRENCH)[2]
Strongylura notata (Poey, 1860)	A	Redfin Needlefish....agujón negro
Strongylura timucu (Walbaum, 1792)	A	Timucú....agujón timucú
Tylosurus acus (Lacepède, 1803)	A	Atlantic Agujón^....agujón del Atlántico
Tylosurus crocodilus (Péron & Lesueur, 1821)	A-PM	Houndfish....agujón lisero
Tylosurus pacificus (Steindachner, 1876)	PM	Pacific Agujón^ ....agujón del Pacífico

Scomberesocidae—En-sauries, Sp-papardas, Fr-balaous

Cololabis saira (Brevoort, 1856)	P	Pacific Saury^....paparda del Pacífico....balaou japonais
Scomberesox saurus (Walbaum, 1792)	A	Atlantic Saury^....balaou

+ORDER CYPRINODONTIFORMES

*Rivulidae—En-New World rivulines, Sp-almirantes, Fr-rivulidés

Kryptolebias marmoratus (Poey, 1880)	A-F:UM	Mangrove Rivulus....almirante de manglar
Millerichthys robustus (Miller & Hubbs, 1974)	F:M	Mexican Rivulus^....almirante mexicano
Rivulus hartii (Boulenger, 1890)	F[I]:U	Giant Rivulus
Rivulus tenuis (Meek, 1904)	F:M	Maya Rivulus^....almirante de El Hule

Profundulidae—En-Middle American killifishes, Sp-escamudos, Fr-profundulidés

Profundulus candalarius Hubbs, 1924	F:M	Headwater Killifish....escamudo de Comitán
Profundulus hildebrandi Miller, 1950	F:M	Chiapas Killifish^....escamudo de San Cristóbal
Profundulus labialis (Günther, 1866)	F:M	Largelip Killifish....escamudo bocón
Profundulus oaxacae (Meek, 1902)	F:M	Oaxaca Killifish^....escamudo oaxaqueño
Profundulus punctatus (Günther, 1866)	F:M	Brownspotted Killifish....escamudo pinto

*Goodeidae—En-goodeids, Sp-mexclapiques, Fr-goodéidés

Allodontichthys hubbsi Miller & Uyeno, 1980	F:M	Whitepatch Splitfin....mexclapique de Tuxpan
Allodontichthys polylepis Rauchenberger, 1988	F:M	Finescale Splitfin....mexclapique escamitas
Allodontichthys tamazulae Turner, 1946	F:M	Peppered Splitfin....mexclapique de Tamazula
Allodontichthys zonistius (Hubbs, 1932)	F:M	Bandfin Splitfin....mexclapique de Colima
Alloophorus robustus (Bean, 1892)	F:M	Bulldog Goodeid....chegua
Allotoca catarinae (de Buen, 1942)	F:M	Catarina Allotoca^....tiro Catarina

SCIENTIFIC NAME	OCCURRENCE[1]	COMMON NAME (ENGLISH, SPANISH, FRENCH)[2]
*Allotoca diazi (Meek, 1902)	F:M	Pátzcuaro Allotoca^......chorumo
Allotoca dugesii (Bean, 1887)	F:M	Bumblebee Allotoca......tiro chato
Allotoca goslinei Smith & Miller, 1987	F:M	Banded Allotoca......tiro listado
Allotoca maculata Smith & Miller, 1980	F:M	Blackspot Allotoca......tiro manchado
*Allotoca meeki (Álvarez, 1959)	F:M	Zirahuén Allotoca^......tiro de Zirahuén
*Allotoca regalis (Álvarez, 1959)	F:M	Balsas Allotoca^......chorumo del Balsas
*Allotoca zacapuensis Meyer, Radda & Domínguez, 2001	F:M	Zacapu Allotoca^......tiro de Zacapu
Ameca splendens Miller & Fitzsimons, 1971	F:M	Butterfly Splitfin......mexclapique mariposa
Ataeniobius toweri (Meek, 1904)	F:M	Bluetail Splitfin......mexclapique cola azul
Chapalichthys encaustus (Jordan & Snyder, 1899)	F:M	Barred Splitfin......pintito de Ocotlán
*Chapalichthys pardalis Álvarez, 1963	F:M	Polka–dot Splitfin......pintito de Tocumbo
*Chapalichthys peraticus Álvarez, 1963	F[X]:M	Alien Splitfin......pintito de San Juanico
Characodon audax Smith & Miller, 1986	F:M	Bold Characodon......mexclapique del Toboso
Characodon garmani Jordan & Evermann, 1898	F[X]:M	Parras Characodon^......mexclapique de Parras
Characodon lateralis Günther, 1866	F:M	Rainbow Characodon......mexclapique arcoiris
Crenichthys baileyi (Gilbert, 1893)	F:U	White River Springfish^
Crenichthys nevadae Hubbs, 1932	F:U	Railroad Valley Springfish^
Empetrichthys latos Miller, 1948	F:U	Pahrump Poolfish^
Empetrichthys merriami Gilbert, 1893	F[X]:U	Ash Meadows Poolfish^
*Girardinichthys ireneae Radda & Meyer, 2003	F:M	Zacapu Splitfin^......mexclapique de Zacapu
Girardinichthys multiradiatus (Meek, 1904)	F:M	Darkedged Splitfin......mexclapique de Zempoala
*Girardinichthys turneri (de Buen, 1940)	F:M	Highland Splitfin......mexclapique michoacano
Girardinichthys viviparus (Bustamante, 1837)	F:M	Chapultepec Splitfin^......mexclapique
Goodea atripinnis Jordan, 1880	F:M	Blackfin Goodea......tiro
Goodea gracilis Hubbs & Turner, 1939	F:M	Dusky Goodea......tiro oscuro
Goodea luitpoldii (Steindachner, 1894)	F:M	Green Goodea......tiro de Pátzcuaro
*Ilyodon cortesae Paulo-Maya & Trujillo-Jiménez, 2000	F:M	Freckled Splitfin......mexclapique pecoso
+Ilyodon furcidens (Jordan & Gilbert, 1882)	F:M	Goldbreast Splitfin......mexclapique del Armería
+Ilyodon lennoni Meyer & Förster, 1983	F:M	Chacambero Splitfin^......mexclapique de Chacambero
Ilyodon whitei (Meek, 1904)	F:M	Balsas Splitfin^......mexclapique cola partida
Skiffia bilineata (Bean, 1887)	F:M	Twoline Skiffia......tiro de dos rayas

SCIENTIFIC NAME	OCCURRENCE[1]	COMMON NAME (ENGLISH, SPANISH, FRENCH)[2]
*Skiffia francesae Kingston, 1978	F[XN]:M	Golden Skiffia .... tiro dorado
Skiffia lermae Meek, 1902	F:M	Olive Skiffia .... tiro olivo
Skiffia multipunctata (Pellegrin, 1901)	F:M	Splotched Skiffia .... tiro pintado
Xenoophorus captivus (Hubbs, 1924)	F:M	Relict Splitfin .... mexclapique viejo
Xenotaenia resolanae Turner, 1946	F:M	Leopard Splitfin .... mexclapique leopardo
Xenotoca eiseni (Rutter, 1896)	F:M	Redtail Splitfin .... mexclapique cola roja
Xenotoca melanosoma Fitzsimons, 1972	F:M	Black Splitfin .... mexclapique negro
Xenotoca variata (Bean, 1887)	F:M	Jeweled Splitfin .... pintada
*Zoogoneticus purhepechus Domínguez-Domínguez, Pérez-Rodríguez & Doadrio, 2008	F:M	Tarascan Splitfin^ .... picote tarasco
Zoogoneticus quitzeoensis (Bean, 1898)	F:M	Picote Splitfin .... picote
Zoogoneticus tequila Webb & Miller, 1998	F:M	Tequila Splitfin^ .... picote de Tequila

Fundulidae—En-topminnows, Sp-sardinillas, Fr-fondules

Adinia xenica (Jordan & Gilbert, 1882)	A	Diamond Killifish
Fundulus albolineatus Gilbert, 1891	F[X]:U	Whiteline Topminnow
Fundulus bifax Cashner & Rogers, 1988	F:U	Stippled Studfish
Fundulus blairae Wiley & Hall, 1975	F:U	Western Starhead Topminnow
Fundulus catenatus (Storer, 1846)	F:U	Northern Studfish
Fundulus chrysotus (Günther, 1866)	F:U	Golden Topminnow
Fundulus cingulatus Valenciennes, 1846	F:U	Banded Topminnow
Fundulus confluentus Goode & Bean, 1879	A-F:U	Marsh Killifish
Fundulus diaphanus (Lesueur, 1817)	F:CU	Banded Killifish .... fondule barré
Fundulus dispar (Agassiz, 1854)	F:U	Starhead Topminnow
Fundulus escambiae (Bollman, 1887)	F:U	Russetfin Topminnow
Fundulus euryzonus Suttkus & Cashner, 1981	F:U	Broadstripe Topminnow
Fundulus grandis Baird & Girard, 1853	A-F:UM	Gulf Killifish^ .... sardinilla del Pánuco
Fundulus grandissimus Hubbs, 1936	AM-F:M	Giant Killifish .... sardinilla gigante
Fundulus heteroclitus (Linnaeus, 1766)	A-F:CU	Mummichog .... choquemort
*Fundulus jenkinsi (Evermann, 1892)	A-F:U	Saltmarsh Topminnow
Fundulus julisia Williams & Etnier, 1982	F:U	Barrens Topminnow^

SCIENTIFIC NAME	OCCURRENCE[1]	COMMON NAME (ENGLISH, SPANISH, FRENCH)[2]
Fundulus kansae Garman, 1895	F:U	Northern Plains Killifish
Fundulus lima Vaillant, 1894	F:M	Baja California Killifish^ ...... sardinilla peninsular
Fundulus lineolatus (Agassiz, 1854)	F:U	Lined Topminnow
Fundulus luciae (Baird, 1855)	A-F:U	Spotfin Killifish
Fundulus majalis (Walbaum, 1792)	A	Striped Killifish
Fundulus notatus (Rafinesque, 1820)	F:CU	Blackstripe Topminnow ...... fondule rayé
Fundulus nottii (Agassiz, 1854)	F:U	Bayou Topminnow
Fundulus olivaceus (Storer, 1845)	F:U	Blackspotted Topminnow
Fundulus parvipinnis Girard, 1854	P-F:UM	California Killifish^ ...... sardinilla chococo
Fundulus persimilis Miller, 1955	AM-F:M	Yucatan Killifish^ ...... sardinilla yucateca
*Fundulus philpisteri García-Ramírez, Contreras-Balderas & Lozano-Vilano, 2007	F:M	Conservationist Killifish ...... sardinilla conservacionista
*Fundulus pulvereus (Evermann, 1892)	A-F:U	Bayou Killifish
Fundulus rathbuni Jordan & Meek, 1889	F:U	Speckled Killifish
Fundulus rubrifrons (Jordan, 1880)	F:U	Redface Topminnow
Fundulus sciadicus Cope, 1865	F:U	Plains Topminnow
Fundulus seminolis Girard, 1859	F:U	Seminole Killifish^
Fundulus similis (Baird & Girard, 1853)	A-F:M	Longnose Killifish ...... sardinilla narigona
Fundulus stellifer (Jordan, 1877)	F:U	Southern Studfish
Fundulus waccamensis Hubbs & Raney, 1946	F:U	Waccamaw Killifish^
*Fundulus zebrinus Jordan & Gilbert, 1883	F:UM[I]	Plains Killifish ...... sardinilla cebra
Leptolucania ommata (Jordan, 1884)	F:U	Pygmy Killifish
Lucania goodei Jordan, 1880	F:U	Bluefin Killifish
*Lucania interioris Hubbs & Miller, 1965	F:M	Cuatro Ciénegas Killifish^ ...... sardinilla de Cuatro Ciénegas
Lucania parva (Baird & Girard, 1855)	A-P[I]-F:UM	Rainwater Killifish^ ...... sardinilla de lluvia

+Cyprinodontidae—En-pupfishes, Sp-cachorritos, Fr-cyprinodontes

Cualac tessellatus Miller, 1956	F:M	Media Luna Pupfish^ ...... cachorrito de La Media Luna
Cyprinodon albivelis Minckley & Miller, 2002	F:M	Whitefin Pupfish ...... cachorrito aletas blancas
*Cyprinodon alvarezi Miller, 1976	F:M	Potosí Pupfish^ ...... cachorrito de Potosí
Cyprinodon arcuatus Minckley & Miller, 2002	F[X]:U	Santa Cruz Pupfish^
*Cyprinodon artifrons Hubbs, 1936	AM-F:M	Yucatan Pupfish^ ...... bolín frentudo

SCIENTIFIC NAME	OCCURRENCE[1]	COMMON NAME (ENGLISH, SPANISH, FRENCH)[2]
*Cyprinodon atrorus Miller, 1968	F:M	Bolsón Pupfish ... cachorrito del bolsón
*Cyprinodon beltrani Álvarez, 1949	F:M	Blackfin Pupfish ... cachorrito lodero
*Cyprinodon bifasciatus Miller, 1968	F:M	Cuatro Ciénegas Pupfish^ ... cachorrito de Cuatro Ciénegas
Cyprinodon bobmilleri Lozano-Vilano & Contreras-Balderas, 1999	F:M	San Ignacio Pupfish^ ... cachorrito de San Ignacio
Cyprinodon bovinus Baird & Girard, 1853	F:U	Leon Springs Pupfish^
*Cyprinodon ceciliae Lozano-Vilano & Contreras-Balderas, 1993	F[X]:M	La Presita Pupfish^ ... cachorrito de La Presita
Cyprinodon diabolis Wales, 1930	F:U	Devils Hole Pupfish^
Cyprinodon elegans Baird & Girard, 1853	F:U	Comanche Springs Pupfish^
Cyprinodon eremus Miller & Fuiman, 1987	F:UM	Sonoyta Pupfish^ ... cachorrito del Sonoyta
Cyprinodon esconditus Strecker, 2002	F:M	Hidden Pupfish ... cachorrito escondido
Cyprinodon eximius Girard, 1859	F:UM	Conchos Pupfish^ ... cachorrito del Conchos
Cyprinodon fontinalis Smith & Miller, 1980	F:M	Carbonera Pupfish^ ... cachorrito de Carbonera
*Cyprinodon inmemoriam Lozano-Vilano & Contreras-Balderas, 1993	F[X]:M	La Trinidad Pupfish^ ... cachorrito de La Trinidad
*Cyprinodon julimes De la Maza-Benignos & Vela-Valladares, 2009	F:M	Julimes Pupfish^ ... cachorrito de Julimes
Cyprinodon labiosus Humphries & Miller, 1981	F:M	Thicklip Pupfish ... cachorrito cangrejero
Cyprinodon latifasciatus Garman, 1881	F[X]:M	Parras Pupfish^ ... cachorrito de Parras
*Cyprinodon longidorsalis Lozano-Vilano & Contreras-Balderas, 1993	F:M	Charco Palma Pupfish^ ... cachorrito de Charco Palma
Cyprinodon macrolepis Miller, 1976	F:M	Bigscale Pupfish ... cachorrito escamudo
Cyprinodon macularius Baird & Girard, 1853	F:UM	Desert Pupfish ... cachorrito del desierto
Cyprinodon maya Humphries & Miller, 1981	F:M	Maya Pupfish^ ... cachorrito gigante
Cyprinodon meeki Miller, 1976	F:M	Mezquital Pupfish^ ... cachorrito del Mezquital
Cyprinodon nazas Miller, 1976	F:M	Nazas Pupfish^ ... cachorrito del Nazas
Cyprinodon nevadensis Eigenmann & Eigenmann, 1889	F:U	Amargosa Pupfish^
Cyprinodon pachycephalus Minckley & Minckley, 1986	F:M	Bighead Pupfish ... cachorrito cabezón
Cyprinodon pecosensis Echelle & Echelle, 1978	F:U	Pecos Pupfish^
Cyprinodon pisteri Miller & Minckley, 2002	F:M	Palomas Pupfish^ ... cachorrito de Palomas

SCIENTIFIC NAME	OCCURRENCE[1]	COMMON NAME (ENGLISH, SPANISH, FRENCH)[2]
Cyprinodon radiosus Miller, 1948	F:U	Owens Pupfish^
Cyprinodon rubrofluviatilis Fowler, 1916	F:U	Red River Pupfish^
Cyprinodon salinus Miller, 1943	F:U	Salt Creek Pupfish^
Cyprinodon salvadori Lozano-Vilano, 2002	F:M	Bocochi Pupfish^......cachorrito de Bocochi
Cyprinodon simus Humphries & Miller, 1981	F:M	Boxer Pupfish......cachorrito boxeador
*Cyprinodon suavium Strecker, 2005	F:M	Kissing Pupfish......cachorrito besucón
Cyprinodon tularosa Miller & Echelle, 1975	F:U	White Sands Pupfish^
*Cyprinodon variegatus Lacepède, 1803	A-F:UM	Sheepshead Minnow......bolín petota
Cyprinodon verecundus Humphries, 1984	F:M	Largefin Pupfish......cachorrito aletón
*Cyprinodon veronicae Lozano-Vilano & Contreras-Balderas, 1993	F:M	Charco Azul Pupfish^......cachorrito de Charco Azul
Floridichthys carpio (Günther, 1866)	A	Goldspotted Killifish
Floridichthys polyommus Hubbs, 1936	AM	Ocellated Killifish......bolín yucateco
Jordanella floridae Goode & Bean, 1879	F:U	Flagfish
Jordanella pulchra (Hubbs, 1936)	F:M	Progreso Flagfish^......cachorrito de Progreso
*Megupsilon aporus Miller & Walters, 1972	F[XN]:M	Catarina Pupfish^......cachorrito enano de Potosí
Anablepidae—En-four-eyed fishes, Sp-cuatrojos, Fr-poissons à quatre yeux		
*Anableps dowi Gill, 1861	PM-F:M	Northern Four-eye......cuatrojos
Poeciliidae—En-livebearers, Sp-topotes y espadas, Fr-poecilies		
Belonesox belizanus Kner, 1860	A-F:U[I]M	Pike Killifish......picudito
Brachyrhaphis hartwegi Rosen & Bailey, 1963	F:M	Soconusco Gambusia^......guayacón del Soconusco
*Carlhubbsia kidderi (Hubbs, 1936)	F:M	Champotón Gambusia^......guayacón del Champotón
Gambusia affinis (Baird & Girard, 1853)	A-F:C[I]UM	Western Mosquitofish......guayacón mosquito......gambusie
Gambusia alvarezi Hubbs & Springer, 1957	F:M	Yellowfin Gambusia......guayacón de San Gregorio
Gambusia amistadensis Peden, 1973	F[X]:U	Amistad Gambusia^
Gambusia atrora Rosen & Bailey, 1963	F:M	Blackfin Gambusia......guayacón de San Luis
Gambusia aurata Miller & Minckley, 1970	F:M	Golden Gambusia......guayacón dorado
*Gambusia clarkhubbsi Garrett & Edwards, 2003	F:U	San Felipe Gambusia^
Gambusia eurystoma Miller, 1975	F:M	Widemouth Gambusia......guayacón del Azufre

SCIENTIFIC NAME	OCCURRENCE[1]	COMMON NAME (ENGLISH, SPANISH, FRENCH)[2]
Gambusia gaigei Hubbs, 1929	F:U	Big Bend Gambusia^
Gambusia geiseri Hubbs & Hubbs, 1957	F:U	Largespring Gambusia
Gambusia georgei Hubbs & Peden, 1969	F[X]:U	San Marcos Gambusia^
Gambusia heterochir Hubbs, 1957	F[X]:U	Clear Creek Gambusia^
Gambusia holbrooki Girard, 1859	A-F:U	Eastern Mosquitofish
Gambusia hurtadoi Hubbs & Springer, 1957	F:M	Crescent Gambusia..........guayacón de Hacienda de Dolores
Gambusia krumholzi Minckley, 1963	F:M	Spotfin Gambusia..........guayacón del Nava
* *Gambusia longispinis* Minckley, 1962	F:M	Cuatro Ciénegas Gambusia^...guayacón de Cuatro Ciénegas
* *Gambusia luma* Rosen & Bailey, 1963	F:M	Sleek Mosquitofish..........guayacón liso
Gambusia marshi Minckley & Craddock, 1962	F:M	Robust Gambusia ....guayacón de los Nadadores
Gambusia nobilis (Baird & Girard, 1853)	F:U	Pecos Gambusia^
* *Gambusia panuco* Hubbs, 1926	F:M	Pánuco Gambusia^..........guayacón del Pánuco
* *Gambusia regani* Hubbs, 1926	F:M	Forlón Gambusia^..........guayacón del Forlón
* *Gambusia rhizophorae* Rivas, 1969	A	Mangrove Gambusia
Gambusia senilis Girard, 1859	F:UM	Blotched Gambusia..........guayacón del Bravo
Gambusia sexradiata Hubbs, 1936	F:M	Stippled Gambusia..........guayacón del sureste
Gambusia speciosa Girard, 1859	F:UM	Tex-Mex Gambusia^..........guayacón de Nuevo León
Gambusia vittata Hubbs, 1926	F:M	Gulf Gambusia^..........guayacón de Victoria
Gambusia yucatana Regan, 1914	F:M	Yucatan Gambusia^..........guayacón yucateco
* *Gambusia zarskei* Meyer, Schories & Schartl, 2010	F:M	Conchos Gambusia^..........guayacón del Conchos
Heterandria bimaculata (Heckel, 1848)	F:M	Spottail Killifish..........guatopete manchado
+ *Heterandria formosa* Agassiz, 1855	F:U	Least Killifish
Heterandria jonesii (Günther, 1874)	F:M	Barred Killifish..........guatopote listado
* *Heterandria tuxtlaensis* McEachran & Dewitt, 2008	F:M	Tuxtlas Killifish^..........guatopote de Catemaco
* *Heterophallus echeagarayi* (Álvarez, 1952)	F:M	Maya Gambusia^..........guayacón maya
Heterophallus milleri Radda, 1987	F:M	Grijalva Gambusia^..........guayacón del Grijalva
Heterophallus rachovii Regan, 1914	F:M	Coatzacoalcos Gambusia^......guayacón jarocho
Phallichthys fairweatheri Rosen & Bailey, 1959	F:M	Picotee Livebearer..........topo
Poecilia butleri Jordan, 1889	F:M	Pacific Molly^..........topote del Pacifico
Poecilia catemaconis Miller, 1975	F:M	Bicolor Molly..........topote de Catemaco
Poecilia chica Miller, 1975	F:M	Dwarf Molly^..........topote del Purificación
Poecilia formosa (Girard, 1859)	F:UM	Amazon Molly^..........topote amazona

SCIENTIFIC NAME	OCCURRENCE[1]	COMMON NAME (ENGLISH, SPANISH, FRENCH)[2]
Poecilia latipinna (Lesueur, 1821)	A-F:C[I]UM	Sailfin Molly ... topote velo negro ... molliénésie à voilure
Poecilia latipunctata Meek, 1904	F:M	Tamesi Molly^ ... topote del Tamesi
Poecilia maylandi Meyer, 1983	F:M	Balsas Molly^ ... topote del Balsas
Poecilia mexicana Steindachner, 1863	F:U[I]M	Shortfin Molly ... topote del Atlántico
Poecilia orri Fowler, 1943	AM-F:M	Mangrove Molly ... topote de manglar
Poecilia petenensis (Günther, 1866)	F:M	Petén Molly^ ... topote lacandón
Poecilia reticulata Peters, 1860	F[I]:UM	Guppy ... gupi
Poecilia sphenops Valenciennes, 1846	F:U[I]M	Mexican Molly^ ... topote mexicano
Poecilia sulphuraria (Álvarez, 1948)	F:M	Sulphur Molly^ ... topote de Teapa
Poecilia velifera (Regan, 1914)	F:M	Yucatan Molly^ ... topote aleta grande
Poeciliopsis baenschi Meyer, Radda, Riehl & Feichtinger, 1986	F:M	Golden Livebearer^ ... guatopote dorado
Poeciliopsis balsas Hubbs, 1926	F:M	Balsas Livebearer^ ... guatopote del Balsas
Poeciliopsis catemaco Miller, 1975	F:M	Catemaco Livebearer^ ... guatopote blanco
Poeciliopsis fasciata (Meek, 1904)	F:M	San Jerónimo Livebearer^ ... guatopote de San Jerónimo
Poeciliopsis gracilis (Heckel, 1848)	F:U[I]M	Porthole Livebearer ... guatopote jarocho
Poeciliopsis hnilickai Meyer & Vogel, 1981	F:M	Upper Grijalva Livebearer^ ... guatopote de Ixtapa
Poeciliopsis infans (Woolman, 1894)	F:M	Lerma Livebearer^ ... guatopote del Lerma
Poeciliopsis latidens (Garman, 1895)	F:M	Lowland Livebearer ... guatopote del Fuerte
Poeciliopsis lucida Miller, 1960	F:M	Clearfin Livebearer ... guatopote del Mocorito
Poeciliopsis lutzi (Meek, 1902)	F:M	Oaxaca Livebearer^ ... guatopote oaxaqueño
Poeciliopsis monacha Miller, 1960	F:M	Headwater Livebearer ... guatopote del Mayo
Poeciliopsis occidentalis (Baird & Girard, 1853)	F:UM	Gila Topminnow^ ... guatopote de Sonora
Poeciliopsis pleurospilus (Günther, 1866)	F:M	Largespot Livebearer ... guatopote manchota
Poeciliopsis presidionis (Jordan & Culver, 1895)	F:M	Sinaloa Livebearer^ ... guatopote de Sinaloa
Poeciliopsis prolifica Miller, 1960	F:M	Blackstripe Livebearer ... guatopote culiche
Poeciliopsis scarlli Meyer, Riehl, Dawes & Dibble, 1985	F:M	Michoacán Livebearer^ ... guatopote michoacano
Poeciliopsis turneri Miller, 1975	F:M	Blackspotted Livebearer ... guatopote de La Huerta
Poeciliopsis turrubarensis (Meek, 1912)	F:M	Barred Livebearer ... guatopote del Pacífico
Poeciliopsis viriosa Miller, 1960	F:M	Chubby Livebearer ... guatopote gordito

SCIENTIFIC NAME	OCCURRENCE[1]	COMMON NAME (ENGLISH, SPANISH, FRENCH)[2]
+*Priapella bonita* (Meek, 1904)	F:M	Graceful Priapella...guayacón bonito
*Priapella chamulae Schartl, Meyer & Wilde, 2006	F:M	Tacotalpa Priapella^...guayacón del Tacotalpa
*Priapella compressa Álvarez, 1948	F:M	Palenque Priapella^...guayacón de Palenque
*Priapella intermedia Álvarez & Carranza, 1952	F:M	Isthmian Priapella...guayacón de Chimalapa
*Priapella lacandonae Meyer, Schories & Schartl, 2011	F:M	Chiapas Priapella^...guayacón de Chiapas
Priapella olmecae Meyer & Espinosa-Pérez, 1990	F:M	Olmec Priapella^...guayacón olmeca
Xenodexia ctenolepis Hubbs, 1950	F:M	Grijalva Studfish^...topo del Grijalva
Xiphophorus alvarezi Rosen, 1960	F:M	Chiapas Swordtail^...espada de Comitán
Xiphophorus andersi Meyer & Schartl, 1979	F:M	Spiketail Platyfish...espada del Atoyac
Xiphophorus birchmanni Lechner & Radda, 1987	F:M	Sheepshead Swordtail...espada del Tempoal
*Xiphophorus clemenciae Álvarez, 1959	F:M	Coatzacoalcos Swordtail^...espada de Clemencia
Xiphophorus continens Rauchenberger, Kallman & Morizot, 1990	F:M	Short-sword Platyfish...espada del Quince
Xiphophorus cortezi Rosen, 1960	F:M	Delicate Swordtail...espada fina
Xiphophorus couchianus (Girard, 1859)	F:M	Monterrey Platyfish^...espada de Monterrey
Xiphophorus evelynae Rosen, 1960	F:M	Reticulate Platyfish...espada del Necaxa
*Xiphophorus gordoni Miller & Minckley, 1963	F:M	Cuatro Ciénegas Platyfish^...espada de Cuatro Ciénegas
Xiphophorus hellerii Heckel, 1848	F:U[I]M	Green Swordtail...cola de espada
*Xiphophorus kallmani Meyer & Schartl, 2003	F:M	Veracruz Swordtail^...espada de Veracruz
Xiphophorus maculatus (Günther, 1866)	F:U[I]M	Southern Platyfish...espada sureña
Xiphophorus malinche Rauchenberger, Kallman & Morizot, 1990	F:M	Highland Swordtail...espada de la Malinche
Xiphophorus meyeri Schartl & Schröder, 1988	F:M	Marbled Swordtail...espada de Múzquiz
Xiphophorus milleri Rosen, 1960	F:M	Catemaco Platyfish^...espada de Catemaco
Xiphophorus montezumae Jordan & Snyder, 1899	F:M	Moctezuma Swordtail^...espada de Moctezuma
Xiphophorus mutilineatus Rauchenberger, Kallman & Morizot, 1990	F:M	Barred Swordtail...espada pigmea rayada
Xiphophorus nezahualcoyotl Rauchenberger, Kallman & Morizot, 1990	F:M	Mountain Swordtail...espada montañesa
*Xiphophorus nigrensis Rosen, 1960	F:M	Pánuco Swordtail^...espada pigmea de El Abra
Xiphophorus pygmaeus Hubbs & Gordon, 1943	F:M	Pygmy Swordtail...espada pigmea delgada

SCIENTIFIC NAME	OCCURRENCE[1]	COMMON NAME (ENGLISH, SPANISH, FRENCH)[2]
Xiphophorus variatus (Meek, 1904)	F:U[I]M	Variable Platyfish .... espada de Valles
Xiphophorus xiphidium (Gordon, 1932)	F:M	Swordtail Platyfish .... espada del Soto La Marina

ORDER BERYCIFORMES

Anomalopidae—En-flashlightfishes, Sp-ojos de linterna, Fr-poissons-phares

Phthanophaneron harveyi (Rosenblatt & Montgomery, 1976)	PM	Panamic Flashlightfish^ .... ojo de linterna panámica

Trachichthyidae—En-roughies, Sp-relojes, Fr-hoplites

Gephyroberyx darwinii (Johnson, 1866)	A	Big Roughy

Berycidae—En-alfonsinos, Sp-alfonsinos, Fr-béryx

Beryx decadactylus Cuvier, 1829	A	Red Bream .... béryx large

Holocentridae—En-squirrelfishes, Sp-candiles, Fr-marignans

Corniger spinosus Agassiz, 1831	A	Spinycheek Soldierfish
Holocentrus adscensionis (Osbeck, 1765)	A	Squirrelfish .... candil de vidrio
Holocentrus rufus (Walbaum, 1792)	A	Longspine Squirrelfish .... candil rufo
Myripristis berndti Jordan & Evermann, 1903	PM	Bigscale Soldierfish .... soldado azotado
Myripristis clarionensis Gilbert, 1897	PM	Yellow Soldierfish .... soldado amarillo
Myripristis jacobus Cuvier, 1829	A	Blackbar Soldierfish .... soldado raya negra
Myripristis leiognathus Valenciennes, 1846	PM	Panamic Soldierfish^ .... soldado panámico
Neoniphon marianus (Cuvier, 1829)	A	Longjaw Squirrelfish .... carajuelo mariano
Ostichthys trachypoma (Günther, 1859)	A	Bigeye Soldierfish
*Plectrypops lima (Valenciennes, 1831)	PM	Shy Soldierfish .... soldado áspero
Plectrypops retrospinis (Guichenot, 1853)	A	Cardinal Soldierfish .... candil cardenal
Sargocentron bullisi (Woods, 1955)	A	Deepwater Squirrelfish^ .... carajuelo profundo
Sargocentron coruscum (Poey, 1860)	A	Reef Squirrelfish .... carajuelo de arrecife
Sargocentron poco (Woods, 1965)	A	Saddle Squirrelfish

SCIENTIFIC NAME	OCCURRENCE[1]	COMMON NAME (ENGLISH, SPANISH, FRENCH)[2]
Sargocentron suborbitalis (Gill, 1863)	PM	Tinsel Squirrelfish............candil sol
Sargocentron vexillarium (Poey, 1860)	A	Dusky Squirrelfish ....carajuelo oscuro

+ORDER ZEIFORMES

Grammicolepidae—En-diamond dories, Sp-oropeles, Fr-poissons-palissades

Grammicolepis brachiusculus Poey, 1873	A	Thorny Tinselfish ....palissade à épines plates
Xenolepidichthys dalgleishi Gilchrist, 1922	A	Spotted Tinselfish

Zeidae—En-dories, Sp-peces de San Pedro, Fr-Saint-Pierre

Cyttopsis rosea (Lowe, 1843)	A	Red Dory ....San Pedro rojo
Zenopsis conchifera (Lowe, 1852)	A	Buckler Dory ....San Pedro plateado ....zée bouclé d'Amérique
Zenopsis nebulosa (Temminck & Schlegel, 1845)	P	Mirror Dory

ORDER GASTEROSTEIFORMES

Aulorhynchidae—En-tubesnouts, Sp-trompudos, Fr-trompes

Aulorhynchus flavidus Gill, 1861	P	Tubesnout............trompudo sargacero ....trompe

Gasterosteidae—En-sticklebacks, Sp-espinochos, Fr-épinoches

Apeltes quadracus (Mitchill, 1815)	A-F:CU	Fourspine Stickleback ....épinoche à quatre épines
Culaea inconstans (Kirtland, 1840)	F:CU	Brook Stickleback ....épinoche à cinq épines
Gasterosteus aculeatus Linnaeus, 1758	A-P-Ar-F:CUM	Threespine Stickleback ....espinocho ....épinoche à trois épines
Gasterosteus wheatlandi Putnam, 1867	A	Blackspotted Stickleback ....épinoche tachetée
Pungitius pungitius (Linnaeus, 1758)	A-P-Ar-F:CU	Ninespine Stickleback ....épinoche à neuf épines

Syngnathidae—En-pipefishes and seahorses, Sp-peces pipa y caballitos de mar, Fr-hippocampes

+*Acentronura dendritica* (Barbour, 1905)	A	Pipehorse ....caballito pipa ....syngnathe dendritique
Anarchopterus criniger (Bean & Dresel, 1884)	A	Fringed Pipefish ....pez pipa orlado
Anarchopterus tectus (Dawson, 1978)	A	Insular Pipefish ....pez pipa isleño
Bryx dunckeri (Metzelaar, 1919)	A	Pugnose Pipefish ....pez pipa ñato
Bryx veleronis Herald, 1940	PM	Offshore Pipefish............pez pipa velero

SCIENTIFIC NAME	OCCURRENCE[1]	COMMON NAME (ENGLISH, SPANISH, FRENCH)[2]
Cosmocampus albirostris (Kaup, 1856)	A	Whitenose Pipefish......pez pipa hocico blanco
Cosmocampus arctus (Jenkins & Evermann, 1889)	P	Snubnose Pipefish......pez pipa chato
Cosmocampus brachycephalus (Poey, 1868)	A	Crested Pipefish......pez pipa crestado
Cosmocampus elucens (Poey, 1868)	A	Shortfin Pipefish......pez pipa aletilla
Cosmocampus hildebrandi (Herald, 1965)	A	Dwarf Pipefish
Cosmocampus profundus (Herald, 1965)	A	Deepwater Pipefish......pez pipa de lo alto
Doryhamphus excisus Kaup, 1856	PM	Fantail Pipefish......pez pipa chico
*Enteliurus aequoreus (Linnaeus, 1758)	A	Snake Pipefish
Halicampus crinitus (Jenyns, 1842)	A	Banded Pipefish......pez pipa payaso
Hippocampus erectus Perry, 1810	A	Lined Seahorse......caballito estriado......hippocampe rayé
Hippocampus ingens Girard, 1858	P	Pacific Seahorse^......caballito del Pacífico
Hippocampus reidi Ginsburg, 1933	A	Longsnout Seahorse......caballito hocico largo
Hippocampus zosterae Jordan & Gilbert, 1882	A	Dwarf Seahorse......caballito enano
Microphis brachyurus (Bleeker, 1853)	A-F:UM	Opossum Pipefish......pez pipa culebra
Penetopteryx nanus (Rosén, 1911)	AM	Worm Pipefish......pez pipa gusano
*Pseudophallus mindii (Meek & Hildebrand, 1923)	F:M	Freshwater Pipefish......pez pipa de estero
Pseudophallus starksii (Jordan & Culver, 1895)	PM-F:M	Yellowbelly Pipefish......pez pipa de río
Syngnathus auliscus (Swain, 1882)	P	Barred Pipefish......pez pipa anillado
Syngnathus californiensis Storer, 1845	P	Kelp Pipefish......pez pipa californiano
Syngnathus caribbaeus Dawson, 1979	AM	Caribbean Pipefish^......pez pipa caribeño
Syngnathus carinatus (Gilbert, 1892)	PM	Cortez Pipefish^......pez pipa de Cortés
*Syngnathus euchrous Fritzsche, 1980	P	Chocolate Pipefish......pez pipa chocolate
Syngnathus exilis (Osburn & Nichols, 1916)	P	Barcheek Pipefish......pez pipa cachete rayado
Syngnathus floridae (Jordan & Gilbert, 1882)	A	Dusky Pipefish......pez pipa prieto
Syngnathus fuscus Storer, 1839	A	Northern Pipefish......syngnathe brun
Syngnathus insulae Fritzsche, 1980	PM	Guadalupe Pipefish^......pez pipa de Guadalupe
Syngnathus leptorhynchus Girard, 1854	P	Bay Pipefish......pez pipa de bahía......syngnathe à lignes grises
Syngnathus louisianae Günther, 1870	A	Chain Pipefish......pez pipa cadena
Syngnathus makaxi Herald & Dawson, 1972	AM	Yucatan Pipefish^......pez pipa yucateco
Syngnathus pelagicus Linnaeus, 1758	A	Sargassum Pipefish......pez pipa oceánico
Syngnathus scovelli (Evermann & Kendall, 1896)	A-F:U	Gulf Pipefish^......pez pipa del Golfo
Syngnathus springeri Herald, 1942	A	Bull Pipefish
*Syngnathus texanus Gilbert, 2013	A	Texas Pipefish^......pez pipa texano

SCIENTIFIC NAME	OCCURRENCE[1]	COMMON NAME (ENGLISH, SPANISH, FRENCH)[2]
		Aulostomidae—En-trumpetfishes, Sp-trompetas, Fr-trompettes
Aulostomus chinensis (Linnaeus, 1766)	PM	Chinese Trumpetfish^ ....trompeta china
Aulostomus maculatus Valenciennes, 1841	A	Atlantic Trumpetfish^ ....trompeta del Atlántico
		Fistulariidae—En-cornetfishes, Sp-cornetas, Fr-fistulaires
Fistularia commersonii Rüppell, 1838	PM	Reef Cornetfish ....corneta pintada
Fistularia corneta Gilbert & Starks, 1904	P	Deepwater Cornetfish ....corneta flautera
Fistularia petimba Lacépède, 1803	A	Red Cornetfish ....corneta colorada
Fistularia tabacaria Linnaeus, 1758	A	Bluespotted Cornetfish ....corneta azul ....fistulaire tabac
		Macroramphosidae— En-snipefishes, Sp-trompeteros, Fr-bécasses de mer
Macroramphosus gracilis (Lowe, 1839)	A-P	Slender Snipefish ....trompetero flaco
Macroramphosus scolopax (Linnaeus, 1758)	A	Longspine Snipefish ....trompetero copete

ORDER SYNBRANCHIFORMES

		*Synbranchidae—En-swamp eels, Sp-anguilas de lodo, Fr-anguilles des mares
Monopterus albus (Zuiew, 1793)	F[I]:U	Asian Swamp Eel^
Ophisternon aenigmaticum Rosen & Greenwood, 1976	F:M	Obscure Swamp Eel ....anguila falsa
Ophisternon infernale (Hubbs, 1938)	F:M	Blind Swamp Eel ....anguila ciega yucateca
Synbranchus marmoratus Bloch, 1795	F:M	Mottled Swamp Eel ....anguila de lodo
		*Mastacembelidae—En-freshwater spiny eels, Sp-anguilas espinosas de pantano, Fr-anguilles épineuses dulcicoles
Macrognathus siamensis (Günther, 1861)	F[I]:U	Spotfin Spiny Eel

ORDER DACTYLOPTERIFORMES

| | | Dactylopteridae—En-flying gurnards, Sp-alones, Fr-grondins volants |
| *Dactylopterus volitans* (Linnaeus, 1758) | A | Flying Gurnard ....alón volador ....dactyloptère |

SCIENTIFIC NAME	OCCURRENCE[1]	COMMON NAME (ENGLISH, SPANISH, FRENCH)[2]

+ORDER SCORPAENIFORMES

Scorpaenidae—En-scorpionfishes, Sp-escorpiones y rocotes, Fr-scorpènes

SCIENTIFIC NAME	OCCURRENCE[1]	COMMON NAME (ENGLISH, SPANISH, FRENCH)[2]
Helicolenus dactylopterus (Delaroche, 1809)	A	Blackbelly Rosefish		chèvre impériale
Neomerinthe hemingwayi Fowler, 1935	A	Spinycheek Scorpionfish	rascacio mejilla espinosa
Pontinus castor Poey, 1860	A	Longsnout Scorpionfish
Pontinus furcirhinus Garman, 1899	PM	Red Scorpionfish	lapón rojo
Pontinus longispinis Goode & Bean, 1896	A	Longspine Scorpionfish	lapón mariposa
Pontinus nematophthalmus (Günther, 1860)	A	Spinythroat Scorpionfish	lapón aleta baja
Pontinus rathbuni Goode & Bean, 1896	A	Highfin Scorpionfish
Pontinus sierra (Gilbert, 1890)	PM	Speckled Scorpionfish	lapón manchado
Pontinus vaughani Barnhart & Hubbs, 1946	PM	Spotback Scorpionfish	lapón lomo manchado
Pterois miles (Bennett, 1828)	A[I]	Devil Firefish	pez de fuego del diablo
Pterois volitans (Linnaeus, 1758)	A[I]	Red Lionfish	pez león rojo
Scorpaena agassizii Goode & Bean, 1896	A	Longfin Scorpionfish	escorpión aleta larga
Scorpaena afuerae Hildebrand, 1946	PM	Peruvian Scorpionfish^	rascacio párlamo
Scorpaena albifimbria Evermann & Marsh, 1900	A	Coral Scorpionfish	escorpión coralino
Scorpaena bergii Evermann & Marsh, 1900	A	Goosehead Scorpionfish	escorpión gansito
Scorpaena brachyptera Eschmeyer, 1965	A	Shortfin Scorpionfish
Scorpaena brasiliensis Cuvier, 1829	A	Barbfish	escorpión pardo
Scorpaena calcarata Goode & Bean, 1882	A	Smoothhead Scorpionfish	escorpión pelón	rascasse dénudée
Scorpaena dispar Longley & Hildebrand, 1940	A	Hunchback Scorpionfish	escorpión jorobado
Scorpaena elachys Eschmeyer, 1965	A	Dwarf Scorpionfish
Scorpaena grandicornis Cuvier, 1829	A	Plumed Scorpionfish	escorpión plumeado
Scorpaena guttata Girard, 1854	P	California Scorpionfish^	escorpión californiano
Scorpaena histrio Jenyns, 1840	PM	Player Scorpionfish	escorpión jueguetón
Scorpaena inermis Cuvier, 1829	A	Mushroom Scorpionfish	escorpión hongo
Scorpaena isthmensis Meek & Hildebrand, 1928	A	Smoothcheek Scorpionfish	escorpión mejilla lisa
Scorpaena mystes Jordan & Starks, 1895	P	Stone Scorpionfish	escorpión roquero
Scorpaena plumieri Bloch, 1789	A	Spotted Scorpionfish	escorpión negro
Scorpaena russula Jordan & Bollman, 1890	PM	Reddish Scorpionfish	escorpión sapo
Scorpaena sonorae Jenkins & Evermann, 1889	PM	Sonora Scorpionfish^	escorpión de Sonora

SCIENTIFIC NAME	OCCURRENCE[1]	COMMON NAME (ENGLISH, SPANISH, FRENCH)[2]
Scorpaenodes caribbaeus Meek & Hildebrand, 1928	A	Reef Scorpionfish......escorpión de arrecife
Scorpaenodes tredecimspinosus (Metzelaar, 1919)	A	Deepreef Scorpionfish......escorpión espinoso
Scorpaenodes xyris (Jordan & Gilbert, 1882)	P	Rainbow Scorpionfish......escorpión arcoiris
+*Sebastes aleutianus* (Jordan & Evermann, 1898)	P	Rougheye Rockfish......sébaste à oeil épineux
Sebastes alutus (Gilbert, 1890)	P	Pacific Ocean Perch^......sébaste à longue mâchoire
Sebastes atrovirens (Jordan & Gilbert, 1880)	P	Kelp Rockfish......rocote sargacero
Sebastes auriculatus Girard, 1854	P	Brown Rockfish......rocote moreno......sébaste brun
Sebastes aurora (Gilbert, 1890)	P	Aurora Rockfish......rocote......sébaste aurore
Sebastes babcocki (Thompson, 1915)	P	Redbanded Rockfish......sébaste à bandes rouges
Sebastes borealis Barsukov, 1970	P	Shortraker Rockfish......sébaste boréal
Sebastes brevispinis (Bean, 1884)	P	Silvergray Rockfish......sébaste argenté
Sebastes carnatus (Jordan & Gilbert, 1880)	P	Gopher Rockfish......rocote amarillo
Sebastes caurinus Richardson, 1844	P	Copper Rockfish......rocote cobrizo......sébaste cuivré
Sebastes chlorostictus (Jordan & Gilbert, 1880)	P	Greenspotted Rockfish......rocote verde......sébaste à taches vertes
Sebastes chrysomelas (Jordan & Gilbert, 1881)	P	Black-and-yellow Rockfish......rocote mulato
+*Sebastes ciliatus* (Tilesius, 1813)	P	Dusky Rockfish......sébaste cilié
Sebastes constellatus (Jordan & Gilbert, 1880)	P	Starry Rockfish......rocote estrellado
Sebastes cortezi (Beebe & Tee-Van, 1938)	PM	Cortez Rockfish^......rocote de Cortés
Sebastes crameri (Jordan, 1897)	P	Darkblotched Rockfish......sébaste tacheté
Sebastes dallii (Eigenmann & Beeson, 1894)	P	Calico Rockfish......rocote algodón
Sebastes diploproa (Gilbert, 1890)	P	Splitnose Rockfish......rocote doble hocico......gueule-de-loup
Sebastes elongatus Ayres, 1859	P	Greenstriped Rockfish......rocote reina......sébaste à rayures vertes
Sebastes emphaeus (Starks, 1911)	P	Puget Sound Rockfish^......sébaste paradeur
Sebastes ensifer Chen, 1971	P	Swordspine Rockfish......rocote espada
Sebastes entomelas (Jordan & Gilbert, 1880)	P	Widow Rockfish......rocote viuda......veuve
Sebastes eos (Eigenmann & Eigenmann, 1890)	P	Pink Rockfish......rocote Santa María
Sebastes exsul Chen, 1971	PM	Buccaneer Rockfish......rocote bucanero
Sebastes fasciatus Storer, 1854	A	Acadian Redfish^......sébaste acadien
Sebastes flavidus (Ayres, 1862)	P	Yellowtail Rockfish......sébaste à queue jaune
Sebastes gilli (Eigenmann, 1891)	P	Bronzespotted Rockfish......rocote bronceado......sébaste à taches bronzées
Sebastes glaucus Hilgendorf, 1880	P	Gray Rockfish
Sebastes goodei (Eigenmann & Eigenmann, 1890)	P	Chilipepper......rocote pimiento......sébaste de Goode

SCIENTIFIC NAME	OCCURRENCE[1]	COMMON NAME (ENGLISH, SPANISH, FRENCH)[2]		
Sebastes helvomaculatus Ayres, 1859	P	Rosethorn Rockfish		sébaste rosacé
Sebastes hopkinsi (Cramer, 1895)	P	Squarespot Rockfish	rocote a cuadros	
Sebastes jordani (Gilbert, 1896)	P	Shortbelly Rockfish	rocote pancita	sébaste à ventre court
Sebastes lentiginosus Chen, 1971	P	Freckled Rockfish	rocote pecoso	
Sebastes levis (Eigenmann & Eigenmann, 1889)	P	Cowcod	rocote vaquilla	
Sebastes macdonaldi (Eigenmann & Beeson, 1893)	P	Mexican Rockfish^	rocote mexicano	
Sebastes maliger (Jordan & Gilbert, 1880)	P	Quillback Rockfish		sébaste à dos épineux
Sebastes melanops Girard, 1856	P	Black Rockfish		sébaste noir
Sebastes melanosema Lea & Fitch, 1979	P	Semaphore Rockfish	rocote semáforo	
*Sebastes melanostictus (Matsubara, 1934)	P	Blackspotted Rockfish		sébaste tacheté
Sebastes melanostomus (Eigenmann & Eigenmann, 1890)	P	Blackgill Rockfish	rocote agalla negra	sébaste à branchies noires
Sebastes mentella (Travin, 1951)	A	Deepwater Redfish		sébaste atlantique
Sebastes miniatus (Jordan & Gilbert, 1880)	P	Vermilion Rockfish	rocote bermejo	sébaste vermillon
Sebastes moseri Eitner, 1999	P	Whitespotted Rockfish	rocote manchas blancas	
Sebastes mystinus (Jordan & Gilbert, 1881)	P	Blue Rockfish	rocote azul	sébaste bleu
Sebastes nebulosus Ayres, 1854	P	China Rockfish^		sébaste à rayures jaunes
Sebastes nigrocinctus Ayres, 1859	P	Tiger Rockfish		sébaste-tigre
Sebastes norvegicus (Ascanius, 1772)	A	Golden Redfish		sébaste orangé
Sebastes notius Chen, 1971	PM	Guadalupe Rockfish^	rocote de Guadalupe	
Sebastes ovalis (Ayres, 1862)	P	Speckled Rockfish	rocote manchado	
Sebastes paucispinis Ayres, 1854	P	Bocaccio	rocote bocaccio	bocaccio
Sebastes peduncularis Chen, 1975	PM	Gulf Rockfish^	rocote del Golfo	
Sebastes phillipsi (Fitch, 1964)	P	Chameleon Rockfish		
Sebastes pinniger (Gill, 1864)	P	Canary Rockfish	rocote canario	sébaste canari
Sebastes polyspinis (Taranetz & Moiseev, 1933)	P	Northern Rockfish		sébaste à quatorze épines
Sebastes proriger (Jordan & Gilbert, 1880)	P	Redstripe Rockfish		sébaste à raie rouge
Sebastes rastrelliger (Jordan & Gilbert, 1880)	P	Grass Rockfish	rocote de olivo	
Sebastes reedi (Westrheim & Tsuyuki, 1967)	P	Yellowmouth Rockfish		sébaste à bouche jaune
Sebastes rosaceus Girard, 1854	P	Rosy Rockfish	rocote rosado	
Sebastes rosenblatti Chen, 1971	P	Greenblotched Rockfish	rocote motas verdes	
Sebastes ruberrimus (Cramer, 1895)	P	Yelloweye Rockfish	rocote ojo amarillo	sébaste aux yeux jaunes
Sebastes rubrivinctus (Jordan & Gilbert, 1880)	P	Flag Rockfish	rocote bandera	

SCIENTIFIC NAME	OCCURRENCE[1]	COMMON NAME (ENGLISH, SPANISH, FRENCH)[2]
Sebastes rufinanus Lea & Fitch, 1972	P	Dwarf-red Rockfish
Sebastes rufus (Eigenmann & Eigenmann, 1890)	P	Bank Rockfish...rocote rojo
Sebastes saxicola (Gilbert, 1890)	P	Stripetail Rockfish...rocote cola listada...sébaste à queue rayée
Sebastes semicinctus (Gilbert, 1897)	P	Halfbanded Rockfish...rocote inspector
Sebastes serranoides (Eigenmann & Eigenmann, 1890)	P	Olive Rockfish...rocote falsa cabrilla
Sebastes serriceps (Jordan & Gilbert, 1880)	P	Treefish...rocote presidiario
Sebastes simulator Chen, 1971	P	Pinkrose Rockfish...rocote rosa
Sebastes sinensis (Gilbert, 1890)	PM	Blackmouth Rockfish...rocote boquinegra
Sebastes spinorbis Chen, 1975	PM	Spinyeye Rockfish...rocote ojo espinoso
Sebastes umbrosus (Jordan & Gilbert, 1882)	P	Honeycomb Rockfish...rocote panal
Sebastes variabilis (Pallas, 1814)	P	Light Dusky Rockfish...sébaste variable
Sebastes variegatus Quast, 1971	P	Harlequin Rockfish...sébaste arlequin
Sebastes varispinis Chen, 1975	PM	Hidden Rockfish...rocote escondido
Sebastes wilsoni (Gilbert, 1915)	P	Pygmy Rockfish...sébaste pygmée
Sebastes zacentrus (Gilbert, 1890)	P	Sharpchin Rockfish...sébaste à menton pointu
Sebastolobus alascanus Bean, 1890	P	Shortspine Thornyhead...chancharro alacrán...sébastolobe à courtes épines
Sebastolobus altivelis Gilbert, 1896	P	Longspine Thornyhead...chancharro espinoso...sébastolobe à longues épines
Sebastolobus macrochir (Günther, 1877)	P	Broadfin Thornyhead
Trachyscorpia cristulata (Goode & Bean, 1896)	A	Atlantic Thornyhead^

Triglidae—En-searobins, Sp-vacas y rubios, Fr-grondins

SCIENTIFIC NAME	OCCURRENCE[1]	COMMON NAME (ENGLISH, SPANISH, FRENCH)[2]
Bellator brachychir (Regan, 1914)	A	Shortfin Searobin...rubio aleticorta
Bellator egretta (Goode & Bean, 1896)	A	Streamer Searobin...rubio gallardete
Bellator gymnostethus (Gilbert, 1892)	PM	Nakedbelly Searobin...vaca enana
Bellator loxias (Jordan, 1897)	PM	Chevron Searobin...vaca angelita
Bellator militaris (Goode & Bean, 1896)	A	Horned Searobin...rubio soldadito
Bellator xenisma (Jordan & Bollman, 1890)	P	Splitnose Searobin...vaca doble hocico
Prionotus alatus Goode & Bean, 1883	A	Spiny Searobin...rubio espinoso
Prionotus albirostris Jordan & Bollman, 1890	PM	Whitesnout Searobin...vaca cariblanca
Prionotus birostratus Richardson, 1844	PM	Twobeak Searobin...vaca dospicos
Prionotus carolinus (Linnaeus, 1771)	A	Northern Searobin...grondin

SCIENTIFIC NAME	OCCURRENCE[1]	COMMON NAME (ENGLISH, SPANISH, FRENCH)[2]
Prionotus evolans (Linnaeus, 1766)	A	Striped Searobin.....prionote strié
Prionotus horrens Richardson, 1844	PM	Bristly Searobin.....vaca polla
Prionotus longispinosus Teague, 1951	A	Bigeye Searobin.....rubio ojón
Prionotus martis Ginsburg, 1950	A	Barred Searobin.....rubio de barras
Prionotus ophryas Jordan & Swain, 1885	A	Bandtail Searobin.....rubio cola bandeada
Prionotus paralatus Ginsburg, 1950	A	Mexican Searobin^.....rubio mexicano
Prionotus punctatus (Bloch, 1793)	AM	Bluewing Searobin.....rubio azul
Prionotus roseus Jordan & Evermann, 1887	A	Bluespotted Searobin.....rubio manchas azules
Prionotus rubio Jordan, 1886	A	Blackwing Searobin.....rubio aletinegra
Prionotus ruscarius Gilbert & Starks, 1904	PM	Rough Searobin.....vaca rasposa
Prionotus scitulus Jordan & Gilbert, 1882	A	Leopard Searobin.....rubio leopardo
Prionotus stearnsi Jordan & Swain, 1885	A	Shortwing Searobin.....rubio pequeño
Prionotus stephanophrys Lockington, 1881	P	Lumptail Searobin.....vaca voladora
Prionotus tribulus Cuvier, 1829	A	Bighead Searobin.....rubio cabezón

+Peristediidae—En-armored searobins, Sp-vaquitas blindadas, Fr-malarmats

SCIENTIFIC NAME	OCCURRENCE[1]	COMMON NAME (ENGLISH, SPANISH, FRENCH)[2]
Peristedion gracile Goode & Bean, 1896	A	Slender Searobin.....vaquita blindada flaca
Peristedion greyae Miller, 1967	A	Alligator Searobin
Peristedion miniatum Goode, 1880	A	Armored Searobin.....malarmat à dix aiguillons
Peristedion paucibarbiger Castro-Aguirre & García-Domínguez, 1984	PM	Cortez Searobin^.....vaquita blindada de Cortés
Peristedion thompsoni Fowler, 1952	A	Rimspine Searobin

Anoplopomatidae—En-sablefishes, Sp-bacalaos negros, Fr-morues noires

SCIENTIFIC NAME	OCCURRENCE[1]	COMMON NAME (ENGLISH, SPANISH, FRENCH)[2]
Anoplopoma fimbria (Pallas, 1814)	P	Sablefish.....bacalao negro.....morue charbonnière
Erilepis zonifer (Lockington, 1880)	P	Skilfish.....morue bariolée

Hexagrammidae—En-greenlings, Sp-molvas, Fr-sourcils

SCIENTIFIC NAME	OCCURRENCE[1]	COMMON NAME (ENGLISH, SPANISH, FRENCH)[2]
Hexagrammos decagrammus (Pallas, 1810)	P	Kelp Greenling.....sourcil de varech
Hexagrammos lagocephalus (Pallas, 1810)	P	Rock Greenling.....sourcil de roche
Hexagrammos octogrammus (Pallas, 1814)	P	Masked Greenling.....sourcil masqué

SCIENTIFIC NAME	OCCURRENCE[1]	COMMON NAME (ENGLISH, SPANISH, FRENCH)[2]		
Hexagrammos stelleri Tilesius, 1810	P-Ar	Whitespotted Greenling		sourcil à taches blanches
Ophiodon elongatus Girard, 1854	P	Lingcod	molva	morue-lingue
Oxylebius pictus Gill, 1862	P	Painted Greenling	molva pinta	sourcil à tête pointue
Pleurogrammus monopterygius (Pallas, 1810)	P	Atka Mackerel^		maquereau d'Atka
Zaniolepis frenata Eigenmann & Eigenmann, 1889	P	Shortspine Combfish	cepillo espina corta	
Zaniolepis latipinnis Girard, 1858	P	Longspine Combfish	cepillo espina larga	sourcil à longues épines
Rhamphocottidae—En-grunt sculpins, Sp-charrascos gruñones, Fr-chabots grogneurs				
Rhamphocottus richardsonii Günther, 1874	P	Grunt Sculpin		chabot grogneur
Cottidae—En-sculpins, Sp-charrascos espinosos, Fr-chabots				
Archistes biseriatus (Gilbert & Burke, 1912)	P	Scaled Sculpin		
Artediellus atlanticus Jordan & Evermann, 1898	A-Ar	Atlantic Hookear Sculpin^		hameçon atlantique
Artediellus gomojunovi Taranetz, 1933	P-Ar	Spinyhook Sculpin		
Artediellus ochotensis Gilbert & Burke, 1912	P	Okhotsk Hookear Sculpin^		
Artediellus pacificus Gilbert, 1896	P	Hookhorn Sculpin		
Artediellus scaber Knipowitsch, 1907	P-Ar	Hamecon		hameçon rude
Artediellus uncinatus (Reinhardt, 1835)	A-Ar	Arctic Hookear Sculpin^		hameçon neigeux
Artedius corallinus (Hubbs, 1926)	P	Coralline Sculpin	charrasco coralino	
Artedius fenestralis Jordan & Gilbert, 1883	P	Padded Sculpin		chabot rembourré
Artedius harringtoni (Starks, 1896)	P	Scalyhead Sculpin		chabot à tête écailleuse
Artedius lateralis (Girard, 1854)	P	Smoothhead Sculpin	charrasco cabeza lisa	chabot à tête lisse
Artedius notospilotus Girard, 1856	P	Bonyhead Sculpin	charrasco huesudo	
Ascelichthys rhodorus Jordan & Gilbert, 1880	P	Rosylip Sculpin		chabot à lèvres roses
Asemichthys taylori Gilbert, 1912	P	Spinynose Sculpin		chabot à museau épineux
Chitonotus pugetensis (Steindachner, 1876)	P	Roughback Sculpin	charrasco espalda rugosa	chabot à dos rugueux
Clinocottus acuticeps (Gilbert, 1896)	P-F:CU	Sharpnose Sculpin		chabot à nez pointu
Clinocottus analis (Girard, 1858)	P	Woolly Sculpin	charrasco lanudo	
Clinocottus embryum (Jordan & Starks, 1895)	P	Calico Sculpin	charrasco angaripola	chabot calico
Clinocottus globiceps (Girard, 1858)	P	Mosshead Sculpin		chabot à tête moussue
Clinocottus recalvus (Greeley, 1899)	P	Bald Sculpin	charrasco pelón	

SCIENTIFIC NAME	OCCURRENCE[1]	COMMON NAME (ENGLISH, SPANISH, FRENCH)[2]
Cottus aleuticus Gilbert, 1896	P-F:CU	Coastrange Sculpin........chabot côtier
Cottus asper Richardson, 1836	P-F:CU	Prickly Sculpin..........chabot piquant
Cottus asperrimus Rutter, 1908	F:U	Rough Sculpin
Cottus baileyi Robins, 1961	F:U	Black Sculpin
+*Cottus bairdii* Girard, 1850	F:CU	Mottled Sculpin..........chabot tacheté
Cottus beldingii Eigenmann & Eigenmann, 1891	F:U	Paiute Sculpin^
Cottus bendirei (Bean, 1881)	F:U	Malheur Sculpin^
Cottus caeruleomentum Kinziger, Raesly & Neely, 2000	F:U	Blue Ridge Sculpin^
+*Cottus carolinae* (Gill, 1861)	F:U	Banded Sculpin
Cottus chattahoochee Neely, Williams & Mayden, 2007	F:U	Chattahoochee Sculpin^
Cottus cognatus Richardson, 1836	F:CU	Slimy Sculpin.....chabot visqueux
Cottus confusus Bailey & Bond, 1963	F:CU	Shorthead Sculpin.....chabot à tête courte
Cottus echinatus Bailey & Bond, 1963	F[X]:U	Utah Lake Sculpin^
Cottus extensus Bailey & Bond, 1963	F:U	Bear Lake Sculpin^
Cottus girardi Robins, 1961	F:U	Potomac Sculpin^
Cottus greenei (Gilbert & Culver, 1898)	F:U	Shoshone Sculpin^
Cottus gulosus (Girard, 1854)	F:U	Riffle Sculpin
Cottus hubbsi Bailey & Dimick, 1949	F:CU	Columbia Sculpin^.......chabot du Columbia
+*Cottus hypselurus* Robins & Robison, 1985	F:U	Ozark Sculpin^
Cottus immaculatus Kinziger & Wood, 2010	F:U	Knobfin Sculpin
Cottus kanawhae Robins, 2005	F:U	Kanawha Sculpin^
Cottus klamathensis Gilbert, 1898	F:U	Marbled Sculpin
Cottus leiopomus Gilbert & Evermann, 1894	F:U	Wood River Sculpin^
Cottus marginatus (Bean, 1881)	F:U	Margined Sculpin
Cottus paulus Williams, 2000	F:U	Pygmy Sculpin
Cottus perplexus Gilbert & Evermann, 1894	F:U	Reticulate Sculpin
Cottus pitensis Bailey & Bond, 1963	F:U	Pit Sculpin^
Cottus princeps Gilbert, 1898	F:U	Klamath Lake Sculpin^
Cottus rhotheus (Smith, 1882)	F:CU	Torrent Sculpin.......chabot de torrent
Cottus ricei (Nelson, 1876)	F:CU	Spoonhead Sculpin.......chabot à tête plate
Cottus tallapoosae Neely, Williams & Mayden, 2007	F:U	Tallapoosa Sculpin^

SCIENTIFIC NAME	OCCURRENCE[1]	COMMON NAME (ENGLISH, SPANISH, FRENCH)[2]		
Cottus tenuis (Evermann & Meek, 1898)	F:U	Slender Sculpin		
Enophrys bison (Girard, 1854)	P	Buffalo Sculpin		chabot-bison
Enophrys diceraus (Pallas, 1788)	P	Antlered Sculpin		
Enophrys lucasi (Jordan & Gilbert, 1898)	P	Leister Sculpin		chabot de leister
Enophrys taurina Gilbert, 1914	P	Bull Sculpin		
Gymnocanthus detrisus Gilbert & Burke, 1912	P	Purplegray Sculpin		
Gymnocanthus galeatus Bean, 1881	P	Armorhead Sculpin		chabot casqué
*Gymnocanthus pistilliger (Pallas, 1814)	P	Threaded Sculpin		
Gymnocanthus tricuspis (Reinhardt, 1830)	A-P-Ar	Arctic Staghorn Sculpin^		tricorne arctique
Hemilepidotus hemilepidotus (Tilesius, 1811)	P	Red Irish Lord^		chabot trilobé rouge
Hemilepidotus jordani Bean, 1881	P	Yellow Irish Lord^		
Hemilepidotus papilio (Bean, 1880)	P	Butterfly Sculpin		
*Hemilepidotus spinosus Ayres, 1854	P	Brown Irish Lord^		chabot trilobé brun
Hemilepidotus zapus Gilbert & Burke, 1912	P	Longfin Irish Lord^		
Icelinus borealis Gilbert, 1896	P	Northern Sculpin		icéline boréale
Icelinus burchami Evermann & Goldsborough, 1907	P	Dusky Sculpin		icéline obscure
Icelinus cavifrons Gilbert, 1890	P	Pit-head Sculpin	charrasco cabeza bacha	
Icelinus filamentosus Gilbert, 1890	P	Threadfin Sculpin		icéline filamenteuse
Icelinus fimbriatus Gilbert, 1890	P	Fringed Sculpin		icéline à grands yeux
*Icelinus limbaughi Rosenblatt & Smith, 2004	P	Canyon Sculpin^		
Icelinus oculatus Gilbert, 1890	P	Frogmouth Sculpin		
Icelinus quadriseriatus (Lockington, 1880)	P	Yellowchin Sculpin	charrasco barbiamarilla	
Icelinus tenuis Gilbert, 1890	P	Spotfin Sculpin	charrasco aletimanchada	icéline à nageoires tachetées
Icelus bicornis (Reinhardt, 1840)	A-P-Ar	Twohorn Sculpin		icèle à deux cornes
Icelus canaliculatus Gilbert, 1896	P	Blacknose Sculpin		
Icelus euryops Bean, 1890	P	Wide-eye Sculpin		
Icelus spatula Gilbert & Burke, 1912	A-P-Ar	Spatulate Sculpin		icèle spatulée
Icelus spiniger Gilbert, 1896	P	Thorny Sculpin		icéline épineuse
Icelus uncinalis Gilbert & Burke, 1912	P	Uncinate Sculpin		
Jordania zonope Starks, 1895	P	Longfin Sculpin		chabot à longues nageoires

SCIENTIFIC NAME	OCCURRENCE[1]	COMMON NAME (ENGLISH, SPANISH, FRENCH)[2]
Leiocottus hirundo Girard, 1856	P	Lavender Sculpin .... charrasco lavanda
Leptocottus armatus Girard, 1854	P-F:CUM	Pacific Staghorn Sculpin^ ...... charrasco de astas .... chabot armé
Megalocottus platycephalus (Pallas, 1814)	P	Belligerent Sculpin
Microcottus sellaris (Gilbert, 1896)	P-Ar	Brightbelly Sculpin
Myoxocephalus aenaeus (Mitchill, 1814)	A-Ar	Grubby .... chaboisseau bronzé
Myoxocephalus jaok (Cuvier, 1829)	P	Plain Sculpin
Myoxocephalus niger (Bean, 1881)	P	Warthead Sculpin
Myoxocephalus octodecemspinosus (Mitchill, 1814)	A-Ar	Longhorn Sculpin............ chaboisseau à dix-huit épines
Myoxocephalus polyacanthocephalus (Pallas, 1814)	P	Great Sculpin........................ grand chaboisseau
Myoxocephalus quadricornis (Linnaeus, 1758)	A-P-Ar-F:C	Fourhorn Sculpin .... chaboisseau à quatre cornes
Myoxocephalus scorpioides (Fabricius, 1780)	A-P-Ar	Arctic Sculpin^ .... chaboisseau arctique
+*Myoxocephalus scorpius* (Linnaeus, 1758)	A-P-Ar	Shorthorn Sculpin............ chaboisseau à épines courtes
Myoxocephalus stelleri Tilesius, 1811	P	Frog Sculpin
Myoxocephalus thompsonii (Girard, 1851)	F:CU	Deepwater Sculpin .... chabot de profondeur
Oligocottus maculosus Girard, 1856	P	Tidepool Sculpin .... chabot de bâche
Oligocottus rimensis (Greeley, 1899)	P	Saddleback Sculpin ...... charrasco ensillado ...... chabot mantelé
Oligocottus rubellio (Greeley, 1899)	P	Rosy Sculpin .... charrasco rosado
Oligocottus snyderi Greeley, 1898	P	Fluffy Sculpin........... charrasco peludo...... chabot pelucheux
Orthonopias triacis Starks & Mann, 1911	P	Snubnose Sculpin............ charrasco chato....... chabot camus
Paricelinus hopliticus Eigenmann & Eigenmann, 1889	P	Thornback Sculpin .... chabot à dos épineux
Phallocottus obtusus Schultz, 1938	P	Spineless Sculpin
Porocottus mednius (Bean, 1898)	P	Aleutian Fringed Sculpin^
Radulinus asprellus Gilbert, 1890	P	Slim Sculpin .... charrasco flaco............ chabot élancé
Radulinus boleoides Gilbert, 1898	P	Darter Sculpin .... chabot-dard
Radulinus vinculus Bolin, 1950	P	Smoothgum Sculpin
Rastrinus scutiger (Bean, 1890)	P	Roughskin Sculpin
Ruscarius creaseri (Hubbs, 1926)	P	Roughcheek Sculpin............ charrasco cachetirugoso
Ruscarius meanyi Jordan & Starks, 1895	P	Puget Sound Sculpin^ .... charrasco à joue écailleuse
Scorpaenichthys marmoratus (Ayres, 1854)	P	Cabezon................................... cabezón
Sigmistes caulias Rutter, 1898	P	Kelp Sculpin
Sigmistes smithi Schultz, 1938	P	Arched Sculpin

SCIENTIFIC NAME	OCCURRENCE[1]	COMMON NAME (ENGLISH, SPANISH, FRENCH)[2]
Stelgistrum beringianum Gilbert & Burke, 1912	P	Smallplate Sculpin
Stelgistrum concinnum Andriashev, 1935	P	Largeplate Sculpin
Synchirus gilli Bean, 1890	P	Manacled Sculpin...chabot menoté
Thyriscus anoplus Gilbert & Burke, 1912	P	Sponge Sculpin
Trichocottus brashnikovi Soldatov & Pavlenko, 1915	P	Hairhead Sculpin
Triglops forficatus (Gilbert, 1896)	P	Scissortail Sculpin
Triglops macellus (Bean, 1884)	P	Roughspine Sculpin...faux-trigle épineux
Triglops metopias Gilbert & Burke, 1912	P	Highbrow Sculpin
Triglops murrayi Günther, 1888	A-Ar	Moustache Sculpin...faux-trigle armé
Triglops nybelini Jensen, 1944	A-P-Ar	Bigeye Sculpin...faux-trigle aux grands yeux
Triglops pingelii Reinhardt, 1837	A-P-Ar	Ribbed Sculpin...faux-trigle bardé
Triglops scepticus Gilbert, 1896	P	Spectacled Sculpin
Triglops xenostethus Gilbert, 1896	P	Scalybreasted Sculpin

Hemitripteridae—En-searavens, Sp-charrascos cuervo, Fr-hémitriptères

Blepsias bilobus Cuvier, 1829	P	Crested Sculpin...chabot bilobé
Blepsias cirrhosus (Pallas, 1814)	P	Silverspotted Sculpin...chabot à taches argentées
Hemitripterus americanus (Gmelin, 1789)	A	Sea Raven...hémitriptère atlantique
Hemitripterus bolini (Myers, 1934)	P	Bigmouth Sculpin...hémitriptère à grande bouche
Nautichthys oculofasciatus (Girard, 1858)	P	Sailfin Sculpin...chabot à grande voile
Nautichthys pribilovius (Jordan & Gilbert, 1898)	P	Eyeshade Sculpin
Nautichthys robustus Peden, 1970	P	Shortmast Sculpin...chabot à petite voile

Agonidae—En-poachers, Sp-bandidos, Fr-poissons-alligators

Agonopsis sterletus (Gilbert, 1898)	P	Southern Spearnose Poacher..bandido narigón
Agonopsis vulsa (Jordan & Gilbert, 1880)	P	Northern Spearnose Poacher...agone foncé
Anoplagonus inermis (Günther, 1860)	P	Smooth Alligatorfish...poisson-alligator lisse
Aspidophoroides monopterygius (Bloch, 1786)	A-P-Ar	Alligatorfish...poisson-alligator atlantique
*Aspidophoroides olrikii Lütken, 1877	A-P-Ar	Arctic Alligatorfish^...poisson-alligator arctique
Bathyagonus alascanus (Gilbert, 1896)	P	Gray Starsnout...astérothèque gris
Bathyagonus infraspinatus (Gilbert, 1904)	P	Spinycheek Starsnout...astérothèque épineux

SCIENTIFIC NAME	OCCURRENCE[1]	COMMON NAME (ENGLISH, SPANISH, FRENCH)[2]
Bathyagonus nigripinnis Gilbert, 1890	P	Blackfin Poacher ..... astérothèque à nageoires noires
Bathyagonus pentacanthus (Gilbert, 1890)	P	Bigeye Poacher ..... astérothèque à cinq épines
Bothragonus swanii (Steindachner, 1876)	P	Rockhead ..... tête-de-roche
Chesnonia verrucosa (Lockington, 1880)	P	Warty Poacher ..... agone verruqueux
Hypsagonus mozinoi (Wilimovsky & Wilson, 1979)	P	Kelp Poacher ..... agone de varech
Hypsagonus quadricornis (Cuvier, 1829)	P	Fourhorn Poacher ..... agone à quatre cornes
Leptagonus decagonus (Bloch & Schneider, 1801)	A-P-Ar.	Atlantic Poacher^ ..... agone atlantique
Leptagonus leptorhynchus (Gilbert, 1896)	P	Longnose Poacher
Occella dodecaedron (Tilesius, 1813)	P-Ar.	Bering Poacher^
Odontopyxis trispinosa Lockington, 1880	P	Pygmy Poacher ..... bandido enano ..... agone pygmée
Pallasina barbata (Steindachner, 1876)	P-Ar.	Tubenose Poacher ..... agone barbu
Percis japonica (Pallas, 1769)	P	Dragon Poacher
Podothecus accipenserinus (Tilesius, 1813)	P	Sturgeon Poacher ..... agone-esturgeon
Podothecus veternus Jordan & Starks, 1895	P-Ar.	Veteran Poacher
*Sarritor frenatus (Gilbert, 1896)	P	Sawback Poacher ..... agone à dos denté
Stellerina xyosterna (Jordan & Gilbert, 1880)	P	Pricklebreast Poacher ..... bandido pechoespinoso ..... agone à poitrine épineuse
Xeneretmus latifrons (Gilbert, 1890)	P	Blacktip Poacher ..... bandido penacho ..... agone à dorsale noire
Xeneretmus leiops Gilbert, 1915	P	Smootheye Poacher ..... agone à nageoire coupée
Xeneretmus ritteri Gilbert, 1915	P	Stripefin Poacher ..... bandido bandera
Xeneretmus triacanthus (Gilbert, 1890)	P	Bluespotted Poacher ..... bandido manchas azules ..... agone à trois épines

Psychrolutidae—En-fathead sculpins, Sp-cabezas gordas, Fr-chabots veloutés

Cottunculus microps Collett, 1875	A-Ar.	Polar Sculpin ..... cotte polaire
*Cottunculus thomsonii (Günther, 1882)	A-Ar.	Pallid Sculpin ..... cotte blême
Dasycottus setiger Bean, 1890	P	Spinyhead Sculpin ..... chabot à tête épineuse
Eurymen gyrinus Gilbert & Burke, 1912	P-Ar.	Smoothcheek Sculpin
Malacocottus kincaidi Gilbert & Thompson, 1905	P	Blackfin Sculpin ..... chabot à nageoires noires
Malacocottus zonurus Bean, 1890	P	Darkfin Sculpin ..... chabot à queue barrée
Psychrolutes paradoxus Günther, 1861	P	Tadpole Sculpin ..... chabot-têtard
Psychrolutes sigalutes (Jordan & Starks, 1895)	P	Soft Sculpin ..... chabot velouté

SCIENTIFIC NAME	OCCURRENCE[1]	COMMON NAME (ENGLISH, SPANISH, FRENCH)[2]
Cyclopteridae—En-lumpfishes, Sp-peces grumo, Fr-poules de mer		
Aptocyclus ventricosus (Pallas, 1769)	P	Smooth Lumpsucker ... poule de mer ventrue
*Cyclopteropsis jordani Soldatov, 1929	Ar	Smooth Lumpfish ... petite poule de mer douce
+Cyclopteropsis mcalpini (Fowler, 1914)	Ar	Arctic Lumpsucker^
Cyclopterus lumpus Linnaeus, 1758	A-Ar	Lumpfish ... grosse poule de mer
Eumicrotremus andriashevi Perminov, 1936	P-Ar	Pimpled Lumpsucker
Eumicrotremus asperrimus (Tanaka, 1912)	P	Siberian Lumpsucker^
Eumicrotremus barbatus (Lindberg & Legeza, 1955)	P	Papillose Lumpsucker
Eumicrotremus derjugini Popov, 1926	A-P-Ar	Leatherfin Lumpsucker^ ... petite poule de mer arctique
Eumicrotremus gyrinops (Garman, 1892)	P	Alaskan Lumpsucker^
Eumicrotremus orbis (Günther, 1861)	P	Pacific Spiny Lumpsucker^ ... petite poule de mer ronde
Eumicrotremus phrynoides Gilbert & Burke, 1912	P	Toad Lumpsucker
+Eumicrotremus spinosus (Fabricius, 1776)	A-P-Ar	Atlantic Spiny Lumpsucker^ ... petite poule de mer atlantique
Eumicrotremus terraenovae Myers & Böhlke, 1950	A	Newfoundland Spiny Lumpsucker^ ... petite poule de Terre-Neuve
Lethotremus muticus Gilbert, 1896	P	Docked Snailfish
Liparidae—En-snailfishes, Sp-peces babosos, Fr-limaces de mer		
*Allocareproctus tanix Orr & Busby, 2006	P	Peach Snailfish
*Allocareproctus unangas Orr & Busby, 2006	P	Goldeneye Snailfish
Careproctus candidus Gilbert & Burke, 1912	P	Bigeye Snailfish
*Careproctus comus Orr & Maslenikov, 2007	P	Comic Snailfish
*Careproctus faunus Orr & Maslenikov, 2007	P	Mischievous Snailfish
Careproctus furcellus Gilbert & Burke, 1912	P	Emarginate Snailfish
Careproctus gilberti Burke, 1912	P	Smalldisk Snailfish
Careproctus longipinnis Burke, 1912	A-Ar	Longfin Snailfish ... limace à longues nageoires
Careproctus melanurus Gilbert, 1892	P	Blacktail Snailfish ... baboso colinegra ... limace à queue noire
Careproctus ostentum Gilbert, 1896	P	Microdisk Snailfish
Careproctus phasma Gilbert, 1896	P	Spectral Snailfish
*Careproctus ramula (Goode & Bean, 1879)	A	Scotian Snailfish^ ... limace acadienne
Careproctus rastrinus Gilbert & Burke, 1912	P	Salmon Snailfish
Careproctus reinhardti (Krøyer, 1862)	A-Ar	Sea Tadpole ... petite limace de mer
Careproctus scottae Chapman & DeLacy, 1934	P	Peachskin Snailfish

SCIENTIFIC NAME	OCCURRENCE[1]	COMMON NAME (ENGLISH, SPANISH, FRENCH)[2]
Careproctus spectrum Bean, 1890	P	Stippled Snailfish
Crystallichthys cyclospilus Gilbert & Burke, 1912	P	Blotched Snailfish
*Liparis adiastolus Stein, Bond & Misitano, 2003	P	Rosybrown Snailfish ... limace rose-brune
Liparis atlanticus (Jordan & Evermann, 1898)	A-Ar	Atlantic Seasnail^ ... limace atlantique
*Liparis bathyarcticus Parr, 1931	A-P-Ar	Nebulous Snailfish ... limace nébuleuse
Liparis beringianus (Gilbert & Burke, 1912)	P	Bering Snailfish^
Liparis bristolensis (Burke, 1912)	P	Bristol Snailfish^
Liparis callyodon (Pallas, 1814)	P	Spotted Snailfish ... limace tachetée
Liparis catharus Vogt, 1973	P	Purity Snailfish
Liparis coheni Able, 1976	A	Gulf Snailfish^ ... limace de Cohen
Liparis cyclopus Günther, 1861	A	Ribbon Snailfish ... limace-ruban
Liparis dennyi Jordan & Starks, 1895	P	Marbled Snailfish ... limace à petits yeux
Liparis fabricii Kroyer, 1847	A-P-Ar	Gelatinous Seasnail ... limace gélatineuse
Liparis florae (Jordan & Starks, 1895)	P	Tidepool Snailfish ... limace de bâche
Liparis fucensis Gilbert, 1896	P	Slipskin Snailfish ... limace de varech
+Liparis gibbus Bean, 1881	A-P-Ar	Variegated Snailfish ... limace marbrée
Liparis greeni (Jordan & Starks, 1895)	P	Lobefin Snailfish ... limace à nageoire lobée
*Liparis herschelinus Scofield, 1898	P-Ar	Bartail Snailfish ... limace à queue barrée
Liparis inquilinus Able, 1973	A	Inquiline Snailfish ... limace des pétoncles
Liparis marmoratus Schmidt, 1950	P	Festive Snailfish
Liparis megacephalus (Burke, 1912)	P	Bighead Snailfish
*Liparis micraspidophorus (Gilbert & Burke, 1912)	P	Thumbtack Snailfish
Liparis mucosus Ayres, 1855	P	Slimy Snailfish ... baboso mucoso ... limace visqueuse
Liparis ochotensis Schmidt, 1904	P	Okhotsk Snailfish^
Liparis pulchellus Ayres, 1855	P	Showy Snailfish ... limace prétentieuse
+Liparis rutteri (Gilbert & Snyder, 1898)	P	Ringtail Snailfish
*Liparis tunicatus Reinhardt, 1836	A-P-Ar	Kelp Snailfish ... limace des laminaires
Lipariscus nanus Gilbert, 1915	P	Pygmy Snailfish ... limace naine
Nectoliparis pelagicus Gilbert & Burke, 1912	P	Tadpole Snailfish ... limace têtard
Paraliparis calidus Cohen, 1968	A	Lowfin Snailfish ... limace ardente
Paraliparis deani Burke, 1912	P	Prickly Snailfish ... limace épineuse

SCIENTIFIC NAME	OCCURRENCE[1]	COMMON NAME (ENGLISH, SPANISH, FRENCH)[2]		

*ORDER PERCIFORMES

Centropomidae—En-snooks, Sp-robalos, Fr-centropomes

Scientific name	Occurrence	English	Spanish	French
*Centropomus armatus Gill, 1863	PM-F:M	Longspine Snook	robalo espina larga	
Centropomus ensiferus Poey, 1860	A-F:UM	Swordspine Snook	robalo de espolón	
*Centropomus medius Günther, 1864	PM-F:M	Blackfin Snook	robalo aleta prieta	
*Centropomus mexicanus Bocourt, 1868	A-F:UM	Largescale Fat Snook	robalo gordo	
*Centropomus nigrescens Günther, 1864	PM-F:M	Black Snook	robalo negro	
Centropomus parallelus Poey, 1860	A-F:UM	Smallscale Fat Snook	chucumite	
Centropomus pectinatus Poey, 1860	A-F:UM	Tarpon Snook	constantino	
Centropomus poeyi Chávez, 1961	AM-F:M	Mexican Snook^	robalo prieto	
*Centropomus robalito Jordan & Gilbert, 1882	PM-F:M	Yellowfin Snook	robalo aleta amarilla	
Centropomus undecimalis (Bloch, 1792)	A-F:UM	Common Snook	robalo blanco	
*Centropomus unionensis Bocourt, 1868	PM-F:M	Humpback Snook	robalo serrano	
*Centropomus viridis Lockington, 1877	PM-F:M	White Snook	robalo plateado	

Moronidae—En-temperate basses, Sp-lobinas norteñas, Fr-bars

Scientific name	Occurrence	English	Spanish	French
Morone americana (Gmelin, 1789)	A-F:CU	White Perch		baret
Morone chrysops (Rafinesque, 1820)	F:CU	White Bass		bar blanc
Morone mississippiensis Jordan & Eigenmann, 1887	F:U	Yellow Bass		
Morone saxatilis (Walbaum, 1792)	A-P[I]-F:CU	Striped Bass	lobina estriada	bar rayé

Acropomatidae—En-lanternbellies, Sp-farolitos, Fr-macondes

Scientific name	Occurrence	English	Spanish	French
Synagrops bellus (Goode & Bean, 1896)	A	Blackmouth Bass		
Synagrops spinosus Schultz, 1940	A	Keelcheek Bass	farolito cachetiquillada	
Synagrops trispinosus Mochizuki & Sano, 1984	A	Threespine Bass	farolito tres espinas	

Symphysanodontidae—En-slopefishes, Sp-pargos del talud, Fr-symphysanodontidés

Scientific name	Occurrence	English	Spanish	French
Symphysanodon berryi Anderson, 1970	A	Slope Bass		

Polyprionidae—En-wreckfishes, Sp-náufragos, Fr-polyprions

Scientific name	Occurrence	English	Spanish	French
Polyprion americanus (Bloch & Schneider, 1801)	A	Wreckfish		cernier de l'Atlantique
Stereolepis gigas Ayres, 1859	P	Giant Sea Bass	pescara	

SCIENTIFIC NAME	OCCURRENCE[1]	COMMON NAME (ENGLISH, SPANISH, FRENCH)[2]

*Epinephelidae—En-groupers, Sp-cabrillas y garropas, Fr-mérous

SCIENTIFIC NAME	OCCURRENCE[1]	COMMON NAME
Alphestes afer (Bloch, 1793)	A	Mutton Hamlet
Alphestes immaculatus Breder, 1936	PM	Pacific Mutton Hamlet^......guaseta del Pacifico
Alphestes multiguttatus (Günther, 1867)	PM	Rivulated Mutton Hamlet......guaseta rayada
Cephalopholis cruentata (Lacepède, 1802)	A	Graysby......cherna enjambre
Cephalopholis fulva (Linnaeus, 1758)	A	Coney......cabrilla roja
Cephalopholis panamensis (Steindachner, 1877)	PM	Panama Graysby^......cabrilla enjambre
Dermatolepis dermatolepis (Boulenger, 1895)	P	Leather Bass......mero cuero
Dermatolepis inermis (Valenciennes, 1833)	A	Marbled Grouper
Epinephelus adscensionis (Osbeck, 1765)	A	Rock Hind......cabrilla payaso
Epinephelus analogus Gill, 1863	P	Spotted Cabrilla......cabrilla pinta
+*Epinephelus cifuentesi* Lavenberg & Grove, 1993	PM	Olive Grouper......cabrilla gallina
Epinephelus clippertonensis Allen & Robertson, 1999	PM	Clipperton Grouper^......cabrilla de Clipperton
+*Epinephelus drummondhayi* Goode & Bean, 1878	A	Speckled Hind......mero pintarroja
Epinephelus guttatus (Linnaeus, 1758)	A	Red Hind......cabrilla colorada
Epinephelus itajara (Lichtenstein, 1822)	A	Atlantic Goliath Grouper^......cherna gigante
Epinephelus labriformis (Jenyns, 1840)	P	Flag Cabrilla......cabrilla piedrera
Epinephelus morio (Valenciennes, 1828)	A	Red Grouper......cherna americana
Epinephelus quinquefasciatus (Bocourt, 1868)	PM	Pacific Goliath Grouper^......mero gigante
Epinephelus striatus (Bloch, 1792)	A	Nassau Grouper^......mero del Caribe
Gonioplectrus hispanus (Cuvier, 1828)	A	Spanish Flag^......cherna bandera
Hyporthodus acanthistius (Gilbert, 1892)	P	Gulf Coney^......baqueta
Hyporthodus exsul (Fowler, 1944)	PM	Tenspine Grouper......cabrilla diez espinas
Hyporthodus flavolimbatus (Poey, 1865)	A	Yellowedge Grouper......mero extraviado
Hyporthodus mystacinus (Poey, 1852)	A	Misty Grouper
Hyporthodus nigritus (Holbrook, 1855)	A	Warsaw Grouper......mero negro
Hyporthodus niphobles (Gilbert & Starks, 1897)	P	Star-studded Grouper......baqueta ploma
Hyporthodus niveatus (Valenciennes, 1828)	A	Snowy Grouper......cherna pintada......mérou neigeux
Mycteroperca acutirostris (Valenciennes, 1828)	A	Western Comb Grouper......cherna peineta
Mycteroperca bonaci (Poey, 1860)	A	Black Grouper......cherna negrillo
Mycteroperca interstitialis (Poey, 1860)	A	Yellowmouth Grouper......cherna boca amarilla

SCIENTIFIC NAME	OCCURRENCE[1]	COMMON NAME (ENGLISH, SPANISH, FRENCH)[2]
Mycteroperca jordani (Jenkins & Evermann, 1889)	P	Gulf Grouper^ — baya
Mycteroperca microlepis (Goode & Bean, 1879)	A	Gag — abadejo
Mycteroperca phenax Jordan & Swain, 1884	A	Scamp — abadejo garropa
Mycteroperca prionura Rosenblatt & Zahuranec, 1967	PM	Sawtail Grouper — cabrilla chiruda
Mycteroperca rosacea (Streets, 1877)	PM	Leopard Grouper — cabrilla sardinera
Mycteroperca tigris (Valenciennes, 1833)	A	Tiger Grouper — cabrilla gato
Mycteroperca venenosa (Linnaeus, 1758)	A	Yellowfin Grouper — guacamayo
Mycteroperca xenarcha Jordan, 1888	P	Broomtail Grouper — cabrilla plomuda
Paranthias colonus (Valenciennes, 1846)	P	Pacific Creolefish^ — sandia
Paranthias furcifer (Valenciennes, 1828)	A	Atlantic Creolefish^ — rabirrubia del Golfo

*Serranidae—En-sea basses, Sp-serranos, Fr-serrans

SCIENTIFIC NAME	OCCURRENCE[1]	COMMON NAME (ENGLISH, SPANISH, FRENCH)[2]
Anthias nicholsi Firth, 1933	A	Yellowfin Bass — mero aleta amarilla — barbier ligne-en-palier
Anthias woodsi Anderson & Heemstra, 1980	A	Swallowtail Bass
Baldwinella aureorubens (Longley, 1935)	A	Streamer Bass — cabrilla cinta
Baldwinella vivanus (Jordan & Swain, 1885)	A	Red Barbier — barbero rojo
Bathyanthias mexicanus (Schultz, 1958)	A	Yellowtail Bass — mero cola amarilla
Centropristis fuscula (Poey, 1861)	A	Twospot Sea Bass
Centropristis ocyurus (Jordan & Evermann, 1887)	A	Bank Sea Bass — cabrilla de banco
Centropristis philadelphica (Linnaeus, 1758)	A	Rock Sea Bass — cabrilla serrana
Centropristis striata (Linnaeus, 1758)	A	Black Sea Bass — bar noir
Choranthias tenuis Nichols, 1920	A	Threadnose Bass — mero naricita
Diplectrum bivittatum (Valenciennes, 1828)	A	Dwarf Sand Perch — serrano guabino
Diplectrum eumelum Rosenblatt & Johnson, 1974	PM	Orange-spotted Sand Perch — serrano carabonita
Diplectrum euryplectrum Jordan & Bollman, 1890	PM	Bighead Sand Perch — serrano extranjero
Diplectrum formosum (Linnaeus, 1766)	A	Sand Perch — serrano arenero
Diplectrum labarum Rosenblatt & Johnson, 1974	PM	Highfin Sand Perch — serrano espinudo
Diplectrum macropoma (Günther, 1864)	PM	Mexican Sand Perch^ — serrano mexicano
Diplectrum maximum Hildebrand, 1946	P	Greater Sand Perch — serrano de altura
Diplectrum pacificum Meek & Hildebrand, 1925	PM	Pacific Sand Perch^ — serrano cabaicucho
Diplectrum rostrum Bortone, 1974	PM	Bridled Sand Perch — serrano frenado

SCIENTIFIC NAME	OCCURRENCE[1]	COMMON NAME (ENGLISH, SPANISH, FRENCH)[2]
Diplectrum sciurus Gilbert, 1892	PM	Squirrel Sand Perch............serrano ardilla
Hemanthias leptus (Ginsburg, 1952)	A	Longtail Bass............cabrilla robalo
Hemanthias peruanus (Steindachner, 1875)	PM	Splittail Bass............cabrilla doblecola
Hemanthias signifer (Garman, 1899)	P	Hookthroat Bass............cabrilla doncella
Hypoplectrus aberrans Poey, 1868	A	Yellowbelly Hamlet............mero panza amarilla
Hypoplectrus castroaguirrei Del Moral Flores, Tello-Musi & Martínez-Pérez, 2011	AM	Bandit Hamlet............mero bandido
Hypoplectrus chlorurus (Cuvier, 1828)	AM	Yellowtail Hamlet............mero solitario
Hypoplectrus gemma Goode & Bean, 1882	A	Blue Hamlet............mero azul
Hypoplectrus guttavarius (Poey, 1852)	A	Shy Hamlet
Hypoplectrus indigo (Poey, 1851)	A	Indigo Hamlet............mero añil
Hypoplectrus nigricans (Poey, 1852)	A	Black Hamlet............mero carbonero
Hypoplectrus puella (Cuvier, 1828)	A	Barred Hamlet............mero barril
Hypoplectrus providencianus Acero P. & Garzón-Ferreira, 1994	AM	Masked Hamlet............mero enmascarado
Hypoplectrus randallorum Lobel, 2011	A	Tan Hamlet............mero café
Hypoplectrus unicolor (Walbaum, 1792)	A	Butter Hamlet............mero mantequilla
Liopropoma aberrans (Poey, 1860)	A	Eyestripe Basslet
Liopropoma carmabi (Randall, 1963)	A	Candy Basslet............cabrilla caramelo
Liopropoma eukrines (Starck & Courtenay, 1962)	A	Wrasse Basslet
Liopropoma fasciatum Bussing, 1980	PM	Rainbow Basslet............cabrilla arcoíris
Liopropoma longilepis Garman, 1899	PM	Scalyfin Basslet............cabrilla aleta escamosa
Liopropoma mowbrayi Woods & Kanazawa, 1951	A	Cave Basslet............cabrilla de cueva
Liopropoma rubre Poey, 1861	A	Peppermint Basslet............cabrilla menta
Paralabrax auroguttatus Walford, 1936	PM	Goldspotted Sand Bass............cabrilla extranjera
Paralabrax clathratus (Girard, 1854)	P	Kelp Bass............cabrilla sargacera
Paralabrax loro Walford, 1936	PM	Parrot Sand Bass............cabrilla cachete amarillo
Paralabrax maculatofasciatus (Steindachner, 1868)	P	Spotted Sand Bass............cabrilla de roca
Paralabrax nebulifer (Girard, 1854)	P	Barred Sand Bass............cabrilla verde de arena
Parasphyraenops incisus (Colin, 1978)	A	Splitfin Bass
Plectranthias garrupellus Robins & Starck, 1961	A	Apricot Bass
Pronotogrammus eos Gilbert, 1890	PM	Bigeye Bass............serrano ojón

SCIENTIFIC NAME	OCCURRENCE[1]	COMMON NAME (ENGLISH, SPANISH, FRENCH)[2]
Pronotogrammus martinicensis (Guichenot, 1868)	A	Roughtongue Bass	serrano lengua rasposa
Pronotogrammus multifasciatus Gill, 1863	P	Threadfin Bass	serrano baga
Pseudogramma gregoryi (Breder, 1927)	A	Reef Bass	jaboncillo arrecifal
Pseudogramma thaumasium (Gilbert, 1900)	PM	Pacific Reef Bass^	jaboncillo ocelado
Rypticus bicolor Valenciennes, 1846	PM	Mottled Soapfish	jabonero moteado
Rypticus bistrispinus (Mitchill, 1818)	A	Freckled Soapfish	jabonero pecoso
Rypticus carpenteri Baldwin & Weigt, 2012	A	Slope Soapfish	
Rypticus courtenayi McCarthy, 1979	PM	Socorro Soapfish^	jabonero de Socorro
Rypticus maculatus Holbrook, 1855	A	Whitespotted Soapfish	jabonero albipunteado
Rypticus nigripinnis Gill, 1861	PM	Twice-spotted Soapfish	jabonero doble punteado
Rypticus saponaceus (Bloch & Schneider, 1801)	A	Greater Soapfish	jabonero grande
Rypticus subbifrenatus Gill, 1861	A	Spotted Soapfish	jabonero punteado
Schultzea beta (Hildebrand, 1940)	A	School Bass	serrano escolar
Serraniculus pumilio Ginsburg, 1952	A	Pygmy Sea Bass	serrano pigmeo
Serranus aequidens Gilbert, 1890	P	Deepwater Serrano	serrano de agua profunda
Serranus annularis (Günther, 1880)	A	Orangeback Bass	serrano naranja
Serranus atrobranchus (Cuvier, 1829)	A	Blackear Bass	serrano oreja negra
Serranus baldwini (Evermann & Marsh, 1899)	A	Lantern Bass	serrano linterna
Serranus chionaraia Robins & Starck, 1961	A	Snow Bass	
Serranus huascarii Steindachner, 1900	PM	Flag Serrano	serrano bandera
Serranus notospilus Longley, 1935	A	Saddle Bass	serrano ensillado
Serranus phoebe Poey, 1851	A	Tattler	serrano diana
Serranus psittacinus Valenciennes, 1846	PM	Barred Serrano	serrano guaseta
Serranus socorroensis Allen & Robertson, 1992	PM	Socorro Serrano^	serrano de Socorro
Serranus subligarius (Cope, 1870)	A	Belted Sandfish	serrano aporreado
Serranus tabacarius (Cuvier, 1829)	A	Tobaccofish	serrano jácome
Serranus tigrinus (Bloch, 1790)	A	Harlequin Bass	serrano arlequín
Serranus tortugarum Longley, 1935	A	Chalk Bass	serrano pálido

Grammatidae—En-basslets, Sp-cabrilletas, Fr-grammatidés

| *Gramma linki* Starck & Colin, 1978 | AM | Yellowcheek Basslet | cabrilleta mejilla amarilla |
| *Gramma loreto* Poey, 1868 | AM | Fairy Basslet | loreto |

SCIENTIFIC NAME	OCCURRENCE[1]	COMMON NAME (ENGLISH, SPANISH, FRENCH)[2]
Gramma melacara Böhlke & Randall, 1963	AM	Blackcap Basslet .... cabrilleta violeta
Lipogramma anabantoides Böhlke, 1960	A	Dusky Basslet .... cabrilleta prieta
+*Lipogramma evides* Robins & Colin, 1979	AM	Banded Basslet .... cabrilleta cinteada
Lipogramma regium Robins & Colin, 1979	A	Royal Basslet
Lipogramma trilineatum Randall, 1963	A	Threeline Basslet .... cabrilleta tres rayas
Opistognathidae—En-jawfishes, Sp-bocones, Fr-tout-en-gueule		
Lonchopisthus micrognathus (Poey, 1860)	A	Swordtail Jawfish .... bocón rayado
Lonchopisthus sinuscalifornicus Castro-Aguirre & Villavicencio-Garayzar, 1988	PM	Longtail Jawfish .... bocón cola larga
Opistognathus aurifrons (Jordan & Thompson, 1905)	A	Yellowhead Jawfish .... bocón cabeza amarilla
Opistognathus brochus Bussing & Lavenberg, 2003	PM	Toothy Jawfish .... bocón dientudo
Opistognathus fossoris Bussing & Lavenberg, 2003	PM	Barred Jawfish .... bocón rayado
Opistognathus lonchurus Jordan & Gilbert, 1882	A	Moustache Jawfish .... bocón bigote
Opistognathus macrognathus Poey, 1860	A	Banded Jawfish
Opistognathus maxillosus Poey, 1860	A	Mottled Jawfish .... bocón moteado
+*Opistognathus megalepis* Smith-Vaniz, 1972	AM	Largescale Jawfish .... bocón escamón
Opistognathus melachasme Smith-Vaniz, 1972	AM	Megamouth Jawfish .... megabocón
Opistognathus nothus Smith-Vaniz, 1997	A	Yellowmouth Jawfish
+*Opistognathus punctatus* Peters, 1869	PM	Finespotted Jawfish .... bocón punteado
Opistognathus rhomaleus Jordan & Gilbert, 1881	PM	Giant Jawfish .... bocón gigante
Opistognathus robinsi Smith-Vaniz, 1997	A	Spotfin Jawfish
Opistognathus rosenblatti Allen & Robertson, 1991	PM	Bluespotted Jawfish .... bocón manchas azules
Opistognathus scops (Jenkins & Evermann, 1889)	PM	Bullseye Jawfish .... bocón ocelado
Opistognathus walkeri Bussing & Lavenberg, 2003	PM	Mexican Jawfish^ .... bocón mexicano
Opistognathus whitehursti (Longley, 1927)	A	Dusky Jawfish .... bocón prieto
Centrarchidae—En-sunfishes, Sp-lobinas, Fr-achigans et crapets		
Acantharchus pomotis (Baird, 1855)	F:U	Mud Sunfish
Ambloplites ariommus Viosca, 1936	F:U	Shadow Bass
Ambloplites cavifrons Cope, 1868	F:U	Roanoke Bass^
Ambloplites constellatus Cashner & Suttkus, 1977	F:U	Ozark Bass^

SCIENTIFIC NAME	OCCURRENCE[1]	COMMON NAME (ENGLISH, SPANISH, FRENCH)[2]		
*Ambloplites rupestris (Rafinesque, 1817)	F:CUM[I]	Rock Bass	lobina de roca	crapet de roche
Archoplites interruptus (Girard, 1854)	F:U	Sacramento Perch^		
Centrarchus macropterus (Lacepède, 1801)	F:U	Flier		
Enneacanthus chaetodon (Baird, 1855)	F:U	Blackbanded Sunfish		
Enneacanthus gloriosus (Holbrook, 1855)	F:U	Bluespotted Sunfish		
Enneacanthus obesus (Girard, 1854)	F:U	Banded Sunfish		
*Lepomis auritus (Linnaeus, 1758)	F:CUM[I]	Redbreast Sunfish	mojarra pecho rojo	crapet rouge
Lepomis cyanellus Rafinesque, 1819	F:CUM[I]	Green Sunfish	pez sol	crapet vert
Lepomis gibbosus (Linnaeus, 1758)	F:CU	Pumpkinseed		crapet-soleil
*Lepomis gulosus (Cuvier, 1829)	F:CUM[I]	Warmouth	mojarra golosa	crapet sac-à-lait
*Lepomis humilis (Girard, 1858)	F:C[I]U	Orangespotted Sunfish		crapet menu
Lepomis macrochirus Rafinesque, 1819	F:CUM	Bluegill	mojarra oreja azul	crapet arlequin
Lepomis marginatus (Holbrook, 1855)	F:U	Dollar Sunfish		
*Lepomis megalotis (Rafinesque, 1820)	F:UM	Longear Sunfish	mojarra orejona	
*Lepomis microlophus (Günther, 1859)	F:UM[I]	Redear Sunfish	mojarra oreja roja	
Lepomis miniatus Jordan, 1877	F:U	Redspotted Sunfish		
*Lepomis peltastes Cope, 1870	F:CU	Northern Sunfish		crapet du nord
*Lepomis punctatus (Valenciennes, 1831)	F:UM[I]	Spotted Sunfish	mojarra manchada	
Lepomis symmetricus Forbes, 1883	*F:U	Bantam Sunfish		
Micropterus cataractae Williams & Burgess, 1999	F:U	Shoal Bass		
Micropterus coosae Hubbs & Bailey, 1940	F:U	Redeye Bass		
*Micropterus dolomieu Lacepède, 1802	F:CUM[I]	Smallmouth Bass	lobina boca chica	achigan à petite bouche
*Micropterus henshalli Hubbs & Bailey, 1940	F:U	Alabama Bass^		
Micropterus notius Bailey & Hubbs, 1949	F:U	Suwannee Bass^		
+Micropterus punctulatus (Rafinesque, 1819)	F:U	Spotted Bass		
+Micropterus salmoides (Lacepède, 1802)	F:CUM	Largemouth Bass	lobina negra	achigan à grande bouche
Micropterus treculii (Vaillant & Bocourt, 1874)	F:U	Guadalupe Bass^		
*Pomoxis annularis Rafinesque, 1818	F:CUM[I]	White Crappie	mojarra blanca	marigane blanche
*Pomoxis nigromaculatus (Lesueur, 1829)	F:CUM[I]	Black Crappie	mojarra negra	marigane noire

+Percidae—En-perches and darters, Sp-percas, Fr-perches et dards

Ammocrypta beanii Jordan, 1877	F:U	Naked Sand Darter	
Ammocrypta bifascia Williams, 1975	F:U	Florida Sand Darter^	

SCIENTIFIC NAME	OCCURRENCE[1]	COMMON NAME (ENGLISH, SPANISH, FRENCH)[2]
Ammocrypta clara Jordan & Meek, 1885	F:U	Western Sand Darter
Ammocrypta meridiana Williams, 1975	F:U	Southern Sand Darter
Ammocrypta pellucida (Agassiz, 1863)	F:CU	Eastern Sand Darter............dard de sable
Ammocrypta vivax Hay, 1882	F:U	Scaly Sand Darter
+Crystallaria asprella (Jordan, 1878)	F:U	Crystal Darter
*Crystallaria cincotta Welsh & Wood, 2008	F:U	Diamond Darter
Etheostoma acuticeps Bailey, 1959	F:U	Sharphead Darter
*Etheostoma akatulo Layman & Mayden, 2009	F:U	Bluemask Darter
Etheostoma aquali Williams & Etnier, 1978	F:U	Coppercheek Darter
Etheostoma artesiae (Hay, 1881)	F:U	Redspot Darter
Etheostoma asprigene (Forbes, 1878)	F:U	Mud Darter
*Etheostoma atripinne (Jordan, 1877)	F:U	Cumberland Snubnose Darter^
Etheostoma australe Jordan, 1889	F:M	Conchos Darter^............perca del Conchos
*Etheostoma autumnale Mayden, 2010	F:U	Autumn Darter
Etheostoma baileyi Page & Burr, 1982	F:U	Emerald Darter
Etheostoma barbouri Kuehne & Small, 1971	F:U	Teardrop Darter
Etheostoma barrenense Burr & Page, 1982	F:U	Splendid Darter
Etheostoma basilare Page, Hardman & Near, 2003	F:U	Corrugated Darter
Etheostoma bellator Suttkus & Bailey, 1993	F:U	Warrior Darter^
Etheostoma bellum Zorach, 1968	F:U	Orangefin Darter
Etheostoma bison Ceas & Page, 1997	F:U	Buffalo Darter^
Etheostoma blennioides Rafinesque, 1819	F:CU	Greenside Darter............dard vert
Etheostoma blennius Gilbert & Swain, 1887	F:U	Blenny Darter
Etheostoma boschungi Wall & Williams, 1974	F:U	Slackwater Darter
Etheostoma brevirostrum Suttkus & Etnier, 1991	F:U	Holiday Darter
*Etheostoma brevispinum (Coker, 1926)	F:U	Carolina Fantail Darter^
Etheostoma burri Ceas & Page, 1997	F:U	Brook Darter
Etheostoma caeruleum Storer, 1845	F:CU	Rainbow Darter............dard arc-en-ciel
Etheostoma camurum (Cope, 1870)	F:U	Bluebreast Darter
Etheostoma cervus Powers & Mayden, 2003	F:U	Chickasaw Darter^
Etheostoma chermocki Boschung, Mayden & Tomelleri, 1992	F:U	Vermilion Darter
Etheostoma chienense Page & Ceas, 1992	F:U	Relict Darter

SCIENTIFIC NAME	OCCURRENCE[1]	COMMON NAME (ENGLISH, SPANISH, FRENCH)[2]
Etheostoma chlorobranchium Zorach, 1972	F:U	Greenfin Darter
Etheostoma chlorosoma (Hay, 1881)	F:U	Bluntnose Darter
Etheostoma chuckwachatte Mayden & Wood, 1993	F:U	Lipstick Darter
+*Etheostoma cinereum* Storer, 1845	F:U	Ashy Darter
Etheostoma collettei Birdsong & Knapp, 1969	F:U	Creole Darter
Etheostoma collis (Hubbs & Cannon, 1935)	F:U	Carolina Darter^
Etheostoma colorosum Suttkus & Bailey, 1993	F:U	Coastal Darter
Etheostoma coosae (Fowler, 1945)	F:U	Coosa Darter^
Etheostoma corona Page & Ceas, 1992	F:U	Crown Darter
Etheostoma cragini Gilbert, 1885	F:U	Arkansas Darter^
Etheostoma crossopterum Braasch & Mayden, 1985	F:U	Fringed Darter
Etheostoma davisoni Hay, 1885	F:U	Choctawhatchee Darter^
Etheostoma denoncourti Stauffer & van Snik, 1997	F:U	Golden Darter
Etheostoma derivativum Page, Hardman & Near, 2003	F:U	Stone Darter
Etheostoma ditrema Ramsey & Suttkus, 1965	F:U	Coldwater Darter
Etheostoma douglasi Wood & Mayden, 1993	F:U	Tuskaloosa Darter^
Etheostoma duryi Henshall, 1889	F:U	Blackside Snubnose Darter
Etheostoma edwini (Hubbs & Cannon, 1935)	F:U	Brown Darter
Etheostoma erythrozonum Switzer & Wood, 2009	F:U	Meramec Saddled Darter^
Etheostoma etnieri Bouchard, 1977	F:U	Cherry Darter
Etheostoma etowahae Wood & Mayden, 1993	F:U	Etowah Darter^
Etheostoma euzonum (Hubbs & Black, 1940)	F:U	Arkansas Saddled Darter^
Etheostoma exile (Girard, 1859)	F:CU	Iowa Darter^ ....dard à ventre jaune
+*Etheostoma flabellare* Rafinesque, 1819	F:CU	Fantail Darter ....dard barré
Etheostoma flavum Etnier & Bailey, 1989	F:U	Saffron Darter
Etheostoma fonticola (Jordan & Gilbert, 1886)	F:U	Fountain Darter
Etheostoma forbesi Page & Ceas, 1992	F:U	Barrens Darter^
Etheostoma fragi Distler, 1968	F:U	Strawberry Darter^
Etheostoma fricksium Hildebrand, 1923	F:U	Savannah Darter^
Etheostoma fusiforme (Girard, 1854)	F:U	Swamp Darter
Etheostoma gracile (Girard, 1859)	F:U	Slough Darter
Etheostoma grahami (Girard, 1859)	F:UM	Rio Grande Darter^ ....perca del Bravo

SCIENTIFIC NAME	OCCURRENCE[1]	COMMON NAME (ENGLISH, SPANISH, FRENCH)[2]
Etheostoma gutselli (Hildebrand, 1932)	F:U	Tuckasegee Darter^
Etheostoma histrio Jordan & Gilbert, 1887	F:U	Harlequin Darter
Etheostoma hopkinsi (Fowler, 1945)	F:U	Christmas Darter^
Etheostoma inscriptum (Jordan & Brayton, 1878)	F:U	Turquoise Darter
Etheostoma jessiae (Jordan & Brayton, 1878)	F:U	Blueside Darter
Etheostoma jordani Gilbert, 1891	F:U	Greenbreast Darter
Etheostoma juliae Meek, 1891	F:U	Yoke Darter
Etheostoma kanawhae (Raney, 1941)	F:U	Kanawha Darter^
Etheostoma kantuckeense Ceas & Page, 1997	F:U	Highland Rim Darter^
Etheostoma kennicotti (Putnam, 1863)	F:U	Stripetail Darter
Etheostoma lachneri Suttkus & Bailey, 1994	F:U	Tombigbee Darter^
Etheostoma lawrencei Ceas & Burr, 2002	F:U	Headwater Darter
*Etheostoma lemniscatum Blanton, 2008	F:U	Tuxedo Darter
Etheostoma lepidum (Baird & Girard, 1853)	F:U	Greenthroat Darter
Etheostoma longimanum Jordan, 1888	F:U	Longfin Darter
Etheostoma lugoi Norris & Minckley, 1997	F:M	Tufa Darter............perca de toba
Etheostoma luteovinctum Gilbert & Swain, 1887	F:U	Redband Darter
Etheostoma lynceum Hay, 1885	F:U	Brighteye Darter
Etheostoma maculatum Kirtland, 1840	F:U	Spotted Darter
Etheostoma mariae (Fowler, 1947)	F:U	Pinewoods Darter
*Etheostoma marmorpinnum Blanton & Jenkins, 2008	F:U	Marbled Darter
*Etheostoma maydeni Powers & Kuhajda, 2012	F:U	Redlips Darter
Etheostoma microlepidum Raney & Zorach, 1967	F:U	Smallscale Darter
Etheostoma microperca Jordan & Gilbert, 1888	F:CU	Least Darter............petit dard
*Etheostoma mihileze Mayden, 2010	F:U	Sunburst Darter
Etheostoma moorei Raney & Suttkus, 1964	F:U	Yellowcheek Darter
Etheostoma neopterum Howell & Dingerkus, 1978	F:U	Lollypop Darter
Etheostoma nianguae Gilbert & Meek, 1887	F:U	Niangua Darter^
Etheostoma nigripinne Braasch & Mayden, 1985	F:U	Blackfin Darter
+Etheostoma nigrum Rafinesque, 1820	F:CU	Johnny Darter............raseux-de-terre noir
Etheostoma nuchale Howell & Caldwell, 1965	F:U	Watercress Darter
Etheostoma obeyense Kirsch, 1892	F:U	Barcheek Darter

SCIENTIFIC NAME	OCCURRENCE[1]	COMMON NAME (ENGLISH, SPANISH, FRENCH)[2]
*Etheostoma occidentale Powers & Mayden, 2007	F:U	Westrim Darter
Etheostoma okaloosae (Fowler, 1941)	F:U	Okaloosa Darter^
Etheostoma olivaceum Braasch & Page, 1979	F:U	Sooty Darter
Etheostoma olmstedi Storer, 1842	F:CU	Tessellated Darter .... raseux-de-terre gris
Etheostoma oophylax Ceas & Page, 1992	F:U	Guardian Darter
*Etheostoma orientale Powers & Mayden, 2007	F:U	Eastrim Darter
Etheostoma osburni (Hubbs & Trautman, 1932)	F:U	Candy Darter
Etheostoma pallididorsum Distler & Metcalf, 1962	F:U	Paleback Darter
Etheostoma parvipinne Gilbert & Swain, 1887	F:U	Goldstripe Darter
+Etheostoma percnurum Jenkins, 1994	F:U	Duskytail Darter
Etheostoma perlongum (Hubbs & Raney, 1946)	F:U	Waccamaw Darter^
Etheostoma phytophilum Bart & Taylor, 1999	F:U	Rush Darter
*Etheostoma planasaxatile Powers & Mayden, 2007	F:U	Duck Darter^
Etheostoma podostemone Jordan & Jenkins, 1889	F:U	Riverweed Darter
Etheostoma potsii (Girard, 1859)	F:M	Mexican Darter^ .... perca mexicana
Etheostoma proeliare (Hay, 1881)	F:U	Cypress Darter
Etheostoma pseudovulatum Page & Ceas, 1992	F:U	Egg-mimic Darter
+Etheostoma punctulatum (Agassiz, 1854)	F:U	Stippled Darter
Etheostoma pyrrhogaster Bailey & Etnier, 1988	F:U	Firebelly Darter
Etheostoma radiosum (Hubbs & Black, 1941)	F:U	Orangebelly Darter
Etheostoma rafinesquei Burr & Page, 1982	F:U	Kentucky Darter^
Etheostoma ramseyi Suttkus & Bailey, 1994	F:U	Alabama Darter^
Etheostoma raneyi Suttkus & Bart, 1994	F:U	Yazoo Darter^
Etheostoma rubrum Raney & Suttkus, 1966	F:U	Bayou Darter
Etheostoma rufilineatum (Cope, 1870)	F:U	Redline Darter
Etheostoma rupestre Gilbert & Swain, 1887	F:CU	Rock Darter
Etheostoma sagitta (Jordan & Swain, 1883)	F:U	Arrow Darter
Etheostoma sanguifluum (Cope, 1870)	F:U	Bloodfin Darter
Etheostoma scotti Bauer, Etnier & Burkhead, 1995	F:U	Cherokee Darter^
Etheostoma segrex Norris & Minckley, 1997	F:M	Salado Darter^ .... perca del Salado
Etheostoma sellare (Radcliffe & Welsh, 1913)	F[X]:U	Maryland Darter^
Etheostoma serrifer (Hubbs & Cannon, 1935)	F:U	Sawcheek Darter
+Etheostoma simoterum (Cope, 1868)	F:U	Snubnose Darter

SCIENTIFIC NAME	OCCURRENCE[1]	COMMON NAME (ENGLISH, SPANISH, FRENCH)[2]
*Etheostoma sitikuense Blanton, 2008	F:U	Citico Darter^
Etheostoma smithi Page & Braasch, 1976	F:U	Slabrock Darter
Etheostoma spectabile (Agassiz, 1854)	F:U	Orangethroat Darter
Etheostoma squamiceps Jordan, 1877	F:U	Spottail Darter
+Etheostoma stigmaeum (Jordan, 1877)	F:U	Speckled Darter
+Etheostoma striatulum Page & Braasch, 1977	F:U	Striated Darter
+Etheostoma susanae (Jordan & Swain, 1883)	F:U	Cumberland Darter^
Etheostoma swaini (Jordan, 1884)	F:U	Gulf Darter^
Etheostoma swannanoa Jordan & Evermann, 1889	F:U	Swannanoa Darter^
Etheostoma tallapoosae Suttkus & Etnier, 1991	F:U	Tallapoosa Darter^
Etheostoma tecumsehi Ceas & Page, 1997	F:U	Shawnee Darter^
*Etheostoma tennesseense Powers & Mayden, 2007	F:U	Tennessee Darter^
+Etheostoma tetrazonum (Hubbs & Black, 1940)	F:U	Missouri Saddled Darter^
Etheostoma thalassinum (Jordan & Brayton, 1878)	F:U	Seagreen Darter
Etheostoma tippecanoe Jordan & Evermann, 1890	F:U	Tippecanoe Darter^
Etheostoma trisella Bailey & Richards, 1963	F:U	Trispot Darter
Etheostoma tuscumbia Gilbert & Swain, 1887	F:U	Tuscumbia Darter^
Etheostoma uniporum Distler, 1968	F:U	Current Darter
Etheostoma variatum Kirtland, 1840	F:U	Variegate Darter
Etheostoma virgatum (Jordan, 1880)	F:U	Striped Darter
Etheostoma vitreum (Cope, 1870)	F:U	Glassy Darter
Etheostoma vulneratum (Cope, 1870)	F:U	Wounded Darter
Etheostoma wapiti Etnier & Williams, 1989	F:U	Boulder Darter
Etheostoma whipplei (Girard, 1859)	F:U	Redfin Darter
Etheostoma zonale (Cope, 1868)	F:U	Banded Darter
Etheostoma zonifer (Hubbs & Cannon, 1935)	F:U	Backwater Darter
Etheostoma zonistium Bailey & Etnier, 1988	F:U	Bandfin Darter
*Gymnocephalus cernua (Linnaeus, 1758)	F[I]:CU	Ruffe......grémille
Perca flavescens (Mitchill, 1814)	F:CU	Yellow Perch......perchaude
Percina antesella Williams & Etnier, 1977	F:U	Amber Darter
*Percina apristis (Hubbs & Hubbs, 1954)	F:U	Guadalupe Darter^
Percina aurantiaca (Cope, 1868)	F:U	Tangerine Darter
Percina aurolineata Suttkus & Ramsey, 1967	F:U	Goldline Darter

SCIENTIFIC NAME	OCCURRENCE[1]	COMMON NAME (ENGLISH, SPANISH, FRENCH)[2]
Percina aurora Suttkus & Thompson, 1994	F:U	Pearl Darter
Percina austroperca Thompson, 1995	F:U	Southern Logperch
*Percina bimaculata Haldeman, 1844	F:U	Chesapeake Logperch^
Percina brevicauda Suttkus & Bart, 1994	F:U	Coal Darter
Percina burtoni Fowler, 1945	F:U	Blotchside Logperch
+Percina caprodes (Rafinesque, 1818)	F:CU	Logperch ... fouille-roche zébré
Percina carbonaria (Baird & Girard, 1853)	F:U	Texas Logperch^
Percina copelandi (Jordan, 1877)	F:CU	Channel Darter ... fouille-roche gris
Percina crassa (Jordan & Brayton, 1878)	F:U	Piedmont Darter^
*Percina crypta Freeman, Freeman & Burkhead, 2008	F:U	Halloween Darter^
Percina cymatotaenia (Gilbert & Meek, 1887)	F:U	Bluestripe Darter
Percina evides (Jordan & Copeland, 1877)	F:U	Gilt Darter
Percina gymnocephala Beckham, 1980	F:U	Appalachia Darter^
Percina jenkinsi Thompson, 1985	F:U	Conasauga Logperch^
Percina kathae Thompson, 1997	F:U	Mobile Logperch^
*Percina kusha Williams & Burkhead, 2007	F:U	Bridled Darter
Percina lenticula Richards & Knapp, 1964	F:U	Freckled Darter
+Percina macrocephala (Cope, 1867)	F:U	Longhead Darter
Percina macrolepida Stevenson, 1971	F:UM	Bigscale Logperch ... perca escamona
Percina maculata (Girard, 1859)	F:CU	Blackside Darter ... dard noir
Percina nasuta (Bailey, 1941)	F:U	Longnose Darter
Percina nevisense (Cope, 1870)	F:U	Chainback Darter
Percina nigrofasciata (Agassiz, 1854)	F:U	Blackbanded Darter
Percina notogramma (Raney & Hubbs, 1948)	F:U	Stripeback Darter
*Percina oxyrhynchus (Hubbs & Raney, 1939)	F:U	Sharpnose Darter
Percina palmaris (Bailey, 1940)	F:U	Bronze Darter
Percina pantherina (Moore & Reeves, 1955)	F:U	Leopard Darter
Percina peltata (Stauffer, 1864)	F:U	Shield Darter
Percina phoxocephala (Nelson, 1876)	F:U	Slenderhead Darter
Percina rex (Jordan & Evermann, 1889)	F:U	Roanoke Logperch^
Percina roanoka (Jordan & Jenkins, 1889)	F:U	Roanoke Darter^
+Percina sciera (Swain, 1883)	F:U	Dusky Darter

SCIENTIFIC NAME	OCCURRENCE[1]	COMMON NAME (ENGLISH, SPANISH, FRENCH)[2]
Percina shumardi (Girard, 1859)	F:CU	River Darter
*Percina sipsi Williams & Neely, 2007	F:U	Bankhead Darter^
**Percina smithvanizi* Williams & Walsh, 2007	F:U	Muscadine Darter^
Percina squamata (Gilbert & Swain, 1887)	F:U	Olive Darter
Percina stictogaster Burr & Page, 1993	F:U	Frecklebelly Darter
Percina suttkusi Thompson, 1997	F:U	Gulf Logperch^
Percina tanasi Etnier, 1976	F:U	Snail Darter
Percina uranidea (Jordan & Gilbert, 1887)	F:U	Stargazing Darter
Percina vigil (Hay, 1882)	F:U	Saddleback Darter
**Percina williamsi* Page & Near, 2007	F:U	Sickle Darter
Sander canadensis (Griffith & Smith, 1834)	F:CU	Sauger ... doré noir
Sander lucioperca (Linnaeus, 1758)	F[I]:U	Zander
Sander vitreus (Mitchill, 1818)	F:CU	Walleye ... doré jaune

Priacanthidae—En-bigeyes, Sp-catalufas, Fr-beauclaires

**Cookeolus japonicus* (Cuvier, 1829)	A-PM	Bulleye ... catalufa aleta larga
Heteropriacanthus cruentatus (Lacepède, 1801)	A-PM	Glasseye Snapper ... catalufa roquera
Priacanthus alalaua Jordan & Evermann, 1903	PM	Hawaiian Bigeye^ ... catalufa alalahua
**Priacanthus arenatus* Cuvier, 1829	A	Bigeye ... catalufa ojona ... priacanthe sablé
Pristigenys alta (Gill, 1862)	A	Short Bigeye ... catalufa de lo alto
Pristigenys serrula (Gilbert, 1891)	P	Popeye Catalufa ... catalufa semáforo

Apogonidae—En-cardinalfishes, Sp-cardenales, Fr-poissons-cardinaux

Apogon affinis (Poey, 1875)	A	Bigtooth Cardinalfish ... cardenal dientón
Apogon atricaudus Jordan & McGregor, 1898	PM	Plain Cardinalfish ... cardenal sencillo
Apogon aurolineatus (Mowbray, 1927)	A	Bridle Cardinalfish ... cardenal frenado
Apogon binotatus (Poey, 1867)	A	Barred Cardinalfish ... cardenal rayado
*Apogon dovii Günther, 1862	PM	Tailspot Cardinalfish ... cardenal colimanchada
Apogon evermanni Jordan & Snyder, 1904	AM	Oddscale Cardinalfish ... cardenal coralero
*Apogon gouldi Smith-Vaniz, 1977	A	Deepwater Cardinalfish ... cardenal de lo alto
Apogon guadalupensis (Osburn & Nichols, 1916)	P	Guadalupe Cardinalfish^ ... cardenal mexicano

SCIENTIFIC NAME	OCCURRENCE[1]	COMMON NAME (ENGLISH, SPANISH, FRENCH)[2]
Apogon lachneri Böhlke, 1959	A	Whitestar Cardinalfish........cardenal estrella blanca
Apogon leptocaulus Gilbert, 1972	A	Slendertail Cardinalfish
Apogon maculatus (Poey, 1860)	A	Flamefish........cardenal manchado
Apogon pacificus (Herre, 1935)	P	Pink Cardinalfish........cardenal morro listado
Apogon phenax Böhlke & Randall, 1968	A	Mimic Cardinalfish........cardenal mimético
Apogon pillionatus Böhlke & Randall, 1968	A	Broadsaddle Cardinalfish........cardenal colirrayada
Apogon planifrons Longley & Hildebrand, 1940	A	Pale Cardinalfish........cardenal pálido
Apogon pseudomaculatus Longley, 1932	A	Twospot Cardinalfish........cardenal dos puntos
Apogon quadrisquamatus Longley, 1934	A	Sawcheek Cardinalfish........cardenal espinoso
Apogon retrosella (Gill, 1862)	PM	Barspot Cardinalfish........cardenal de Cortés
Apogon townsendi (Breder, 1927)	A	Belted Cardinalfish........cardenal cincho
Astrapogon alutus (Jordan & Gilbert, 1882)	A	Bronze Cardinalfish........cardenal bronceado
Astrapogon puncticulatus (Poey, 1867)	A	Blackfin Cardinalfish........cardenal punteado
Astrapogon stellatus (Cope, 1867)	A	Conchfish........cardenal del cobo
Phaeoptyx conklini (Silvester, 1915)	A	Freckled Cardinalfish........cardenal pecoso
Phaeoptyx pigmentaria (Poey, 1860)	A	Dusky Cardinalfish........cardenal prieto
Phaeoptyx xenus (Böhlke & Randall, 1968)	A	Sponge Cardinalfish........cardenal esponjero

Malacanthidae—En-tilefishes, Sp-blanquillos, Fr-tiles

Caulolatilus affinis Gill, 1865	P	Pacific Golden-eyed Tilefish^........conejo
Caulolatilus chrysops (Valenciennes, 1833)	A	Goldface Tilefish........blanquillo ojo amarillo
Caulolatilus cyanops Poey, 1866	A	Blackline Tilefish........domingo
Caulolatilus intermedius Howell Rivero, 1936	A	Anchor Tilefish........blanquillo payaso
Caulolatilus microps Goode & Bean, 1878	A	Blueline Tilefish........blanquillo lucio
+*Caulolatilus princeps* (Jenyns, 1840)	P	Ocean Whitefish........pierna........tile océanique
Lopholatilus chamaeleonticeps Goode & Bean, 1879	A	Tilefish........conejo amarillo........tile
Malacanthus plumieri (Bloch, 1786)	A	Sand Tilefish........matajuelo blanco

Pomatomidae—En-bluefishes, Sp-anjovas, Fr-tassergals

Pomatomus saltatrix (Linnaeus, 1766)	A	Bluefish........anjova........tassergal

SCIENTIFIC NAME	OCCURRENCE[1]	COMMON NAME (ENGLISH, SPANISH, FRENCH)[2]
Nematistiidae—En-roosterfishes, Sp-papagallos, Fr-plumières		
Nematistius pectoralis Gill, 1862	P	Roosterfish ... papagallo
+Carangidae—En-jacks, Sp-jureles y pámpanos, Fr-carangues		
Alectis ciliaris (Bloch, 1787)	A-PM	African Pompano^ ... pámpano de hebra
*Carangoides orthogrammus (Jordan & Gilbert, 1882)	PM	Island Jack ... jurel isleño
Caranx bartholomaei Cuvier, 1833	A	Yellow Jack ... cojinuda amarilla
Caranx caballus Günther, 1868	P	Green Jack ... jurel bonito
Caranx caninus Günther, 1867	P	Pacific Crevalle Jack^ ... jurel toro
Caranx crysos (Mitchill, 1815)	A	Blue Runner ... cojinuda negra ... carangue jaune
Caranx hippos (Linnaeus, 1766)	A	Crevalle Jack ... jurel común
Caranx latus Agassiz, 1831	A	Horse-eye Jack ... jurel blanco
Caranx lugubris Poey, 1860	A-PM	Black Jack ... jurel negro
Caranx melampygus Cuvier, 1833	PM	Bluefin Trevally ... jurel aleta azul
Caranx otrynter Jordan & Gilbert, 1883	PM	Threadfin Jack ... jurel chicuaca
Caranx ruber (Bloch, 1793)	A	Bar Jack ... cojinuda carbonera
Caranx sexfasciatus Quoy & Gaimard, 1825	P	Bigeye Trevally ... jurel voraz
Caranx vinctus Jordan & Gilbert, 1882	P	Cocinero ... cocinero
Chloroscombrus chrysurus (Linnaeus, 1766)	A	Atlantic Bumper^ ... horqueta del Atlántico
Chloroscombrus orqueta Jordan & Gilbert, 1883	P	Pacific Bumper^ ... horqueta del Pacífico
Decapterus macarellus (Cuvier, 1833)	A-PM	Mackerel Scad ... macarela caballa ... décaptère faux-maquereau
Decapterus macrosoma Bleeker, 1851	PM	Shortfin Scad ... macarela alicorta
Decapterus muroadsi (Temminck & Schlegel, 1844)	P	Amberstripe Scad ... macarela plátano
Decapterus punctatus (Cuvier, 1829)	A	Round Scad ... macarela chuparaco ... comète quiaquia
Decapterus tabl Berry, 1968	A	Redtail Scad ... macarela salmón
Elagatis bipinnulata (Quoy & Gaimard, 1825)	A-PM	Rainbow Runner ... jurel dorado
Gnathanodon speciosus (Forsskål, 1775)	PM	Golden Trevally ... jurelito chato
Hemicaranx amblyrhynchus (Cuvier, 1833)	A	Bluntnose Jack ... jurelito aletiamarilla
Hemicaranx leucurus (Günther, 1864)	PM	Yellowfin Jack ... jurelito chocho
Hemicaranx zelotes Gilbert, 1898	PM	Blackfin Jack ... pez piloto
Naucrates ductor (Linnaeus, 1758)	A-P	Pilotfish ... poisson pilote

SCIENTIFIC NAME	OCCURRENCE[1]	COMMON NAME (ENGLISH, SPANISH, FRENCH)[2]
Oligoplites altus (Günther, 1868)	PM	Longjaw Leatherjack....piña bocona
Oligoplites refulgens Gilbert & Starks, 1904	PM	Shortjaw Leatherjack....piña flaca
Oligoplites saurus (Bloch & Schneider, 1801)	A-PM	Leatherjack....piña sietecueros
Pseudocaranx dentex (Bloch & Schneider, 1801)	A	White Trevally
Selar crumenophthalmus (Bloch, 1793)	A-PM	Bigeye Scad....charrito ojón....sélar à grandes paupières
Selene brevoortii (Gill, 1863)	P	Mexican Lookdown^....jorobado mexicano
Selene brownii (Cuvier, 1816)	AM	Caribbean Moonfish^....jorobado luna
Selene orstedii Lütken, 1880	PM	Mexican Moonfish^....jorobado carite
Selene peruviana (Guichenot, 1866)	P	Pacific Moonfish^....jorobado papelillo
Selene setapinnis (Mitchill, 1815)	A	Atlantic Moonfish^....jorobado caballa....musso atlantique
Selene vomer (Linnaeus, 1758)	A	Lookdown....jorobado penacho
Seriola dumerili (Risso, 1810)	A	Greater Amberjack....medregal coronado....sériole
Seriola fasciata (Bloch, 1793)	A	Lesser Amberjack....medregal listado
Seriola lalandi Valenciennes, 1833	P	Yellowtail Jack....medregal rabo amarillo....sériole à queue jaune
Seriola peruana Steindachner, 1881	PM	Fortune Jack....medregal fortuno
Seriola rivoliana Valenciennes, 1833	A-P	Almaco Jack....medregal limón
Seriola zonata (Mitchill, 1815)	A	Banded Rudderfish....medregal rayado....sériole à ceintures
Trachinotus carolinus (Linnaeus, 1766)	A	Florida Pompano^....pámpano amarillo
Trachinotus falcatus (Linnaeus, 1758)	A	Permit....pámpano palometa
Trachinotus goodei Jordan & Evermann, 1896	A	Palometa....pámpano listado
Trachinotus kennedyi Steindachner, 1876	PM	Blackblotch Pompano....pámpano gitano
Trachinotus paitensis Cuvier, 1832	P	Paloma Pompano....pámpano paloma
Trachinotus rhodopus Gill, 1863	P	Gafftopsail Pompano....pámpano fino
Trachinotus stilbe (Jordan & MacGregor, 1898)	PM	Steel Pompano....pámpano acerado
Trachurus lathami Nichols, 1920	A	Rough Scad....charrito garretón
Trachurus symmetricus (Ayres, 1855)	P	Jack Mackerel....charrito chícharo....saurel maxécus
Uraspis helvola (Forster, 1801)	PM	Whitemouth Jack....jurel lengua blanca....carangue symétrique
Uraspis secunda (Poey, 1860)	A-P	Cottonmouth Jack....jurel volantín

Rachycentridae—En-cobias, Sp-cobias, Fr-cobilos

Rachycentron canadum (Linnaeus, 1766)	A	Cobia....cobia

SCIENTIFIC NAME	OCCURRENCE[1]	COMMON NAME (ENGLISH, SPANISH, FRENCH)[2]
+Coryphaenidae—En-dolphinfishes, Sp-dorados, Fr-coryphènes		
Coryphaena equiselis Linnaeus, 1758	A-PM	Pompano Dolphinfish........dorado enano
Coryphaena hippurus Linnaeus, 1758	A-P	Dolphinfish........dorado........coryphène commune
Echeneidae—En-remoras, Sp-rémoras, Fr-rémoras		
Echeneis naucrates Linnaeus, 1758	A-P	Sharksucker........rémora rayada........naucrate
Echeneis neucratoides Zuiew, 1786	A	Whitefin Sharksucker........rémora filoblanco
Phtheirichthys lineatus (Menzies, 1791)	A-P	Slender Suckerfish........rémora delgada
+Remora albescens (Temminck & Schlegel, 1850)	A-P	White Suckerfish........rémora blanca
Remora australis (Bennett, 1840)	A-P	Whalesucker........rémora ballenera
Remora brachyptera (Lowe, 1839)	A-P	Spearfish Remora........rémora robusta........rémora brun
Remora osteochir (Cuvier, 1829)	A-P	Marlinsucker........rémora marlinera
Remora remora (Linnaeus, 1758)	A-P	Remora........rémora tiburonera........rémora noir
Bramidae—En-pomfrets, Sp-tristones, Fr-castagnoles		
Brama brama (Bonnaterre, 1788)	A	Atlantic Pomfret^........grande castagnole
Brama caribbea Mead, 1972	A	Caribbean Pomfret^........tristón del Caribe
Brama dussumieri Cuvier, 1831	A	Lowfin Pomfret
Brama japonica Hilgendorf, 1878	P	Pacific Pomfret^........tristón del Pacifico........castagnole mince
Brama orcini Cuvier, 1831	P	Bigtooth Pomfret
Pteraclis aesticola (Jordan & Snyder, 1901)	P	Pacific Fanfish^........abanico del Pacifico
Pterycombus brama Fries, 1837	A	Atlantic Fanfish^........poisson-écaille atlantique
Taractes asper Lowe, 1843	P	Rough Pomfret........castagnole rugueuse
Taractes rubescens (Jordan & Evermann, 1887)	A	Keeltail Pomfret........tristón coliquillada
Taractichthys longipinnis (Lowe, 1843)	A	Bigscale Pomfret........tristón aletudo........castagnole fauchoir
Taractichthys steindachneri (Döderlein, 1884)	P	Sickle Pomfret........tristón segador
Emmelichthyidae—En-rovers, Sp-andorreros, Fr-poissons-rubis		
Emmelichthys ruber (Trunov, 1976)	A	Red Rover
Erythrocles monodi Poll & Cadenat, 1954	A	Crimson Rover
Lutjanidae—En-snappers, Sp-pargos y huachinangos, Fr-vivaneaux		
Apsilus dentatus Guichenot, 1853	A	Black Snapper........pargo lamparita

SCIENTIFIC NAME	OCCURRENCE[1]	COMMON NAME (ENGLISH, SPANISH, FRENCH)[2]
Etelis oculatus (Valenciennes, 1828)	A	Queen Snapper...pargo cachucho
Hoplopagrus guentherii Gill, 1862	PM	Barred Pargo...pargo coconaco
Lutjanus analis (Cuvier, 1828)	A	Mutton Snapper...pargo criollo
Lutjanus apodus (Walbaum, 1792)	A	Schoolmaster...pargo canchix
Lutjanus aratus (Günther, 1864)	PM	Mullet Snapper...pargo raicero
Lutjanus argentiventris (Peters, 1869)	P	Amarillo Snapper...pargo amarillo
Lutjanus buccanella (Cuvier, 1828)	A	Blackfin Snapper...pargo sesí
Lutjanus campechanus (Poey, 1860)	A	Red Snapper...huachinango del Golfo
Lutjanus colorado Jordan & Gilbert, 1882	P	Colorado Snapper...pargo colorado
Lutjanus cyanopterus (Cuvier, 1828)	A	Cubera Snapper...pargo cubera...vivaneau cubéra
Lutjanus griseus (Linnaeus, 1758)	A-F:UM	Gray Snapper...pargo mulato
Lutjanus guttatus (Steindachner, 1869)	PM	Spotted Rose Snapper...pargo flamenco
Lutjanus inermis (Peters, 1869)	PM	Golden Snapper...pargo rabirrubia
Lutjanus jocu (Bloch & Schneider, 1801)	A	Dog Snapper...pargo caballera
Lutjanus jordani (Gilbert, 1898)	PM	Whipper Snapper...pargo colmillón
Lutjanus mahogoni (Cuvier, 1828)	A	Mahogany Snapper...pargo ojón
Lutjanus novemfasciatus Gill, 1862	P	Pacific Dog Snapper^...pargo prieto
Lutjanus peru (Nichols & Murphy, 1922)	P	Pacific Red Snapper^...huachinango del Pacífico
Lutjanus purpureus (Poey, 1866)	A	Caribbean Red Snapper^...pargo rojo
Lutjanus synagris (Linnaeus, 1758)	A	Lane Snapper...pargo biajaiba
Lutjanus viridis (Valenciennes, 1846)	PM	Blue-and-gold Snapper...pargo azul-dorado
Lutjanus vivanus (Cuvier, 1828)	A	Silk Snapper...huachinango ojo amarillo
Ocyurus chrysurus (Bloch, 1791)	A	Yellowtail Snapper...rubia
Pristipomoides aquilonaris (Goode & Bean, 1896)	A	Wenchman...huachinango navaja
Pristipomoides freemani Anderson, 1966	A	Slender Wenchman
Pristipomoides macrophthalmus (Müller & Troschel, 1848)	AM	Cardinal Snapper...pargo panchito
Rhomboplites aurorubens (Cuvier, 1829)	A	Vermilion Snapper...besugo

Lobotidae—En-tripletails, Sp-dormilonas, Fr-croupias

Lobotes pacificus Gilbert, 1898	P	Pacific Tripletail^...dormilona del Pacífico
Lobotes surinamensis (Bloch, 1790)	A	Atlantic Tripletail^...dormilona del Atlántico...croupia roche

SCIENTIFIC NAME	OCCURRENCE[1]	COMMON NAME (ENGLISH, SPANISH, FRENCH)[2]	
Gerreidae—En-mojarras, Sp-mojarras, Fr-blanches			
Diapterus auratus Ranzani, 1842	A-F:UM	Irish Pompano^	mojarra guacha
Diapterus aureolus (Jordan & Gilbert, 1882)	PM	Golden Mojarra	mojarra palometa
*Diapterus brevirostris (Sauvage, 1879)	PM-F:M	Shortnose Mojarra	mojarra aletas amarillas
*Diapterus rhombeus (Cuvier, 1829)	A-F:M	Rhombic Mojarra	mojarra de estero
Eucinostomus argenteus Baird & Girard, 1855	A-F:M	Spotfin Mojarra	mojarra plateada
Eucinostomus currani Zahuranec, 1980	P-F:M	Pacific Flagfin Mojarra^	mojarra tricolor
Eucinostomus dowii (Gill, 1863)	P	Pacific Spotfin Mojarra^	mojarra manchita
Eucinostomus entomelas Zahuranec, 1980	PM	Darkspot Mojarra	mojarra mancha negra
Eucinostomus gracilis (Gill, 1862)	PM	Graceful Mojarra	mojarra charrita
Eucinostomus gula (Quoy & Gaimard, 1824)	A	Silver Jenny	mojarra española
Eucinostomus harengulus Goode & Bean, 1879	A-F:UM	Tidewater Mojarra	mojarra costera
Eucinostomus havana (Nichols, 1912)	A	Bigeye Mojarra	mojarra cubana
Eucinostomus jonesii (Günther, 1879)	A	Slender Mojarra	mojarra flaca
Eucinostomus lefroyi (Goode, 1874)	A	Mottled Mojarra	mojarra pinta
Eucinostomus melanopterus (Bleeker, 1863)	A-F:M	Flagfin Mojarra	mojarra de ley
*Eugerres awlae Schultz, 1949	AM-F:M	Maracaibo Mojarra	mojarra del Maracaibo
Eugerres axillaris (Günther, 1864)	PM-F:M	Black Axillary Mojarra	mojarra malacapa
+Eugerres brasilianus (Cuvier, 1830))	AM	Brazilian Mojarra^	mojarra brasileña
Eugerres brevimanus (Günther, 1864)	PM	Shortfin Mojarra	mojarra aleta corta
Eugerres lineatus (Humboldt, 1821)	PM-F:M	Streaked Mojarra	mojarra china
Eugerres mexicanus (Steindachner, 1863)	F:M	Mexican Mojarra^	mojarra mexicana
+Eugerres plumieri (Cuvier, 1830)	A-F:UM	Striped Mojarra	mojarra rayada
Gerres cinereus (Walbaum, 1792)	A-PM-F:M	Yellowfin Mojarra	mojarra trompetera
+Haemulidae—En-grunts, Sp-burros y roncos, Fr-grogneurs			
Anisotremus caesius (Jordan & Gilbert, 1882)	PM	Silvergray Grunt	burro mojarro
Anisotremus davidsonii (Steindachner, 1876)	P	Sargo	sargo rayado
Anisotremus interruptus (Gill, 1862)	PM	Burrito Grunt	burro bacoco
Anisotremus surinamensis (Bloch, 1791)	A	Black Margate	burriquete
Anisotremus taeniatus Gill, 1861	PM	Panamic Porkfish^	burro bandera
Anisotremus virginicus (Linnaeus, 1758)	A	Porkfish	burro payaso
Conodon nobilis (Linnaeus, 1758)	A	Barred Grunt	ronco canario

SCIENTIFIC NAME	OCCURRENCE[1]	COMMON NAME (ENGLISH, SPANISH, FRENCH)[2]
Conodon serrifer Jordan & Gilbert, 1882	P	Armed Grunt...ronco ofensivo
*Emmelichthyops atlanticus Schultz, 1945	A	Bonnetmouth
*Genyatremus dovii (Günther, 1864)	PM	Blackbarred Grunt...burro rompepaila
*Genyatremus pacifici (Günther, 1864)	PM	Carruco Grunt...burro carruco
*Haemulon album Cuvier, 1830	A	Margate...ronco jallao
*Haemulon aurolineatum Cuvier, 1830	A	Tomtate...ronco jeníguaro
*Haemulon bonariense Cuvier, 1830	AM	Black Grunt...ronco prieto
*Haemulon californiensis (Steindachner, 1876)	P	Salema...salema
*Haemulon carbonarium Poey, 1860	A	Caesar Grunt...ronco carbonero
*Haemulon chrysargyreum Günther, 1859	A	Smallmouth Grunt...ronco boquichica
*Haemulon flaviguttatum Gill, 1862	P	Cortez Grunt^...burro de Cortés
*Haemulon flavolineatum (Desmarest, 1823)	A	French Grunt^...ronco condenado
*Haemulon macrostomum Günther, 1859	A	Spanish Grunt^...ronco español
*Haemulon maculicauda (Gill, 1862)	PM	Spottail Grunt...burro rasposo
*Haemulon melanurum (Linnaeus, 1758)	A	Cottonwick...ronco lomo manchado
*Haemulon parra (Desmarest, 1823)	A	Sailors Choice...boquilla
*Haemulon plumierii (Lacepède, 1801)	A	White Grunt...chac-chí
*Haemulon sciurus (Shaw, 1803)	A	Bluestriped Grunt...ronco carite
*Haemulon scudderii Gill, 1862	PM	Mojarra Grunt...burro pecoso
*Haemulon sexfasciatum Gill, 1862	PM	Graybar Grunt...burro almejero
*Haemulon steindachneri (Jordan & Gilbert, 1882)	PM	Latin Grunt^...burro latino
*Haemulon striatum (Linnaeus, 1758)	A	Striped Grunt...ronco pinto
*Haemulon vittatum (Poey, 1860)	A	Boga
*Haemulopsis axillaris (Steindachner, 1869)	PM	Yellowstripe Grunt...ronco callana
*Haemulopsis elongatus (Steindachner, 1879)	PM	Elongate Grunt...ronco alargado
*Haemulopsis leuciscus (Günther, 1864)	PM	Raucous Grunt...ronco ruco
*Haemulopsis nitidus (Steindachner, 1869)	PM	Shining Grunt...ronco brillante
*Microlepidotus brevipinnis (Steindachner, 1869)	PM	Brassy Grunt...ronco bronceado
*Microlepidotus inornatus Gill, 1862	P	Wavyline Grunt...ronco rayadillo
*Orthopristis cantharinus (Jenyns, 1840)	PM	Sheephead Grunt...teniente
*Orthopristis chalceus (Günther, 1864)	PM	Humpback Grunt...burrito corcovado
*Orthopristis chrysoptera (Linnaeus, 1766)	A-F:UM	Pigfish...corocoro armado
*Orthopristis reddingi Jordan & Richardson, 1895	PM	Bronzestriped Grunt...burrito rayado

SCIENTIFIC NAME	OCCURRENCE[1]	COMMON NAME (ENGLISH, SPANISH, FRENCH)[2]
Pomadasys bayanus Jordan & Evermann, 1898	PM-F:M	Purplemouth Grunt........roncacho boquimorado
Pomadasys branickii (Steindachner, 1879)	PM	Sand Grunt........roncacho arenero
Pomadasys crocro (Cuvier, 1830)	A-F:M	Burro Grunt........corocoro crocro
Pomadasys macracanthus (Günther, 1864)	PM	Longspine Grunt........roncacho gordo
Pomadasys panamensis (Steindachner, 1876)	PM	Panamic Grunt^........roncacho mapache
Pomadasys ramosus (Poey, 1860)	AM-F:M	Western Atlantic Grunt^........roncacho caribeño
Xenichthys xanti Gill, 1863	PM	Longfin Salema........chula
Sparidae—En-porgies, Sp-plumas, Fr-dorades		
Archosargus probatocephalus (Walbaum, 1792)	A-F:UM	Sheepshead........sargo chopa........spare tête-de-mouton
Archosargus rhomboidalis (Linnaeus, 1758)	A	Sea Bream........sargo amarillo
Calamus arctifrons Goode & Bean, 1882	A	Grass Porgy
Calamus bajonado (Bloch & Schneider, 1801)	A	Jolthead Porgy........pluma
Calamus brachysomus (Lockington, 1880)	P	Pacific Porgy^........pluma marotilla
Calamus calamus (Valenciennes, 1830)	A	Saucereye Porgy........pluma calamo
Calamus campechanus Randall & Caldwell, 1966	AM	Campeche Porgy^........pluma campechana
Calamus leucosteus Jordan & Gilbert, 1885	A	Whitebone Porgy........pluma golfina
Calamus nodosus Randall & Caldwell, 1966	A	Knobbed Porgy........mojarrón pecoso
Calamus penna (Valenciennes, 1830)	A	Sheepshead Porgy........pluma manchada
Calamus pennatula Guichenot, 1868	AM	Pluma Porgy........pluma del Caribe
Calamus proridens Jordan & Gilbert, 1884	A	Littlehead Porgy........pluma jorobada
Diplodus argenteus (Valenciennes, 1830)	A	Silver Porgy........pluma plateada
Diplodus holbrookii (Bean, 1878)	A	Spottail Pinfish........sargo cotonero
Lagodon rhomboides (Linnaeus, 1766)	A-F:UM	Pinfish........xlavitia
Pagrus pagrus (Linnaeus, 1758)	A	Red Porgy........sargo rojo
Stenotomus caprinus Jordan & Gilbert, 1882	A	Longspine Porgy........sargo espinudo
Stenotomus chrysops (Linnaeus, 1766)	A	Scup........spare doré
Polynemidae—En-threadfins, Sp-barbudos, Fr-capitaines		
Polydactylus approximans (Lay & Bennett, 1839)	P	Blue Bobo........barbudo seis barbas
Polydactylus octonemus (Girard, 1858)	A	Atlantic Threadfin^........barbudo ocho barbas
Polydactylus oligodon (Günther, 1860)	A	Littlescale Threadfin........barbudo siete barbas

SCIENTIFIC NAME	OCCURRENCE[1]	COMMON NAME (ENGLISH, SPANISH, FRENCH)[2]
Polydactylus opercularis (Gill, 1863)	P	Yellow Bobo....barbudo nueve barbas
Polydactylus virginicus (Linnaeus, 1758)	A	Barbu....barbudo barbú
Sciaenidae—En-drums and croakers, Sp-corvinas y berrugatas, Fr-tambours		
Aplodinotus grunniens Rafinesque, 1819	F:CUM	Freshwater Drum....roncador de agua dulce....malachigan
Atractoscion nobilis (Ayres, 1860)	P	White Seabass....corvina cabaicucho....acoupa blanc
Bairdiella armata Gill, 1863	PM	Armed Croaker....ronco armado
Bairdiella chrysoura (Lacepède, 1802)	AM-F:UM	Silver Perch....ronco amarillo
Bairdiella ensifera (Jordan & Gilbert, 1882)	PM	Swordspine Croaker....ronco barbirrubia
*Bairdiella icistia (Jordan & Gilbert, 1882)	PM	Bairdiella....ronco roncacho
Bairdiella ronchus (Cuvier, 1830)	AM	Ground Croaker....ronco rayado
Cheilotrema saturnum (Girard, 1858)	P	Black Croaker....corvinata negra
*Corvula batabana (Poey, 1860)	A	Blue Croaker....ronco azul
Corvula macrops (Steindachner, 1876)	PM	Vacuoqua Croaker....corvineta vacuoqua
*Corvula sanctaeluciae Jordan, 1890	A	Striped Croaker....ronco caribeño
Cynoscion albus (Günther, 1864)	PM	Queen Corvina....corvina chiapaneca
Cynoscion arenarius Ginsburg, 1930	A	Sand Seatrout....corvina arenera
Cynoscion jamaicensis (Vaillant & Bocourt, 1883)	AM	Jamaica Weakfish^....corvina jamaica
Cynoscion nannus Castro-Aguirre & Arvizu-Martínez, 1976	PM	Dwarf Corvina....corvina enana
Cynoscion nebulosus (Cuvier, 1830)	A-F:U	Spotted Seatrout....corvina pinta
Cynoscion nothus (Holbrook, 1848)	A	Silver Seatrout....corvina plateada
Cynoscion othonopterus Jordan & Gilbert, 1882	PM	Gulf Corvina^....corvina golfina
Cynoscion parvipinnis Ayres, 1861	P	Shortfin Corvina....corvina aleta corta
Cynoscion phoxocephalus Jordan & Gilbert, 1882	PM	Sharpnose Corvina....corvina picuda
Cynoscion regalis (Bloch & Schneider, 1801)	A	Weakfish....acoupa royal
Cynoscion reticulatus (Günther, 1864)	PM	Striped Corvina....corvina rayada
Cynoscion squamipinnis (Günther, 1867)	PM	Scalyfin Corvina....corvina aguada
Cynoscion stolzmanni (Steindachner, 1879)	PM	Yellowtail Corvina....corvina coliamarilla
*Cynoscion xanthulus Jordan & Gilbert, 1882	PM	Orangemouth Corvina....corvina boquinaranja
Elattarchus archidium (Jordan & Gilbert, 1882)	PM	Bluestreak Drum....corvineta gallinita
Equetus lanceolatus (Linnaeus, 1758)	A	Jackknife-fish....payasito obispo

SCIENTIFIC NAME	OCCURRENCE[1]	COMMON NAME (ENGLISH, SPANISH, FRENCH)[2]
Equetus punctatus (Bloch & Schneider, 1801)	A	Spotted Drum....payasito punteado
Genyonemus lineatus (Ayres, 1855)	P	White Croaker....corvineta blanca.........tambour rayé
Isopisthus remifer Jordan & Gilbert, 1882	PM	Bigeye Corvina....corvina ojona
Larimus acclivis Jordan & Bristol, 1898	PM	Steeplined Drum....boquinete
Larimus argenteus (Gill, 1863)	PM	Silver Drum....boquinete chato
Larimus effulgens Gilbert, 1898	PM	Shining Drum....boquinete boca de novia
Larimus fasciatus Holbrook, 1855	A	Banded Drum....boquinete listado
Larimus pacificus Jordan & Bollman, 1890	PM	Pacific Drum^....boquinete del Pacífico
Leiostomus xanthurus Lacepède, 1802	A-F:UM	Spot....croca
Menticirrhus americanus (Linnaeus, 1758)	A	Southern Kingfish....berrugato zorro
Menticirrhus elongatus (Günther, 1864)	PM	Slender Kingfish....berrugato fino
Menticirrhus littoralis (Holbrook, 1847)	A	Gulf Kingfish^....berrugato del Golfo
Menticirrhus nasus (Günther, 1868)	PM	Highfin Kingfish^....berrugato real
Menticirrhus paitensis Hildebrand, 1946	PM	Paita Kingfish^....berrugato chulo
Menticirrhus panamensis (Steindachner, 1875)	PM	Panama Kingfish^....berrugato panameño
Menticirrhus saxatilis (Bloch & Schneider, 1801)	A	Northern Kingfish....berrugato ratón
Menticirrhus undulatus (Girard, 1854)	P	California Corbina^....berrugato californiano
Micropogonias altipinnis (Günther, 1864)	PM	Golden Croaker....chano sureño
Micropogonias ectenes (Jordan & Gilbert, 1882)	PM	Slender Croaker....chano mexicano
*Micropogonias furnieri (Desmarest, 1823)	A-F:U	Whitemouth Croaker
Micropogonias megalops (Gilbert, 1890)	PM	Gulf Croaker^....chano norteño
Micropogonias undulatus (Linnaeus, 1766)	A-F:UM	Atlantic Croaker^....gurrubata.........tambour brésilien
Nebris occidentalis Vaillant, 1897	PM	Pacific Smalleye Croaker^....corvina guavina
*Odontoscion dentex (Cuvier, 1830)	A	Reef Croaker....corvineta de roca
*Odontoscion xanthops Gilbert, 1898	PM	Yelloweye Croaker....corvineta ojiamarillo
*Ophioscion imiceps (Jordan & Gilbert, 1882)	PM	Blinkard Croaker....corvineta ronca
Ophioscion scierus (Jordan & Gilbert, 1884)	PM	Dusky Croaker....corvineta parda
Ophioscion strabo Gilbert, 1897	PM	Squint-eyed Croaker....corvineta bizca
Ophioscion typicus Gill, 1863	PM	Racer Croaker....corvineta corredora
Ophioscion vermicularis (Günther, 1867)	PM	Wormlined Croaker....corvineta cococha
Paralonchurus goodei Gilbert, 1898	PM	Angel Croaker....corvineta ángel
*Paralonchurus rathbuni (Jordan & Bollman, 1890)	PM	Bearded Banded Croaker....corvineta barbón

SCIENTIFIC NAME	OCCURRENCE[1]	COMMON NAME (ENGLISH, SPANISH, FRENCH)[2]		
Pareques acuminatus (Bloch & Schneider, 1801)	A	High-hat	payasito largo	
Pareques fuscovittatus (Kendall & Radcliffe, 1912)	PM	Festive Drum	payasito lindo	
Pareques iwamotoi Miller & Woods, 1988	A	Blackbar Drum	payasito rayado	
Pareques umbrosus (Jordan & Eigenmann, 1889)	A	Cubbyu	payasito prieto	
Pareques viola (Gilbert, 1898)	PM	Rock Croaker	payasito gungo	
Pogonias cromis (Linnaeus, 1766)	A	Black Drum	tambor negro	grand tambour
Roncador stearnsii (Steindachner, 1876)	P	Spotfin Croaker	roncador aleta manchada	
Sciaenops ocellatus (Linnaeus, 1766)	A-F-UM	Red Drum	corvineta ocelada	
Seriphus politus Ayres, 1860	P	Queenfish	corvineta reina	tambour royal
Stellifer chrysoleuca (Günther, 1867)	PM	Shortnose Stardrum	corvinilla chata	
Stellifer ericymba (Jordan & Gilbert, 1882)	PM	Hollow Stardrum	corvinilla hueca	
Stellifer illecebrosus Gilbert, 1898	PM	Silver Stardrum	corvinilla plateada	
Stellifer lanceolatus (Holbrook, 1855)	A	Star Drum	corvinilla lanza	
Stellifer walkeri Chao, 2001	PM	Professor Stardrum	corvinilla del profesor	
Stellifer wintersteenorum Chao, 2001	PM	Amigo Stardrum	corvinilla amigable	
Totoaba macdonaldi (Gilbert, 1890)	PM	Totoaba	totoaba	
Umbrina analis Günther, 1868	PM	Longspine Croaker	berrugata espinuda	
Umbrina bussingi López, 1980	PM	Bigeye Croaker	berrugata ojona	
Umbrina coroides Cuvier, 1830	A	Sand Drum	berrugata arenera	
Umbrina dorsalis Gill, 1862	PM	Longfin Croaker	berrugata aleta larga	
Umbrina roncador Jordan & Gilbert, 1882	P	Yellowfin Croaker	berrugata aleta amarilla	
Umbrina wintersteeni Walker & Radford, 1992	PM	Cortez Croaker^	berrugata de Cortés	
Umbrina xanti Gill, 1862	PM	Surf Croaker	berrugata roncadora	

Mullidae—En-goatfishes, Sp-chivos, Fr-surmulets

Mulloidichthys dentatus (Gill, 1862)	PM	Mexican Goatfish^	chivo barbón	
Mulloidichthys martinicus (Cuvier, 1829)	A	Yellow Goatfish	chivo amarillo	
Mullus auratus Jordan & Gilbert, 1882	A	Red Goatfish	chivo colorado	rouget doré
Pseudupeneus grandisquamis (Gill, 1863)	P	Bigscale Goatfish	chivo escamudo	
Pseudupeneus maculatus (Bloch, 1793)	A	Spotted Goatfish	chivo manchado	
Upeneus parvus Poey, 1852	A	Dwarf Goatfish	chivo rayuelo	

SCIENTIFIC NAME	OCCURRENCE[1]	COMMON NAME (ENGLISH, SPANISH, FRENCH)[2]		

Pempheridae—En-sweepers, Sp-barrenderos, Fr-poissons-balayeurs

Scientific name	Occ.	English	Spanish	French
Pempheris schomburgkii Müller & Troschel, 1848	A	Glassy Sweeper	barrendero transparente	

Kyphosidae—En-sea chubs, Sp-chopas, Fr-kyphoses

Scientific name	Occ.	English	Spanish	French
Girella nigricans (Ayres, 1860)	P	Opaleye	chopa verde	
Girella simplicidens Osburn & Nichols, 1916	PM	Gulf Opaleye^	chopa ojo azul	
Hermosilla azurea Jenkins & Evermann, 1889	P	Zebraperch	chopa bonita	
Kyphosus analogus (Gill, 1862)	P	Blue-bronze Chub	chopa rayada	
Kyphosus elegans (Peters, 1869)	PM	Cortez Sea Chub^	chopa de Cortés	
Kyphosus incisor (Cuvier, 1831)	A	Yellow Chub	chopa amarilla	
Kyphosus lutescens (Jordan & Gilbert, 1882)	PM	Revillagigedo Sea Chub^	chopa de Revillagigedo	
Kyphosus saltatrix (Linnaeus, 1758)	A	Bermuda Chub^	chopa blanca	kyphose des Bermudes
Medialuna californiensis (Steindachner, 1876)	P	Halfmoon	chopa medialuna	demi-lune
Sector ocyurus (Jordan & Gilbert, 1882)	P	Bluestriped Chub	chopa salema	

(* before *Kyphosus saltatrix*)

Chaetodontidae—En-butterflyfishes, Sp-peces mariposa, Fr-poissons-papillons

Scientific name	Occ.	English	Spanish	French
Chaetodon capistratus Linnaeus, 1758	A	Foureye Butterflyfish	mariposa ocelada	
Chaetodon humeralis Günther, 1860	P	Threebanded Butterflyfish	mariposa muñeca	
Chaetodon ocellatus Bloch, 1787	A	Spotfin Butterflyfish	mariposa perla amarilla	palhala
Chaetodon sedentarius Poey, 1860	A	Reef Butterflyfish	mariposa parche	
Chaetodon striatus Linnaeus, 1758	A	Banded Butterflyfish	mariposa rayada	
Forcipiger flavissimus Jordan & McGregor, 1898	PM	Forcepsfish	mariposa hocicona	
Johnrandallia nigrirostris (Gill, 1862)	PM	Barberfish	mariposa barbero	
Prognathodes aculeatus (Poey, 1860)	A	Longsnout Butterflyfish	mariposa narigona	
Prognathodes aya (Jordan, 1886)	A	Bank Butterflyfish	mariposa de banco	
Prognathodes falcifer (Hubbs & Rechnitzer, 1958)	P	Scythe Butterflyfish	mariposa guadaña	
Prognathodes guyanensis (Durand, 1960)	A	Guyana Butterflyfish^		

Pomacanthidae—En-angelfishes, Sp-ángeles, Fr-demoiselles

Scientific name	Occ.	English	Spanish	French
Centropyge argi Woods & Kanazawa, 1951	A	Cherubfish	angelote pigmeo	
Holacanthus bermudensis Goode, 1876	A	Blue Angelfish	chabelita azul	

SCIENTIFIC NAME	OCCURRENCE[1]	COMMON NAME (ENGLISH, SPANISH, FRENCH)[2]
Holacanthus ciliaris (Linnaeus, 1758)	A	Queen Angelfish....................ángel reina
Holacanthus clarionensis Gilbert, 1891	PM	Clarion Angelfish^...........ángel de Clarión
Holacanthus passer Valenciennes, 1846	PM	King Angelfish..........................ángel real
Holacanthus tricolor (Bloch, 1795)	A	Rock Beauty ....chabelita tricolor
Pomacanthus arcuatus (Linnaeus, 1758)	A	Gray Angelfish....................gallineta café
Pomacanthus paru (Bloch, 1787)	A	French Angelfish^.............gallineta negra
Pomacanthus zonipectus (Gill, 1862)	P	Cortez Angelfish^..........ángel de Cortés

Pentacerotidae—En-armorheads, Sp-espartanos, Fr-têtes casquées

Pseudopentaceros wheeleri Hardy, 1983	P	North Pacific Armorhead^

Kuhliidae—En-flagtails, Sp-daras, Fr-crocros

Kuhlia mugil (Forster, 1801)	PM	Barred Flagtail....................dara bandera

Cirrhitidae—En-hawkfishes, Sp-halcones, Fr-poissons-éperviers

Amblycirrhitus pinos (Mowbray, 1927)	A	Redspotted Hawkfish ....halcón rayadito
Cirrhitichthys oxycephalus (Bleeker, 1855)	PM	Coral Hawkfish.................halcón de coral
Cirrhitus rivulatus Valenciennes, 1846	PM	Giant Hawkfish.........................chino mero
Oxycirrhites typus Bleeker, 1857	PM	Longnose Hawkfish..........halcón narigón

Elassomatidae—En-pygmy sunfishes, Sp-solecitos, Fr-crapets-pygmées

Elassoma alabamae Mayden, 1993	F:U	Spring Pygmy Sunfish
Elassoma boehlkei Rohde & Arndt, 1987	F:U	Carolina Pygmy Sunfish^
+Elassoma evergladei Jordan, 1884	F:U	Everglades Pygmy Sunfish^
*Elassoma gilberti Snelson, Krabbenhoft & Quattro, 2009	F:U	Gulf Coast Pygmy Sunfish^
Elassoma okatie Rohde & Arndt, 1987	F:U	Bluebarred Pygmy Sunfish
+Elassoma okefenokee Böhlke, 1956	F:U	Okefenokee Pygmy Sunfish^
Elassoma zonatum Jordan, 1877	F:U	Banded Pygmy Sunfish

+Cichlidae—En-cichlids and tilapias, Sp-tilapias y mojarras de agua dulce, Fr-cichlidés

*Amatitlania nigrofasciata (Günther, 1867)	F[I]:UM	Convict Cichlid ....mojarra congo

SCIENTIFIC NAME	OCCURRENCE[1]	COMMON NAME (ENGLISH, SPANISH, FRENCH)[2]		
*Amphilophus citrinellus (Günther, 1864)	F[I]:U	Midas Cichlid		
*Amphilophus macracanthus (Günther, 1864)	F:M	Blackthroat Cichlid	mojarra de Guamuchal	
*Amphilophus nourissati (Allgayer, 1989)	F:M	Bluemouth Cichlid	mojarra de labios gruesos	
*Amphilophus robertsoni (Regan, 1905)	F:M	Honduras Cichlid^	mojarra hondureña	
*Amphilophus trimaculatus (Günther, 1867)	F:M	Threespot Cichlid	mojarra prieta	
Astronotus ocellatus (Agassiz, 1831)	F[I]:U	Oscar		
Cichla ocellaris Bloch & Schneider, 1801	F[I]:U	Butterfly Peacock Bass		
+Cichlasoma beani (Jordan, 1889)	F:M	Sinaloa Cichlid^	mojarra de Sinaloa	
+Cichlasoma bimaculatum (Linnaeus, 1758)	F[I]:U	Black Acara		
+Cichlasoma grammodes Taylor & Miller, 1980	F:M	Chiapa de Corzo Cichlid^	mojarra del Chiapa de Corzo	
+Cichlasoma istlanum (Jordan & Snyder, 1899)	F:M	Redside Cichlid	mojarra del Balsas	
+Cichlasoma nebuliferum (Günther, 1860)	F:M	Papaloapan Cichlid^	mojarra del Papaloapan	
+Cichlasoma urophthalmus (Günther, 1862)	A-F:U[I]M	Mayan Cichlid^	mojarra del sureste	
*Cryptoheros chetumalensis Schmitter-Soto, 2007	F:M	Chetumal Cichlid^	mojarra chetumaleña	
Geophagus surinamensis (Bloch, 1791)	F[I]:U	Redstriped Eartheater		
Hemichromis guttatus Günther, 1862	F[I]:M	Spotted Jewelfish	pez joya manchado	
Hemichromis letourneuxi Sauvage, 1880	F[I]:CU	African Jewelfish^		cichlide à deux taches
*Herichthys bartoni (Bean, 1892)	F:M	Media Luna Cichlid^	mojarra caracolera	
*Herichthys carpintis (Jordan & Snyder, 1899)	F:M	Lowland Cichlid	mojarra tampiqueña	
*Herichthys cyanoguttatus Baird & Girard, 1854	F:UM	Rio Grande Cichlid^	mojarra del norte	
*Herichthys deppii (Heckel, 1840)	F:M	Nautla Cichlid^	mojarra del sur	
*Herichthys labridens (Pellegrin, 1903)	F:M	Blackcheek Cichlid	mojarra huasteca	
*Herichthys minckleyi (Kornfield & Taylor, 1983)	F:M	Cuatro Ciénegas Cichlid^	mojarra de Cuatro Ciénegas	
*Herichthys pantostictus (Taylor & Miller, 1983)	F:M	Chairel Cichlid^	mojarra de Chairel	
*Herichthys steindachneri (Jordan & Snyder, 1899)	F:M	Slender Cichlid	mojarra del Ojo Frío	
*Herichthys tamasopoensis Artigas Azas, 1993	F:M	Tamasopo Cichlid^	mojarra del Tamasopo	
Heros severus Heckel, 1840	F[I]:U	Banded Cichlid		
Oreochromis aureus (Steindachner, 1864)	F[I]:UM	Blue Tilapia	tilapia azul	
Oreochromis mossambicus (Peters, 1852)	P[I]-F[I]:UM	Mozambique Tilapia^	tilapia de Mozambique	
Oreochromis niloticus (Linnaeus, 1758)	F[I]:UM	Nile Tilapia^	tilapia del Nilo	
Oreochromis urolepis (Norman, 1922)	F[I]:U	Wami Tilapia		
*Parachromis friedrichsthalii (Heckel, 1840)	F:M	Yellowjacket	mojarra del San Juan	
*Parachromis managuensis (Günther, 1867)	F[I]:UM	Jaguar Guapote	mojarra de Managua	

SCIENTIFIC NAME	OCCURRENCE[1]	COMMON NAME (ENGLISH, SPANISH, FRENCH)[2]
*Parachromis motaguensis (Günther, 1867)	F:M	Motagua Cichlid^ ... mojarra del Motagua
*Parachromis salvini (Günther, 1862)	F:U[I]M	Yellowbelly Cichlid ... guapote tricolor
*Paraneetroplus argenteus (Allgayer, 1991)	F:M	White Cichlid ... mojarra pozolera
*Paraneetroplus bifasciatus (Steindachner, 1864)	F:M	Twoband Cichlid ... mojarra panza colorada
*Paraneetroplus breidohri (Werner & Stawikowski, 1987)	F:M	Angostura Cichlid^ ... mojarra de la Angostura
*Paraneetroplus bulleri Regan, 1905	F:M	Sarabia Cichlid^ ... mojarra del Sarabia
*Paraneetroplus fenestratus (Günther, 1860)	F:M	Blackstripe Cichlid ... mojarra de La Lana
*Paraneetroplus gibbiceps (Steindachner, 1864)	F:M	Teapa Cichlid^ ... mojarra del Teapa
*Paraneetroplus guttulatus (Günther, 1864)	F:M	Amatitlán Cichlid^ ... mojarra de Amatitlán
*Paraneetroplus hartwegi (Taylor & Miller, 1980)	F:M	Tailbar Cichlid ... mojarra del Grande de Chiapas
*Paraneetroplus melanurus (Günther, 1862)	F:M	Redhead Cichlid ... mojarra paleta
*Paraneetroplus regani (Miller, 1974)	F:M	Almoloya Cichlid^ ... mojarra del Almoloya
*Paraneetroplus zonatus (Meek, 1905)	F:M	Oaxaca Cichlid^ ... mojarra oaxaqueña
Petenia splendida Günther, 1862	F:M	Giant Cichlid ... tenguayaca
*Rocio gemmata Contreras-Balderas & Schmitter-Soto, 2007	F:M	Leona Vicario Cichlid^ ... mojarra de Leona Vicario
*Rocio ocotal Schmitter-Soto, 2007	F:M	Ocotal Cichlid^ ... mojarra del Ocotal
*Rocio octofasciata (Regan, 1903)	F:U[I]M	Jack Dempsey ... mojarra castarrica
Sarotherodon melanotheron Rüppell, 1852	F[I]:U	Blackchin Tilapia
*Theraps heterospilus (Hubbs, 1936)	F:M	Montecristo Cichlid^ ... mojarra de Montecristo
*Theraps intermedius (Günther, 1862)	F:M	Petén Cichlid^ ... mojarra del Petén
*Theraps irregularis Günther, 1862	F:M	Arroyo Cichlid ... canchay
*Theraps lentiginosus (Steindachner, 1864)	F:M	Freckled Cichlid ... mojarra gachupina
*Theraps pearsei (Hubbs, 1936)	F:M	Pantano Cichlid ... mojarra zacatera
*Theraps rheophilus Seegers & Staeck, 1985	F:M	Palenque Cichlid^ ... mojarra de Palenque
*Theraps ufermanni (Allgayer, 2002)	F:M	Usumacinta Cichlid^ ... mojarra del Usumacinta
*Thorichthys affinis (Günther, 1862)	F:M	Golden Cichlid ... mojarra dorada
*Thorichthys callolepis (Regan, 1904)	F:M	San Domingo Cichlid^ ... mojarra de San Domingo
*Thorichthys ellioti Meek, 1904	F:M	Spotcheek Cichlid ... chescla
*Thorichthys helleri (Steindachner, 1864)	F:M	Yellow Cichlid ... mojarra amarilla
*Thorichthys meeki Brind, 1918	F:U[I]M	Firemouth Cichlid ... mojarra boca de fuego
*Thorichthys pasionis (Rivas, 1962)	F:M	Blackgullet Cichlid ... mojarra de La Pasión

SCIENTIFIC NAME	OCCURRENCE[1]	COMMON NAME (ENGLISH, SPANISH, FRENCH)[2]
*Thorichthys socolofi (Miller & Taylor, 1984)	F:M	Chiapas Cichlid[^] ...... mojarra del Misalá
Tilapia mariae (Boulenger, 1899)	F[I]:U	Spotted Tilapia
*Tilapia zillii (Gervais, 1848)	F[I]:UM	Redbelly Tilapia ...... tilapia vientre rojo

Embiotocidae—En-surfperches, Sp-mojarras vivíparas, vivíparas, Fr-perches vivipares

SCIENTIFIC NAME	OCCURRENCE[1]	COMMON NAME (ENGLISH, SPANISH, FRENCH)[2]
Amphistichus argenteus Agassiz, 1854	P	Barred Surfperch ...... mojarra de bandas
Amphistichus koelzi (Hubbs, 1933)	P	Calico Surfperch ...... mojarra angaripola
Amphistichus rhodoterus (Agassiz, 1854)	P	Redtail Surfperch ...... ditrème rosé
Brachyistius frenatus Gill, 1862	P	Kelp Perch ...... mojarra sargacera ...... perche de varech
Cymatogaster aggregata Gibbons, 1854	P-F:CUM	Shiner Perch ...... mojarra brillosa ...... perche-méné
*Damalichthys vacca Girard, 1855	P	Pile Perch ...... mojarra muellera ...... perche de pilotis
Embiotoca jacksoni Agassiz, 1853	P	Black Perch ...... mojarra rayas negras
Embiotoca lateralis Agassiz, 1854	P	Striped Seaperch ...... mojarra azul ...... ditrème rayé
Hyperprosopon anale Agassiz, 1861	P	Spotfin Surfperch ...... mojarra aletimanchada
Hyperprosopon argenteum Gibbons, 1854	P	Walleye Surfperch ...... mojarra ojona
Hyperprosopon ellipticum (Gibbons, 1854)	P	Silver Surfperch ...... mojarra ovalada ...... ditrème argenté
+Hypsurus caryi (Agassiz, 1853)	P	Rainbow Seaperch ...... mojarra arcoiris
Hysterocarpus traskii Gibbons, 1854	F:U	Tule Perch
Micrometrus aurora (Jordan & Gilbert, 1880)	P	Reef Perch ...... mojarra de arrecife
Micrometrus minimus (Gibbons, 1854)	P	Dwarf Perch ...... mojarra enana
Phanerodon atripes (Jordan & Gilbert, 1880)	P	Sharpnose Seaperch ...... mojarra picuda
Phanerodon furcatus Girard, 1854	P	White Seaperch ...... mojarra lomo rayado ...... ditrème fourchu
Rhacochilus toxotes Agassiz, 1854	P	Rubberlip Seaperch ...... mojarra labios de hule
Zalembius rosaceus (Jordan & Gilbert, 1880)	P	Pink Seaperch ...... mojarra rosada

Pomacentridae—En-damselfishes, Sp-castañetas y jaquetas, Fr-sergents

SCIENTIFIC NAME	OCCURRENCE[1]	COMMON NAME (ENGLISH, SPANISH, FRENCH)[2]
Abudefduf declivifrons (Gill, 1862)	PM	Mexican Night Sergeant[^] ...... petaca mexicana
Abudefduf saxatilis (Linnaeus, 1758)	A	Sergeant Major ...... petaca rayada
Abudefduf taurus (Müller & Troschel, 1848)	A	Night Sergeant ...... petaca toro
Abudefduf troschelii (Gill, 1862)	P	Panamic Sergeant Major[^] ...... petaca banderita
Azurina hirundo Jordan & McGregor, 1898	P	Swallow Damselfish ...... castañuela golondrina
Chromis alta Greenfield & Woods, 1980	P	Silverstripe Chromis ...... castañeta alta

SCIENTIFIC NAME	OCCURRENCE[1]	COMMON NAME (ENGLISH, SPANISH, FRENCH)[2]
Chromis atrilobata Gill, 1862	PM	Scissortail Chromis......castañeta cola de tijera
Chromis cyanea (Poey, 1860)	A	Blue Chromis......castañeta azul
Chromis enchrysura Jordan & Gilbert, 1882	A	Yellowtail Reeffish......castañeta coliamarilla
Chromis insolata (Cuvier, 1830)	A	Sunshinefish......castañeta sol
Chromis limbaughi Greenfield & Woods, 1980	PM	Blue-and-yellow Chromis......castañeta mexicana
Chromis multilineata (Guichenot, 1853)	A	Brown Chromis......castañeta parda
Chromis punctipinnis (Cooper, 1863)	P	Blacksmith......castañeta herrera
Chromis scotti Emery, 1968	A	Purple Reeffish......castañeta púrpura
Hypsypops rubicundus (Girard, 1854)	P	Garibaldi^......jaqueta garibaldi
Microspathodon bairdii (Gill, 1862)	PM	Bumphead Damselfish......jaqueta vistosa
Microspathodon chrysurus (Cuvier, 1830)	A	Yellowtail Damselfish......jaqueta coliamarilla
Microspathodon dorsalis (Gill, 1862)	PM	Giant Damselfish......jaqueta gigante
Stegastes acapulcoensis (Fowler, 1944)	PM	Acapulco Damselfish^......jaqueta acapulqueña
Stegastes adustus (Troschel, 1865)	A	Dusky Damselfish......jaqueta prieta
Stegastes diencaeus (Jordan & Rutter, 1897)	A	Longfin Damselfish......jaqueta miel
Stegastes flavilatus (Gill, 1862)	PM	Beaubrummel......jaqueta de dos colores
Stegastes leucorus (Gilbert, 1892)	PM	Whitetail Damselfish......jaqueta rabo blanco
Stegastes leucostictus (Müller & Troschel, 1848)	A	Beaugregory......jaqueta bonita
Stegastes partitus (Poey, 1868)	A	Bicolor Damselfish......jaqueta bicolor
Stegastes planifrons (Cuvier, 1830)	A	Threespot Damselfish......jaqueta de tres puntos
Stegastes rectifraenum (Gill, 1862)	PM	Cortez Damselfish^......jaqueta de Cortés
Stegastes redemptus (Heller & Snodgrass, 1903)	PM	Clarion Damselfish^......jaqueta azafranada
Stegastes variabilis (Castelnau, 1855)	A	Cocoa Damselfish......jaqueta castaña

*Labridae—En-wrasses and parrotfishes, Sp-doncellas, señoritas y loros, Fr-labres et perroquets

Bodianus diplotaenia (Gill, 1862)	PM	Mexican Hogfish^......vieja mexicana
Bodianus pulchellus (Poey, 1860)	A	Spotfin Hogfish......vieja lomo negro
Bodianus rufus (Linnaeus, 1758)	A	Spanish Hogfish^......vieja española
Calotomus carolinus (Valenciennes, 1840)	PM	Stareye Parrotfish......pococho perico
Clepticus parrae (Bloch & Schneider, 1801)	A	Creole Wrasse......doncella mulata
Cryptotomus roseus Cope, 1871	A	Bluelip Parrotfish......loro chimuelo
Decodon melasma Gomon, 1974	P	Blackspot Wrasse......viejita manchada

SCIENTIFIC NAME	OCCURRENCE[1]	COMMON NAME (ENGLISH, SPANISH, FRENCH)[2]	
Decodon puellaris (Poey, 1860)	A	Red Hogfish	doncella de lo alto
Doratonotus megalepis Günther, 1862	A	Dwarf Wrasse	doncella enana
Halichoeres adustus (Gilbert, 1890)	PM	Black Wrasse	señorita negra
Halichoeres aestuaricola Bussing, 1972	PM	Mangrove Wrasse	señorita de manglar
Halichoeres bathyphilus (Beebe & Tee-Van, 1932)	A	Greenband Wrasse	doncella cintaverde
+*Halichoeres bivittatus* (Bloch, 1791)	A	Slippery Dick	doncella rayada
Halichoeres burekae Weaver & Rocha, 2007	A	Mardi Gras Wrasse^	doncella carnaval
Halichoeres caudalis (Poey, 1860)	A	Painted Wrasse	doncella pintada
Halichoeres chierchiae di Caporiacco, 1947	PM	Wounded Wrasse	señorita herida
Halichoeres cyanocephalus (Bloch, 1791)	A	Yellowcheek Wrasse	doncella lomo amarillo
Halichoeres dispilus (Günther, 1864)	PM	Chameleon Wrasse	señorita camaleón
Halichoeres garnoti (Valenciennes, 1839)	A	Yellowhead Wrasse	doncella cabeciamarilla
Halichoeres insularis Allen & Robertson, 1992	PM	Socorro Wrasse^	señorita de Socorro
Halichoeres maculipinna (Müller & Troschel, 1848)	A	Clown Wrasse	doncella payaso
Halichoeres melanotis (Gilbert, 1890)	PM	Golden Wrasse	señorita dorada
Halichoeres nicholsi (Jordan & Gilbert, 1882)	PM	Spinster Wrasse	señorita solterona
Halichoeres notospilus (Günther, 1864)	PM	Banded Wrasse	señorita listada
Halichoeres pictus (Poey, 1860)	A	Rainbow Wrasse	doncella arcoiris
Halichoeres poeyi (Steindachner, 1867)	A	Blackear Wrasse	doncella orejinegra
Halichoeres radiatus (Linnaeus, 1758)	A	Puddingwife	doncella azulada
Halichoeres semicinctus (Ayres, 1859)	P	Rock Wrasse	señorita piedrera
Iniistius pavo (Valenciennes, 1840)	PM	Peacock Razorfish	cuchillo pavo real
Lachnolaimus maximus (Walbaum, 1792)	A	Hogfish	boquinete
Nicholsina denticulata (Evermann & Radcliffe, 1917)	P	Loosetooth Parrotfish	pococho beriquete
Nicholsina usta (Valenciennes, 1840)	A	Emerald Parrotfish	loro esmeralda
Novaculichthys taeniourus (Lacepède, 1801)	PM	Rockmover Wrasse	cuchillo dragón
Oxyjulis californica (Günther, 1861)	P	Señorita	señorita californiana
Polylepion cruentum Gomon, 1977	PM	Bleeding Wrasse	vieja sangradora
Pseudojuloides inornatus (Gilbert, 1890)	PM	Cape Wrasse^	señorita del Cabo
Scarus coelestinus Valenciennes, 1840	A	Midnight Parrotfish	loro de medianoche
Scarus coeruleus (Bloch, 1786)	A	Blue Parrotfish	loro azul

SCIENTIFIC NAME	OCCURRENCE[1]	COMMON NAME (ENGLISH, SPANISH, FRENCH)[2]		
Scarus compressus (Osburn & Nichols, 1916)	PM	Azure Parrotfish	loro chato	
Scarus ghobban Forsskål, 1775	PM	Bluechin Parrotfish	loro barbazul	
Scarus guacamaia Cuvier, 1829	A	Rainbow Parrotfish	loro guacamayo	
Scarus iseri (Bloch, 1789)	A	Striped Parrotfish	loro listado	
Scarus perrico Jordan & Gilbert, 1882	PM	Bumphead Parrotfish	loro jorobado	
Scarus rubroviolaceus Bleeker, 1847	PM	Bicolor Parrotfish	loro bicolor	
*Scarus taeniopterus Desmarest, 1831	A	Princess Parrotfish	loro princesa	
Scarus vetula Bloch & Schneider, 1801	A	Queen Parrotfish	loro reina	
Semicossyphus pulcher (Ayres, 1854)	P	California Sheephead^	vieja californiana	
Sparisoma atomarium (Poey, 1861)	A	Greenblotch Parrotfish	loro mancha verde	
Sparisoma aurofrenatum (Valenciennes, 1840)	A	Redband Parrotfish	loro manchado	
Sparisoma chrysopterum (Bloch & Schneider, 1801)	A	Redtail Parrotfish	loro verde	
Sparisoma radians (Valenciennes, 1840)	A	Bucktooth Parrotfish	loro dientudo	
Sparisoma rubripinne (Valenciennes, 1840)	A	Yellowtail Parrotfish	loro coliamarillo	
Sparisoma viride (Bonnaterre, 1788)	A	Stoplight Parrotfish	loro brilloso	
*Stethojulis bandanensis (Bleeker, 1851)	PM	Red-shoulder Wrasse	vieja manga roja	
Tautoga onitis (Linnaeus, 1758)	A	Tautog		tautogue noir
Tautogolabrus adspersus (Walbaum, 1792)	A	Cunner		tanche-tautogue
Thalassoma bifasciatum (Bloch, 1791)	A	Bluehead	cara de cotorra	
Thalassoma grammaticum Gilbert, 1890	PM	Sunset Wrasse	señorita crepúsculo	
Thalassoma lucasanum (Gill, 1862)	PM	Cortez Rainbow Wrasse^	arcoiris de Cortés	
Thalassoma virens Gilbert, 1890	PM	Emerald Wrasse	señorita esmeralda	
Xyrichtys martinicensis Valenciennes, 1840	A	Rosy Razorfish	cuchillo llorón	
Xyrichtys mundiceps Gill, 1862	PM	Cape Razorfish^	cuchillo desnudo	
Xyrichtys novacula (Linnaeus, 1758)	A	Pearly Razorfish	cuchillo perlino	
Xyrichtys splendens Castelnau, 1855	A	Green Razorfish	cuchillo de lunar	

Bathymasteridae—En-ronquils, Sp-roncos pelones, Fr-ronquilles

Bathymaster caeruleofasciatus Gilbert & Burke, 1912	P	Alaskan Ronquil^		ronquille à nageoires bleues
Bathymaster leurolepis McPhail, 1965	P	Smallmouth Ronquil		ronquille à petite bouche
Bathymaster signatus Cope, 1873	P	Searcher		chercheur aux yeux bleus

SCIENTIFIC NAME	OCCURRENCE[1]	COMMON NAME (ENGLISH, SPANISH, FRENCH)[2]
Rathbunella alleni Gilbert, 1904	P	Stripefin Ronquil ... ronco pelón aletirrayada
Rathbunella hypoplecta (Gilbert, 1890)	P	Bluebanded Ronquil ... ronco pelón rayado
Ronquilus jordani (Gilbert, 1889)	P	Northern Ronquil ... ronquille du nord
Zoarcidae—En-eelpouts, Sp-viruelas, Fr-lycodes		
Bothrocara brunneum (Bean, 1890)	P	Twoline Eelpout ... viruela dos rayas ... lycode à deux lignes
Bothrocara pusillum (Bean, 1890)	P	Alaska Eelpout^ ... lycode à oeil ovale
Eucryphycus californicus (Starks & Mann, 1911)	P	Persimmon Eelpout
Gymnelus hemifasciatus Andriashev, 1937	P	Halfbarred Pout
Gymnelus popovi (Taranetz & Andriashev, 1935)	P	Aleutian Pout^
Gymnelus retrodorsalis Le Danois, 1913	A-P-Ar	Aurora Pout ... unernak aurore
Gymnelus viridis (Fabricius, 1780)	A-P-Ar	Fish Doctor ... unernak caméléon
Lycenchelys paxillus (Goode & Bean, 1879)	A-Ar	Common Wolf Eel ... lycode commune
*Lycenchelys sarsii (Collett, 1871)	A-Ar	Theologian Eelpout ... lycode de Sars
Lycenchelys verrillii (Goode & Bean, 1877)	A	Wolf Eelpout ... lycode à tête longue
Lycodapus fierasfer Gilbert, 1890	P	Blackmouth Eelpout ... lycode nacrée
Lycodapus mandibularis Gilbert, 1915	P	Pallid Eelpout ... lycode à longues branchiospines
Lycodapus parviceps Gilbert, 1896	P	Smallhead Eelpout ... lycode à petite tête
Lycodapus psarostomatus Peden & Anderson, 1981	P	Specklemouth Eelpout
*Lycodes akuugun Stevenson & Orr, 2006	P	Bicolor Eelpout
Lycodes brevipes Bean, 1890	P	Shortfin Eelpout ... lycode à courtes nageoires
Lycodes concolor Gill & Townsend, 1897	P	Ebony Eelpout
Lycodes cortezianus (Gilbert, 1890)	P	Bigfin Eelpout ... lycode à grandes nageoires
Lycodes diapterus Gilbert, 1892	P	Black Eelpout ... lycode noire
Lycodes esmarkii Collett, 1875	A-Ar	Greater Eelpout ... grande lycode
*Lycodes eudipleurostictus Jensen, 1902	A-Ar	Doubleline Eelpout
Lycodes fasciatus (Schmidt, 1904)	P	Banded Eelpout
*Lycodes gracilis Sars, 1867	A	Gracile Eelpout ... lycode gracile
Lycodes jugoricus Knipowitsch, 1906	P-Ar	Shulupaoluk ... lycode plume
Lycodes lavalaei Vladykov & Tremblay, 1936	A-Ar	Newfoundland Eelpout^ ... lycode du Labrador
*Lycodes luetkenii Collett, 1880	A-Ar	Pink Eelpout ... lycode rose

SCIENTIFIC NAME	OCCURRENCE[1]	COMMON NAME (ENGLISH, SPANISH, FRENCH)[2]
*Lycodes marisalbi Knipowitsch, 1906	Ar	White Sea Eelpout^ .... lycode de la mer Blanche
Lycodes mucosus Richardson, 1855	A-P-Ar	Saddled Eelpout .... lycode à selles
Lycodes pacificus Collett, 1879	P	Blackbelly Eelpout ...... viruela panza negra ..... lycode à ventre noir
Lycodes palearis Gilbert, 1896	P	Wattled Eelpout .... lycode tressée
Lycodes pallidus Collett, 1879	A-P-Ar	Pale Eelpout .... lycode pâle
Lycodes polaris (Sabine, 1824)	A-P	Canadian Eelpout^ .... lycode polaire
Lycodes raridens Taranetz & Andriashev, 1937	P	Marbled Eelpout
Lycodes reticulatus Reinhardt, 1835	A-P-Ar	Arctic Eelpout^ .... lycode arctique
Lycodes rossi Malmgren, 1865	P-Ar	Threespot Eelpout .... lycode à trois taches
*Lycodes seminudus Reinhardt, 1837	A-Ar	Longear Eelpout .... lycode à oreilles
Lycodes turneri Bean, 1879	A-P-Ar	Polar Eelpout .... lycode de Turner
+Lycodes vahlii Reinhardt, 1831	A-Ar	Checker Eelpout .... lycode à carreaux
Lyconema barbatum Gilbert, 1896	P	Bearded Eelpout ...... viruela barbona
Melanostigma atlanticum Koefoed, 1952	A	Atlantic Soft Pout^ .... mollasse atlantique
Melanostigma pammelas Gilbert, 1896	PM	Midwater Eelpout ...... viruela carbonera
Zoarces americanus (Bloch & Schneider, 1801)	A-Ar	Ocean Pout .... loquette d'Amérique

Stichaeidae—En-pricklebacks, Sp-peces abrojo, Fr-stichées

Acantholumpenus mackayi (Gilbert, 1896)	P-Ar	Blackline Prickleback .... terrassier à six lignes
Alectrias alectrolophus (Pallas, 1814)	P	Stone Cockscomb
Alectridium aurantiacum Gilbert & Burke, 1912	P	Lesser Prickleback
Anisarchus medius (Reinhardt, 1837)	A-P-Ar	Stout Eelblenny .... lompénie naine
Anoplarchus insignis Gilbert & Burke, 1912	P	Slender Cockscomb .... crête-de-coq mince
Anoplarchus purpurescens Gill, 1861	P	High Cockscomb .... crête-de-coq pourpre
Bryozoichthys lysimus (Jordan & Snyder, 1902)	P	Nutcracker Prickleback
Bryozoichthys marjorius McPhail, 1970	P	Pearly Prickleback .... stichée perlée
Cebidichthys violaceus (Girard, 1854)	P	Monkeyface Prickleback ...... abrojo cara de mono
Chirolophis ascanii (Walbaum, 1792)	Ar	Atlantic Warbonnet^
Chirolophis decoratus (Jordan & Snyder, 1902)	P	Decorated Warbonnet .... toupet marbré
Chirolophis nugator (Jordan & Williams, 1895)	P	Mosshead Warbonnet .... toupet décoré
Chirolophis snyderi (Taranetz, 1938)	P	Bearded Warbonnet .... toupet élégant
Chirolophis tarsodes (Jordan & Snyder, 1902)	P	Matcheek Warbonnet .... bonnet à joues touffues

SCIENTIFIC NAME	OCCURRENCE[1]	COMMON NAME (ENGLISH, SPANISH, FRENCH)[2]
Ernogrammus walkeri Follett & Powell, 1988	P	Masked Prickleback
Esselenichthys carli (Follett & Anderson, 1990)	P	Threeline Prickleback........abrojo tres rayas
Esselenichthys laurae (Follett & Anderson, 1990)	P	Twoline Prickleback........abrojo dos rayas
Eumesogrammus praecisus (Krøyer, 1837)	A-P-Ar	Fourline Snakeblenny........quatre-lignes atlantique
Gymnoclinus cristulatus Gilbert & Burke, 1912	P	Trident Prickleback
Kasatkia seigeli Posner & Lavenberg, 1999	P	Sixspot Prickleback
Leptoclinus maculatus (Fries, 1837)	A-P-Ar	Daubed Shanny .... lompénie tachetée
Lumpenella longirostris (Evermann & Goldsborough, 1907)	P	Longsnout Prickleback........stichée à long nez
*Lumpenopsis clitella Hastings & Walker, 2003	P	Saddled Prickleback
*Lumpenopsis hypochroma (Hubbs & Schultz, 1932)	P	Y-Prickleback........stichée-Y
Lumpenus fabricii Reinhardt, 1836	A-P-Ar	Slender Eelblenny........lompénie de Fabricius
Lumpenus lampretaeformis (Walbaum, 1792)	A-Ar	Snakeblenny........lompénie-serpent
Lumpenus sagitta Wilimovsky, 1956	P	Snake Prickleback........lompénie élancée
Phytichthys chirus (Jordan & Gilbert, 1880)	P	Ribbon Prickleback........lompénie ruban
Plagiogrammus hopkinsii Bean, 1894	P	Crisscross Prickleback
Plectobranchus evides Gilbert, 1890	P	Bluebarred Prickleback........lompénie à barres bleues
Poroclinus rothrocki Bean, 1890	P	Whitebarred Prickleback........lompénie à barres blanches
Stichaeus punctatus (Fabricius, 1780)	A-P-Ar	Arctic Shanny^........stichée arctique
Ulvaria subbifurcata (Storer, 1839)	A	Radiated Shanny........ulvaire deux-lignes
Xiphister atropurpureus (Kittlitz, 1858)	P	Black Prickleback........abrojo negro........lompénie noire
Xiphister mucosus (Girard, 1858)	P	Rock Prickleback........lompénie de roche

Cryptacanthodidae—En-wrymouths, Sp-risueños, Fr-terrassiers

Cryptacanthodes aleutensis (Gilbert, 1896)	P	Dwarf Wrymouth........terrassier nain
Cryptacanthodes giganteus (Kittlitz, 1858)	P	Giant Wrymouth........terrassier géant
Cryptacanthodes maculatus Storer, 1839	A	Wrymouth........terrassier tacheté

Pholidae—En-gunnels, Sp-espinosos de marea, Fr-sigouines

Apodichthys flavidus Girard, 1854	P	Penpoint Gunnel........sigouine jaunâtre
Apodichthys fucorum Jordan & Gilbert, 1880	P	Rockweed Gunnel........espinoso de marea zacatero ... sigouine de varech
Pholis clemensi Rosenblatt, 1964	P	Longfin Gunnel........sigouine à longue nageoire

SCIENTIFIC NAME	OCCURRENCE[1]	COMMON NAME (ENGLISH, SPANISH, FRENCH)[2]
Pholis fasciata (Bloch & Schneider, 1801)	A-P-Ar	Banded Gunnel......sigouine rubanée
Pholis gunnellus (Linnaeus, 1758)	A	Rock Gunnel......sigouine de roche
Pholis laeta (Cope, 1873)	P	Crescent Gunnel......sigouine lunée
Pholis ornata (Girard, 1854)	P	Saddleback Gunnel......sigouine mantelée
Pholis schultzi Schultz, 1931	P	Red Gunnel......sigouine rouge
Rhodymenichthys dolichogaster (Pallas, 1814)	P	Stippled Gunnel
Ulvicola sanctaerosae Gilbert & Starks, 1897	P	Kelp Gunnel......espinoso de marea sargacero
Anarhichadidae—En-wolffishes, Sp-peces lobo, Fr-poissons-loups		
Anarhichas denticulatus Krøyer, 1845	A-P-Ar	Northern Wolffish......loup à tête large
Anarhichas lupus Linnaeus, 1758	A-Ar	Atlantic Wolffish^......loup atlantique
Anarhichas minor Olafsen, 1772	A-Ar	Spotted Wolffish......loup tacheté
Anarhichas orientalis Pallas, 1814	P-Ar	Bering Wolffish^......loup de Béring
*Anarrhichthys ocellatus Ayres, 1855	P	Wolf-eel......anguila lobo......loup ocellé
Ptilichthyidae—En-quillfishes, Sp-peces púa, Fr-fouette-queues		
Ptilichthys goodei Bean, 1881	P	Quillfish......fouette-queue
Zaproridae—En-prowfishes, Sp-peces proa, Fr-zaproridés		
Zaprora silenus Jordan, 1896	P	Prowfish......zaprora
Scytalinidae—En-graveldivers, Sp-peces topo, Fr-blennies fouisseuses		
Scytalina cerdale Jordan & Gilbert, 1880	P	Graveldiver......blennie fouisseuse
Trichodontidae—En-sandfishes, Sp-areneros, Fr-trichodontes		
Arctoscopus japonicus (Steindachner, 1881)	P	Sailfin Sandfish
Trichodon trichodon (Tilesius, 1813)	P	Pacific Sandfish^......trichodonte
Percophidae—En-flatheads, Sp-picos de pato, Fr-platêtes		
Bembrops anatirostris Ginsburg, 1955	A	Duckbill Flathead......pico de pato
Bembrops gobioides (Goode, 1880)	A	Goby Flathead......pico de pala

SCIENTIFIC NAME	OCCURRENCE[1]	COMMON NAME (ENGLISH, SPANISH, FRENCH)[2]
Ammodytidae—En-sand lances, Sp-peones, Fr-lançons		
Ammodytes americanus DeKay, 1842	A	American Sand Lance^ .... lançon d'Amérique
Ammodytes dubius Reinhardt, 1837	A-Ar	Northern Sand Lance .... lançon du nord
Ammodytes hexapterus Pallas, 1814	P-Ar	Pacific Sand Lance^ .... lançon gourdeau
Ammodytoides gilli (Bean, 1895)	PM	Panamic Sand Lance^ .... peon panámico
Uranoscopidae—En-stargazers, Sp-miracielos, Fr-uranoscopes		
Astroscopus guttatus Abbott, 1860	A	Northern Stargazer
Astroscopus y-graecum (Cuvier, 1829)	A	Southern Stargazer .... miracielo del sureste
Astroscopus zephyreus Gilbert & Starks, 1897	P	Pacific Stargazer^ .... miracielo perro
Kathetostoma albigutta (Bean, 1892)	A	Lancer Stargazer .... miracielo sargacero
Kathetostoma averruncus Jordan & Bollman, 1890	P	Smooth Stargazer .... miracielo buldog
*Xenocephalus egregius (Jordan & Thompson, 1905)	A	Freckled Stargazer
Tripterygiidae—En-triplefins, Sp-tres aletas, Fr-triptérygiidés		
Axoclinus lucillae Fowler, 1944	PM	Panamic Triplefin^ .... tres aletas bigote
Axoclinus multicinctus Allen & Robertson, 1992	PM	Multibarred Triplefin .... tres aletas listado
Axoclinus nigricaudus Allen & Robertson, 1991	PM	Cortez Triplefin^ .... tres aletas colinegra
*Axoclinus storeyae (Brock, 1940)	PM	Carmine Triplefin .... tres aletas carmín
Crocodilichthys gracilis Allen & Robertson, 1991	PM	Lizard Triplefin .... lagartija tres aletas
Enneanectes altivelis Rosenblatt, 1960	A	Lofty Triplefin .... tres aletas de barras
Enneanectes atrorus Rosenblatt, 1960	AM	Blackedge Triplefin .... tres aletas orleado
Enneanectes boehlkei Rosenblatt, 1960	A	Roughhead Triplefin .... tres aletas rugoso
*Enneanectes carminalis (Jordan & Gilbert, 1882)	PM	Delicate Triplefin .... tres aletas manchada
Enneanectes jordani (Evermann & Marsh, 1899)	AM	Mimic Triplefin .... tres aletas escondido
Enneanectes pectoralis (Fowler, 1941)	A	Redeye Triplefin .... tres aletas aletón
Enneanectes reticulatus Allen & Robertson, 1991	PM	Flag Triplefin .... tres aletas bandera
Dactyloscopidae—En-sand stargazers, Sp-miraestrellas, Fr-télescopes		
Dactylagnus mundus Gill, 1862	PM	Giant Stargazer .... miraestrellas gigante

SCIENTIFIC NAME	OCCURRENCE[1]	COMMON NAME (ENGLISH, SPANISH, FRENCH)[2]
Dactylagnus parvus Dawson, 1976	PM	Panamic Stargazer^ ....miraestrellas panámica
Dactyloscopus amnis Miller & Briggs, 1962	PM	Riverine Stargazer ....miraestrellas ribereña
+*Dactyloscopus byersi* Dawson, 1969	PM	Notchtail Stargazer ....miraestrellas colirranurada
Dactyloscopus crossotus Starks, 1913	A	Bigeye Stargazer
*Dactyloscopus elongatus Myers & Wade, 1946	PM	Fringed Stargazer ....miraestrellas orleada
*Dactyloscopus fallax Dawson, 1975	PM	Deceitful Stargazer ....miraestrellas de Chacala
Dactyloscopus foraminosus Dawson, 1982	A	Reticulate Stargazer
*Dactyloscopus heraldi Dawson, 1975	PM	Baja Stargazer^ ....miraestrellas de la Baja
*Dactyloscopus insulatus Dawson, 1975	PM	Island Stargazer ....miraestrellas isleño
Dactyloscopus lunaticus Gilbert, 1890	PM	Moonstruck Stargazer ....miraestrellas lunática
Dactyloscopus metoecus Dawson, 1975	PM	Mexican Stargazer^ ....miraestrellas mexicana
Dactyloscopus minutus Dawson, 1975	PM	Tiny Stargazer ....miraestrellas chiquita
Dactyloscopus moorei (Fowler, 1906)	A	Speckled Stargazer
+*Dactyloscopus pectoralis* Gill, 1861	PM	Whitesaddle Stargazer ....miraestrellas fisgona
Dactyloscopus tridigitatus Gill, 1859	A	Sand Stargazer ....miraestrellas ojilargo
Gillellus arenicola Gilbert, 1890	PM	Sandloving Stargazer ....miraestrellas fina
Gillellus greyae Kanazawa, 1952	A	Arrow Stargazer ....miraestrellas flecha
Gillellus healae Dawson, 1982	A	Masked Stargazer
Gillellus ornatus Gilbert, 1892	PM	Ornate Stargazer ....miraestrellas ornada
Gillellus searcheri Dawson, 1977	PM	Searcher Stargazer^ ....miraestrellas rayada
Gillellus semicinctus Gilbert, 1890	PM	Halfbanded Stargazer ....miraestrellas mediafranjada
Gillellus uranidea Böhlke, 1968	A	Warteye Stargazer ....miraestrellas ojiverrugado
Heteristius cinctus (Osburn & Nichols, 1916)	PM	Banded Stargazer ....miraestrellas vendada
Myxodagnus macrognathus Hildebrand, 1946	PM	Longjaw Stargazer ....miraestrellas bocona
+*Myxodagnus opercularis* Gill, 1861	PM	Dart Stargazer ....miraestrellas virote
*Myxodagnus walkeri Dawson, 1976	PM	Professor Stargazer ....miraestrellas del profesor
*Platygillellus rubrocinctus (Longley, 1934)	A	Saddle Stargazer ....miraestrellas triste

Blenniidae—En-combtooth blennies, Sp-borrachos, Fr-blennies à dents de peigne

| *Chasmodes bosquianus* (Lacepède, 1800) | A | Striped Blenny |
| *Chasmodes longimaxilla* Williams, 1983 | A | Stretchjaw Blenny ....borracho bocón |

SCIENTIFIC NAME	OCCURRENCE[1]	COMMON NAME (ENGLISH, SPANISH, FRENCH)[2]
Chasmodes saburrae Jordan & Gilbert, 1882	A	Florida Blenny^
Entomacrodus chiostictus (Jordan & Gilbert, 1882)	PM	Notchfin Blenny ... borracho aleta mocha
Entomacrodus nigricans Gill, 1859	A	Pearl Blenny ... borracho perlado
Hypleurochilus bermudensis Beebe & Tee-Van, 1933	A	Barred Blenny ... borracho de barras
Hypleurochilus caudovittatus Bath, 1994	A	Zebratail Blenny
Hypleurochilus geminatus (Wood, 1825)	A	Crested Blenny
Hypleurochilus multifilis (Girard, 1858)	A	Featherduster Blenny ... borracho plumero
Hypleurochilus pseudoaequipinnis Bath, 1994	A	Oyster Blenny ... borracho ostionero
Hypleurochilus springeri Randall, 1966	A	Orangespotted Blenny
Hypsoblennius brevipinnis (Günther, 1861)	PM	Barnaclebill Blenny^ ... borracho vacilón
Hypsoblennius gentilis (Girard, 1854)	P	Bay Blenny ... borracho de bahía
Hypsoblennius gilberti (Jordan, 1882)	P	Rockpool Blenny ... borracho de poza
Hypsoblennius hentz (Lesueur, 1825)	A	Feather Blenny
Hypsoblennius invemar Smith-Vaniz & Acero-P., 1980	A	Tessellated Blenny
Hypsoblennius ionthas (Jordan & Gilbert, 1882)	A	Freckled Blenny
Hypsoblennius jenkinsi (Jordan & Evermann, 1896)	P	Mussel Blenny ... borracho mejillonero
Hypsoblennius proteus (Krejsa, 1960)	PM	Socorro Blenny^ ... borracho de Socorro
Lupinoblennius nicholsi (Tavolga, 1954)	A	Highfin Blenny ... borracho aletón
Lupinoblennius vinctus (Poey, 1867)	A	Mangrove Blenny
Ophioblennius macclurei (Silvester, 1915)	A	Redlip Blenny ... borracho labio rojo
Ophioblennius steindachneri Jordan & Evermann, 1898	PM	Panamic Fanged Blenny^ ... borracho mono
Parablennius marmoreus (Poey, 1876)	A	Seaweed Blenny ... borracho marmóreo ... blennie des algues
Plagiotremus azaleus (Jordan & Bollman, 1890)	P	Sabertooth Blenny ... diente sable
Scartella cristata (Linnaeus, 1758)	A	Molly Miller ... borracho peineta

Clinidae—En-kelp blennies, Sp-sargaceros, Fr-clinies

Gibbonsia elegans (Cooper, 1864)	P	Spotted Kelpfish ... sargacero manchado
Gibbonsia metzi Hubbs, 1927	P	Striped Kelpfish ... sargacero rayado ... clinide rayé
Gibbonsia montereyensis Hubbs, 1927	P	Crevice Kelpfish ... sargacero de Monterey ... clinide de crevasse
Heterostichus rostratus Girard, 1854	P	Giant Kelpfish ... sargacero gigante

SCIENTIFIC NAME	OCCURRENCE[1]	COMMON NAME (ENGLISH, SPANISH, FRENCH)[2]
Labrisomidae—En-labrisomid blennies, Sp-trambollos, Fr-labrisomidés		
Alloclinus holderi (Lauderbach, 1907)	P	Island Kelpfish .... trambollo isleño
Cryptotrema corallinum Gilbert, 1890	P	Deepwater Blenny .... trambollo de profundidad
Cryptotrema seftoni Hubbs, 1954	PM	Hidden Blenny .... trambollo escondido
Dialommus macrocephalus (Günther, 1861)	PM	Foureye Rockskipper .... trambollo listo
Exerpes asper (Jenkins & Evermann, 1889)	PM	Sargassum Blenny .... trambollo sargacero
Haptoclinus apectolophus Böhlke & Robins, 1974	AM	Uncombed Blenny .... trambollo despeinado
Labrisomus albigenys Beebe & Tee-Van, 1928	AM	Whitecheek Blenny .... trambollo cachete blanco
Labrisomus bucciferus Poey, 1868	A	Puffcheek Blenny .... trambollo fumador
Labrisomus gobio (Valenciennes, 1836)	A	Palehead Blenny .... trambollo caripálido
Labrisomus guppyi (Norman, 1922)	A	Mimic Blenny .... trambollo mímico
Labrisomus haitiensis Beebe & Tee-Van, 1928	A	Longfin Blenny .... trambollo príncipe
Labrisomus kalisherae (Jordan, 1904)	A	Downy Blenny .... trambollo velloso
Labrisomus multiporosus Hubbs, 1953	PM	Porehead Blenny .... trambollo cabeza porosa
Labrisomus nigricinctus Howell Rivero, 1936	A	Spotcheek Blenny .... trambollo lunado
Labrisomus nuchipinnis (Quoy & Gaimard, 1824)	A	Hairy Blenny .... trambollo peludo
Labrisomus socorroensis Hubbs, 1953	PM	Misspelled Blenny .... trambollo de Socorro
Labrisomus striatus Hubbs, 1953	PM	Green Blenny^ .... trambollo listado
Labrisomus wigginsi Hubbs, 1953	PM	Baja Blenny^ .... trambollo bajacaliforniano
Labrisomus xanti Gill, 1860	PM	Largemouth Blenny .... chalapo
Malacoctenus aurolineatus Smith, 1957	A	Goldline Blenny .... trambollo lineado
Malacoctenus boehlkei Springer, 1959	AM	Diamond Blenny .... trambollo diamantino
Malacoctenus ebisui Springer, 1959	PM	Fishgod Blenny .... trambollo dorado
Malacoctenus erdmani Smith, 1957	AM	Imitator Blenny .... trambollo imitador
Malacoctenus gigas Springer, 1959	PM	Sonora Blenny^ .... trambollo de Sonora
Malacoctenus gilli (Steindachner, 1867)	AM	Dusky Blenny .... trambollo pardo
+*Malacoctenus hubbsi* Springer, 1959	PM	Redside Blenny .... trambollo rojo
Malacoctenus macropus (Poey, 1868)	A	Rosy Blenny .... trambollo rosado
*Malacoctenus mexicanus Springer, 1959	PM	Mexican Margarita Blenny^ .... trambollo margarita mexicana
*Malacoctenus polyporosus Springer, 1959	PM	Chinpore Blenny .... trambollo aujereado
Malacoctenus tetranemus (Cope, 1877)	PM	Throatspotted Blenny .... trambollo pintado
Malacoctenus triangulatus Springer, 1959	A	Saddled Blenny .... trambollo ensillado

SCIENTIFIC NAME	OCCURRENCE[1]	COMMON NAME (ENGLISH, SPANISH, FRENCH)[2]	
Malacoctenus versicolor (Poey, 1876)	AM	Barfin Blenny	trambollo multicolor
Malacoctenus zacae Springer, 1959	PM	Zaca Blenny^	trambollo aletiamarilla
Malacoctenus zonifer (Jordan & Gilbert, 1882)	PM	Glossy Blenny	trambollo brilloso
Nemaclinus atelestos Böhlke & Springer, 1975	A	Threadfin Blenny	
Paraclinus altivelis (Lockington, 1881)	PM	Topgallant Blenny	trambollito juanete
Paraclinus beebei Hubbs, 1952	PM	Pink Blenny	trambollito clavel
Paraclinus cingulatus (Evermann & Marsh, 1899)	A	Coral Blenny	trambollito coralino
Paraclinus ditrichus Rosenblatt & Parr, 1969	PM	Leastfoot Blenny	trambollito pocas patas
Paraclinus fasciatus (Steindachner, 1876)	A	Banded Blenny	trambollito ocelado
Paraclinus grandicomis (Rosén, 1911)	A	Horned Blenny	
Paraclinus infrons Böhlke, 1960	A	Bald Blenny	trambollito pelón
Paraclinus integripinnis (Smith, 1880)	P	Reef Finspot	trambollito de arrecife
Paraclinus magdalenae Rosenblatt & Parr, 1969	PM	Magdalena Blenny^	trambollito de Magdalena
Paraclinus marmoratus (Steindachner, 1876)	A	Marbled Blenny	
Paraclinus mexicanus (Gilbert, 1904)	PM	Mexican Blenny^	trambollito mexicano
Paraclinus naeorhegmis Böhlke, 1960	AM	Surf Blenny	trambollito de la resaca
Paraclinus nigripinnis (Steindachner, 1867)	A	Blackfin Blenny	trambollito aletinegra
Paraclinus sini Hubbs, 1952	PM	Flapscale Blenny	trambollito frondoso
Paraclinus stephensi Rosenblatt & Parr, 1969	PM	Professor Blenny	trambollito del maestro
Paraclinus tanygnathus Rosenblatt & Parr, 1969	PM	Longjaw Blenny	trambollito adornado
*Paraclinus walkeri Hubbs, 1952	PM	San Quintín Blenny^	trambollito de San Quintín
Starksia cremnobates (Gilbert, 1890)	PM	Fugitive Blenny	trambollito fugaz
Starksia fasciata (Longley, 1934)	AM	Blackbar Blenny	trambollito barra oscura
Starksia grammilaga Rosenblatt & Taylor, 1971	PM	Pinstriped Blenny	trambollito estilográfo
Starksia guadalupae Rosenblatt & Taylor, 1971	PM	Guadalupe Blenny^	trambollito de Guadalupe
Starksia hoesei Rosenblatt & Taylor, 1971	PM	Hose Blenny	trambollito manguera
*Starksia langi Castillo & Baldwin, 2011	AM	Longblotch Blenny	trambollito manchón
Starksia lepidogaster Rosenblatt & Taylor, 1971	PM	Scalybelly Blenny	trambollito panza escamosa
Starksia nanodes Böhlke & Springer, 1961	AM	Dwarf Blenny	trambollito enano
Starksia occidentalis Greenfield, 1979	AM	Occidental Blenny	trambollito occidental
Starksia ocellata (Steindachner, 1876)	A	Checkered Blenny	
Starksia posthon Rosenblatt & Taylor, 1971	PM	Brownspotted Blenny	trambollito moteado
*Starksia sangreyae Castillo & Baldwin, 2011	AM	Barred Smootheye Blenny	trambollito chino

SCIENTIFIC NAME	OCCURRENCE[1]	COMMON NAME (ENGLISH, SPANISH, FRENCH)[2]
Starksia spinipenis (Al-Uthman, 1960)	PM	Phallic Blenny......trambollito macho
Starksia starcki Gilbert, 1971	A	Key Blenny......trambollito de cayo
Starksia weigti Baldwin & Castillo, 2011	AM	Whitelip Blenny......trambollito bocablanca
Xenomedea rhodopyga Rosenblatt & Taylor, 1971	PM	Redrump Blenny......trambollito nalga roja
+Chaenopsidae—En-tube blennies, Sp-trambollos tubícolas, Fr-chaenopsidés		
Acanthemblemaria aspera (Longley, 1927)	A	Roughhead Blenny
Acanthemblemaria balanorum Brock, 1940	PM	Clubhead Barnacle Blenny......tubícola espinudo
Acanthemblemaria chaplini Böhlke, 1957	A	Papillose Blenny
Acanthemblemaria crockeri Beebe & Tee-Van, 1938	PM	Browncheek Blenny......tubícola cachetón
Acanthemblemaria greenfieldi Smith-Vaniz & Palacio, 1974	AM	Stalk Blenny......tubícola palito
Acanthemblemaria hastingsi Lin & Galland, 2010	PM	Cortez Barnacle Blenny^......tubícola de Cortés
Acanthemblemaria macrospilus Brock, 1940	PM	Mexican Barnacle Blenny^......tubícola mexicano
Acanthemblemaria mangognatha Hastings & Robertson, 1999	PM	Revillagigedo Barnacle Blenny^...tubícola mango
Acanthemblemaria spinosa Metzelaar, 1919	AM	Spinyhead Blenny......tubícola cabeza espinosa
Chaenopsis alepidota (Gilbert, 1890)	P	Orangethroat Pikeblenny......tubícola lucio
Chaenopsis coheni Böhlke, 1957	PM	Cortez Pikeblenny^......tubícola picudo
Chaenopsis limbaughi Robins & Randall, 1965	A	Yellowface Pikeblenny
Chaenopsis ocellata Poey, 1865	A	Bluethroat Pikeblenny......tubícola afilado
Chaenopsis roseola Hastings & Shipp, 1981	A	Flecked Pikeblenny
Cirriemblemaria lucasana (Stephens, 1963)	PM	Plume Blenny......tubícola plumoso
Coralliozetus angelicus (Böhlke & Mead, 1957)	PM	Angel Blenny......tubícola ángel
Coralliozetus boehlkei Stephens, 1963	PM	Barcheek Blenny......tubícola cachete rayado
Coralliozetus micropes (Beebe & Tee-Van, 1938)	PM	Zebraface Blenny......tubícola cara de cebra
Coralliozetus rosenblatti Stephens, 1963	PM	Spikefin Blenny......tubícola de espiga
Ekemblemaria myersi Stephens, 1963	PM	Reef-sand Blenny......tubícola de cejas
Emblemaria atlantica Jordan & Evermann, 1898	A	Banner Blenny
Emblemaria hypacanthus (Jenkins & Evermann, 1889)	PM	Gulf Signal Blenny^......tubícola flamante
Emblemaria pandionis Evermann & Marsh, 1900	A	Sailfin Blenny......tubícola dragón

SCIENTIFIC NAME	OCCURRENCE[1]	COMMON NAME (ENGLISH, SPANISH, FRENCH)[2]
Emblemaria piratica Ginsburg, 1942	PM	Sailfin Signal Blenny...tubícola bandera
Emblemaria piratula Ginsburg & Reid, 1942	A	Pirate Blenny
Emblemaria walkeri Stephens, 1963	PM	Elusive Signal Blenny...tubícola fugaz
Emblemariopsis bahamensis Stephens, 1961	A	Blackhead Blenny...tubícola cabecinegra
Emblemariopsis diaphana Longley, 1927	A	Glass Blenny
Emblemariopsis occidentalis Stephens, 1970	AM	Redspine Blenny...tubícola espina roja
Emblemariopsis pricei Greenfield, 1975	AM	Seafan Blenny...tubícola gorgonio
Emblemariopsis signifera (Ginsburg, 1942)	AM	Flagfin Blenny...tubícola aletón
*Hemiemblemaria simula Longley & Hildebrand, 1940	A	Wrasse Blenny...tubícola doncella
Neoclinus blanchardi Girard, 1858	P	Sarcastic Fringehead...tubícola chusco
Neoclinus stephensae Hubbs, 1953	P	Yellowfin Fringehead...tubícola aletiamarilla
Neoclinus uninotatus Hubbs, 1953	P	Onespot Fringehead...tubícola mancha singular
*Protemblemaria bicirrus (Hildebrand, 1946)	PM	Warthead Blenny...tubícola tupido
Stathmonotus gymnodermis Springer, 1955	AM	Naked Blenny...tubícola esperanza
*Stathmonotus hemphillii Bean, 1885	A	Blackbelly Blenny
Stathmonotus lugubris Böhlke, 1953	PM	Mexican Worm Blenny^...tubícola lombríz
Stathmonotus sinuscalifornici (Chabanaud, 1942)	PM	Gulf Worm Blenny^...tubícola gusano
*Stathmonotus tekla Nichols, 1910	A	Eelgrass Blenny...tubícola anguila
Icosteidae—En-ragfishes, Sp-peces harapo, Fr-icostéidés		
Icosteus aenigmaticus Lockington, 1880	P	Ragfish...torchon mou
Gobiesocidae—En-clingfishes, Sp-chupapiedras, Fr-crampons		
Acyrtops amplicirrus Briggs, 1955	AM	Flarenostril Clingfish...chupapiedras nariz crestada
*Acyrtops beryllinus (Hildebrand & Ginsburg, 1926)	A	Emerald Clingfish...chupapiedras esmeralda
Acyrtus artius Briggs, 1955	AM	Papillate Clingfish...chupapiedras papilosa
Acyrtus rubiginosus (Poey, 1868)	AM	Red Clingfish...chupapiedras roja
Arcos erythrops (Jordan & Gilbert, 1882)	PM	Rockwall Clingfish...chupapiedras de cantil
Arcos macrophthalmus (Günther, 1861)	AM	Padded Clingfish...chupapiedras acojinada
Derilissus kremmobates Fraser, 1970	AM	Whiskereye Clingfish...chupapiedras ojo estriado
Gobiesox adustus Jordan & Gilbert, 1882	PM	Panamic Clingfish^...chupapiedras panámica

SCIENTIFIC NAME	OCCURRENCE[1]	COMMON NAME (ENGLISH, SPANISH, FRENCH)[2]
Gobiesox aethus (Briggs, 1951)	PM	Clarion Clingfish^...chupapiedras de Clarión
Gobiesox barbatulus Starks, 1913	AM	Lappetlip Clingfish...chupapiedras aristada
Gobiesox canidens (Briggs, 1951)	PM	Socorro Clingfish^...chupapiedras de Socorro
Gobiesox eugrammus Briggs, 1955	P	Lined Clingfish...chupapiedras estriada
Gobiesox fluviatilis Briggs & Miller, 1960	F:M	Mountain Clingfish...cucharita de río
Gobiesox juniperoserrai Espinosa-Pérez & Castro-Aguirre, 1996	F:M	Peninsular Clingfish^...cucharita peninsular
Gobiesox maeandricus (Girard, 1858)	P	Northern Clingfish...chupapiedras norteña...crampon bariolé
Gobiesox marijeanae Briggs, 1960	PM	Lonely Clingfish...chupapiedras solita
Gobiesox mexicanus Briggs & Miller, 1960	F:M	Mexican Clingfish^...cucharita mexicana
Gobiesox papillifer Gilbert, 1890	P	Bearded Clingfish...chupapiedras barbona
Gobiesox pinniger Gilbert, 1890	PM	Tadpole Clingfish...chupapiedras renacuajo
Gobiesox punctulatus (Poey, 1876)	A	Stippled Clingfish...chupapiedras punteada
Gobiesox rhessodon Smith, 1881	P	California Clingfish^...chupapiedras californiana
Gobiesox schultzi Briggs, 1951	PM	Smoothlip Clingfish...chupapiedras labioliso
Gobiesox strumosus Cope, 1870	A	Skilletfish...cazoleta
Pherallodiscus funebris (Gilbert, 1890)	PM	Northern Fraildisc Clingfish...chupapiedras discofrágil norteña
Pherallodiscus varius Briggs, 1955	PM	Southern Fraildisc Clingfish...chupapiedras discofrágil sureña
Rimicola cabrilloi Briggs, 2002	P	Channel Islands Clingfish^
Rimicola dimorpha Briggs, 1955	P	Southern Clingfish...chupapiedras chiquita
Rimicola eigenmanni (Gilbert, 1890)	P	Slender Clingfish...chupapiedras flaca
Rimicola muscarum (Meek & Pierson, 1895)	P	Kelp Clingfish...chupapiedras sargacera...crampon de varech
Rimicola sila Briggs, 1955	PM	Guadalupe Clingfish^...chupapiedras de Guadalupe
Tomicodon absitus Briggs, 1955	PM	Distant Clingfish...chupapiedras lejana
Tomicodon boehlkei Briggs, 1955	PM	Cortez Clingfish^...chupapiedras de Cortés
*Tomicodon eos (Jordan & Gilbert, 1882)	PM	Rosy Clingfish...chupapiedras rosada
Tomicodon humeralis (Gilbert, 1890)	PM	Sonora Clingfish^...chupapiedras de Sonora
Tomicodon myersi Briggs, 1955	PM	Blackstripe Clingfish...chupapiedras raya negra
Tomicodon petersii (Garman, 1875)	PM	Hourglass Clingfish...chupapiedras clepsidra
*Tomicodon reitzae Briggs, 2001	AM	Accidental Clingfish...chupapiedras accidental
*Tomicodon rupestris (Poey, 1860)	AM	Barred Clingfish...chupapiedras de barras
Tomicodon zebra (Jordan & Gilbert, 1882)	PM	Zebra Clingfish...chupapiedras cebra

SCIENTIFIC NAME	OCCURRENCE[1]	COMMON NAME (ENGLISH, SPANISH, FRENCH)[2]
Callionymidae—En-dragonets, Sp-dragoncillos, Fr-dragonnets		
Diplogrammus pauciradiatus (Gill, 1865)	A	Spotted Dragonet...........dragonnet à trois épines
Foetorepus agassizii (Goode & Bean, 1888)	A	Spotfin Dragonet...........callionyme à nageoire tachetée
Foetorepus goodenbeani Nakabo & Hartel, 1999	A	Palefin Dragonet
Paradiplogrammus bairdi (Jordan, 1888)	A	Lancer Dragonet...........dragoncillo coralino
Synchiropus atrilabiatus (Garman, 1899)	P	Blacklip Dragonet ....dragoncillo de asta
+Eleotridae—En-sleepers, Sp-guavinas, Fr-dormeurs		
Dormitator latifrons (Richardson, 1844)	P:F:M	Pacific Fat Sleeper^...........puyeki
Dormitator maculatus (Bloch, 1792)	A-F:UM	Fat Sleeper...........naca
Eleotris amblyopsis (Cope, 1871)	A-F:UM	Largescaled Spinycheek Sleeper..dormilón oscuro
Eleotris perniger (Cope, 1871)	A-F:UM	Smallscaled Spinycheek Sleeper..guavina espinosa
Eleotris picta Kner, 1863	PM-F:UM	Spotted Sleeper...........guavina manchada
Erotelis armiger (Jordan & Richardson, 1895)	PM-F:M	Flathead Sleeper...........guavina cabeza plana
Erotelis smaragdus (Valenciennes, 1837)	A-F:M	Emerald Sleeper...........guavina de concha
Gobiomorus dormitor Lacepède, 1800	A-F:UM	Bigmouth Sleeper...........guavina bocona
Gobiomorus maculatus (Günther, 1859)	PM-F:M	Pacific Sleeper^...........dormilón manchado
Gobiomorus polylepis Ginsburg, 1953	PM-F:M	Finescale Sleeper...........guavina cristalina
Guavina guavina (Valenciennes, 1837)	AM-F:UM	Guavina ....guavina
+Gobiidae—En-gobies, Sp-gobios, Fr-gobies		
Aboma etheostoma Jordan & Starks, 1895	PM	Scaly Goby...........gobio escamoso
Acanthogobius flavimanus (Temminck & Schlegel, 1845)	P[I]-F[I]:UM	Yellowfin Goby...........gobio extranjero
*Antillogobius nikkiae Van Tassell & Colin, 2012	AM	Sabre Goby...........gobio sable
Aruma histrio (Jordan, 1884)	PM	Slow Goby...........gobio lento
+Awaous banana (Valenciennes, 1837)	F:UM	River Goby...........gobio de río
Barbulifer antennatus Böhlke & Robins, 1968	AM	Whiskered Goby...........gobio antenado
Barbulifer ceuthoecus (Jordan & Gilbert, 1884)	A	Bearded Goby
*Barbulifer mexicanus Hoese & Larson, 1985	PM	Saddlebanded Goby ....gobio alambrón
Barbulifer pantherinus (Pellegrin, 1901)	PM	Panther Goby...........gobio pantera

SCIENTIFIC NAME	OCCURRENCE[1]	COMMON NAME (ENGLISH, SPANISH, FRENCH)[2]
*Bathygobius antilliensis Tornabene, Baldwin & Pezold, 2010	A	Antilles Frillfin^
Bathygobius curacao (Metzelaar, 1919)	A	Notchtongue Goby ... gobio jaspeado
*Bathygobius geminatus Tornabene, Baldwin & Pezold, 2010	A	Twinspotted Frillfin
*Bathygobius lacertus (Poey, 1860)	A	Checkerboard Frillfin ... gobio tablero
Bathygobius mystacium Ginsburg, 1947	A	Island Frillfin ... gobio bandeado
Bathygobius ramosus Ginsburg, 1947	PM	Panamic Frillfin^ ... mapo panámico
+Bathygobius soporator (Valenciennes, 1837)	A	Frillfin Goby ... mapo aguado
*Bollmannia boqueronensis Evermann & Marsh, 1899	A	White-eye Goby ... gobio ojiblanco
Bollmannia communis Ginsburg, 1942	A	Ragged Goby ... gobio andrajoso
Bollmannia eigenmanni (Garman, 1896)	A	Shelf Goby
Bollmannia macropoma Gilbert, 1892	PM	Frailscale Goby ... gobio pedernal
Bollmannia marginalis Ginsburg, 1939	PM	Apostrophe Goby ... gobio sellado
Bollmannia ocellata Gilbert, 1892	PM	Pennant Goby ... gobio penacho
Bollmannia stigmatura Gilbert, 1892	PM	Tailspot Goby ... gobio colimanchado
Bollmannia umbrosa Ginsburg, 1939	PM	Dusky Goby ... gobio prieto
Chriolepis benthonis Ginsburg 1953	AM	Deepwater Goby ... gobio de agua profunda
Chriolepis cuneata Bussing, 1990	PM	Rail Goby ... gobio carril
Chriolepis minutillus Gilbert, 1892	PM	Rubble Goby ... gobio conchalero
Chriolepis vespa Hastings & Bortone, 1981	A	Wasp Goby
Chriolepis zebra Ginsburg, 1938	PM	Gecko Goby ... gobio salamanquesa
Clevelandia ios (Jordan & Gilbert, 1882)	P-F:U	Arrow Goby ... gobio flecha ... gobie-flèche
Coryphopterus alloides Böhlke & Robins, 1960	A	Barfin Goby
Coryphopterus dicrus Böhlke & Robins, 1960	A	Colon Goby ... gobio dos puntos
Coryphopterus eidolon Böhlke & Robins, 1960	A	Pallid Goby ... gobio pálido
Coryphopterus glaucofraenum Gill, 1863	A	Bridled Goby ... gobio de riendas
Coryphopterus hyalinus Böhlke & Robins, 1962	A	Glass Goby ... gobio cristal
*Coryphopterus kuna Victor, 2007	A	Kuna Goby
*Coryphopterus lipernes Böhlke & Robins, 1962	A	Peppermint Goby ... gobio linterna
*Coryphopterus personatus (Jordan & Thompson, 1905)	A	Masked Goby ... gobio mapache

SCIENTIFIC NAME	OCCURRENCE[1]	COMMON NAME (ENGLISH, SPANISH, FRENCH)[2]
Coryphopterus punctipectophorus Springer, 1960	A	Spotted Goby...gobio punteado
Coryphopterus thrix Böhlke & Robins, 1960	A	Bartail Goby...gobio listado
+*Coryphopterus tortugae* (Jordan, 1904)	A	Sand Goby
Coryphopterus urospilus Ginsburg, 1938	PM	Redlight Goby...gobio semáforo
Ctenogobius boleosoma (Jordan & Gilbert, 1882)	A-F:UM	Darter Goby...madrejuile
Ctenogobius claytonii (Meek, 1902)	A-F:UM	Mexican Goby^...gobio mexicano
Ctenogobius fasciatus Gill, 1858	F:U	Blotchcheek Goby
Ctenogobius manglicola (Jordan & Starks, 1895)	PM	Mangrove Goby...gobio de manglar
Ctenogobius pseudofasciatus (Gilbert & Randall, 1971)	A-F:U	Slashcheek Goby
Ctenogobius saepepallens (Gilbert & Randall, 1968)	A	Dash Goby...gobio guión
Ctenogobius sagittula (Günther, 1861)	P	Longtail Goby...gobio aguzado
Ctenogobius shufeldti (Jordan & Eigenmann, 1887)	A-F:U	Freshwater Goby
Ctenogobius smaragdus (Valenciennes, 1837)	A	Emerald Goby
Ctenogobius stigmaticus (Poey, 1860)	A	Marked Goby
Ctenogobius stigmaturus (Goode & Bean, 1882)	A	Spottail Goby
Elacatinus digueti (Pellegrin, 1901)	PM	Banded Cleaning Goby...gobio barbero
Elacatinus illecebrosus (Böhlke & Robins, 1968)	AM	Barsnout Goby...gobio seductor
Elacatinus janssi Bussing, 1982	PM	Spotback Goby...gobio lomopintado
Elacatinus jarocho Taylor & Akins, 2007	AM	Jarocho Goby^...gobio jarocho
Elacatinus limbaughi Hoese & Reader, 2001	PM	Widebanded Cleaning Goby...gobio insólito
Elacatinus lobeli Randall & Colin, 2009	AM	Belize Goby^...gobio beliceño
Elacatinus louisae (Böhlke & Robins, 1968)	AM	Spotlight Goby...gobio farol
Elacatinus macrodon (Beebe & Tee-Van, 1928)	A	Tiger Goby...gobio tigre
Elacatinus oceanops Jordan, 1904	A	Neon Goby
Elacatinus prochilos (Böhlke & Robins, 1968)	AM	Broadstripe Goby...gobio bordeado
Elacatinus puncticulatus (Ginsburg, 1938)	PM	Redhead Goby...gobio cabeza roja
Elacatinus redimiculus Taylor & Akins, 2007	AM	Cinta Goby...gobio listón
+*Elacatinus xanthiprora* (Böhlke & Robins, 1968)	A	Yellowprow Goby
Enypnias seminudus (Günther, 1861)	PM	Silt Goby...gobio cienoso
Eucyclogobius newberryi (Girard, 1856)	P-F:U	Tidewater Goby
Evermannia longipinnis (Steindachner, 1879)	PM	Enigmatic Goby...gobio enigmático
Evermannia zosterura (Jordan & Gilbert, 1882)	PM	Bandedtail Goby...gobio colirrayado

SCIENTIFIC NAME	OCCURRENCE[1]	COMMON NAME (ENGLISH, SPANISH, FRENCH)[2]		
Evermannichthys spongicola (Radcliffe, 1917)	A	Sponge Goby	gobio esponjero	
Evorthodus lyricus (Girard, 1858)	A-F:M	Lyre Goby	tismiche	
Evorthodus minutus Meek & Hildebrand, 1928	PM	Small Goby	gobio pequeño	
Gillichthys detrusus Gilbert & Scofield, 1898	PM-F:M	Delta Mudsucker^	chupalodo delta	
Gillichthys mirabilis Cooper, 1864	P-F:UM	Longjaw Mudsucker	chupalodo grande	
Gillichthys seta (Ginsburg, 1938)	PM	Shortjaw Mudsucker	chupalodo chico	
Ginsburgellus novemlineatus (Fowler, 1950)	AM	Ninelined Goby	gobio nueve rayas	
Gnatholepis thompsoni Jordan, 1904	A	Goldspot Goby	gobio puntadorada	
Gobioides broussonetii Lacepède, 1800	A-F:UM	Violet Goby	gobio violeta	
Gobionellus microdon (Gilbert, 1892)	PM-F:M	Palmtail Goby	gobio cola de palma	
Gobionellus oceanicus (Pallas, 1770)	A	Highfin Goby	madrejuile flecha	
Gobiosoma bosc (Lacepède, 1800)	A-F:UM	Naked Goby	gobio desnudo	
Gobiosoma chiquita (Jenkins & Evermann, 1889)	PM	Sonora Goby^	gobio chiquito	
Gobiosoma ginsburgi Hildebrand & Schroeder, 1928	A	Seaboard Goby		
Gobiosoma grosvenori (Robins, 1964)	A	Rockcut Goby		
Gobiosoma longipala Ginsburg, 1933	A	Twoscale Goby		
Gobiosoma nudum (Meek & Hildebrand, 1928)	PM	Knobchin Goby	gobio bulto	
Gobiosoma paradoxum (Günther, 1861)	PM	Paradox Goby	gobio paradoja	
Gobiosoma robustum Ginsburg, 1933	A	Code Goby	gobio clave	
Gobiosoma yucatanum Dawson, 1971	AM	Yucatan Goby^	gobio yucateco	
Gobulus crescentalis (Gilbert, 1892)	PM	Crescent Goby	gobio creciente	
Gobulus hancocki Ginsburg, 1938	PM	Sandtop Goby	gobio invertido	
Gobulus myersi Ginsburg, 1939	A	Paleback Goby		
Gymneleotris seminuda (Günther, 1864)	PM	Splitbanded Goby	gobio blanco y negro	
Ilypnus gilberti (Eigenmann & Eigenmann, 1889)	P	Cheekspot Goby	gobio mejilla manchada	
Ilypnus luculentus Ginsburg, 1938	PM	Bright Goby	gobio brillante	
Lepidogobius lepidus (Girard, 1858)	P	Bay Goby	gobio frío	gobie de baie
Lethops connectens Hubbs, 1926	P	Halfblind Goby	gobio sargacero	
Lophogobius cyprinoides (Pallas, 1770)	A-F:UM	Crested Goby	gobio gallo	
Lythrypnus dalli (Gilbert, 1890)	P	Bluebanded Goby	gobio bonito	
Lythrypnus elasson Böhlke & Robins, 1960	A	Dwarf Goby	gobio enano	
Lythrypnus insularis Bussing, 1990	PM	Distant Goby	gobio isleño	

SCIENTIFIC NAME	OCCURRENCE[1]	COMMON NAME (ENGLISH, SPANISH, FRENCH)[2]
Lythrypnus nesiotes Böhlke & Robins, 1960.	A	Island Goby .... gobio insular
Lythrypnus phorellus Böhlke & Robins, 1960.	A	Convict Goby .... gobio reo
Lythrypnus pulchellus Ginsburg, 1938.	PM	Gorgeous Goby .... gobio coquetón
Lythrypnus rhizophora (Heller & Snodgrass, 1903)	PM	Spottedcheek Goby .... gobio ligero
Lythrypnus spilus Böhlke & Robins, 1960.	A	Bluegold Goby .... gobio marcado
Lythrypnus zebra (Gilbert, 1890)	P	Zebra Goby .... gobio cebra
Microgobius brevispinis Ginsburg, 1939.	PM	Balboa Goby^ .... gobio de Balboa
Microgobius carri Fowler, 1945.	A	Seminole Goby^ ....
Microgobius cyclolepis Gilbert, 1890.	PM	Roundscale Goby .... gobio escamas redondas
Microgobius emblematicus (Jordan & Gilbert, 1882)	PM	Emblem Goby .... gobio emblema
Microgobius erectus Ginsburg, 1938.	PM	Erect Goby .... gobio chato
Microgobius gulosus (Girard, 1858).	A-F:U	Clown Goby .... gobio payaso
Microgobius microlepis Longley & Hildebrand, 1940.	A	Banner Goby ....
Microgobius miraflorensis Gilbert & Starks, 1904.	PM-F:M	Miraflores Goby^ .... gobio de Miraflores
Microgobius tabogensis Meek & Hildebrand, 1928	PM	Taboga Goby^ .... gobio de Taboga
Microgobius thalassinus (Jordan & Gilbert, 1883)	A	Green Goby ....
+*Neogobius melanostomus* (Pallas, 1814).	F[I]:CU	Round Goby .... gobie à taches noires
Nes longus (Nichols, 1914)	A	Orangespotted Goby .... gobio camaronícola
Oxyurichthys stigmalophius (Mead & Böhlke, 1958)	A	Spotfin Goby .... gobio aleta manchada
Palatogobius paradoxus Gilbert, 1971.	A	Mauve Goby ....
Parrella ginsburgi Wade, 1946.	PM	Darkblotch Goby .... gobio lunarejo
Parrella lucretiae (Eigenmann & Eigenmann, 1888)	PM	Maculated Goby .... gobio maculado
Parrella maxillaris Ginsburg, 1938.	PM	Doublestripe Goby .... gobio veteado
Priolepis hipoliti (Metzelaar, 1922)	A	Rusty Goby .... gobio oxidado
*Proterorhinus semilunaris (Heckel, 1837).	F[I]:CU	Freshwater Tubenose Goby .... gobie à nez tubulaire
Psilotris alepis Ginsburg, 1953	AM	Scaleless Goby .... gobio sin escamas
Psilotris batrachodes Böhlke, 1963	AM	Toadfish Goby .... gobio sapito
Psilotris celsus Böhlke, 1963	A	Highspine Goby .... gobio espina alta
Pycnomma semisquamatum Rutter, 1904	PM	Secret Goby .... gobio furtivo
*Quietula guaymasiae (Jenkins & Evermann, 1889)	PM	Guaymas Goby^ .... gobio guaymense
Quietula y-cauda (Jenkins & Evermann, 1889)	P	Shadow Goby .... gobio sombreado
Rhinogobiops nicholsii (Bean, 1882)	P	Blackeye Goby .... gobio triste .... gobie aux yeux noirs

SCIENTIFIC NAME	OCCURRENCE[1]	COMMON NAME (ENGLISH, SPANISH, FRENCH)[2]
Risor ruber (Rosén, 1911)	A	Tusked Goby — gobio boquita
**Robinsichthys arrowsmithensis* Birdsong, 1988	AM	Arrowsmith Goby^ — gobio cuatrorayas
Sicydium gymnogaster Ogilvie-Grant, 1884	F:M	Smoothbelly Goby — dormilón de Veracruz
Sicydium multipunctatum Regan, 1906	F:M	Multispotted Goby — dormilón pecoso
Tridentiger barbatus (Günther, 1861)	P[I]-F[I]:U	Shokihaze Goby^
Tridentiger bifasciatus Steindachner, 1881	F[I]:U	Shimofuri Goby
Tridentiger trigonocephalus (Gill, 1859)	P[I]	Chameleon Goby
Typhlogobius californiensis Steindachner, 1879	P	Blind Goby — gobio ciego
Varicus marilynae Gilmore, 1979	A	Orangebelly Goby
Microdesmidae—En-wormfishes, Sp-peces lombriz, Fr-poissons-lombrics		
Cerdale floridana Longley, 1934	A	Pugjaw Wormfish
Clarkichthys bilineatus (Clark, 1936)	PM	Flagtail Wormfish — pez lombriz colibandera
Microdesmus affinis Meek & Hildebrand, 1928	PM	Olivaceous Wormfish — pez lombriz oliváceo
Microdesmus carri Gilbert, 1966	AM	Stippled Wormfish — pez lombriz punteado
Microdesmus dipus Günther, 1864	PM	Banded Wormfish — pez lombriz rayado
Microdesmus dorsipunctatus Dawson, 1968	PM	Spotback Wormfish — pez lombriz lomo punteado
Microdesmus lanceolatus Dawson, 1962	A	Lancetail Wormfish
Microdesmus longipinnis (Weymouth, 1910)	A	Pink Wormfish
Microdesmus retropinnis Jordan & Gilbert, 1882	PM	Rearfin Wormfish — pez lombriz aletatrasera
Microdesmus suttkusi Gilbert, 1966	PM	Spotside Wormfish — pez lombriz manchado
Ptereleotridae—En-dartfishes, Sp-gobios dardos, Fr-ptéréléotridés		
Ptereleotris calliura (Jordan & Gilbert, 1882)	A	Blue Dartfish — gobio dardo azul
Ptereleotris carinata Bussing, 2001	PM	Panamic Dartfish^ — gobio dardo panámico
Ptereleotris helenae (Randall, 1968)	A	Hovering Dartfish
Ephippidae—En-spadefishes, Sp-peluqueros, Fr-chèvres de mer		
Chaetodipterus faber (Broussonet, 1782)	A	Atlantic Spadefish^ — chabela
Chaetodipterus zonatus (Girard, 1858)	P	Pacific Spadefish^ — chambo
Parapsettus panamensis Steindachner, 1876	PM	Panama Spadefish^ — zapatero

SCIENTIFIC NAME	OCCURRENCE[1]	COMMON NAME (ENGLISH, SPANISH, FRENCH)[2]
		Luvaridae—En-louvars, Sp-emperadores, Fr-louvereaux
Luvarus imperialis Rafinesque, 1810	A-P	Louvar ....emperador
		Zanclidae—En-Moorish idols, Sp-ídolos moros, Fr-cochers
Zanclus cornutus (Linnaeus, 1758)	PM	Moorish Idol^ ....ídolo moro
		Acanthuridae—En-surgeonfishes, Sp-cirujanos, Fr-poissons-chirurgiens
Acanthurus achilles Shaw, 1803	PM	Achilles Tang^ ....cirujano encendido
Acanthurus chirurgus (Bloch, 1787)	A	Doctorfish ....cirujano rayado
Acanthurus coeruleus Bloch & Schneider, 1801	A	Blue Tang ....cirujano azul
Acanthurus nigricans (Linnaeus, 1758)	PM	Goldrim Surgeonfish ....cirujano cariblanco
*Acanthurus tractus Poey, 1860	A	Ocean Surgeon ....cirujano pardo
Acanthurus triostegus (Linnaeus, 1758)	PM	Convict Surgeonfish ....cirujano reo
Acanthurus xanthopterus Valenciennes, 1835	PM	Yellowfin Surgeonfish ....cirujano aleta amarilla
*Ctenochaetus marginatus (Valenciennes, 1835)	PM	Bluespotted Surgeonfish ....cirujano estriado
Prionurus laticlavius (Valenciennes, 1846)	PM	Razor Surgeonfish ....cochinito barbero
Prionurus punctatus Gill, 1862	PM	Yellowtail Surgeonfish ....cochinito punteado
		Sphyraenidae—En-barracudas, Sp-barracudas, Fr-barracudas
Sphyraena argentea Girard, 1854	P	Pacific Barracuda^ ....barracuda plateada..............barracuda argenté
Sphyraena barracuda (Edwards, 1771)	A	Great Barracuda^ ....barracuda
*Sphyraena borealis DeKay, 1842	A	Sennet ....picudilla
Sphyraena ensis Jordan & Gilbert, 1882	P	Mexican Barracuda^ ....barracuda mexicana
Sphyraena guachancho Cuvier, 1829	A	Guaguanche ....tolete
Sphyraena idiastes Heller & Snodgrass, 1903	PM	Pelican Barracuda ....barracuda pelicano
Sphyraena lucasana Gill, 1863	PM	Cortez Barracuda^ ....barracuda de Cortés
*Sphyraena qenie Klunzinger, 1870	PM	Blackfin Barracuda ....barracuda aleta negra
		Gempylidae—En-snake mackerels, Sp-escolares, Fr-escolars
Diplospinus multistriatus Maul, 1948	A	Striped Escolar ....escolar rayado
Epinnula magistralis Poey, 1854	AM	Domine ....dominó

SCIENTIFIC NAME	OCCURRENCE[1]	COMMON NAME (ENGLISH, SPANISH, FRENCH)[2]		
Gempylus serpens Cuvier, 1829	A-P	Snake Mackerel	escolar de canal	
Lepidocybium flavobrunneum (Smith, 1843)	A-P	Escolar	escolar negro	escolar
Nealotus tripes Johnson, 1865	A-PM	Black Snake Mackerel	escolar listado	coelho tripode
Neoepinnula americana (Grey, 1953)	A	American Sackfish^	escolar americano	
Nesiarchus nasutus Johnson, 1862	A	Black Gemfish	escolar narigudo	
Ruvettus pretiosus Cocco, 1833	A-P	Oilfish	escolar clavo	rouvet

Trichiuridae—En-cutlassfishes, Sp-sables, Fr-sabres de mer

Assurger anzac (Alexander, 1917)	P	Razorback Scabbardfish	sable aserrado	
Benthodesmus pacificus Parin & Becker, 1970	P	North Pacific Frostfish^	cintilla del Pacífico	poisson sabre nord-pacifique
Benthodesmus simonyi (Steindachner, 1891)	A	North Atlantic Frostfish^	cintilla del Atlántico	poisson sabre ganse
+*Evoxymetopon taeniatus* Poey, 1863	A	Channel Scabbardfish		poisson sabre canal
Lepidopus altifrons Parin & Collette, 1993	A	Crested Scabbardfish		
Lepidopus fitchi Rosenblatt & Wilson, 1987	P	Pacific Scabbardfish^	pez cinto	
Trichiurus lepturus Linnaeus, 1758	A	Atlantic Cutlassfish^	sable del Atlántico	
Trichiurus nitens Garman, 1899	P	Pacific Cutlassfish^	sable del Pacífico	

Scombridae—En-mackerels, Sp-macarelas, Fr-maquereaux

Acanthocybium solandri (Cuvier, 1832)	A-PM	Wahoo	peto	
Allothunnus fallai Serventy, 1948	P	Slender Tuna	atún lanzón	
Auxis rochei (Risso, 1810)	A-P	Bullet Mackerel	melvera	bonitou
Auxis thazard (Lacepède, 1800)	A-P	Frigate Mackerel	melva	
Euthynnus affinis (Cantor, 1849)	P	Kawakawa	bacoreta oriental	
Euthynnus alletteratus (Rafinesque, 1810)	A	Little Tunny	bacoreta	thonine commune
Euthynnus lineatus Kishinouye, 1920	P	Black Skipjack	barrilete negro	
Katsuwonus pelamis (Linnaeus, 1758)	A-P	Skipjack Tuna	barrilete listado	bonite à ventre rayé
Sarda chiliensis (Cuvier, 1832)	P	Pacific Bonito^	bonito del Pacífico oriental	bonite du Pacifique
Sarda orientalis (Temminck & Schlegel, 1844)	PM	Striped Bonito	bonito mono	
Sarda sarda (Bloch, 1793)	A	Atlantic Bonito^	bonito del Atlántico	bonite à dos rayé
Scomber australasicus Cuvier, 1832	PM	Spotted Chub Mackerel	macarela pintoja	
Scomber colias Gmelin, 1789	A	Atlantic Chub Mackerel^	macarela estornino	maquereau blanc
Scomber japonicus Houttuyn, 1782	P	Pacific Chub Mackerel^	macarela estornino	maquereau du Pacifique

SCIENTIFIC NAME	OCCURRENCE[1]	COMMON NAME (ENGLISH, SPANISH, FRENCH)[2]		
Scomber scombrus Linnaeus, 1758	A	Atlantic Mackerel^		maquereau bleu
Scomberomorus brasiliensis Collette, Russo & Zavala-Camin, 1978	AM	Serra	serra	
Scomberomorus cavalla (Cuvier, 1829)	A	King Mackerel	carito	thazard
Scomberomorus concolor (Lockington, 1879)	P	Gulf Sierra^	sierra golfina	
Scomberomorus maculatus (Mitchill, 1815)	A	Spanish Mackerel^	sierra común	thazard tacheté
Scomberomorus regalis (Bloch, 1793)	A	Cero	sierra	
Scomberomorus sierra Jordan & Starks, 1895	P	Pacific Sierra^	sierra del Pacifico	
Thunnus alalunga (Bonnaterre, 1788)	A-P	Albacore	albacora	germon atlantique
Thunnus albacares (Bonnaterre, 1788)	A-P	Yellowfin Tuna	atún aleta amarilla	albacore à nageoires jaunes
Thunnus atlanticus (Lesson, 1831)	A	Blackfin Tuna	atún aleta negra	
Thunnus obesus (Lowe, 1839)	A-P	Bigeye Tuna	patudo	thon obèse
Thunnus orientalis (Temminck & Schlegel, 1844)	P	Pacific Bluefin Tuna^	atún cimarrón	
Thunnus thynnus (Linnaeus, 1758)	A	Bluefin Tuna	atún aleta azul	thon rouge

Xiphiidae—En-swordfishes, Sp-espadas, Fr-espadons

SCIENTIFIC NAME	OCCURRENCE	ENGLISH	SPANISH	FRENCH
Xiphias gladius Linnaeus, 1758	A-P	Swordfish	pez espada	espadon

*Istiophoridae—En-billfishes, Sp-picudos, Fr-voiliers

SCIENTIFIC NAME	OCCURRENCE	ENGLISH	SPANISH	FRENCH
*Istiompax indica (Cuvier, 1832)	P	Black Marlin	marlin negro	
Istiophorus platypterus (Shaw, 1792)	A-P	Sailfish	pez vela	
*Kajikia albida (Poey, 1860)	A	White Marlin	marlin blanco	makaire blanc
*Kajikia audax (Philippi, 1887)	P	Striped Marlin	marlin rayado	
+Makaira nigricans Lacepède, 1802	A-P	Blue Marlin	marlin azul	makaire bleu
Tetrapturus angustirostris Tanaka, 1915	P	Shortbill Spearfish	marlin trompa corta	
*Tetrapturus georgii Lowe, 1841	A	Roundscale Spearfish		
Tetrapturus pfluegeri Robins & de Sylva, 1963	A	Longbill Spearfish	marlin trompa larga	

Centrolophidae—En-medusafishes, Sp-cojinobas, Fr-pompiles

SCIENTIFIC NAME	OCCURRENCE	ENGLISH	SPANISH	FRENCH
Centrolophus niger (Gmelin, 1789)	A	Black Ruff		pompile noir
Hyperoglyphe bythites (Ginsburg, 1954)	A	Black Driftfish		
Hyperoglyphe perciformis (Mitchill, 1818)	A	Barrelfish		pompile d'Amérique

SCIENTIFIC NAME	OCCURRENCE[1]	COMMON NAME (ENGLISH, SPANISH, FRENCH)[2]		
Icichthys lockingtoni Jordan & Gilbert, 1880	P	Medusafish	cojinoba medusa	stromatée-méduse
Schedophilus medusophagus (Cocco, 1839)	A	Brown Ruff		pompile brun
Schedophilus pemarco (Poll, 1959)	A	Pemarco Blackfish^		
Nomeidae—En-driftfishes, Sp-derivantes, Fr-physaliers				
Cubiceps capensis (Smith, 1845)	A	Cape Cigarfish^		pompile du cap
Cubiceps paradoxus Butler, 1979	P	Longfin Cigarfish	derivante colón	
Cubiceps pauciradiatus Günther, 1872	A-PM	Bigeye Cigarfish	derivante ojón	pompile paucirayonné
Nomeus gronovii (Gmelin, 1789)	A-PM	Man-of-war Fish	derivante fragata portuguesa	
Psenes cyanophrys Valenciennes, 1833	A	Freckled Driftfish	derivante rayado	
Psenes maculatus Lütken, 1880	A	Silver Driftfish		psène maculé
Psenes pellucidus Lütken, 1880	A-P	Bluefin Driftfish	derivante aleta azul	
Psenes sio Haedrich, 1970	PM	Twospine Driftfish	derivante dos espinas	
Ariommatidae—En-ariommatids, Sp-pastorcillos, Fr-poissons pailletés				
Ariomma bondi Fowler, 1930	A	Silver-rag	pastorcillo lucía	semble-coulirou
Ariomma melanum (Ginsburg, 1954)	A	Brown Driftfish	pastorcillo café	
Ariomma regulus (Poey, 1868)	A	Spotted Driftfish	pastorcillo aquillado	
Tetragonuridae—En-squaretails, Sp-colicuadrados, Fr-tétragonures				
Tetragonurus atlanticus Lowe, 1839	A	Bigeye Squaretail		
Tetragonurus cuvieri Risso, 1810	P	Smalleye Squaretail	colicuadrado ojito	tétragonure lilas
Stromateidae—En-butterfishes, Sp-palometas, Fr-stromatées				
Peprilus burti Fowler, 1944	A	Gulf Butterfish^	palometa del Golfo	
Peprilus medius (Peters, 1869)	PM	Pacific Harvestfish^	palometa	
Peprilus ovatus Horn, 1970	PM	Cortez Butterfish^	palometa de Cortés	
Peprilus paru (Linnaeus, 1758)	A	Harvestfish	palometa pámpano	
Peprilus simillimus (Ayres, 1860)	P	Pacific Pompano^	palometa plateada	pompano du Pacifique
Peprilus snyderi Gilbert & Starks, 1904	PM	Salema Butterfish	palometa salema	
Peprilus triacanthus (Peck, 1804)	A-Ar	Butterfish		stromatée à fossettes

SCIENTIFIC NAME	OCCURRENCE[1]	COMMON NAME (ENGLISH, SPANISH, FRENCH)[2]
	*Osphronemidae—En-gouramies, Sp-guramis, Fr-gouramies	
Trichopsis vittata (Cuvier, 1831)	F[I]:U	Croaking Gourami
	Channidae—En-snakeheads, Sp-cabezas de serpiente, Fr-têtes-de-serpent	
Channa argus (Cantor, 1842)	F[I]:U	Northern Snakehead
Channa marulius (Hamilton, 1822)	F[I]:U	Bullseye Snakehead
	+Caproidae—En-boarfishes, Sp-verracos, Fr-sangliers	
Antigonia capros Lowe, 1843	A	Deepbody Boarfish	verraco alto
Antigonia combatia Berry & Rathjen, 1959	A	Shortspine Boarfish
	+ORDER PLEURONECTIFORMES	
	Scophthalmidae—En-turbots, Sp-rodaballos, Fr-scophthalmidés	
Scophthalmus aquosus (Mitchill, 1815)	A	Windowpane	turbot de sable
	Paralichthyidae—En-sand flounders, Sp-lenguados areneros, Fr-flétans de sable	
Ancylopsetta dendritica Gilbert, 1890	PM	Threespot Sand Flounder	lenguado tresojos
Ancylopsetta dilecta (Goode & Bean, 1883)	A	Three-eye Flounder	lenguado tres manchas
Ancylopsetta quadrocellata Gill, 1864	A	Ocellated Flounder	lenguado cuatro manchas
Citharichthys abbotti Dawson, 1969	AM	Veracruz Whiff^	lenguado veracruzano
Citharichthys arctifrons Goode, 1880	A	Gulf Stream Flounder^	lenguado golfino	plie du Gulf Stream
Citharichthys arenaceus Evermann & Marsh, 1900	A	Sand Whiff
Citharichthys cornutus (Günther, 1880)	A	Horned Whiff	lenguado cornudo
Citharichthys dinoceros Goode & Bean, 1886	A	Spined Whiff	lenguado espinoso
Citharichthys fragilis Gilbert, 1890	P	Gulf Sanddab^	lenguado flaco
Citharichthys gilberti Jenkins & Evermann, 1889	PM	Bigmouth Sanddab	lenguado tapadera
Citharichthys gordae Beebe & Tee-Van, 1938	PM	Mimic Sanddab	lenguado escondido
Citharichthys gymnorhinus Gutherz & Blackman, 1970	A	Anglefin Whiff
Citharichthys macrops Dresel, 1885	A	Spotted Whiff	lenguado manchado

SCIENTIFIC NAME	OCCURRENCE[1]	COMMON NAME (ENGLISH, SPANISH, FRENCH)[2]
Citharichthys mariajorisae van der Heiden & Mussot, 1995	PM	Five-rayed Sanddab...lenguado cinco radios
Citharichthys platophrys Gilbert, 1891	PM	Small Sanddab...lenguado frentón
Citharichthys sordidus (Girard, 1854)	P	Pacific Sanddab^...lenguado moteado...limande sordide
Citharichthys spilopterus Günther, 1862	A-F:U	Bay Whiff...lenguado pardo
Citharichthys stigmaeus Jordan & Gilbert, 1882	P	Speckled Sanddab...lenguado pecoso...limande tachetée
Citharichthys uhleri Jordan, 1889	AM	Voodoo Whiff...lenguado albimoteado
Citharichthys xanthostigma Gilbert, 1890	P	Longfin Sanddab...lenguado alón
Cyclopsetta chittendeni Bean, 1895	A	Mexican Flounder^...lenguado mexicano
Cyclopsetta fimbriata (Goode & Bean, 1885)	A	Spotfin Flounder^...lenguado aleta sucia
Cyclopsetta panamensis (Steindachner, 1876)	PM	Panamic Flounder^...lenguado panámico
*Cyclopsetta querna (Jordan & Bollman, 1890)	PM	Toothed Flounder...lenguado dientón
*Etropus ciadi van der Heiden & Plascencia-González, 2005	PM	Intermediate Flounder...lenguado intermedio
Etropus crossotus Jordan & Gilbert, 1882	A-PM	Fringed Flounder...lenguado ribete
Etropus cyclosquamus Leslie & Stewart, 1986	A	Shelf Flounder
Etropus microstomus (Gill, 1864)	A	Smallmouth Flounder
Etropus peruvianus Hildebrand, 1946	PM	Peruvian Flounder^...lenguado zapatilla
Etropus rimosus Goode & Bean, 1885	A	Gray Flounder...lenguado sombreado
Gastropsetta frontalis Bean, 1895	A	Shrimp Flounder...lenguado gambero
Hippoglossina bollmani Gilbert, 1890	PM	Spotted Flounder...lenguado pintado
Hippoglossina stomata Eigenmann & Eigenmann, 1890	P	Bigmouth Sole...lenguado bocón
Hippoglossina tetrophthalma (Gilbert, 1890)	PM	Foureye Flounder...lenguado cuatrojos
Paralichthys aestuarius Gilbert & Scofield, 1898	PM	Cortez Halibut^...lenguado de Cortés
Paralichthys albigutta Jordan & Gilbert, 1882	A	Gulf Flounder^...lenguado panzablanca
Paralichthys californicus (Ayres, 1859)	P	California Halibut^...lenguado californiano
Paralichthys dentatus (Linnaeus, 1766)	A	Summer Flounder...cardeau d'été
Paralichthys lethostigma Jordan & Gilbert, 1884	A-F:U	Southern Flounder...lenguado limpio
Paralichthys oblongus (Mitchill, 1815)	A	Fourspot Flounder...cardeau à quatre ocelles
Paralichthys squamilentus Jordan & Gilbert, 1882	A	Broad Flounder...lenguado huarachón
Paralichthys woolmani Jordan & Williams, 1897	PM	Dappled Flounder...lenguado huarache
Syacium gunteri Ginsburg, 1933	A	Shoal Flounder...lenguado arenoso

SCIENTIFIC NAME	OCCURRENCE[1]	COMMON NAME (ENGLISH, SPANISH, FRENCH)[2]		
Syacium latifrons (Jordan & Gilbert, 1882)	PM	Beach Flounder	lenguado playero	
Syacium longidorsale Murakami & Amaoka, 1992	PM	Pompadour Flounder	lenguado copetón	
Syacium micrurum Ranzani, 1842	A	Channel Flounder	lenguado anillado	fausse limande pâté
Syacium ovale (Günther, 1864)	PM	Oval Flounder	lenguado ovalado	
Syacium papillosum (Linnaeus, 1758)	A	Dusky Flounder	lenguado moreno	
Xystreurys liolepis Jordan & Gilbert, 1880	P	Fantail Sole	lenguado cola de abanico	

Pleuronectidae—En-righteye flounders, Sp-platijas, Fr-plies

SCIENTIFIC NAME	OCCURRENCE[1]	COMMON NAME (ENGLISH, SPANISH, FRENCH)[2]		
Atheresthes evermanni Jordan & Starks, 1904	P	Kamchatka Flounder^		plie à grande bouche
Atheresthes stomias (Jordan & Gilbert, 1880)	P	Arrowtooth Flounder		plie de profondeur
Embassichthys bathybius (Gilbert, 1890)	P	Deepsea Sole		plie de Californie
Eopsetta jordani (Lockington, 1879)	P	Petrale Sole	platija petrale	plie grise
Glyptocephalus cynoglossus (Linnaeus, 1758)	A-Ar	Witch Flounder		plie royale
Glyptocephalus zachirus Lockington, 1879	P	Rex Sole	platija rey	plie à tête plate
Hippoglossoides elassodon Jordan & Gilbert, 1880	P	Flathead Sole		plie canadienne
Hippoglossoides platessoides (Fabricius, 1780)	A-Ar	American Plaice^		plie de Béring
Hippoglossoides robustus Gill & Townsend, 1897	P-Ar	Bering Flounder^		flétan atlantique
Hippoglossus hippoglossus (Linnaeus, 1758)	A-Ar	Atlantic Halibut^		flétan du Pacifique
Hippoglossus stenolepis Schmidt, 1904	P	Pacific Halibut^	alabato del Pacifico	plie à écailles régulières
Isopsetta isolepis (Lockington, 1880)	P	Butter Sole		fausse limande du Pacifique
Lepidopsetta bilineata (Ayres, 1855)	P	Rock Sole		limande du nord
Lepidopsetta polyxystra Orr & Matarese, 2000	P	Northern Rock Sole		limande à nageoires jaunes
Limanda aspera (Pallas, 1814)	P	Yellowfin Sole		limande à queue jaune
Limanda ferruginea (Storer, 1839)	A	Yellowtail Flounder		limande carline
Limanda proboscidea Gilbert, 1896	P-Ar	Longhead Dab		
Limanda sakhalinensis Hubbs, 1915	P	Sakhalin Sole^		
Lyopsetta exilis (Jordan & Gilbert, 1880)	P	Slender Sole	platija flaca	plie mince
Microstomus kitt (Walbaum, 1792)	A	Lemon Sole		limande-sole
Microstomus pacificus (Lockington, 1879)	P	Dover Sole^	platija resbalosa	carlottin anglais
Parophrys vetulus (Girard, 1854)	P	English Sole^	platija limón	flet étoilé
Platichthys stellatus (Pallas, 1788)	P-Ar-F-CU	Starry Flounder^		plie arctique
Pleuronectes glacialis Pallas, 1776	P-Ar	Arctic Flounder^		

SCIENTIFIC NAME	OCCURRENCE[1]	COMMON NAME (ENGLISH, SPANISH, FRENCH)[2]
Pleuronectes putnami (Gill, 1864)	A-Ar	Smooth Flounder ... plie lisse
Pleuronectes quadrituberculatus Pallas, 1814	P	Alaska Plaice^
Pleuronichthys coenosus Girard, 1854	P	C-O Sole^ ... platija de fango ... plie vaseuse
Pleuronichthys decurrens Jordan & Gilbert, 1881	P	Curlfin Sole ... platija aleta de rizo ... plie à nageoires frisées
Pleuronichthys guttulatus Girard, 1856	P	Diamond Turbot ... platija diamante
Pleuronichthys ocellatus Starks & Thompson, 1910	PM	Ocellated Turbot ... platija ocelada
Pleuronichthys ritteri Starks & Morris, 1907	P	Spotted Turbot ... platija moteada
Pleuronichthys verticalis Jordan & Gilbert, 1880	P	Hornyhead Turbot ... platija cornuda
Psettichthys melanostictus Girard, 1854	P	Sand Sole ... sole de sable
Pseudopleuronectes americanus (Walbaum, 1792)	A	Winter Flounder ... plie rouge
Reinhardtius hippoglossoides (Walbaum, 1792)	A-P-Ar	Greenland Halibut^ ... platija negra ... flétan du Groenland

Bothidae—En-lefteye flounders, Sp-lenguados chuecos, Fr-turbots

Bothus constellatus (Jordan, 1889)	PM	Pacific Eyed Flounder^ ... lenguado hoja
Bothus leopardinus (Günther, 1862)	PM	Pacific Leopard Flounder^ ... lenguado leopardo del Pacífico
Bothus lunatus (Linnaeus, 1758)	A	Peacock Flounder ... lenguado lunado
Bothus mancus (Broussonet, 1782)	PM	Tropical Flounder ... lenguado tropical
Bothus ocellatus (Agassiz, 1831)	A	Eyed Flounder ... chueco playón ... plie oculée
Bothus robinsi Topp & Hoff, 1972	A	Twospot Flounder ... chueco dos manchas
Engyophrys sanctilaurentii Jordan & Bollman, 1890	P	Speckledtail Flounder ... lenguado colimanchada
Engyophrys senta Ginsburg, 1933	A	Spiny Flounder ... lenguado ojicornudo
Monolene antillarum Norman, 1933	A	Slim Flounder
Monolene asaedai Clark, 1936	PM	Dark Flounder ... lenguado carbón
Monolene dubiosa Garman, 1899	PM	Acapulco Flounder^ ... lenguado acapulqueño
*Monolene maculipinna Garman, 1899	PM	Pacific Deepwater Flounder^ ... lenguado de profundidad
Monolene sessilicauda Goode, 1880	A	Deepwater Flounder ... cardeau des profondeurs
Perissias taeniopterus (Gilbert, 1890)	PM	Flag Flounder ... lenguado bandera
Trichopsetta ventralis (Goode & Bean, 1885)	A	Sash Flounder ... lenguado de punto

Poecilopsettidae—En-bigeye flounders, Sp-lenguados ojones, Fr-plies à grands yeux

Poecilopsetta beanii (Goode, 1881)	A	Deepwater Dab ... lenguado ojón

SCIENTIFIC NAME	OCCURRENCE[1]	COMMON NAME (ENGLISH, SPANISH, FRENCH)[2]
Achiridae—En-American soles, Sp-lenguados suelas, Fr-soles américaines		
Achirus klunzingeri (Steindachner, 1879)	PM	Brown Sole...suela plomiza
Achirus lineatus (Linnaeus, 1758)	A	Lined Sole...suela listada
Achirus mazatlanus (Steindachner, 1869)	PM	Pacific Lined Sole^...tepalcate
Achirus scutum (Günther, 1862)	PM	Network Sole...comal
Achirus zebrinus Clark, 1936	PM	Tehuantepec Sole^...suela cebra
Gymnachirus melas Nichols, 1916	A	Naked Sole...suela desnuda
Gymnachirus nudus Kaup, 1858	AM	Flabby Sole...suela fofa
Gymnachirus texae (Gunter, 1936)	A	Fringed Sole...suela texana
Trinectes fimbriatus (Günther, 1862)	PM	Whitespotted Sole...suela pintada
Trinectes fonsecensis (Günther, 1862)	PM-F:M	Spottedfin Sole...suela rayada
Trinectes inscriptus (Gosse, 1851)	A	Scrawled Sole...suela garabato
Trinectes maculatus (Bloch & Schneider, 1801)	A-F:UM	Hogchoker...suela tortilla
Trinectes paulistanus (Miranda-Ribeiro, 1915)	AM	Southern Hogchoker...suela carioca
Soleidae—En-soles, Sp-suelas soles, Fr-soles		
Aseraggodes herrei Seale, 1940	PM	Reticulated Sole...sol reticulado
Cynoglossidae—En-tonguefishes, Sp-lenguas, Fr-soles-langues		
Symphurus arawak Robins & Randall, 1965	A	Caribbean Tonguefish^...lengua caribeña
Symphurus atramentatus Jordan & Bollman, 1890	PM	Halfspotted Tonguefish...lengua mediomanchada
Symphurus atricaudus (Jordan & Gilbert, 1880)	P	California Tonguefish^...lengua californiana...sole californienne
Symphurus billykrietei Munroe, 1998	A	Chocolatebanded Tonguefish...lengua boba...sole de Kriete
Symphurus callopterus Munroe & Mahadeva, 1989	PM	Chocolate Tonguefish...lengua chocolate
Symphurus chabanaudi Mahadeva & Munroe, 1990	PM	Darkcheek Tonguefish...lengua cachete prieto
Symphurus civitatium Ginsburg, 1951	A	Offshore Tonguefish...lengua gatita
Symphurus diomedeanus (Goode & Bean, 1885)	A	Spottedfin Tonguefish...lengua filonegro...sole tachetée
Symphurus elongatus (Günther, 1868)	PM	Elongate Tonguefish...lengua esbelta
Symphurus fasciolaris Gilbert, 1892	PM	Banded Tonguefish...lengua listada
Symphurus gorgonae Chabanaud, 1948	PM	Dwarf Tonguefish...lengua enana
Symphurus leei Jordan & Bollman, 1890	PM	Blacktail Tonguefish...lengua colinegra

SCIENTIFIC NAME	OCCURRENCE[1]	COMMON NAME (ENGLISH, SPANISH, FRENCH)[2]
Symphurus marginatus (Goode & Bean, 1886)	A	Margined Tonguefish
Symphurus melanurus Clark, 1936	PM	Drab Tonguefish.........lengua lucia
Symphurus melasmatotheca Munroe & Nizinski, 1990	PM	Darkbelly Tonguefish.........lengua tripa negra
Symphurus minor Ginsburg, 1951	A	Largescale Tonguefish
Symphurus oligomerus Mahadeva & Munroe, 1990	PM	Whitetail Tonguefish.........lengua coliblanca
Symphurus parvus Ginsburg, 1951	A	Pygmy Tonguefish.........lengua pigmea
Symphurus pelicanus Ginsburg, 1951	A	Longtail Tonguefish.........lengua colilarga
Symphurus piger (Goode & Bean, 1886)	A	Deepwater Tonguefish.........lengua perezosa
Symphurus plagiusa (Linnaeus, 1766)	A	Blackcheek Tonguefish.........lengua gris
Symphurus prolatinaris Munroe, Nizinski & Mahadeva, 1991	PM	Halfstriped Tonguefish.........lengua narigona
Symphurus pusillus (Goode & Bean, 1885)	A	Northern Tonguefish
Symphurus stigmosus Munroe, 1998	A	Blotchfin Tonguefish
Symphurus undecimplerus Munroe & Nizinski, 1990	PM	Imitator Tonguefish.........lengua imitador
Symphurus urospilus Ginsburg, 1951	A	Spottail Tonguefish.........lengua colipunteada
Symphurus williamsi Jordan & Culver, 1895	PM	Yellow Tonguefish.........lengua amarillenta

ORDER TETRAODONTIFORMES

Triacanthodidae—En-spikefishes, Sp-cochis espinosos, Fr-triacanthodidés

Hollardia meadi Tyler, 1966	A	Spotted Spikefish
Parahollardia lineata (Longley, 1935)	A	Jambeau.........cochi rombo

Balistidae—En-triggerfishes, Sp-cochitos, Fr-balistes

Balistes capriscus Gmelin, 1789	A	Gray Triggerfish.........pejepuerco blanco.........baliste capri
Balistes polylepis Steindachner, 1876	P	Finescale Triggerfish.........cochi
Balistes vetula Linnaeus, 1758	A	Queen Triggerfish.........cochino.........baliste royal
Canthidermis maculata (Bloch, 1786)	A-PM	Rough Triggerfish.........cochito manchado
Canthidermis sufflamen (Mitchill, 1815)	A	Ocean Triggerfish.........sobaco lija
Melichthys niger (Bloch, 1786)	A-P	Black Durgon.........cochito negro
Melichthys vidua (Richardson, 1845)	PM	Pinktail Durgon.........cochito cola rosada

SCIENTIFIC NAME	OCCURRENCE[1]	COMMON NAME (ENGLISH, SPANISH, FRENCH)[2]
Pseudobalistes naufragium (Jordan & Starks, 1895)	PM	Blunthead Triggerfish..........cochito bota
Sufflamen verres (Gilbert & Starks, 1904)	PM	Orangeside Triggerfish..........cochito naranja
Xanthichthys mento (Jordan & Gilbert, 1882)	P	Redtail Triggerfish..........cochito cuadriculado
Xanthichthys ringens (Linnaeus, 1758)	A	Sargassum Triggerfish..........cocuyo

Monacanthidae—En-filefishes, Sp-lijas, Fr-poissons-bourses

SCIENTIFIC NAME	OCCURRENCE[1]	COMMON NAME (ENGLISH, SPANISH, FRENCH)[2]
Aluterus heudelotii Hollard, 1855	A	Dotterel Filefish..........lija jaspeada
Aluterus monoceros (Linnaeus, 1758)	A-PM	Unicorn Filefish..........lija barbuda
Aluterus schoepfii (Walbaum, 1792)	A	Orange Filefish..........lija naranja
Aluterus scriptus (Osbeck, 1765)	A-PM	Scrawled Filefish..........lija trompa
Cantherhines dumerilii (Hollard, 1854)	PM	Barred Filefish..........lija vagabunda
Cantherhines macrocerus (Hollard, 1853)	A	Whitespotted Filefish
Cantherhines pullus (Ranzani, 1842)	A	Orangespotted Filefish..........lija colorada
Monacanthus ciliatus (Mitchill, 1818)	A	Fringed Filefish..........lija de clavo..........lime frangée
Monacanthus tuckeri Bean, 1906	A	Slender Filefish..........lija reticulada
Stephanolepis hispidus (Linnaeus, 1766)	A	Planehead Filefish..........lija áspera
Stephanolepis setifer (Bennett, 1831)	A	Pygmy Filefish..........lija de hebra

Ostraciidae—En-boxfishes, Sp-peces cofre, Fr-coffres

SCIENTIFIC NAME	OCCURRENCE[1]	COMMON NAME (ENGLISH, SPANISH, FRENCH)[2]
Acanthostracion polygonius Poey, 1876	A	Honeycomb Cowfish..........torito hexagonal
Acanthostracion quadricornis (Linnaeus, 1758)	A	Scrawled Cowfish..........torito cornudo
Lactophrys bicaudalis (Linnaeus, 1758)	A	Spotted Trunkfish..........chapín pintado
Lactophrys trigonus (Linnaeus, 1758)	A	Trunkfish..........chapín búfalo
Lactophrys triqueter (Linnaeus, 1758)	A	Smooth Trunkfish..........chapín baqueta
Lactoria diaphana (Bloch & Schneider, 1801)	P	Spiny Boxfish..........cofre espinoso
Ostracion meleagris Shaw, 1796	PM	Spotted Boxfish..........cofre moteado

Tetraodontidae—En-puffers, Sp-botetes, Fr-sphéroides

SCIENTIFIC NAME	OCCURRENCE[1]	COMMON NAME (ENGLISH, SPANISH, FRENCH)[2]
Arothron hispidus (Linnaeus, 1758)	PM	Stripebelly Puffer..........botete panza rayada
Arothron meleagris (Lacèpede, 1798)	PM	Guineafowl Puffer..........botete aletas punteadas
Canthigaster jamestyleri Moura & Castro, 2002	A	Goldface Toby
Canthigaster punctatissima (Günther, 1870)	PM	Spotted Sharpnose Puffer..........botete bonito

SCIENTIFIC NAME	OCCURRENCE[1]	COMMON NAME (ENGLISH, SPANISH, FRENCH)[2]
Canthigaster rostrata (Bloch, 1786)	A	Sharpnose Puffer........tamborín narizón
Lagocephalus laevigatus (Linnaeus, 1766)	A	Smooth Puffer ....botete grande
Lagocephalus lagocephalus (Linnaeus, 1758)	A-P	Oceanic Puffer........botete oceánico........orbe étoilé
Sphoeroides annulatus (Jenyns, 1842)	P	Bullseye Puffer........botete diana
Sphoeroides dorsalis Longley, 1934	A	Marbled Puffer........botete jaspeado
Sphoeroides lispus Walker, 1996	PM	Naked Puffer........botete liso
Sphoeroides lobatus (Steindachner, 1870)	P	Longnose Puffer........botete verrugoso
Sphoeroides maculatus (Bloch & Schneider, 1801)	A	Northern Puffer........sphéroïde du nord
Sphoeroides nephelus (Goode & Bean, 1882)	A	Southern Puffer........botete fruta
Sphoeroides pachygaster (Müller & Troschel, 1848)	A	Blunthead Puffer........botete chato........sphéroïde trogne
Sphoeroides parvus Shipp & Yerger, 1969	A	Least Puffer........botete xpú
Sphoeroides sechurae Hildebrand, 1946	PM	Peruvian Puffer^........botete peruano
Sphoeroides spengleri (Bloch, 1785)	A	Bandtail Puffer........botete collarete
Sphoeroides testudineus (Linnaeus, 1758)	A	Checkered Puffer........botete sapo
Sphoeroides trichocephalus (Cope, 1870)	PM	Pygmy Puffer........botete enano

Diodontidae—En-porcupinefishes, Sp-peces erizo, Fr-poissons porcs-épics

SCIENTIFIC NAME	OCCURRENCE[1]	COMMON NAME (ENGLISH, SPANISH, FRENCH)[2]
Chilomycterus antennatus (Cuvier, 1816)	A	Bridled Burrfish........pez erizo de riendas
Chilomycterus antillarum Jordan & Rutter, 1897	A	Web Burrfish........guanábana caribeña
Chilomycterus reticulatus (Linnaeus, 1758)	A-P	Spotfin Burrfish........pez erizo enano
Chilomycterus schoepfi (Walbaum, 1792)	A	Striped Burrfish........guanábana rayada
Diodon eydouxii Brisout de Barneville, 1846	P	Pelagic Porcupinefish........pez erizo pelágico
Diodon holocanthus Linnaeus, 1758	A-P	Balloonfish........pez erizo mapache
Diodon hystrix Linnaeus, 1758	A-P	Porcupinefish........pez erizo pecoso

Molidae—En-molas, Sp-molas, Fr-poissons-lune

SCIENTIFIC NAME	OCCURRENCE[1]	COMMON NAME (ENGLISH, SPANISH, FRENCH)[2]
Mola lanceolata (Liénard, 1840)	A-PM	Sharptail Mola........mola coliaguda
Mola mola (Linnaeus, 1758)	A-P	Ocean Sunfish........mola........môle
Ranzania laevis (Pennant, 1776)	A-P	Slender Mola........mola flaca

PART II

Appendix 1
Changes from Sixth Edition (2004) and Comments

The comments and explanatory notes below are keyed to the appropriate scientific name as indicated by an asterisk (*) or plus sign (+) in the main list, Part I. Entries are in the same order as in the list and are grouped by page. Information provided in pages 65–87 *in* the Appendix in the Third Edition, 1970, American Fisheries Society, Special Publication 6, Bethesda, Maryland; in pages 68–92 *in* Appendix 1 in the Fourth Edition, 1980, American Fisheries Society, Special Publication 12, Bethesda, Maryland; in pages 71–96 *in* Appendix 1 in the Fifth Edition, 1991, American Fisheries Society, Special Publication 20, Bethesda, Maryland; and in pages 187–253 *in* Appendix 1 in the Sixth Edition, 2004, American Fisheries Society, Special Publication 29, Bethesda, Maryland, is not repeated here except where considered necessary. Literature citations occur in standard form (e.g., author, year), with the cited work given in "References," or in abbreviated text form as in previous editions when not in References. The fourth edition of the International Code of Zoological Nomenclature is referred to as the "International Code," whereas ICZN refers to the International Commission on Zoological Nomenclature. Abbreviations for fish collections are as follows: ANSP = Academy of Natural Sciences of Philadelphia; ARC = Atlantic Reference Centre, St. Andrews, New Brunswick; CAS = California Academy of Sciences, San Francisco; ECOCH = El Colegio de la Frontera Sur (ECOSUR), Chetumal, Quintana Roo; FMNH = Field Museum of Natural History, Chicago; GCRL = Gulf Coast Research Laboratory, The University of Southern Mississippi, Ocean Springs; IBUNAM-P = Colección Nacional de Peces, Instituto de Biología, Universidad Nacional Autónoma de México, Mexico, D.F.; LACM = Natural History Museum of Los Angeles County; NCSM = North Carolina Museum of Natural Sciences, Raleigh; SIO = Scripps Institution of Oceanography, Marine Vertebrate Collection, La Jolla, California; UAZ = University of Arizona, Tucson; UF = University of Florida, Florida Museum of Natural History, Gainesville; UMMZ = University of Michigan Museum of Zoology, Ann Arbor; USNM = Smithsonian Institution National Museum of Natural History, Washington, D.C.; UW = University of Washington, Seattle.

Page 47

Branchiostomatidae. Common name in French changed to be consistent with general use (C. B. Renaud, personal communication, 2010). See Epigonichthyidae.

Epigonichthyidae. Recognized as a family by Nelson (2006:18) and included here for *Epigonichthys lucayanus*, removed from Branchiostomatidae. Common name in English proposed by N. Holland (personal communication, 2007).

Page 48

Petromyzontida. Change in class name following Nelson (2006).

Petromyzontidae. Transfers to *Entosphenus*, *Lethenteron*, and *Tetrapleurodon* of species recognized in *Lampetra* in the 2004 list and, in some cases, changes in endings of species names are based on H. S. Gill, C. B. Renaud, F. Chapleau, R. L. Mayden, and I. C. Potter, 2003, Copeia 2003(3):687–703.

Entosphenus folletti. Added to the list following C. B. Renaud, 2011, Lampreys of the world, Food and Agriculture Organization of the United Nations, FAO Species Catalogue for Fishery Purposes No. 5, Rome.

Entosphenus lethophagus. See Petromyzontidae; change in genus.

Entosphenus macrostomus. See Petromyzontidae; change in genus.

Entosphenus minimus. See Petromyzontidae; change change in genus.

Entosphenus similis. See Petromyzontidae; change in genus.

Entosphenus tridentatus. See Petromyzontidae; change in genus. Recognition of Gairdner as the author, not Richardson as given in Eschmeyer (2012), was explained in the 2004 list (p. 188).

Lampetra ayresii. Common name changed from river lamprey to Western River Lamprey as used in C. B. Renaud, M. F. Docker, and N. E. Mandrak, 2009, Taxonomy, distribution and conservation of lampreys in Canada, Pages 293–309 *in* L. R. Brown, S. Chase, M. Mesa, R. Beamish and P. Moyle, editors, Biology, management and conservation of lamreys in North America, American Fisheries Society, Bethesda, Maryland.

Lampetra hubbsi. We retain this species in *Lam-*

193

petra, as in N. J. Lang, K. J. Roe, C. B. Renaud, H. S. Gill, I. C. Potter, J. Freyhof, A. M. Naseka, P. Cochran, H. Espinosa Pérez, E. M. Habit, B. R. Kuhajda, D. A. Neely, Y. S. Reshetnikov, V. B. Salnikov, M. T. Stoumboudi, and R. L. Mayden, 2010, Pages 41–55 *in* L. R. Brown, S. Chase, M. Mesa, R. Beamish and P. Moyle, editors, Biology, management, and conservation of lampreys in North America, American Fisheries Society, Bethesda, Maryland. The phylogenetic analysis of lampreys by H. S. Gill, C. B. Renaud, F. Chapleau, R. L. Mayden, and I. C. Potter, 2003, Copeia 2003(3):687–703, examined only parasitic species and provided no evidence for relationships of this species. Likewise, the classification provided by C. B. Renaud, 2011, Lampreys of the world, Fish and Agriculture Organization of the United Nations, FAO Species Catalogue for Fishery Purposes No. 5, Rome, in which this species was placed in *Entosphenus*, was not based on published phylogenetic information.

Lampetra pacifica. Removed from the synonymy of *L. richardsoni* by S. B. Reid, D. Boguski, D. Goodman, and M. F. Docker, Zootaxa 3091:42–50. It was recognized as valid in the 1980 edition but deleted in the 1991 edition following C. E. Bond and T. T. Kan, 1986, Systematics and evolution of the lampreys of Oregon, Page 919 *in* T. Uyeno, R. Arai, T. Taniuchi, and K. Matsuura, editors, Indo-Pacific fish biology, Proceedings of the second international conference on Indo-Pacific fishes, Ichthyological Society of Japan, Tokyo.

Lampetra richardsoni. See *L. pacifica*.

Lethenteron alaskense. Populations previously recognized as *Lampetra appendix* in Alaska were recognized as *Lampetra alaskensis* in Mecklenburg et al. (2002), and in Alaska and Canada as *Lethenteron alaskense*, the Alaskan Brook Lamprey, in Page and Burr (2011). Conforming to present use, the species is recognized here in *Lethenteron*.

Lethenteron appendix. See Petromyzontidae; change in genus.

Lethenteron camtschaticum. See Petromyzontidae; change in genus.

Tetrapleurodon geminis. Correction of orthography of author's name from Alvarez to Álvarez. See Petromyzontidae; change in genus.

Tetrapleurodon spadiceus. See Petromyzontidae; change in genus.

Page 49

Chondrichthyes. The change in sequence of the orders Heterodontiformes, Orectolobiformes, Lamniformes, Carcharhiniformes, Hexanchiformes, Squaliformes (with removal of Echinorhinidae), and Squatiniformes and recognition of Echinorhiniformes follow Nelson (2006), and that work should be consulted for the literature used. The term "shark" is used as a collective term for members of the families Heterodontidae to Squatinidae (in eight orders); the term "ray" is used as a collective term for members of the families Torpedinidae to Myliobatidae (in four orders). Skates are members of one family of rays, the Rajidae.

Hydrolagus melanophasma. This new species was described by K. C. James, D. A. Ebert, D. J. Long, and D. A. Didier, 2009, Zootaxa 2218:60. The holotype was collected in Mexico, Gulf of California, Baja California Sur, off Punta Pescadero, at 30.5-m depth, in 1977. The species is also known from southern California and the outer coast of the Baja California peninsula but at depths exceeding 200 m.

Odontaspis ferox. Occurrence in Atlantic waters of United States was noted in T. F. Sheehan, 1998, Mar. Fish. Rev. 60(1):33–34, and F. J. Schwartz, 2003, Sharks, skates, and rays of the Carolinas, University of North Carolina Press, Chapel Hill.

Page 50

Alopias vulpinus. Common name in English is changed from thresher shark to Common Thresher Shark based on current general use and to avoid confusion with the other two members of the family Alopiidae. Without a modifying adjective, this species is frequently confused with Bigeye Thresher and Pelagic Thresher.

Carcharodon carcharias. Often referred to as the great white shark. We retain the established name White Shark.

Page 51

Mustelus albipinnis. This new species was described from off Bahía Magdalena, Baja California Sur, from depths of 103–111 m by J. L. Castro-Aguirre, A. Antuna-Mendiola, A. González-Acosta, and J. De la Cruz-Agüero, 2005, Hidrobiologica 15(2 Especial):126. *Mustelus hacat*, described from the Gulf of California by J. C. Pérez-Jimenez, O. S. Nishizaki, and J. L. Castillo-Geniz, Copeia, 2005(4):836, is considered a junior synonym of *M. albipinnis* by J. I. Castro, 2011, The sharks of North America, Oxford University Press, New York.

Carcharhinus cerdale. This species, originally described from the Pacific off Panama, was resurrected from the synonymy of *C. porosus* by J. I. Castro, 2011, Aqua, International Journal of Ichthyology 17(1):1–10, thus restricting that species to the western Atlantic.

Carcharhinus galapagensis. Previously included for Atlantic on unpublished records. F. J. Schwartz, 1998, J. Elisha Mitchell Sci. Soc. 114(3):149–158, recorded it off North Carolina.

Carcharhinus perezii. Often referred to as the Caribbean reef shark (e.g., W. B. Driggers, III, E. R. Hoffmayer, E. L. Hickerson, T. I. Martin, and C. T. Gledhill, 2011, Zootaxa 2933:65–68 [as *C. perezi*], who validated its occurrence in the northern Gulf of Mexico).

Page 52

Carcharhinus porosus. This species is restricted to the Atlantic Ocean and is replaced in the eastern Pacific by the sister-species *C. cerdale* (J. I. Castro, 2011, Aqua, International Journal of Ichthyology 17(1):1–10). Year of description changed from 1840 to 1839 following Eschmeyer (2012).

Page 53

Echinorhiniformes. See Chondrichthyes.

Echinorhinus brucus. Confirmation in our area is based on F. J. Schwartz, 1993, J. Elisha Mitchell Sci. Soc. 109(3):158–162 (e.g., off North Carolina at 111 m) and F. J. Schwartz, 2003, Sharks, skates, and rays of the Carolinas, University of North Carolina Press, Chapel Hill.

Squaliformes. See Chondrichthyes.

Squalus acanthias. See *S. suckleyi.*

Squalus suckleyi. Previously considered a subspecies or junior synonym of *S. acanthias* but treated as a species by D. A. Ebert, W. T. White, K. J. Goldman, L. J. V. Compagno, T. S. Daly-Engel, and R. D. Ward, 2010, Zootaxa 2612:22–40, based on differences in morphology and mitochondrial DNA. *Squalus suckleyi* is endemic to both sides of the North Pacific and, within our area of coverage, ranges from Alaska south to southern Baja California. Its geographic range is separate from that of *S. acanthias*, a widespread species that in our region is confined to the

Atlantic (not including the Gulf of Mexico) from southern Florida north to Canada.

Etmopteridae. This family included the species *Euprotomicrus bispinatus* in the 2004 list, which is now placed in Dalatiidae.

Euprotomicrus bispinatus. See Etmopteridae.

Page 54

Squatina heteroptera. This new species was described from the Gulf of Mexico, off Tamaulipas and Tabasco states, by J. L. Castro-Aguirre, H. Espinosa Pérez, and L. Huidobro Campos, 2007 [dated 2006], Rev. Biol. Trop. 54(3):1036. Common names proposed by H. Espinosa Pérez.

Squatina mexicana. This new species was described from the Gulf of Mexico, off Tamaulipas, Tabasco, and Yucatan states, by J. L. Castro-Aguirre, H. Espinosa Pérez, and L. Huidobro Campos, 2007 [dated 2006], Rev. Biol. Trop. 54(3):1032. Common names proposed by H. Espinosa Pérez.

Rajiformes. See Platyrhynidae below.

Page 55

Rhinobatos percellens. This Caribbean species is added on basis of occurrence off eastern Yucatan recorded by J. J. Schmitter-Soto, L. Vásquez-Yeomans, A. Aguilar-Perera, C. Curiel-Mondragón, and J. A. Caballero-Vázquez, 2000, An. Inst. Biol. Univ. Nac. Auton. Mex. Ser. Zool. 71(2):146.

Rhinobatos prahli. Originally described from Isla Gorgona, Colombia. Added to the list based on documentation of its presence in the Gulf of Tehuantepec in southern Mexico by M. Carrera-Fernández, F. Galván-Magaña, and O. Escobar-Sánchez, 2012, Mar. Biodiv. Rec. 5:e6, DOI: 10.1017/S1755267211001072.

Zapteryx xyster. Added to the list based on occurrence in shallow waters of the eastern Pacific from the southeastern Gulf of California, Mexico to Peru (Robertson and Allen 2008; D. R. Robertson, personal communication, 2011). Three collections off southern mainland Mexico are in the Marine Vertebrate Collection at Scripps Institution of Oceanography (SIO 63-515, 73-237, 73-244).

Bathyraja mariposa. This new species was described from the Aleutian Islands by D. E. Stevenson, J. W. Orr, G. R. Hoff, and J. D. McEachran, 2004, Copeia 2004(2):306, but appeared too late for inclusion in the 2004 list.

Bathyraja minispinosa. Added to the list based on

a record from the western Gulf of Alaska proximal to the eastern Aleutian Islands, 106-m depth, collected by the National Marine Fisheries Service, and deposited in the University of Washington Fish Collection, UW 42107 (D. Stevenson, personal communication, 2009).

Page 56

Rajella fyllae. Inadvertently omitted from previous lists. The type locality is Greenland, Davis Strait, from 80 fathoms [146 m]. Canadian records are from K. J. Sulak, D. P. MacWhirter, K. E. Luke, A. D. Norem, J. M. Miller, J. A. Cooper, and L. E. Harris, 2009, Can. Tech. Rep. Fish. Aquat. Sci. 2850.

Myliobatiformes. Change in sequence of families and composition; see Nelson (2006) for references.

Platyrhynidae. Moved from Rajiformes to Myliobatiformes based on references in Nelson (2006:76).

Urotrygonidae. Species formerly placed in Urolophidae (which remains a valid family outside our area). Changes in family common names result from addition of modifiers pertaining to the Americas.

Page 57

Myliobatidae. The formerly recognized Rhinopteridae and Mobulidae are now considered to be subfamilies of Myliobatidae; see Nelson (2006) for references. Expansions of common names of the family reflect this taxonomic change.

Rhinoptera brasiliensis. Inadvertently omitted from the 2004 edition and is added here based on J. D. McEachran and M. R. de Carvalho, 2003 (dated 2002), Rhinopteridae, Pages 583–585 *in* Carpenter (2003a). A confirmatory record from Tuxpan, Veracruz, Mexico is catalogued as CNPE-IBUNAM7006 in the Instituto de Biología, Universidad Nacional Autónoma de México, in Mexico City.

Page 58

Polyodon spathula. Extirpated in Canada (Ontario); last reported in 1917.

Atractosteus spatula. As noted by J. D. McEachran and J. D. Fechhelm, 1998, Fishes of the Gulf of Mexico, volume 1, University of Texas Press, Austin, this species, *Lepisosteus platostomus*, and *L. osseus* are occasionally found in the Gulf of Mexico.

Lepisosteus osseus. See *Atractosteus spatula.*
Lepisosteus platostomus. See *Atractosteus spatula.*

Page 59

Elops smithi. This new species, formerly in *E. saurus*, was described from the northern coast of South America, Caribbean Sea, Bahamas, Gulf of Mexico, and the eastern seaboard of North America by R. S. McBride, C. R. Rocha, R. Ruiz-Carus, and B. W. Bowen, 2010, Zootaxa 2346:31.

Albulidae. Information is presented below on a genetically characterized but undescribed western Atlantic species in the *Albula vulpes* complex (see *A. vulpes*). In addition, and although outside our area of geographical coverage, K. Hidaka, Y. Iwatsuki, and J. E. Randall, 2008, Ichthyol. Res. 55:53–64, in dealing with Indo-Pacific species of *Albula*, showed that *A. argentea* is a senior synonym of the nominal *A. forsteri* and *A. neoguinaica*, that *A. glossodonta* is a valid species as is *A. virgata* (Hawaiian endemic), and described *A. oligolepis* (widespread in Indian Ocean to northeastern Australia). Subsequently, Kwun and Kim, 2011, Zootaxa 2903:57–63, described *A. koreana* from Korea and Taiwan.

Albula esuncula. Added due to its resurrection from the *A. vulpes* complex of cryptic species as one of the two genetically distinct eastern Pacific species (given in the 2004 list, in part, as "*Albula* species," with a "P" distribution—now restricted to PM) by E. Pfeiler, B. G. Bitler, R. Ulloa, A. M. van der Heiden, and P. A. Hastings, 2008, Copeia 2008(4):763–770. This species, originally described in 1899 from two leptocephalous larvae and erroneously considered a synonym of *A. vulpes* by most subsequent workers, has appeared in several recent publications as the genetically characterized "*Albula* species C." It is now known to occur from Ecuador (perhaps farther south) northward to northwestern Mexico off Mazatlán, Sinaloa, in the southeastern Gulf of California, where it slightly overlaps in distribution with the more northerly occurring *A. gilberti.* Adults of *A. esuncula* recently have been described in a redescription of that species by E. Pfeiler and A. van der Heiden in E. Pfeiler, A. van der Heiden, R. S. Ruboyianes, and T. Watts, 2011, Zootaxa 3088:1–14.

Albula gilberti. Added due to its resurrection from the *A. vulpes* complex of cryptic species as one of the two genetically distinct eastern Pacific species (given in the 2004 list, in part, as "*Albula* species," with a "P" distribution) by Pfeiler et al., 2008 (cited above), and its formal description, genetic characterization, and comparisons with several relatives by E. Pfeiler and A. van der Heiden in Pfeiler et al., 2011 (cited above). It has been referred to as "*Albula* species A" in several recent publications. This species appeared in the 1960–1991 lists as "*Albula vulpes*" with occurrence as "P" and was referred to in the 2004 list as "*Albula* species, Cortez bonefish, macabí de Cortés" with a "P" distribution. It occurs throughout the Gulf of California and as far north as Morro Bay, California. Following warmwater years, it is a sport fish of some significance in southern California.

Albula pacifica. Added following study by E. Pfeiler, 2008, Rev. Biol. Trop. 56(2):839–844, who resurrected *A. pacifica* from the synonymy of *A. nemoptera* (Fowler, 1911), thus restricting the latter species to the Atlantic. Records of *A. nemoptera* are lacking from our area of coverage, and it is thus deleted from the list (see note for that species in the 2004 list, p. 194).

Albula vulpes. Occurring in western Atlantic waters of the United States and Mexico. As with *A. gilberti* and *A. esuncula*, another close relative of *A. vulpes* is the genetically well-defined species (but awaiting formal description) referred to as "*Albula* species B" in several recent publications (e.g., E. Pfeiler, B. G. Bitler, R. Ulloa, A. M. van der Heiden, and P. A. Hastings, 2008, Copeia 2008(4):763–770; E. Pfeiler, A. van der Heiden, R. S. Ruboyianes, and T. Watts, 2011, Zootaxa 3088:1–14). It is widely distributed in the Atlantic, including Mexico and the United States, where it at least partially overlaps in distribution (Florida Keys) with *A. vulpes* (A. J. Adams, R. K. Wolfe, M. D. Tringali, E. M. Wallace, and G. T. Kellison, 2008, Pages 203–214 *in* J. S. Ault, editor, Biology and management of the world tarpon and bonefish fisheries, CRC Press, Boca Raton, Florida). A common name in English for that (undescribed) species in Florida was given as "Big-eye Bonefish" in B. W. Bowen, S. A. Karl, and E. Pfeiler, 2008, Pages 147–157 *in* J. S. Ault, editor, Biology and management of the world tarpon and bonefish fisheries, CRC Press, Boca Raton, Florida. A literal translation of that name into Spanish would be *macabí ojón*.

Notacanthidae. Change in common names for family. Species in Notacanthidae and in Mastacembelidae are commonly known as "spiny eels" (a name used in previous editions for Notacanthidae). To avoid confusion, the modifier "deep-sea" is added for Notacanthidae and "freshwater" for Mastacembelidae, with similar names in Spanish and French.

Page 60

Neoconger vermiformis. Inadvertently omitted from the 2004 list, this species was described from soft bottoms in the northern Gulf of California, Mexico, from a depth of 55 m. It occurs from there southward to Colombia (Robertson and Allen [2008] and D. R. Robertson, personal communication, 2011).

Chlopsis kazuko. Inadvertently omitted from the 2004 list, this species was described from the southwestern Gulf of California, in the cape region of the Baja California peninsula, from a depth of ca. 95 m. It also occurs on mainland Mexico off Jalisco state and southward to (at least) Costa Rica (Robertson and Allen [2008] and D. R. Robertson, personal communication, 2011).

Page 61

Gymnothorax flavimarginatus. New to the list. Widespread in the tropical Indo-Pacific, occurring from East Africa eastward to the Americas. In the eastern Pacific, it is known from the tip of the Baja California peninsula and Costa Rica and Panama, as well as all of the oceanic islands, including the Revillagigedo Archipelago of Mexico (Robertson and Allen [2008] and D. R. Robertson, personal communication, 2011).

Gymnothorax pictus. New to the list. Widespread in the tropical Indo-Pacific, occurring from East Africa eastward to the Americas. In the eastern Pacific known mainly from the oceanic islands, including the Revillagigedo Archipelago of Mexico (Robertson and Allen [2008] and D. R. Robertson, personal communication, 2011).

Gymnothorax undulatus. New to the list. Widespread in the tropical Indo-Pacific, occurring from East Africa eastward to the Americas. In the eastern Pacific known from Costa Rica to Colombia and the Revillagigedo Archipelago of Mexico (Robertson and Allen [2008] and D. R. Robertson, personal communication, 2011).

Muraena argus. Recorded from waters of southern California by J. E. McCosker and D. G. Smith, 2003, Proc. Calif. Acad. Sci. 55:248–249.

Page 62

Ophichthidae. This list is probably incomplete for Atlantic species; many species are known from above 200-m depth from leptocephali only and, as noted by D. G. Smith (personal communication, 2002), "Leptocephali are usually a good indicator of the presence of eel species that are cryptic or difficult to collect as adults." The following species, which are not included in our list, have been recorded from our area of coverage only as leptocephali by M. M. Leiby, 1989, Leptocephali, Pages 764–897 *in* E. B. Böhlke, editor, Fishes of the western North Atlantic, Memoir 1, part 9, volume 2, Sears Foundation for Marine Research, Yale University, New Haven, Connecticut: *Asarcenchelys longimanus, Gordiichthys randalli, Letharchus aliculatus, Mixomyrophis pusillipinna, Ophichthus menezesi, O. spinicauda, Phaenomonas longissima, Pseudomyrophis frio, Quassiremus ascensionis*, and *Stictorhinus potamius*. The following species are listed as occurring only in the United States but have been recorded from Mexico as leptocephali: *Aprognathodon platyventris, Apterichtus kendalli, Bascanichthys scuticaris, Caralophia loxochila*, and *Pseudomyrophis fugesae*. The following species are listed as occurring only in Mexico but have been recorded from Canada and the United States as leptocephali: *Callechelys bilinearis* and *Myrophis platyrhynchus*.

Page 63

Ophichthus frontalis. Parentheses are removed from around the author's name.

Page 65

Serrivomeridae. Added to the list for the species noted.

Serrivomer beanii. Added based on a collection in the Atlantic Reference Centre (ARC 8600337) of a 286-mm-standard-length adult taken at 121-m bottom depth in the Atlantic Ocean off Canada, and from specimens from less than 200 m in the Gulf of St. Lawrence (R. Miller, personal communication). It also occurs in deeper waters (beyond 200 m) in our area at more southern latitudes.

Clupeiformes. Change in sequence of families; see Nelson (2006) for references.

Page 66

Anchoa analis. Although indicated as occurring in freshwater in the 2004 list, this has not been documented. The species was not included in Miller et al. (2006).

Anchoa exigua. Parentheses were inadvertently omitted from authors' names in the 2004 list; this species was described in *Stolephorus*.

Anchoa walkeri. Known from freshwater as well as the Pacific coast of Mexico (W. J. Baldwin and N. H. C. Chang, 1970, Pac. Sci. 24(1):139–143; Miller et al. 2006).

Anchovia macrolepidota. Known from freshwater as well as the Pacific coast of Mexico (Miller et al. 2006).

Page 67

Engraulis eurystole. Change in year of description follows Eschmeyer (2012).

Page 68

Lile stolifera. Presence in freshwater based on Miller et al. (2006) and Minckley and Marsh (2009).

Chanos chanos. Change in diacritic mark in orthography of author's name (from Forsskäl to Forsskål).

Cyprinidae. In a molecular phylogenetic study of many North American cyprinid genera and species, R. L. Mayden, A. M. Simons, R. M. Wood, P. M. Harris, and B. R. Kuhajda, 2007 [dated 2006], Pages 72–101 *in* M. L. Lozano-Vilano and A. J. Contreras-Balderas, editors, Studies of North American desert fishes in honor of E. P. (Phil) Pister, Conservationist, Universidad Autónoma de Nuevo León, México, provided results from phylogenetic analyses of variation in cytochrome *b* sequences supporting several changes in generic placement of species and the monophyly of currently recognized genera. Following the publication of these results, additional molecular data from mitochondrial and nuclear genes have been examined and yield additional evidence for revising the generic taxonomy of the family, but they are not consistent with all of the revisions recommended by Mayden et al. (2007). Major revisions to North American cyprinid taxonomy at this time would be premature.

Algansea amecae. This new species, formerly considered to be a population of *A. tincella*, was described from the Ameca River in central

Mexico by R. Pérez-Rodríguez, G. Pérez-Ponce de León, O. Domínguez-Domínguez, and I. Doadrio, 2009, Revista Mexicana de Biodiversidad 80:485.

Algansea barbata. Correction of orthography of Álvarez from Alvarez.

Algansea tincella. We retain the spelling of the common name in Spanish as pupo del Valle and do not change to "pupo de valle," as in H. L. Jelks, et al. 2008, Fisheries 33:327–407. "Valle" refers to a specific valley, the Valley of Mexico, the species being described from the environs of Mexico City, where it no longer occurs. See *A. amecae.*

Campostoma anomalum. In a study of variation in the mitochondrial cytochrome *b* gene in the genus *Campostoma*, M. J. Blum, D. A. Neely, P. M. Harris, and R. L. Mayden, 2008, Copeia 2008(2):360–369, concluded that "at least nine lineages could be recognized as distinct taxa" in this genus and recommended recognition of several populations at the specific level, including *C. pullum, C. plumbeum, C. michauxi,* and *C. griseum.* However, we choose not to recognize those nominal species because of incomplete sampling (acknowledged by Blum et al. 2008) and absence of diagnoses. Also, authors studying morphological variation have reached different taxonomic conclusions. For example, B. M. Burr and R. C. Cashner, 1983, Copeia 1983(1):101–116, recognized *C. anomalum michauxi* as a subspecies occupying the Santee and Savannah River drainages, North Carolina, South Carolina, and Georgia. The Santee drainage is the type locality for *michauxi*, but Blum et al. (2008) analyzed no samples from the Santee. D. A. Etnier and W. C. Starnes, 2008, Update for 2001 printing for The fishes of Tennessee, University of Tennessee Press, Knoxville, recognized *C. pullum* as a species occurring west of the Mississippi River and in northern Illinois, southern Wisconsin, the Great Lakes basin, and the Wabash River. In contrast, Blum et al. (2008) assigned western populations to *C. plumbeum* and populations east of the Mississippi River to *C. pullum*; however, the type locality for *C. pullum* is Burlington, Iowa. We feel that the assignment of names to populations for which genetic, phenetic, and distributional boundaries are undefined is premature. Populations from highland areas of Oklahoma and Arkansas are referable to the recently resurrected *C. spadiceum.*

Page 69

Campostoma spadiceum. R. C. Cashner, W. J. Matthews, E. Marsh-Matthews, P. J. Unmack, and F. M. Cashner, 2010, Copeia 2010(3):300–311, removed this species from the synonymy of *C. anomalum* and suggested the common name.

Chrosomus cumberlandensis. R. M. Strange and R. L. Mayden, 2009, Copeia 2009(3):494–501, in a revision of the genus *Phoxinus*, concluded that the genus is not monophyletic and recognized all North American species in *Chrosomus.* The genus *Phoxinus*, which is valid for Eurasian species, had been recognized in past lists since 1970 (for reasons given on page 70, for the four species recognized, of the 1970 list), but the 1960 list recognized those four species in *Chrosomus.*

Chrosomus eos. See *C. cumberlandensis.*

Chrosomus erythrogaster. See *C. cumberlandensis.*

Chrosomus neogaeus. See *C. cumberlandensis.*

Chrosomus oreas. See *C. cumberlandensis.*

Chrosomus saylori. See *C. cumberlandensis.*

Chrosomus tennesseensis. See *C. cumberlandensis.*

Codoma ornata. Based on a multigene molecular phylogenetic analysis by S. Schönhuth, I. Doadrio, O. Domínguez-Domínguez, D. M. Hillis, and R. L. Mayden, 2008, Mol. Phylogenet. Evol. 47:729–756, *C. ornata* is not closely related to *Cyprinella* but forms the sister group to *Tampichthys.* Identical results were obtained in the study discussed under *Cyprinella lutrensis.*

Page 70

Cyprinella lutrensis. In a molecular phylogenetic analysis of species relationships in *Cyprinella*, using mitochondrial and nuclear gene sequences, S. Schönhuth and R. L. Mayden, 2010, Mol. Phylogenet. Evol. 55(1):77–98, recognized *C. forlonensis* and *C. suavis.* These two taxa traditionally are treated as subspecies of *C. lutrensis* and occur in coastal-plain rivers of the western Gulf of Mexico. However, treatment of these forms as species seems premature until individuals from a broader area have been examined.

Erimystax x-punctatus. Extirpated from Canada (Ontario); last reported there in 1958.

Page 71

Gila conspersa. Clarification of name in Spanish.

Gila jordani. A. S. Gerber, C. A. Tibbets, and T. E. Dowling, 2001, Evol. 55:2028–2039, recognized this form as a species of hybrid origin. Although not recognized in the 2004 list, the taxon is added following more general recognition (e.g., Minckley and Marsh 2009). The common name refers to the White River where the species is endemic.

Gila robusta. Miller et al. (2006) record this species as likely to have occurred in Mexico, although no specimens are known.

Hesperoleucus symmetricus. Although some authors place this species in *Lavinia* (e.g., Moyle 2002), the lack of a comprehensive phylogenetic study of western cyprinids suggests that a change in genus is premature.

Hybognathus amarus. Miller et al. (2006:127) reported this species as extirpated from Mexico.

Hybognathus placitus. Reported as occurring in Canada in a tributary of the Milk River in Grasslands National Park, Saskatchewan by R. M. Sylvester, S. E. Freeling, and C. R. Berry, Jr., 2004, Can. Field-Nat. 119(2):219–223.

Hybognathus regius. Common name in French changed to reflect distribution and name in English.

Page 72

Hypophthalmichthys nobilis. Some authors recognize this species in the monotypic genus *Aristichthys*. However, we follow the phylogenetic analysis of G. Howes, 1981, Bull. Br. Mus. (Nat. Hist.) Zool. 41(1):1–52, who placed *nobilis* in *Hypophthalmichthys*.

Lepidomeda aliciae. J. B. Johnson, T. E. Dowling, and M. C. Belk, 2004, Syst. Biol. 53(6):841–855, resurrected this species from the synonymy of *Snyderichthys copei* and placed both species in the genus *Lepidomeda*.

Lepidomeda copei. J. B. Johnson, T. E. Dowling, and M. C. Belk, 2004, Syst. Biol. 53(6):841–855, transferred this species, formerly in *Snyderichthys*, to the genus *Lepidomeda*. See also *L. aliciae*.

Luxilus zonatus. Species described as new in the publication by Putnam, 1863, Bull. Mus. Comp. Zool. 1(1):1–16, appear either as Agassiz, MS (e.g., *Alburnus zonatus* Agassiz, MS; *Pleurolepis pellucidus* Agassiz, MS) or Putnam, MS (e.g., *Catonotus kennicotti* Putnam, MS). Some have interpreted inclusion of "MS" to mean that the indicated individual was only responsible for the name and that Putnam (as author of the paper) prepared all

included descriptions (see the 1960–1991 lists and Eschmeyer 2012). Although it is impossible to determine who prepared the descriptions, Putnam's intentions were obvious from the preface to his paper. We therefore continue to recognize, in the interests of nomenclatural stability (as in the 2004 list), Agassiz as the describer of both *Luxilus zonatus* (Cyprinidae) and *Ammocrypta pellucida* (Percidae), and Putnam as the describer of *Etheostoma kennicotti* (Percidae).

Page 73

Margariscus margarita. Alteration of common name in English reflects geographic separation from *M. nachtriebi*. See *M. nachtriebi*.

Margariscus nachtriebi. Removed from synonymy of *M. margarita* by R. M. Bailey, W. C. Latta, and G. R. Smith, 2004, Misc. Publ. Mus. Zool. Univ. Mich. 192:1–215. Common name in English proposed by Bailey et al. (2004).

Meda fulgida. Miller et al. (2006) recorded this species as likely to have occurred in Mexico, although no specimens are known.

Mylopharyngodon piceus. This species has been found for more than a decade in the lower Mississippi basin and is probably established (L. G. Nico, J. D. Williams, and H. L. Jelks, 2005, Black carp: biological synopsis and risk assessment of an introduced fish, American Fisheries Society, Special Publication 32, Bethesda, Maryland).

Notropis amecae. This species, listed as extinct in the 2004 list, has been rediscovered (E. López López and P. Maya, 2001, J. Freshw. Ecol. 16:179–187). Treated by Miller et al. (2006) as *Hybopsis amecae*.

Page 74

Notropis amplamala. This new species, formerly considered to be the disjunct southern population of *N. buccatus*, was described from the southeastern United States (from Mississippi to Florida and Georgia) by T. P. Pera and J. W. Armbruster, 2006, Copeia 2006(3):424.

Notropis buccatus. See *N. amplamala*.

Notropis calabazas. This new species was described from the Río Pánuco basin of central Mexico by J. Lyons and N. Mercado-Silva, Copeia 2004(4):869. Common name in Spanish partly modified from that proposed in original description.

Notropis calientis. See *N. grandis* and *N. marhabatiensis*.

Notropis cumingii. This species, whose precise type locality is unknown, was regarded as a senior synonym of *N. imeldae* Cortés, 1968 by Gilbert (1998, Fla. Mus. Nat. Hist. Spec. Publ. 1, p. 95). This was recognized in the 2004 list and was confirmed by Miller et al. (2006). S. Schönhuth and I. Doadrio, 2003, Biol. J. Linnean Soc. 80:323–337, apparently unaware of Gilbert's publication, considered *N. imeldae* (originally described from the Río Atoyac) as valid and made no mention of *N. cumingii*.

Page 75

Notropis grandis. O. Domínguez-Domínguez, R. Pérez-Rodríguez, L. H. Escalera-Vázquez, and I. Doadrio, 2009, Hidrobiológica 19(2):159–172 described this species, endemic to Zacapu Lake and its outlet, Río Lerma drainage, Michoacán, Mexico. The species previously was part of *N. calientis*. Common name in English was recommended by the authors.

Notropis marhabatiensis. O. Domínguez-Domínguez, R. Pérez-Rodríguez, L. H. Escalera-Vázquez, and I. Doadrio, 2009, Hidrobiológica 19(2):159–172 described this species, endemic to San Miguel Spring, in the town of Marhabatio (= Maravatío), Río Lerma drainage, Michoacán, Mexico. The species was part of *N. calientis*. Common name in English was recommended by the authors.

Notropis moralesi. Common name in Spanish misspelled (by one letter) in 2004 list; correct orthography is carpita del Tepelmeme.

Page 76

Notropis sallaei. Recognized in *Aztecula* in the 2004 list. S. Schönhuth and I. Doadrio, 2003, Biol. J. Linn. Soc. 80(2):323–337, presented molecular data placing this species in *Notropis*.

Page 77

Plagopterus argentissimus. Although Miller et al. (2006) record this species as likely to have occurred in Mexico, no specimens are known.

Pteronotropis hypselopterus. See *P. metallicus* and *P. stonei*.

Pteronotropis metallicus. Removed from synonymy of *P. hypselopterus* by R. D. Suttkus, B. A. Porter, and B. J. Freeman, 2003, Proc. Am. Philos. Soc. 147(4):354–376. Common name proposed in that paper.

Pteronotropis stonei. Removed from synonymy of *P. hypselopterus* by R. D. Suttkus, B. A. Porter, and B. J. Freeman, 2003, Proc. Am. Philos. Soc. 147(4):354–376. Common name proposed in that paper.

Rhinichthys atratulus. Recent arguments for recognizing *R. obtusus* as distinct from *R. atratulus* have been varied and inconsistent, as discussed in the Appendix to the 2004 list. Some publications treat *obtusus* as a subspecies of *R. atratulus* (W. J. Matthews, R. E. Jenkins, and J. T. Styron, 1982, Copeia 1982(4):902–920; R. E. Jenkins and N. M. Burkhead, 1994, Freshwater fishes of Virginia, American Fisheries Society, Bethesda, Maryland). Others recognize *R. obtusus* (R. M. Bailey, W. C. Latta, and G. R. Smith, 2004, Univ. Mich. Mus. Zool. Misc. Publ. 192:1–215) or *R. meleagris* (C. L. Smith, 1986 [dated 1985], The inland fishes of New York State, New York State Department of Environmental Conservation, Albany) as distinct from *R. atratulus*. D. A. Etnier and W. C. Starnes, 1994 [dated 1993], The fishes of Tennessee, The University of Tennessee Press, Knoxville, and H. T. Boschung, Jr. and R. L. Mayden, 2004, Fishes of Alabama, Smithsonian Books, Washington, D.C., recognized three subspecies, *R. a. atratulus*, *R. a. meleagris* and *R. a. obtusus*, but describe different ranges for them. A study of 20 Canadian populations, covering the ranges of two putative taxa, could not differentiate the taxa using characters presented in those publications (B. A. Fraser, N. E. Mandrak, and R. L. McLaughlin, 2005, Can. J. Zool. 83:1502–1510). Although it seems likely that several populations within *R. atratulus* deserve taxonomic recognition, we remove *R. obtusus* from the list pending a comprehensive study of variation and return to the long-standing common name of Blacknose Dace for *R. atratulus*.

Rhinichthys osculus. This widespread species, with many geographically disjunct populations, has been accorded a total of 23 formal descriptions, of which at least 15 involve recently recognized subspecies (C. R. Gilbert, 1998, Fla. Mus. Nat. Hist. Spec. Publ. 1:32–33). In addition, three other members of the complex are currently recognized as valid species, in two cases by virtue of demonstrated sympatry with *R. osculus* (*R. falcatus* and *R. umatilla*) and in the other case largely because of extinction of the only known population (*R. deaconi*). The extraordinary and confusing morphological variability exhibited by

R. osculus, as presently recognized, has until now resisted all attempts at a formal resolution. However, the recent study by D. D. Oakey, M. E. Douglas, and M. R. Douglas (2004, Copeia 2004(2):207–223), involving analysis of mitochondrial DNA, has gone far to clarify the situation. It was found that the species complex is divisible into three well-defined genetic units, as follows: (1) a northern group, including the Columbia and Klamath River basins; (2) a combined southern-eastern group, involving the entire Colorado River basin and the geographically disjunct Los Angeles River system; and (3) a geographically intermediate group, which includes the Lahontan and Bonneville basins, together with the isolated Death Valley.

Page 78

Rhodeus sericeus. This introduced species has been known as *R. sericeus*, with widely disjunct populations in Europe and Asia. However, Kottelat and Freyhof (2007) recognized *R. sericeus* as occurring in eastern Asia and *R. amarus* as the form native to the basins of the North, Baltic, Black, Caspian, and Aegean seas, and the Mediterranean basin in northern Rhone (France) and Drin river drainages in Albania, Montenegro and Macedonia, with introduced populations throughout Europe. No study has confirmed which species has been introduced in North America (C. Scharpf, personal communication, 2011).

Siphateles alvordensis. *Siphateles* is recognized to include *S. alvordensis*, *S. bicolor*, and *S. boraxobius* based on A. M. Simons, P. B. Berendzen, and R. L. Mayden, 2003, Zool. J. Linn. Soc. 139:63–80. These species formerly were in *Gila*. Although not all species of *Gila* were included in the study by Simons et al., suggesting that other changes in genera of western cyprinids may be forthcoming, authors are recognizing *Siphateles* (e.g., Moyle 2002; Page and Burr 2011).

Siphateles bicolor. See *S. alvordensis*.

Siphateles boraxobius. See *S. alvordensis*.

Tampichthys catostomops. In a phylogenetic analysis of the genus *Dionda* and other southwestern cyprinid genera by S. Schönhuth, I. Doadrio, O. Domínguez-Domínguez, D. M. Hillis, and R. L. Mayden, 2008, Mol. Phylogenet. Evol. 47:729–756, using nuclear and mitochondrial genes, six species formerly in *Dionda* and endemic to rivers of northeastern Mex-

ico were allocated to the newly described genus *Tampichthys* (*T. catostomops*, *T. dichroma*, *T. erimyzonops*, *T. ipni*, *T. mandibularis*, and *T. rasconis*). The remaining species of *Dionda* were found to form a monophyletic group.

Tampichthys dichroma. See *T. catostomops*.

Tampichthys erimyzonops. See *T. catostomops*.

Tampichthys ipni. Correction of orthography of Álvarez (from Alvarez); in 2004 list as *Dionda ipni* (Alvarez & Navarro, 1953). See *T. catostomops*.

Tampichthys mandibularis. See *T. catostomops*.

Tampichthys rasconis. See *T. catostomops*.

Yuriria alta. S. Schönhuth and I. Doadrio, 2003, Biol. J. Linn. Soc. 80(2):323–337, presented molecular data placing this species within *Notropis* (as *N. altus*); however, the change is not made pending examination of other species in *Yuriria*. Based on overall physical appearance, *Y. alta* is quite unlike any species currently referred to *Notropis*.

Yuriria amatlana. This new species was described from the Ameca River in western central Mexico by O. Domínguez-Domínguez, A. Pompa-Domínguez, and I. Doadrio, 2007, Graellsia 63:263.

Catostomus ardens. See *Chasmistes liorus*.

Page 79

Catostomus clarkii. Although Minckley and Marsh (2009) recognized *Pantosteus intermedius* (Tanner, 1942) as separate from *C. clarkii*, they provided no diagnostic characteristics. In his revision of western U.S. suckers, G. R. Smith, 1966, Univ. Mich. Mus. Zool. Misc. Publ. 129, found no basis for recognition of the White River population, and we continue to consider *intermedius* to be a synonym of *C. clarkii*.

Catostomus commersonii. See *C. utawana*.

Catostomus latipinnis. Once occurred in the Colorado River basin in northern Mexico but is now extirpated (W. L. Minckley, 2002, Fishes of the lower Colorado River, its delta, and estuary: a commentary on biotic change, Pages 63–78 *in* M. L. Lozano-Vilano, editor, Libro jubilar en honor al Dr. Salvador Contreras Balderas, Universidad Autónoma de Nuevo León, Monterrey, Mexico).

Catostomus macrocheilus. See *C. tsiltcoosensis*.

Catostomus tsiltcoosensis. Removed from the synonymy of *C. macrocheilus* as a species endemic to coastal drainages of Oregon by J. Kettratad and D. F. Markle, 2010, West. N.

Am. Nat. 2010:273–287. Kettratad and Markle used the common name Tyee Sucker.

Catostomus utawana. Formerly synonymized with *C. commersonii.* Recognized as a species endemic to the St. Lawrence-Lake Ontario drainages of the Adirondack Mountains, New York by R. S. Morse and R. A. Daniels, 2009, Copeia, 2009:214–220. Morse and Daniels used the common name Summer Sucker.

Catostomus wigginsi. Change in orthography of names in English and Spanish to agree with cultural (tribal) name in Mexico (from Opata Sucker and matalote opata).

Chasmistes cujus. The common name cui-ui is pronounced "kweé-wee."

Chasmistes liorus. This species, endemic to Utah Lake, Utah, has recently (i.e., over the past 60 years) experienced a shift in certain meristic characters compared to those of the species at the time of its original description. R. R. Miller and G. R. Smith, 1981, Occ. Pap. Mus. Zool. Univ. Mich. 696:1–46, addressed this situation, which may have come about in response to ecological changes in the lake, and chose to resolve the problem by erection of a new subspecies, *mictus*, to replace the typical subspecies originally present. Miller and Smith also determined that *Catostomus fecundus*, a distinctive form once present in the lake, was based on a hyrid: *Catostomus ardens* × *Chasmistes liorus.* The latter decision was disputed by A. G. Cook, 2001, J. Zool. (Lond.) 254:293–308, who provided evidence to support recognition of *Catostomus fecundus* as a valid but now-extinct species also endemic to Utah Lake. Since specimens of *C. fecundus* are not available for genetic or protein analyses, the question of its true identity may never be resolved. Considering this, we choose to follow the 1991 list, in which the putative hybrid status of *fecundus* was accepted and the species name accordingly deleted from the list.

Erimyzon claviformis. Removed from synonymy of *E. oblongus* by R. M. Bailey, W. C. Latta, and G. R. Smith, 2004. Misc. Publ. Mus. Zool. Univ. Mich. 192:1–215. Common name proposed by Bailey et al. (2004).

Page 80

Erimyzon oblongus. The modifier "eastern" is added to the common name. See *E. claviformis.*

Ictiobus bubalus. Very few buffaloes with subterminal mouths have been collected in Canada, all in the lower Great Lakes (E. Holm, N. E. Mandrak, and M. E. Burridge, 2010, The ROM guide to freshwater fishes of Ontario, Royal Ontario Museum, Toronto). All appear to be hybrids of *I. cyprinellus* with *I. bubalus* or *I. niger* (H. L. Bart, Jr., M. D. Clements, R. E. Blanton, K. R. Piller, and D. L. Hurley, 2010, Mol. Phylogenet. Evol. 56:808–820). No pure specimens of *I. bubalus* or *I. niger* are known from Canada.

Ictiobus niger. See *I. bubalus.*

Page 81

Misgurnus anguillicaudatus. Caught in the Alouette River, British Columbia, 2008–2010, and considered established (S. Cope, 2011, Alouette River salmonid smolt migration enumeration: 2010 data report, Westslope Fisheries, Cranbrook, BC).

Characidae. Common names for family in English and Spanish are changed to reflect use.

Astyanax aeneus. J. J. Schmitter-Soto, M. E. Valdez-Moreno, R. Rodiles-Hernández, and A. A. González-Díaz, 2008, Copeia 2008(2):409–413, synonymzed *Astyanax armandoi* Lozano-Vilano & Contreras-Balderas, 1990, the Penjamo Tetra or sardinita de Pénjamo (listed in 2004), with *A. aeneus.*

Astyanax mexicanus. There is disagreement on the taxonomic status of populations assigned to this species. *Asytanax mexicanus* was recognized by Miller et al. (2006) but was synonymized with the more southern-occurring *A. fasciatus* (Cuvier, 1819) in earlier publications. Also, some authors recognize blind cave populations within the range of *A. mexicanus* as *A. jordani* (Hubbs and Innes, 1936); for example, G. S. Proudlove, 2006, Subterranean fishes of the world: an account of the subterranean (hypogean) fishes described up to 2003 with a bibliography 1541–2004, International Society for Subterranean Biology, Moulis, France; and Reis et al., editors (2003). We recognize the complexity of this problem but follow general use and arguments by A. Romero, 2008, Environ. Biol. Fishes (62):43–71, for not recognizing *A. jordani* as a separate species.

Siluriformes. Recognition of the catfish families follows J. P. Sullivan, J. G. Lundberg, and M. Hardman, 2006, Mol. Phylogenet. Evol. 41: 636–662, and J. G. Lundberg, J. P. Sullivan, R. Rodiles-Hernández, and D. A. Hendrickson, 2007, Proc. Acad. Nat. Sci. Phila. 156:39–53, which differs from Nelson (2006) only in placement of Ictaluridae and Lacantuniidae.

Hypostomus plecostomus. Identification is provisional. *Hypostomus* species are native to Middle and South America from Costa Rica south to Río de la Plata drainage. One or more species are established in the United States and Mexico.

Pterygoplichthys anisitsi. This species and *P. disjunctivus*, *P. multiradiatus*, and *P. pardalis* were recorded as established in Mexico by R. Mendoza Alfaro, J. P. Fisher, W. Courtenay, C. Ramírez Martínez, A. Orbe-Mendoza, C. Escalera Gallardo, P. Álvarez Torres, P. Koleff Osorio, and S. Contreras Balderas, 2009, Armored catfish (Loricariidae) trinational risk assessment, Pages 25–37 *in* R. E. Mendoza Alfaro et al., editors, Trinational risk assessment guidelines for aquatic alien invasive species, Commission for Environmental Cooperation, Montreal.

Pterygoplichthys disjunctivus. See *P. anisitsi*.

Page 82

Pterygoplichthys multiradiatus. See *P. anisitsi*.

Pterygoplichthys pardalis. See *P. anisitsi*.

Clariidae. Correction of family name in French with addition of "e" in "labyrinthes" (C. B. Renaud, personal communication, 2008).

Clarias batrachus. The identity of our populations is uncertain given that several species in Asia are confused under the name *C. batrachus* (H. H. Ng and M. Kottelat, 2008, Zool. J. Linn. Soc. 153:725–732). H. H. Ng and M. Kottelat established the type locality of *C. batrachus* as Bandung, Java (Indonesia) by virtue of neotype designation.

Ariidae. Several species of *Cathorops* and *Galeichthys peruvianus* are deleted from the list based on information in A. P. Marceniuk and C. J. Ferraris, Jr., 2003, *in* Reis et al., editors (2003); R. Betancur-R. and A. Acero P., 2005, Zootaxa 1045:45–60; A. P. Marceniuk, R. Betancur-R., and A. Acero-P., 2009, Bull. Mar. Sci. 85(3):245–280; and R. Betancur-R., A. Acero P., E. Bermingham, and R. Cooke, 2007, Mol. Phylogenet. Evol. 45:339–357. *Cathorops fuerthii* (Steindachner, 1877) is restricted to the Pacific coast of Central America. *Cathorops melanopus* (Günther, 1864) is restricted to Guatemala. *Cathorops spixii* (Agassiz, 1829) is restricted to Brazil. *Galeichthys peruvianus* Lütken, 1874 is restricted to the Pacific coast of South America.

Cathorops belizensis. This new species was described from the western Caribbean by A. P. Marceniuk and R. Betancur-R., 2008, Neotropical Ichthyology 6(1):29.

Cathorops dasycephalus. Change in genus from *Ariopsis* following R. Betancur-R., A. Acero P., E. Bermingham, and R. Cooke, 2007, Mol. Phylogenet. Evol. 45:339–357, who placed the species in a new (monotypic) subgenus *Precathorops*. Presence of this species in waters off Pacific Mexico is based on 16 specimens identified by Arturo Acero P. in the fish collection of the University of Arizona, Tucson: UAZ 68-135, Tartar Shoals, 16°21'N, 96°88.6'W, 10–14 fathoms, 22 May 1968, C. Lehner (collector) aboard R/V *Te Vega*.

Cathorops kailolae. This new species was described from the Río Usumacinta basin in Guatemala and Mexico by A. P. Marceniuk and R. Betancur-R., 2008, Neotropical Ichthyology 6(1):36. Common names are based on the diagnostic fleshy papillae intercalated with gill rakers on first two gill arches.

Cathorops liropus. This species occurs along the Pacific coast of Mexico (A. P. Marceniuk, R. Betancur-R., and A. Acero-P., 2009, Bull. Mar. Sci. 85(3):245–280).

Cathorops raredonae. This new species from Mexico and El Salvador was described by A. P. Marceniuk, R. Betancur-R., and A. Acero P., 2009, Bull. Mar. Sci. 85(3):245–280. Common names are modified from those used by authors to honor S. J. Raredon, U.S. National Museum of Natural History.

Notarius kessleri. Change in genus from *Ariopsis* following R. Betancur-R., A. Acero P., E. Bermingham, and R. Cooke, 2007, Mol. Phylogenet. Evol. 45:339–357.

Notarius planiceps. Change in genus from *Ariopsis* following R. Betancur-R., A. Acero P., E. Bermingham, and R. Cooke, 2007, Mol. Phylogenet. Evol. 45:339–357.

Notarius troschelii. Change in genus from *Sciadeops* following R. Betancur-R., A. Acero P., E. Bermingham, and R. Cooke, 2007, Mol. Phylogenet. Evol. 45:339–357.

Occidentarius platypogon. Change in genus from *Ariopsis* following R. Betancur-R., A. Acero P., E. Bermingham, and R. Cooke, 2007, Mol. Phylogenet. Evol. 45:339–357.

Potamarius nelsoni. Contrary to the 2004 list, this species occurs only in freshwater (J. L. Castro Aguirre, H. S. Espinosa-Pérez, and J. J. Schmitter-Soto, 1999, Ictiofauna estuarino-lagunar y vicaria de México, Editorial Limusa-Noriega/IPN, México).

Potamarius usumacintae. This new species was described from the Río Usumacinta basin in Guatemala and Mexico by R. Betancur-R. and P. W. Willink, 2007, Copeia 2007(4):820. Names in English and Spanish were proposed in the species description.

Page 83

Sciades dowii. Taxonomy of this species from the Pacific coast of Mexico is uncertain. Treated as *S. hymenorrhinos*—misspelled as *hymenorrhinus* (Bleeker, 1862) in the 2004 list, but as *S. dowii* by R. Betancur-R., A. Acero P., E. Bermingham, and R. Cooke, 2007, Mol. Phylogenet. Evol. 45:339–357.

Heptapteridae. Recognition of *Rhamdia* in this family rather than in Pimelodidae (still a valid family although not in our area) follows Nelson (2006), and that work should be consulted for relevant literature. Names in English and French for the family are translations of the family name; juiles is an Aztec name.

Rhamdia laluchensis. This new troglobitic species was described by A. Weber, G. Allegrucci, and V. Sbordoni, 2003, Ichthyol. Explor. Freshwat. 14(3):275 from Chiapas, Mexico.

Rhamdia parryi. Change in orthography of name in English to agree with geographic name in Mexico (from Tonala Catfish).

Rhamdia reddelli. Name in Spanish changed to accurately describe distribution, in contrast to that of *R. zongolicensis.*

Rhamdia zongolicensis. Common names Oaxaca catfish and juil oaxaqueño in the 2004 list are changed to Zongolica Catfish and juil ciego de Zongolica because the Zongolica cave type locality is in Veracruz, not in Oaxaca (H. Wilkens, 1993, Mitt. Hamb. Zool. Mus. Inst. 90:375–378, and J. J. Schmitter-Soto, personal communication, 2007).

Lacantuniidae. This new family of freshwater catfishes was described by R. Rodiles-Hernández, D. A. Hendrickson, and J. G. Lundberg *in* R. Rodiles-Hernández, D. A. Hendrickson, J. G. Lundberg, and J. M. Humphries, 2005, Zootaxa 1000:1–24. See *Lacantunia enigmatica.*

Lacantunia enigmatica. This new genus and species of freshwater catfish was described from the Río Lacantún and Río Lacanjá of the Río Usumacinta basin, Chiapas, Mexico, by R. Rodiles-Hernández, D. A. Hendrickson, and J. G. Lundberg *in* R. Rodiles-Hernández, D. A. Hendrickson, J. G. Lundberg, and J. M. Humphries, 2005, Zootaxa 1000:1–24.

Ictalurus australis. Change in orthography of name in English to agree with geographic name in Mexico (from Panuco Catfish).

Ictalurus furcatus. According to Eschmeyer (2012), the author of this species is Valenciennes, 1840, and not Lesueur, 1840, with the species originally described as *Pimelodus furcatus* Valenciennes (ex Lesueur) in Cuvier and Valenciennes, 1840. We retain Lesueur, as in the 1960–2004 lists, as being responsible for the description in the interests of nomenclatural stability. See *I. meridionalis.*

Ictalurus meridionalis. R. Rodiles-Hernández, J. G. Lundberg, and J. P. Sullivan *in* P. J. Gutiérrez-Yurrita, editor, 2006, Memorias del X Congreso Nacional de Ictiología, Sociedad Ictiológica Mexicana, A. C. (SIMAC), Universidad Autónoma de Querétaro, suggested removal of this species from the synonymy of *I. furcatus.* Its recognition was accepted by A. Á. González-Díaz, R. M. Quiñones, J. Velázquez-Martínez, and R. Rodiles-Hernández, 2008, Zootaxa 1685:47–54, and its relationships within the *I. furcatus* group of three species were described by R. Rodiles-Hernández, J. G. Lundberg, and J. P. Sullivan, 2010, Proc. Acad. Nat. Sci. Phila. 159:67–82. Common names refer to southern distribution of the species relative to that of *I. furcatus.*

Page 84

Noturus albater. See *N. maydeni.*

Noturus baileyi. Common name treated as a proper noun as it refers to the Smoky Mountains from which the species was described, as noted in the 1970 list. The listing as "smoky madtom" in the 1980, 1991, and 2004 lists was an orthographic error.

Noturus crypticus. This new species, formerly considered to be a population of *N. elegans*, was described from Little Chucky Creek, in the upper Tennessee River drainage of eastern Tennessee, by B. M. Burr, D. J. Eisenhour, and J. M. Grady, 2005, Copeia 2005(4):794.

Noturus elegans. Now known only from the Green River drainage of central Kentucky and north-central Tennessee. See *N. crypticus* and *N. fasciatus.*

Noturus fasciatus. This new species was described from the lower Tennessee River drainage of western Tennessee by B. M. Burr, D. J. Eisenhour, and J. M. Grady, 2005, Copeia 2005(4):783.

Noturus gladiator. This new species, described from the lower Mississippi Valley (western Tennessee and western Mississippi) by M. R. Thomas and B. M. Burr, 2004, Ichthyol. Explor. Freshwat. 15(4):353, was formerly considered to be a southern population of *N. stigmosus*.

Noturus maydeni. This new species was described from the Black River system of southeastern Missouri and northeastern Arkansas by Egge *in* J. J. D. Egge and A. M. Simons, 2006, Zool. Scri. 35(6):588. Previously recognized as an eastern population of *N. albater*, it is genetically distinguishable, but is indistinguishable from *N. albater* on the basis of external morphological characters and pigmentation.

Noturus stigmosus. See *N. gladiator.*

Page 85

Pylodictis olivaris. Probably not native to Canada, having been first recorded there in 1978, and there is no evidence of reproduction (COSEWIC, 2008, COSEWIC assessment and update status report on the flathead catfish (*Pylodictis olivaris*) in Canada, Committee on the Status of Endangered Wildlife in Canada, Ottawa). Spelling of name in Spanish changed.

Argentiniformes. Sequence of this order changed following Nelson (2006), and that work should be consulted for relevant literature.

Argentina georgei. Added to the list based on a specimen collected in May 1998 and identified by F. F. Snelson, Jr., between 182-m and 195-m depths from the Straits of Florida (UF 109365).

Microstomatidae. *Leuroglossus* is now recognized in this family (subfamily Bathylaginae) following Nelson (2006).

Osmeriformes. Formerly in Salmoniformes. Now recognized as a separate order following Nelson (2006), and that work should be consulted for relevant literature.

Page 86

Osmerus dentex. Elevated from a subspecies of *O. mordax* based on analyses of mitochondrial cytochrome *b* by E. B. Taylor and J. J. Taylor (1994, Mol. Ecol. 3:235–248) and of cytochrome oxidase c subunit 1 (COI) by C. M. Mecklenburg, P. R. Møller and D. Steinke (2011, Mar. Biodiv. 41:109–140). Common

name in English from Kottelat and Freyhof (2007).

Osmerus mordax. See *O. dentex.* Also, change in distribution based on data in E. B. Taylor and J. J. Taylor (1994, cited above) and C. M. Mecklenburg et al. (2011, cited above).

Salmoniformes. Recognizing this order only for Salmonidae follows Nelson (2006), and that work should be consulted for relevant literature.

Coregonus artedi. The adoption of "cisco" in the 2004 list for this species created some confusion between this and other species with cisco as part of the name. Capitalization of common names in English in the present list should remove ambiguities with other species. *Coregonus nipigon* was listed as a species in the 1970 and earlier lists. It was considered a junior synonym of *C. artedi* by Scott and Crossman (1973), and the Nipigon cisco was removed from the 1980 and subsequent lists. D. A. Etnier and C. E. Skelton, 2003, Copeia 2003(4):739–749, identified one of three morphs of cisco caught in Lake Saganaga, Minnesota and Ontario, as *C. nipigon.* However, they did not explain why *C. nipigon* is not a junior synonym of *C. artedi.* We continue to recognize *Leucichthys nipigon* Koelz as a junior synonym of *C. artedi.*

Coregonus clupeaformis. Several nominal species are probably conspecific with this species, but they could prove to be valid (e.g., *C. nelsonii* Bean, 1884, the Alaska Whitefish, is recognized as valid by Mecklenburg et al. 2002). However, J. L. McDermid, J. D. Reist, and R. A. Bodaly, 2007, Arch. Hydrobiol. Spec. Issues Advanc. Limnol. 60:91–109, in a study of morphological and genetic characters, do not recommend species status for *C. nelsonii* or *C. pidschian* but provisionally recognize them as subspecies of *C. clupeaformis.* We do not change what was recognized in the 2004 list and continue to recognize *C. pidschian* pending broader studies that also consider Siberian forms.

Coregonus pidschian. See *C. clupeaformis.*

Oncorhynchus aguabonita. Treated as a subspecies of *O. mykiss* in the 2004 list. Recognized as a species by L. M. Page and B. M. Burr (2011) and herein because of lack of evidence of intergradation with *O. mykiss.* In Canada, only known from introduced populations established in at least three lakes in Alberta as a result of stocking in the late 1970s (J. D.

Stelfox and S. Herman, personal communication, 2010).

Oncorhynchus apache. Treated as a subspecies of *O. gilae* in the 2004 list. Recognized as a species by L. M. Page and B. M. Burr (2011) and herein because of lack of evidence of intergradation with *O. gilae*.

Oncorhynchus gilae. See *O. apache*.

Page 87

Oncorhynchus mykiss. The term "steelhead" is applied to Pacific slope sea-run Rainbow Trout and some populations in large lakes in eastern North America (and running to the Atlantic), where they were introduced.

Oncorhynchus nerka. Lacustrine stocks of Sockeye Salmon are known as kokanee (kokani in French).

Stenodus leucichthys. M. Kottelat and J. Freyhof (2007) recognized the species of *Stenodus* in North America as *S. nelma* (Pallas, 1773). We continue to recognize our North American populations as *S. leucichthys* until data are published demonstrating the distinctiveness of *S. leucichthys* from *S. nelma*.

Esocidae. Esox is nested within a clade with umbrid genera that renders Umbridae, as previously recognized, paraphyletic (J. A. López, P. Bentzen, and T. W. Pietsch, 2000, Copeia 2000(3):420–431; J. A. López, W. J. Chen, and G. Ortí, 2004, Copeia 2004(2):449–464). Although these authors continued to recognize Umbridae for *Umbra*, J. A. Lopez (personal communication, 2011) now feels that all species of esociforms should be in one family, a move followed by Page and Burr (2011). Family common names listed accordingly.

Esox americanus. The subspecies *E. americanus vermiculatus* Lesueur, 1846, is commonly referred to as the Grass Pickerel (brochet vermiculé in French).

Page 88

Maurolicus muelleri. Added based on beach-cast specimens (A. G. Huntsman, 1922, Contrib. Canadian Biol. 1921(3):49–72) and several collections from less than 200-m depths by Fisheries and Oceans Canada trawl surveys.

Stomiidae. A number of oceanic species in this and other families normally occur much deeper than 200 m during the day but migrate above 200 m at night and may occur as strays over our continental shelf. Therefore, the list for stomiids

is somewhat arbitrary, as are those for other mesopelagic fishes. See Myctophidae below.

Aulopiformes. Sequence of families in this order is changed following Nelson (2006), and that work should be consulted for literature. See Paralepididae.

Page 89

Paralepididae. The inclusion of the two species of *Anotopterus* in this family follows Nelson (2006); they were formerly recognized in Anotopteridae (accordingly deleted from the list and family common names expanded).

Anotopterus nikparini. See Paralepididae.

Anotopterus pharao. See Paralepididae.

Macroparalepis johnfitchi. Inadvertently omitted from earlier lists. The type locality is East End Anchorage, San Clemente Island, California, and the specimen was taken in 27 m at night by purse seine. A second specimen (SIO 73-410; 393 mm standard length) was collected alive in the surf zone at Mission Beach, California.

Myctophidae. This list is somewhat arbitrary, as are those for other families of mesopelagic and oceanic fishes, because of the uncertainty as to which species occasionally occur within the 200-m continental shelf contour. Other species could possibly be added, including the Atlantic *Diaphus dumerilii* (Bleeker, 1856), *D. garmani* Gilbert, 1906, *D. mollis* Tåning, 1928, *D. rafinesquii* (Cocco, 1838), and *D. taaningi* Norman, 1930 (J. E. Craddock and K. E. Hartel, personal communication, 2008), as well as several Pacific species. Most myctophids that occur at depths shallower than 200 m in the water column are vertical migrators living in areas of open ocean with bottom depths greatly exceeding 200 m. However, a number of the mesopelagic vertical-migrating myctophids can be found close to land in certain areas of the Americas, such as submarine canyons of the Pacific West Coast, the edge of the Gulf Stream or its ring eddies off Cape Hatteras, the Florida Current, and the Yucatan Channel.

Benthosema panamense. In October 2007, a specimen of *B. panamense* was found on the beach at Cabo Pulmo, Baja California Sur, Mexico (SIO 07-184). An earlier beach-cast specimen, from February 1964 and also from the Gulf of California, is in the Marine Vertebrate Collection at Scripps Institution of Oceanography (SIO 64-96).

Ceratoscopelus maderensis. Added based on many collections in the Atlantic Reference Centre from various bottom depths, including less than 100 m, in Canadian waters of the Atlantic Ocean.

Page 90

Gonichthys cocco. Added based on several collections in the Atlantic Reference Centre from various bottom depths, including less than 150 m, in Canadian waters of the Atlantic Ocean.

Hygophum hygomii. Added based on a collection in the Atlantic Reference Centre (ARC 156546) of 23 adults from 149-m bottom depth in Canadian waters of the Atlantic Ocean.

Lobianchia dofleini. Added based on several collections in the Atlantic Reference Centre from various bottom depths less than 200 m in the Canadian waters of the Atlantic Ocean.

Lampriformes. Orthography of ordinal and family names changed from 2004 list following Nelson (2006), and that work should be consulted for reasons in changing from Lampridiformes and Lamprididae. Not all workers accept these spellings.

Lampridae. See Lampriformes.

Stylephorus chordatus. Evidence was provided by M. Miya, N. I. Holcroft, T. P. Satoh, M. Yamaguchi, M. Nishida, and E. O. Wiley, 2007, Ichthyol. Res. 54:323–332, that *S. chordatus* is more closely related to the Gadiformes than to the Lampriformes and should be placed in its own order, Stylephoriformes. However, E. O. Wiley and G. D. Johnson, 2010, A teleost classification based on monophyletic groups, Pages 123–182 *in* J. S. Nelson, H.-P. Schultze, and M. V. H. Wilson, editors, Origin and phylogenetic interrelationships of teleosts, Verlag Dr. Friedrich Pfeil, Munich, Germany, provide synapomorphies for Lampriformes, including the monotypic *Stylephorus.*

Page 91

Trachipterus jacksonensis. Added based on a specimen (IBUNAM-P 15620) trapped on the surface off the coast of Colima, Mexico and identified by J. L. Castro-Aguirre and H. S. Espinosa Pérez.

Page 92

Gadiformes. Change in sequence of Gadiformes (and families within) and Ophidiiformes follows Nelson (2006), and that work should be consulted for relevant literature.

Coelorinchus caelorinchus. T. Iwamoto, Page xi *in* A. M. Orlov and T. Iwamoto, editors, 2008, Grenadiers of the world: biology, stock assessment, and fisheries, American Fisheries Society, Symposium 63, Bethesda, Maryland, discussed the confusion in the spelling of the genus; *Coelorinchus* vs. *Caelorinchus.* His recommendation is to employ *Coelorinchus* as the original intent of the author (Giorna). The spelling of the specific name, *caelorinchus,* is indisputedly correct.

Coelorinchus caribbaeus. See *C. caelorinchus.*

Coelorinchus scaphopsis. See *C. caelorinchus.*

Coryphaenoides pectoralis. The inclusion of *Albatrossia* in the genus *Coryphaenoides* was proposed by R. R. Wilson and P. Attia, 2003, Mol. Phylogenet. Evol. 27:343–347, based on allozyme, peptide mapping and DNA sequence data. Treated as *Albatrossia pectoralis* in the 2004 list and by D. M. Clausen *in* A. M. Orlov and T. Iwamoto, editors, Grenadiers of the world: biology, stock assessment, and fisheries, 2008, American Fisheries Society, Symposium 63, Bethesda, Maryland. However, in that same work, Clausen (p. 414) stated that "subsequent biochemical and DNA phylogenetic studies have concluded that giant grenadier do indeed bear such close affinity to *Coryphaenoides* that the species should be returned to this genus (Wilson 1994; Morita 1999, and Wilson and Attia 2003)."

Page 93

Merlucciidae. Reasons for placing *Steindachneria,* with one species in our area, in this family (instead of Steindachneriidae as in the 2004 list) follows Nelson (2006), and that work should be consulted for relevant literature. See Gadiformes.

Merluccius productus. D. Lloris, J. Matallanas, and P. Oliver, 2005, synonymized *M. hernandezi* Matthews, 1985, with *M. angustimanus* Garman, 1899, Page 19 *in* Hakes of the world (family Merluccidae), Food and Agriculture Organization of the United Nations, FAO Species Catalogue for Fishery Purposes No. 2, Rome. Subsequently, C. A. Silva-Segundo, M. Brito-Chavarria, E. F. Balart, I. A. Barriga-Sosa, R. Rojas-Esquivel, M. I. Roldán, G. Murugan, and F. J. García de León, 2011, Rev. Fish Biol. Fish. 21:259–282, proposed that *M. productus* is the only species of hake present along the North American and north Central American coast. They synonymized *M.*

angustimanus with *M. productus* (p. 279), stating that morphological and genetic data suggest a single taxonomic entity with a minor degree of morphological and genetic intraspecific variation in the northeastern Pacific.

Steindachneria argentea. See Merlucciidae.

Phycis chesteri. In the 2004 list, we noted that this species, then in *Urophycis*, was placed in *Phycis* by many recent authors. This has become generally accepted and is adopted here.

Arctogadus glacialis. Arctogadus borisovi Dryagin, which appeared in the 2004 list, was synonymized with *A. glacialis* by A. D. Jordan, P. R. Møller, and J. G. Nielsen (2003, J. Fish Biol. 62:1339–1352) based on genetic and morphometric evidence.

Gadus chalcogrammus. Previously listed as *Theragra chalcogramma* but returned to *Gadus* on the basis of genetic studies by M. W. Coulson, H. D. Marshall, P. Pepin, and S. M. Carr (2006, Genome 49:1115–1130), and S. M. Carr and H. D. Marshall (2008, Genetics 180:381–389), and as discussed by C. M. Mecklenburg, P. R. Møller, and D. Steinke (2011, Mar. Biodiv. 41:109–140).

Gadus macrocephalus. C. M. Mecklenburg, P. R. Møller, and D. Steinke (2011, Mar. Biodiv. 41:109–140) concluded, on the basis of earlier DNA studies (S. M. Carr, D. S. Kivlichan, P. Pepin, and D. C. Crutcher, 1999, Can. J. Zool. 77:19–26; P. R. Møller, A. D. Jordan, P. Gravlund, and J. F. Steffensen, 2002, Polar Biol. 25:342–349) and early life-history information (S. A. Evseenko, B. Laurel, J. A. Brown, and D. Y. U. Malikova, 2006, J. Ichthyol. 46:351–358), that *G. ogac* Richardson, 1836, does not warrant species separation from *G. macrocephalus.*

Gaidropsarus argentatus. Added based on its presence in 100+ m depths in the western North Atlantic and eastern Arctic oceans (B. W. Coad and J. D. Reist, 2004, Can. Manuscr. Rep. Fish. Aquat. Sci. 2674; P. R. Møller, J. G. Nielsen, S. W. Knudsen, J. W. Poulsen, K. Sünksen, and O. A. Jørgensen, 2010, Zootaxa 2378:1–84; and C. M. Mecklenburg, P. R. Møller, and D. Steinke, 2011, Mar. Biodiv. 41:109–140).

Gaidropsarus ensis. Added based on several collections from Canadian waters in the Atlantic Reference Centre and St. Andrews Biological Station, some from bottom depths less than 100 m in the Atlantic Ocean, and two specimens from less than 200 m in the Gulf of St. Lawrence (D. Clark and R. Miller, personal communication).

Lota lota. M. Kottelat and J. Freyhof (2007) recognize the Burbot in North America as *Lota maculosa* but provide no supporting evidence for separating the North American population from the Eurasian population.

Merlangius merlangus. Recorded from the southwestern coast of Greenland by P. R. Møller, J. G. Nielsen, S. W. Knudsen, J. Y. Poulsen, K. Sünksen, and O. A. Jørgensen, 2010, Zootaxa 2378:1–84.

Page 94

Ophidiiformes. See Gadiformes above.

Brotula clarkae. Recorded off southern California based on two specimens from depths of 223 and 65 m, taken in 2001 and 2003, respectively (R. N. Lea, M. J. Allen, and W. Power, 2009, Bull. So. Calif. Acad. Sci. 108(3):163–167).

Lepophidium marmoratum. Based on two specimens (UF 229552) collected off Quintana Roo (Pillsbury station 598) between 155-m and 205-m trawl depth. Name in English suggested by C. R. Robins (personal communication).

Lepophidium staurophor. Range extended into U.S. waters based on a collection from 192 m off western coast of Florida (UF 152799). Two other collections known from U.S. waters off Alabama and North Carolina (A. M. Quattrini, S. W. Ross, J. Sulak, A. M. Necaise, T. L. Casazza, and G. D. Dennis, 2004, Southeast. Nat. 3(1):161), are from depths greater than 200 m.

Page 95

Ophidion lagochila. In *Parophidion* in the last edition; we now follow J. G. Nielsen and C. R. Robins, 2003 [dated 2002], Ophidiidae (cuskeels), Pages 965–972 *in* Carpenter (2003b).

Calamopteryx robinsorum. Known depth of occurrence above 200 m not definite.

Page 96

Ogilbia boydwalkeri. This new species was described from the Pacific of Mexico and El Salvador by P. R. Møller, W. Schwarzhans, and J. G. Nielsen, 2005, Aqua, International Journal of Ichthyology 10(4):139.

Ogilbia cayorum. Occurrence in Mexican waters, as reported in the 2004 list, is based on the species subsequently described as *O. suarezae* by P. R. Møller, W. Schwarzhans, and J. G. Nielsen, 2005, Aqua, International Journal of Ichthyology 10(4):194. See *O. suarezae*.

Ogilbia davidsmithi. This new species was described from the Gulf of California by P. R. Møller, W. Schwarzhans, and J. G. Nielsen, 2005, Aqua, International Journal of Ichthyology 10(4):145.

Ogilbia nigromarginata. This new species was described from the Gulf of California by P. R. Møller, W. Schwarzhans, and J. G. Nielsen, 2005, Aqua, International Journal of Ichthyology 10(4):157.

Ogilbia nudiceps. This new species was described from the Gulf of California by P. R. Møller, W. Schwarzhans, and J. G. Nielsen, 2005, Aqua, International Journal of Ichthyology 10(4):160.

Ogilbia robertsoni. This new species was described from the eastern Pacific from Mexico to Costa Rica by P. R. Møller, W. Schwarzhans, and J. G. Nielsen, 2005, Aqua, International Journal of Ichthyology 10(4):164.

Ogilbia sabaji. This new species was described from the western Atlantic from the Florida Keys and elsewhere by P. R. Møller, W. Schwarzhans, and J. G. Nielsen, 2005, Aqua, International Journal of Ichthyology 10(4): 192.

Ogilbia sedorae. This new species was described from the eastern Pacific off Mexico and farther south by P. R. Møller, W. Schwarzhans, and J. G. Nielsen, 2005, Aqua, International Journal of Ichthyology 10(4):166.

Ogilbia suarezae. This new species was described from the Gulf of Mexico and the Caribbean Sea by P. R. Møller, W. Schwarzhans, and J. G. Nielsen, 2005; Aqua, International Journal of Ichthyology 10(4):194. Mexican Atlantic populations previously identified as *O. cayorum* are this species.

Ogilbia ventralis. Parentheses were inadvertently omitted from around the author's name in the 2004 list; it was described in *Brosmophycis*.

Typhliasina pearsei. Placed in *Ogilbia* in the 2004 list; now placed in the monotypic genus *Typhliasina* following the revisionary study by P. R. Møller, W. Schwarzhans, and J. G. Nielsen, 2004, Aqua, International Journal of Ichthyology 8(4):141–192.

Page 97

Lophius americanus. Called "monkfish" when commercialized as a food fish.

Antennarius commerson. New to the list. Widespread in the tropical Indo-Pacific and occurring from East Africa eastward to the Americas. In the eastern Pacific known (but rare) from central Mexico to Colombia (Isla Gorgona), as well as several of the oceanic islands, including the Revillagigedo Archipelago of Mexico (Robertson and Allen 2008; D. R. Robertson, personal communication, 2011). Although several authors attribute the species name to Latreille, 1804, we follow Eschmeyer (2012) in attributing it to Lacepède, 1798.

Antennatus coccineus. New to the list. Widespread in the tropical Indo-Pacific, occurring from East Africa eastward to the Americas. In the eastern Pacific known (but rare) from central Mexico to Panama and some of the oceanic islands (Robertson and Allen 2008), including two oceanic islands off Chile evidently based on SIO records (Eschmeyer, 2012). The central Mexican record is from Puerto Vallarta, Jalisco, in the southeasternmost Gulf of California (D. R. Robertson, personal communication, 2011). Until recently, this species was placed in the genus *Antennarius*, but in a study utilizing DNA sequences from the mitochondrial 16S and cytochrome oxidase c subunit 1 (COI) genes, and the nuclear recombination activating gene 2 (RAG2), R. J. Arnold and T. W. Pietsch, 2012, Mol. Phylogenet Evol. 62:117–129, transferred it to *Antennatus*.

Antennatus sanguineus. In a study utilizing DNA sequences from the mitochondrial 16S and cytochrome oxidase c subunit 1 (COI) genes, and the nuclear recombination activating gene 2 (RAG2), R. J. Arnold and T. W. Pietsch, 2012, Mol. Phylogenet. Evol. 62:117–129, transferred this species from *Antennarius* to *Antennatus*.

Fowlerichthys avalonis. In a study utilizing DNA sequences from the mitochondrial 16S and cytochrome oxidase c subunit 1 (COI) genes, and the nuclear recombination activating gene 2 (RAG2), R. J. Arnold and T. W. Pietsch, 2012, Mol. Phylogenet. Evol. 62:117–129, transferred this species from *Antennarius* to *Fowlerichthys*.

Fowlerichthys ocellatus. In a study utilizing DNA sequences from the mitochondrial 16S and cytochrome oxidase c subunit 1 (COI) genes, and the nuclear recombination activating gene 2 (RAG2), R. J. Arnold and T. W. Pietsch, 2012, Mol. Phylogenet. Evol. 62:117–129, transferred this species from *Antennarius* to *Fowlerichthys*.

Fowlerichthys radiosus. In a study utilizing DNA sequences from the mitochondrial 16S and cytochrome oxidase c subunit 1 (COI) genes, and the nuclear recombination activating gene 2 (RAG2), R. J. Arnold and T. W. Pietsch, 2012, Mol. Phylogenet. Evol. 62:117–129, transferred this species from *Antennarius* to *Fowlerichthys*.

Page 98

Halieutichthys aculeatus. See *H. bispinosus* and *H. intermedius*.

Halieutichthys bispinosus. This species, related to *H. aculeatus*, was described by H.-C. Ho, P. Chakrabarty, and J. S. Sparks, 2010, J. Fish Biol. 77:853, with material from the Atlantic coast of the United States, Gulf of Mexico and off the Yucatan Peninsula, Mexico.

Halieutichthys intermedius. This species, related to *H. aculeatus*, was described by H.-C. Ho, P. Chakrabarty, and J. S. Sparks, 2010, J. Fish Biol. 77:854. It is known only from the upper Gulf of Mexico from northwestern Florida to Texas.

Ceratias holboelli. This species is added based on four specimens from less than 200 m from the Gulf of St. Lawrence, in Canada (R. Miller, personal communication). There are numerous records from deeper depths farther south, and it is known from the eastern North Pacific but at depths beyond our range of coverage.

Page 99

Mugil hospes. This species is listed as occurring only in Pacific Mexico, from where it was described. However, the species is stated to also occur from Brazil, the Guianas, and Caribbean coasts of South and Central America as far north as Belize (I. J. Harrison, 2003 [dated 2002], Mugilidae (mullets), Pages 1071–1085 *in* Carpenter (2003b).

Mugil rubrioculus. This new species, the type locality of which is Venezuela, was described by I. J. Harrison, M. Nirchio, C. Oliveira, E. Ron, and J. Gavina, 2007, J. Fish Biol. 71(Supplement A):80, with one specimen reported from southeastern Florida (ANSP 152244). It is primarily distinguished by a red iris and is the mullet listed as *M. gaimardianus* in earlier (1960–1991) lists and as *Mugil* species in the 2004 list. Also see appendix note for *Mugil* species in 2004 list.

Mugil trichodon. *Mugil gyrans*, included in the 2004 list but with an appendix note questioning its validity, was included in the synonymy of *M. trichodon* by I. J. Harrison, M. Nirchio, C. Oliveira, E. Ron, and J. Gavina, 2007, J. Fish Biol. 71(Supplement A):76–97. Eight syntypes of *Querimana gyrans* Jordan and Gilbert, 1884 (USNM 34966) were included (without comment) in the material examined of *M. trichodon*.

Atherinella callida. Recent efforts to find this species at the type locality (the only known locality) have been unsuccessful, and the species is thought to be extinct (K. R. Piller, personal communication, 2011).

Atherinella schultzi. Correction of orthography of Álvarez (from Alvarez).

Page 100

Chirostoma melanoccus. Correction of orthography of Álvarez (from Alvarez).

Chirostoma patzcuaro. Change in orthography of name in English to agree with geographic name in Mexico (from Patzcuaro silverside).

Menidia audens. Although the recognition of this species as separate from *M. beryllina* has been controversial, R. D. Suttkus, B. A. Thompson, and J. K. Blackburn, 2005, Southeastern Fishes Council Proceedings 48:1–9, presented data to support the premise that they are separate, with *M. beryllina* being a brackish or tidewater inhabitant and *M. audens* a freshwater inhabitant. No hybrids were found in the area of sympatry.

Menidia conchorum. Based on electrophoretic data, C. F. Duggins, A. A. Karlin, K. Relyea, and R. W. Yerger, 1986, Tulane Stud. Zool. Bot. 25:133–150, showed *M. conchorum* to be indistinguishable from *M. peninsulae*, but specifically distinct from *M. beryllina* and *M. colei*. D. D. Bloom, K. R. Piller, J. Lyons, N. Mercado-Silva, and M. Medina-Nava, 2009, Copeia 2009(2):408–417, reached a similar conclusion based on the mitochondrially encoded ND2 gene. However, C. R. Gilbert, 1992, Pages 213–217 *in* Rare and endangered biota of Florida, volume 2, Fishes, showed that *M. conchorum*, in addition to being widely separated geographically, differs trenchantly from *M. peninsulae* in three meristic characters (numbers of anal rays, branchial lateral-line scales, and total vertebrae), as well as reaching a smaller size. We view the identical gene sequence of these two forms as the retention of a plesiomorphic haplotype and consider it appropriate to continue the recognition of *M. conchorum*.

Page 101

Poblana letholepis. Correction of orthography of Álvarez (from Alvarez).

Poblana squamata. Correction of orthography of Álvarez (from Alvarez).

Beloniformes. Change in sequence of families and composition. See Nelson (2006) for relevant literature.

Page 102

Hyporhamphus mexicanus. Correction of orthography of Álvarez (from Alvarez).

Hyporhamphus roberti. Occurrence based on J. J. Schmitter-Soto, 1998, Catálogo de los peces continentales de Quintana Roo, El Colegio de la Frontera Sur, San Cristóbal de las Casas, Chiapas, Mexico (pp. 80–81, catalog number ECOCH 3086, Lago Bacalar, Quintana Roo, Mexico). Common names from B. B. Collette, 2003 [dated 2002], Hemiramphidae (halfbeaks), Pages 1135–1144 *in* Carpenter (2003b).

Hyporhamphus unifasciatus. Date of original description corrected from 1842 to 1841.

Oxyporhamphus micropterus. Placed in Exocoetidae in the 2004 list based on J. C. Dasilao, Jr. and K. Sasaki, 1998, Ichthyol. Res. 45(4):347–353. However, it was moved to Hemiramphidae by N. R. Lovejoy, M. Iranpour, and B. B. Collette, 2004, Integr. Comp. Biol. 44(5):366–377.

Page 103

Strongylura timucu. Change in orthography of name in English to agree with its form in Spanish (from timucu).

Tylosurus acus. The application by B. B. Collette and N. V. Parin to conserve the name *Sphyraena acus* (currently *T. acus*), as employed in the last list (see 2004 list, p. 215, for history) was approved as Opinion 2169 (Bull. Zool. Nomencl. 64(1):75–76). Change in orthography of name in English to agree with its form in Spanish (agujón).

Tylosurus pacificus. Change in orthography of name in English to agree with its form in Spanish (agujón).

Cyprinodontiformes. Changes in sequence of families and composition follow Nelson (2006),

and that work should be consulted for relevant literature.

Rivulidae. Species placed in Aplocheilidae in the last edition are now recognized in Rivulidae for reasons given in Nelson (2006:284). Aplocheilidae is a valid family for Asian and African rivulines.

Kryptolebias marmoratus. *Cryptolebias* was erected by W. J. E. M. Costa, 2004, Ichthyol. Explor. Freshwat. 15(2):105–120, for the reception of *Rivulus marmoratus* and several closely related species. However, *Cryptolebias* Costa is preoccupied by *Cryptolebias* (a fossil cyprinodontoid genus from Europe described by J. Gaudant in 1978), and W. J. E. M. Costa, 2004, Neotrop. Ichthyol. 2(2):107–108, proposed the substitute name *Kryptolebias*.

Goodeidae. The spelling of "mexcalpique" is corrected to "mexclapique," as used in the original description of *Girardinichthys viviparus* (Bustamante, 1837), in 22 common names in Spanish on pages 103–105. The genera *Crenichthys* and *Empetrichthys*, with four species endemic to the southwestern United States, are sometimes placed in their own family, the Empetrichthyidae, most recently by Minckley and Marsh (2009). However, L. R. Parenti (1981, Bull. Amer. Mus. Nat. Hist. 168) demonstrated the close relationship of these genera to others in the family Goodeidae.

Page 104

Allotoca diazi. Change in orthography of name in English to agree with geographic name in Mexico (from Patzcuaro allotoca).

Allotoca meeki. Correction of orthography of Álvarez (from Alvarez). Change in orthography of name in English to agree with geographic name in Mexico (from Zirahuen allotoca).

Allotoca regalis. Placed in the monotypic genus *Neoophorus* by M. K. Meyer, A. C. Radda, and O. Domínguez-Domínguez, 2001, Ann. Naturhist. Mus. Wien 103B:453–460. Although these authors note that this species lacks derived characteristics of other species of *Allotoca*, we follow recent use (e.g., Miller et al. 2006) and retain it in *Allotoca*. Correction of orthography of Álvarez (from Alvarez).

Allotoca zacapuensis. Correction of spelling of Radda.

Chapalichthys pardalis. Correction of orthography of Álvarez (from Alvarez).

Chapalichthys peraticus. Correction of orthography of Álvarez (from Alvarez). Although Miller et al. (2006) considered *C. peraticus* to be a synonym of *C. pardalis*, we continue to consider *C. peraticus* valid in the absence of a study of variation within *Chapalichthys*.

Girardinichthys ireneae. This new species was described from Laguna de Zacapu, Michoacán, Mexico, by A. C. Radda and M. K. Meyer, 2003, Ann. Naturhist. Mus. Wien 104 B:7. These authors give reasons for recognizing *Hubbsina* as a subgenus (to which this species and *G. turneri* belong) of *Girardinichthys*.

Girardinichthys turneri. Formerly recognized in *Hubbsina*. According to O. Domínguez-Domínguez, N. Mercado-Silva, J. Lyons, and H. J. Grier, 2005, The viviparous goodeid fishes, Pages 525–569 *in* M. C. Uribe and H. J. Grier, editors, Viviparous fishes, New Life Publications, Homestead, Florida, this species is critically endangered. See *G. ireneae*.

Ilyodon cortesae. Parentheses removed from around authors' names. Although Miller et al. (2006) considered *I. cortesae* and *I. lennoni* to be synonyms of *I. whitei*, we continue to consider them valid in the absence of a study of variation within *Ilyodon*.

Ilyodon furcidens. *Ilyodon xantusi* was placed in the synonymy of this species by B. J. Turner, T. A. Grudzien, K. P. Adkisson, and M. M. White, 1983, Environ. Biol. Fish. 9:159–172. See also B. J. Turner, T. A. Grudzien, K. P. Adkisson, and R. A. Worrell, 1985, Evol. 39:122–134.

Ilyodon lennoni. See *Ilyodon cortesae*.

Page 105

Skiffia francesae. Extinct in nature but captive population maintained at the Universidad Autónoma de Nuevo León in Monterrey, Mexico.

Zoogoneticus purhepechus. This new species was described from La Luz Spring, Zamora, Michoacán, Mexico by O. Domínguez-Domínguez, R. Pérez-Rodríguez, and I. Doadrio, 2008, Revista Mexicana de Biodiversidad 79:377. Names in English and Spanish refer to indigenous people of the area where the species occurs.

Fundulus jenkinsi. Change in area of occurrence; there are apparently no verified records of this species in Mexico.

Page 106

Fundulus philpisteri. This new species was described from Baño de San Ignacio and neighboring springs, Río San Fernando basin, Nuevo León, Mexico, by M. E. García-Ramírez, S. Contreras-Balderas, and M. L. Lozano-Vilano, 2007 [dated 2006], Pages 13–19 *in* M. L. Lozano-Vilano and A. J. Contreras-Balderas, editors, Studies of North American desert fishes in honor of E. P. (Phil) Pister, conservationist, Universidad Autónoma de Nuevo León, Monterrey, Mexico.

Fundulus pulvereus. Change in area of occurrence; there are apparently no verified records of this species in Mexico.

Fundulus zebrinus. Minckley and Marsh (2009) note the introduction and wide dispersion of this species (as *Plancterus zebrinus*) in the Rio Grande (Río Bravo) basin, including northeastern Mexico. It had been listed earlier for Mexico by H. Espinosa-Pérez, M. T. Gaspar-Dillanes, and P. Fuentes-Mata, 1993, Listados faunísticos de México III, Los peces dulceacuícolas mexicanos, Instituto de Biología, Universidad Nacional Autónoma de México, Mexico, D.F.

Lucania interioris. Change in orthography of name in English to agree with geographic name in Mexico (from Cuatro Cienegas killifish).

Cyprinodontidae. See Cyprinodontiformes.

Cyprinodon alvarezi. Change in orthography of name in English to agree with geographic name in Mexico (from Potosi pupfish).

Cyprinodon artifrons. Change in name in Spanish for clarity of name origin (from bolín petota); the adjective petota now transferred to name in Spanish for *C. variegatus*.

Page 107

Cyprinodon atrorus. Change in orthography of name in English to agree with geographic name in Mexico (from bolson pupfish).

Cyprinodon beltrani. Correction of orthography of Álvarez (from Alvarez).

Cyprinodon bifasciatus. Change in orthography of name in English to agree with geographic name in Mexico (from Cuatro Cienegas pupfish).

Cyprinodon ceciliae. Change in names in English and Spanish from those in the 2004 list to accurately reflect area of occurrence.

Cyprinodon inmemoriam. Change in names in English and in Spanish from those in the 2004 list to accurately reflect area of occurrence.

Cyprinodon julimes. This new species was described from the thermal spring El Pandeño de los Pando in the municipality of Julimes, Río Conchos basin, Chihuahua, Mexico, by M. De la Maza-Benignos and L. Vela-Valladares, 2009, Pages 185–189 (Appendix D) *in* M. De la Maza Benignos, editor, Los peces del Río Conchos, Alianza WWF (World Wildlife Fund)-Fundación Gonzalo Rio Aronte y Gobierno del Estado de Chihuahua, Jiutepec, Morelos, Mexico.

Cyprinodon longidorsalis. Change in names in English and in Spanish from those erroneously given in the 2004 list to accurately reflect area of occurrence.

Page 108

Cyprinodon suavium. This new species, the seventh endemic species of *Cyprinodon* known from Lake Chichancanab, Yucatan, Mexico, was described by U. Strecker, 2005, Hydrobiologia 541:109.

Cyprinodon variegatus. Change in name in Spanish for clarity about origin of name (from bolín). See *C. artifrons*.

Cyprinodon veronicae. Change in names in English and in Spanish from those erroneously given in the 2004 list to accurately reflect area of occurrence.

Megupsilon aporus. Extinct in nature, but captive population maintained at the Universidad Autónoma de Nuevo León in Monterrey, Mexico.

Anableps dowi. Listed in 2004 as occurring only in freshwater; however, the species was cited as occurring in mangrove forests at river mouths by Robertson and Allen (2008). For discussion of retaining the spelling of the species name as *dowi*, rather than *dowei*, as used by several authors (e.g., Eschmeyer 2012), see the 2004 list, Appendix 1:217.

Carlhubbsia kidderi. Change in orthography of name in English to agree with geographic name in Mexico (from Champoton gambusia).

Gambusia clarkhubbsi. This new species was described from San Felipe Spring, at Del Rio, Val Verde County, Texas, by G. P. Garrett and R. J. Edwards, 2003, Copeia 2003(4):783.

Page 109

Gambusia longispinis. Change in orthography of name in English to agree with geographic name in Mexico (from Cuatro Cienegas gambusia).

Gambusia luma. Collected in the Río Hondo, Belize (D. W. Greenfield and J. E. Thomerson, 1997, Fishes of the continental waters of Belize, University of Florida Press, Gainesville). Because this stream forms the boundary between Belize and Quintana Roo, Mexico, the presence of this species on the Belizean side of the stream is considered as sufficient evidence for its presence in Mexico. Name in English proposed by Greenfield and Thomerson (1997).

Gambusia panuco. Change in orthography of name in English to agree with geographic name in Mexico (from Panuco gambusia).

Gambusia regani. Change in orthography of name in English to agree with geographic name in Mexico (from Forlon gambusia).

Gambusia rhizophorae. Although listed as occurring in freshwater (United States) in past lists, no documentation is known.

Gambusia zarskei. This new species, endemic to the upper Río Conchos, Chihuahua, Mexico, was described by M. K. Meyer, S. Schories, and M. Schartl, 2010, Vert. Zool. 60(1):13. Common names refer to the Río Conchos.

Heterandria formosa. Although Eschmeyer (2012) gives reasons why the original description of this species should date from Girard, 1859, the reference to small size alone in Agassiz's 1855 description seems sufficient to establish the identity of the fish he was describing.

Heterandria tuxtlaensis. This new species, endemic to Lago de Catemaco and tributaries of the lake and the Río Grande de Catemaco above the falls at El Salto de Eyipantla, in the Tuxtla Mountains of southern Veracruz, Mexico, was described by J. D. McEachran and T. J. Dewitt, 2008, Zootaxa 1824:49. Common name in English refers to the only known locality of the species, the Tuxtla Mountains of Veracruz.

Heterophallus echeagarayi. Correction of orthography of Álvarez (from Alvarez).

Page 110

Poecilia latipunctata. Change in orthography of name in English to agree with geographic name in Mexico (from Tamesi molly).

Poecilia petenensis. Change in orthography of name in English to agree with geographic name in Mexico (from Peten molly).

Poecilia sulphuraria. Correction of orthography of Álvarez (from Alvarez).

Poeciliopsis fasciata. Change in orthography of name in English to agree with geographic name in Mexico (from San Jeronimo livebearer).

Poeciliopsis occidentalis. As noted in the 2004 list (Appendix 1:218), P. W. Hedrick, K. M. Parker, and R. N. Lee, 2001, Mol. Ecol. 10(6): 1399–1412, provided molecular evidence that *P. occidentalis occidentalis* (Baird & Girard, 1853) and *P. occidentalis sonoriensis* (Girard, 1859), "Yaqui topminnow," should be recognized as valid species. However, P. H. F. Lucinda *in* Reis et al. (2003, p. 250) regarded *P. sonoriensis* as a synonym of *P. occidentalis*, and although Miller et al. (2006:249) recognized *P. sonoriensis* as a species, they did not distinguish it morphologically from *P. occidentalis*. Although *P. sonoriensis* may be a valid taxon, we defer species recognition pending further studies.

Poeciliopsis scarlli. Change in orthography of name in English to agree with geographic name in Mexico (from Michoacan livebearer). This species was considered by Miller et al. (2006) to be a synonym of *P. turrubarensis*.

Poeciliopsis turrubarensis. See *Poeciliopsis scarlli*.

Page 111

Priapella bonita. This species may be extinct (Miller et al., 2006:251–252).

Priapella chamulae. This new species was described from the upper Grijalva River system, Tabasco and Chiapas, Mexico, by M. Schartl, M. K. Meyer, and B. Wilde, 2006, Zool. Abh. (Dresden) 55:61.

Priapella compressa. Correction of orthography of Álvarez (from Alvarez).

Priapella intermedia. Correction of orthography of Álvarez (from Alvarez).

Priapella lacandonae. This new species was described from Chiapas, Mexico, by M. K. Meyer, S. Schories, and M. Schartl, 2011, Vert. Zool. 61:93.

Xiphophorus clemenciae. Correction of orthography of Álvarez (from Alvarez).

Xiphophorus gordoni. Change in orthography of name in English to agree with geographic name in Mexico (from Cuatro Cienegas platyfish).

Xiphophorus kallmani. This new species was described from near Lake Catemaco, Veracruz, Mexico, by M. K. Meyer and M. Schartl, 2003, Zool. Abh. (Dresden) 53:59.

Xiphophorus nigrensis. Change in orthography of

name in English to agree with geographic name in Mexico (from Panuco swordtail).

Page 112

Plectrypops lima. New to the list. Widespread in the Indo-Pacific, occurring from eastern Africa eastward to the Americas. In the eastern Pacific known from the oceanic islands of Isla del Coco, Clipperton Atoll, and the Revillagigedo Archipelago of Mexico (Robertson and Allen 2008; D. R. Robertson, personal communication, 2011).

Page 113

Zeiformes. Change in sequence of families and transfer of Caproidae to Perciformes follow Nelson (2006), and that work should be consulted for literature.

Acentronura dendritica. Many recent authors follow C. E. Dawson (1982, Syngnathidae, Pages 1–172 *in* J. E. Böhlke, editor, Fishes of the western North Atlantic, Memoir 1, part 8, Sears Foundation for Marine Research, Yale University, New Haven, Connecticut) in assigning this species to the genus *Amphelikturus* Parr, 1930, perhaps unaware that Dawson (1984, Japan. J. Ichthyol. 31(2):158 and 1985, Indo-Pacific pipefishes [Red Sea to the Americas], Gulf Coast Research Laboratory, Ocean Springs, Mississippi) subsequently treated *Amphelikturus* as a subgenus of *Acentronura* Kaup, 1853.

Page 114

Entelurus aequoreus. Recorded from the southwestern coast of Greenland by P. R. Møller, J. G. Nielsen, S. W. Knudsen, J. Y. Poulsen, K. Sünksen, and O. A. Jørgensen, 2010, Zootaxa 2378:1–84.

Pseudophallus mindii. Added due to its collection in the Río Hondo, Belize (D. W. Greenfield and J. E. Thomerson, 1997, Fishes of the continental waters of Belize, University of Florida Press, Gainesville). Because this stream forms the boundary between Belize and Quintana Roo, Mexico, the presence of this species on the Belizean side of the stream is considered as sufficient evidence for its presence in Mexico. Name in English proposed by Greenfield and Thomerson (1997).

Syngnathus euchrous. Correction of spelling of Fritzsche (from Fritzche); also incorrect in the 1991 list.

Syngnathus texanus. C. R. Gilbert, new name. This name replaces *Syngnathus affinis* Günther, 1870, which Eschmeyer (2012) has determined to be a junior homonym of *Syngnathus affinis* Eichwald, 1831, a valid species of pipefish endemic to the Black Sea (R. H. Kuiter, 2009, A comprehensive guide to Syngnathiformes, TMC Publishing, Chorleywood, UK; R. H. Kuiter, 2009, Seahorses and their relatives, Aquatic Photographics, Seaford, Australia). C. E. Dawson (1982, Syngnathidae, Pages 1–172 *in* J. E. Böhlke, editor, Fishes of the western North Atlantic, Memoir 1, part 8, Sears Foundation for Marine Research, Yale University, New Haven, Connecticut) considered Günther's *S. affinis* to be a valid but rare species, distinguished from its geographically close congeners by discrete meristic and mensural characters but most closely related to the widely allopatric *S. fuscus*. Although J. Tolan (2008, Texas J. Sci. 60(2):83–96) considered this species to be a junior synonym of *S. scovelli*, we follow Dawson and recognize the Texas Pipefish.

Page 115

Aulostomus maculatus. Year of publication corrected following C. F. Cowan, 1976, J. Soc. Bibliog. Nat. Hist. 8:32–64.

Synbranchidae. Correction in spelling of family common name in Spanish (from anguillas de lodo).

Mastacembelidae. Added for the species listed. See Notacanthidae above (appendix notes for p. 59).

Macrognathus siamensis. This Asian species is established in southern Florida.

Page 116

Scorpaeniformes. There is considerable evidence that this order as given here and classically recognized is not monophyletic. Major changes in the classification of this order and that of the Perciformes as recognized herein are in order, but we do not make changes pending agreement in the scientific literature. E. O. Wiley and G. D. Johnson, 2010, A teleost classification based on monophyletic groups, Pages 123–182 *in* J. S. Nelson, H.-P. Schultze, and M. V. H. Wilson, editors, Origin and phylogenetic interrelationships of teleosts, Verlag Dr. Friedrich Pfeil, Munich, Germany, recognize the order Scorpaeniformes with a new composition, comprising two suborders, Scor-

paenoidei and Serranoidei, and recognize a new order, Cottiformes with two suborders, Cottoidei and Zoarcoidei. See also W. L. Smith and W. C. Wheeler, 2004, Mol. Phylogenet. Evol. 32:627–646; W. L. Smith and M. T. Craig, 2007, Copeia 2007(1):35–55; and G. Shinohara and H. Imamura, 2007, Ichthyol. Res. 54:92–99.

Pterois miles. This species, along with the previously listed *P. volitans*, is established along the East Coast of the United States and elsewhere in Atlantic waters as documented by R. M. Hamner, D. W. Freshwater, and P. E. Whitfield, 2007, J. Fish Biol. 71 (Supplement B):214–222, and W. R. Courtenay, Jr., B. B. Collette, T. E. Essington, R. Hilborn, J. W. Orr, D. Pauly, J. E. Randall, and W. F. Smith-Vaniz, 2009, Fisheries 34(4):181–186. Both species recently have become established in Mexico (Comité Asesor Nacional sobre Especies Invasoras, 2010, Estratégia nacional sobre especies invasoras en México: prevención, control y erradicación, Comisión Nacional para el Conocimiento y Uso de la Biodiversidad, Comisión Nacional de Áreas Protegidas, Secretaría de Medio Ambiente y Recursos Naturales, Mexico).

Pterois volitans. See *P. miles*.

Scorpaena afuerae. Added based on three specimens collected off the western coast of Baja California Sur and deposited at Scripps Institution of Oceanography (SIO 08-135), La Jolla, California (H. J. Walker, Jr., personal communication, 2009). It occurs from Mexico to Peru and at the oceanic Isla del Coco off Costa Rica.

Page 117

Sebastes aleutianus. J. W. Orr and S. Hawkins, 2008, Fish. Bull. 106:111–134, showed this name, as previously used, to refer to a complex of two closely related species. See *S. melanostictus*.

Sebastes ciliatus. See *S. variabilis*.

Page 118

Sebastes melanostictus. Removed from the synonymy of *S. aleutianus* by J. W. Orr and S. Hawkins, 2008, Fish. Bull. 106:111–134. The range of *S. melanostictus* extends from the central coast of Japan, through the Kuril and Aleutian Islands and Bering Sea to 60.5°N, and southward to southern California.

Page 119

Sebastes variabilis. Resurrected from the synonymy of *S. ciliatus* by J. W. Orr and J. E. Blackburn, 2004, Fish. Bull. 102:328–348, as part of the Dusky Rockfish complex. We apply the name Light Dusky Rockfish, as was done when this species was considered a light color variant of *S. ciliatus*.

Page 120

Peristediidae. The common name "armored gurnards" is used for this group by some authors.

Page 122

Cottus bairdii. See *C. chattahoochee* and *C. tallapoosae*.

Cottus carolinae. See *C. kanawhae*.

Cottus chattahoochee. This new species, restricted to the Chattahoochee River drainage above the Fall Line in Georgia and formerly considered part of *C. bairdii*, was described by D. A. Neely, J. D. Williams, and R. L. Mayden, 2007, Copeia 2007(3):649.

Cottus hypselurus. See *C. immaculatus*.

Cottus immaculatus. This new species, previously considered a population of *C. hypselurus*, from the White River system of Arkansas and Missouri, was described by A. P. Kinziger and R. M. Wood, 2010, Zootaxa 2340:51.

Cottus kanawhae. This new species, previously considered part of *C. carolinae*, was described from the New River system of West Virginia and Virginia by C. R. Robins, 2005, Zootaxa 987:1.

Cottus tallapoosae. This new species, restricted to the Tallapoosa River drainage above the Fall Line in east-central Alabama and west-central Georgia and formerly considered part of *C. bairdii*, was described by D. A. Neely, J. D. Williams, and R. L. Mayden, 2007, Copeia 2007(3):642.

Page 123

Gymnocanthus galeatus. Parentheses are removed from around the author's name (species name was originally combined with an incorrect spelling, *Gymnacanthus*, and parentheses are not appropriate).

Hemilepidotus spinosus. Parentheses are removed from around the author's name.

Icelinus limbaughi. This new species was described from off southern California at depths between 20 and 86 m by R. H. Rosenblatt and W. L. Smith, 2004, Copeia 2004(3):556.

Page 124

Myoxocephalus scorpius. *Myoxocephalus verrucosus* was recognized in the 2004 list; however, C. W. Mecklenburg, P. R. Møller, and D. Steinke, 2011, Mar. Biodiv. 41:109–140, concluded that clinal variation in morphology and cytochrome oxidase c subunit 1 (COI) data did not support separation of that form from *M. scorpius*.

Page 125

Aspidophoroides olrikii. Originally described in *Aspidophoroides*, this species had been assigned to *Ulcina* (as in the 2004 list); however, C. M. Mecklenburg, P. R. Møller, and D. Steinke, 2011, Mar. Biodiv. 41:109–140, synonymized *Ulcina* with *Aspidophoroides*. Correction in year of description based on Eschmeyer (2012).

Page 126

Sarritor frenatus. Change in genus from *Leptagonus* follows B. A. Sheiko and C. W. Mecklenburg, 2004, Family Agonidae Swainson 1839—poachers, California Academy of Sciences Annotated Checklists of Fishes 30:1–27. As *Sarritor* in the 1960, 1970, 1980, and 1991 editions.

Cottunculus thomsonii. This North Atlantic species was inadvertently omitted from the 2004 list and is added based on W. B. Scott and M. G. Scott, 1988, Atlantic fishes of Canada, University of Toronto Press, Toronto; known from depths of 182–1,462 m off the North American coast.

Page 127

Cyclopteropsis jordani. This Arctic species is added based on B. W. Coad and J. D. Reist, 2004, Can. Manuscr. Rep. Fish. Aquat. Sci. 2674.

Cyclopteropsis mcalpini. The holotype, one of two known specimens, is from northwestern Greenland (P. R. Møller, J. G. Nielsen, S. W. Knudsen, J. Y. Poulsen, K. Sünksen, and O. A. Jørgensen, 2010, Zootaxa 2378:1–84).

Eumicrotremus spinosus. *Eumicrotremus eggvinii*, which was included in the 2004 list, was synonymized with *E. spinosus* by I. Byrkjedal, D. J. Rees, and E. Willassen, 2007, J. Fish. Biol. 71 (Supplement A):111–131, who determined, based on mitochondrial and nuclear DNA evidence, that *E. eggvinii* was based on sexually dimorphic males of *E. spinosus*.

Allocareproctus tanix. This new species was described from a depth range of 104–620 m from the Aleutian Islands by J. W. Orr and M. S. Busby, 2006, Zootaxa 1173:20, in their revision of *Allocareproctus*. Other species in this genus occur within our range of coverage but from depths greater than 200 m.

Allocareproctus unangas. This new species was described from the Aleutian Islands by J. W. Orr and M. S. Busby, 2006, Zootaxa 1173:27. They reported one collection from a depth of 176 m (CAS 223485).

Careproctus comus. This new species was described from the Aleutian Islands, at depths of 189–400 m, by J. W. Orr and K. P. Maslenikov, 2007, Copeia 2007(3):700.

Careproctus faunus. This new species was described from the central and eastern Aleutian Islands, at depths of 120–422 m, by J. W. Orr and K. P. Maslenikov, 2007, Copeia 2007(3):706.

Careproctus ranula. Inadvertently omitted in previous editions, this species was described by Goode and Bean in 1897 from a specimen from Nova Scotia taken off the mouth of Halifax Harbor at 52 fathoms (95 m). It was also collected from bottom depths less than 200 m in Canadian waters of the Atlantic in 2009 (D. Clark, personal communication, 2011).

Page 128

Liparis adiastolus. This new species, previously part of *L. rutteri* and known from northern California to Washington, was described by D. L. Stein, C. E. Bond, and D. Misitano, 2003, Copeia 2003(4):818.

Liparis bathyarcticus. Previously considered a synonym of *L. gibbus* but recognized as valid by N. V. Chernova, 2008, J. Ichthyol. 48(10):831–852.

Liparis gibbus. See *L. bathyarcticus*.

Liparis herschelinus. Long considered a junior synonym of *L. tunicatus*, this species was resurrected by N. V. Chernova, 2008, J. Ichthyol. 48(10):831–852, an action followed herein. However, C. W. Mecklenburg, P. R. Møller, and D. Steinke, 2011, Mar. Biodiv. 41:109–140, felt that Chernova's data were insufficient to clarify the status of *L. herschelinus* and that the situation re-

quires further study. The type locality for *L. herschelinus* is Herschel Island, Yukon Territory, Canada.

Liparis micraspidophorus. Correction of authorship (from Burke, 1912).

Liparis rutteri. See *L. adiastolus*.

Liparis tunicatus. Correction of year of publication (from 1837). Also, see *L. herschelinus*.

Page 129

Perciformes. Changes in addition to those discussed below have been suggested by E. O. Wiley and G. D. Johnson, 2010, Pages 123–182 *in* J. S. Nelson, H.-P. Schultze, and M. V. H. Wilson, editors, Origin and phylogenetic interrelationships of teleosts, Verlag Dr. Friedrich Pfeil, Munich, Germany.

Centropomus armatus. Corrected occurrence. The freshwater occurrence of the six species of Mexican Pacific *Centropomus*, as indicated by J. L. Castro Aguirre, H. S. Espinosa-Pérez, and J. J. Schmitter-Soto, 1999, Ictiofauna estuarino-lagunar y vicaria de México, Editorial Limusa-Noriega/IPN, México, and Miller et al. (2006) was inadvertenly omitted from the 2004 list.

Centropomus medius. Corrected occurrence. See *C. armatus*.

Centropomus mexicanus. Change in distribution; it has been found in the Loxahatchee, St. Lucie, and St. Sebastian rivers, Florida (R. G. Gilmore, personal communication, 2011).

Centropomus nigrescens. Corrected occurrence. See *C. armatus*.

Centropomus robalito. Corrected occurrence. See *C. armatus*.

Centropomus unionensis. Corrected occurrence. See *C. armatus*.

Centropomus viridis. Corrected occurrence. See *C. armatus*.

Page 130

Epinephelidae. Recognition of Epinephelidae (as separate from Serranidae) and its composition is based on M. T. Craig and P. A. Hastings, 2007, Ichthyol. Res. 54:1–17, and W. L. Smith and M. T. Craig, 2007, Copeia 2007(1):35–55. Family common names reflect changes in compositions, especially regarding those names applied to Serranidae in the 2004 list.

Epinephelus cifuentesi. Although Craig and Hastings (2007, Ichthyol. Res. 54:9) demonstrated a close relationship between this species and a group containing *E. drummondhayi*, *Alphestes*, *Dermatolepis*, *Hyporthodus*, and *Triso*, we follow those authors in retaining it in *Epinephelus*.

Epinephelus clippertonensis. Originally thought to be endemic to Clipperton Atoll, it was reported from Alijos Rocks, off the Pacific coast of Baja California Sur by M. T. Craig, P. H. Hastings, D. J. Pondella, D. R. Robertson, and J. A. Rosales-Casián, 2006, J. Biogeogr. 33:969–979, and reported as occurring in the Revillagigedo Archipelago of Mexico, far to the southwest of the tip of the Baja California peninsula, by Robertson and Allen (2008). Common names are based on type locality.

Epinephelus drummondhayi. Although Craig and Hastings (2007, Ichthyol. Res. 54:9) demonstrated a close relationship between this species and a group containing *E. cifuentesi*, *Alphestes*, *Dermatolepis*, *Hyporthodus*, and *Triso*, we follow those authors in retaining it in *Epinephelus*.

Epinephelus itajara. See *E. quinquefasciatus*.

Epinephelus labriformis. Reported from San Diego, California by M. T. Craig, D. J. Pondella, II, and R. N. Lea, 2006, California Fish and Game 92(2):91–97.

Epinephelus quinquefasciatus. M. T. Craig, R. T. Graham, R. A. Torres, J. R. Hyde, M. O. Freitas, B. P. Ferreira, M. Hostim-Silva, L. C. Gerhardinger, A. A. Bertoncini, and D. R. Robertson, 2009, Endangered Species Research 7:167–174, concluded that the goliath grouper (as given for *E. itajara* in the 2004 list) in the eastern Pacific, the Pacific Goliath Grouper or mero gigante, is a valid species, separate from *E. itajara* of the western Atlantic, which we now refer to as the Atlantic Goliath Grouper or cherna gigante, based on strong evidence from both nuclear and mitochondrial DNA sequences (although morphological differences have yet to be found).

Hyporthodus acanthistius. Seven species are transferred to *Hyporthodus* from *Epinephelus* following W. L. Smith and M. T. Craig, 2007, Copeia 2007(1):35–55, and M. T. Craig and P. A. Hastings, 2007, Ichthyol. Res. 54:1–17.

Hyporthodus exsul. See *H. acanthistius*.

Hyporthodus flavolimbatus. See *H. acanthistius*.

Hyporthodus mystacinus. See *H. acanthistius*.

Hyporthodus nigritus. See *H. acanthistius*.

Hyporthodus niphobles. See *H. acanthistius*.

Hyporthodus niveatus. See *H. acanthistius*.

Page 131

Serranidae. See Epinephelidae.

Baldwinella aureorubens. Formerly *Hemanthias aureorubens*. This species and *H. vivanus* were placed in the new genus *Baldwinella* by W. D. Anderson, Jr. and P. C. Heemstra, 2012, Trans. Am. Philos. Soc. 102(2):1–173.

Baldwinella vivanus. See *B. aureorubens*.

Choranthias tenuis. Formerly *Anthias tenuis*. This species was placed in the new genus *Choranthias* by W. D. Anderson, Jr. and P. C. Heemstra, 2012, Trans. Am. Philos. Soc. 102(2):1–173.

Page 132

Hypoplectrus aberrans. Occurrence in Mexico based on J. J. Schmitter-Soto, L. Vásquez-Yeomans, A. Aguilar-Perera, C. Curiel-Mondragón, and J. A. Caballero-Vázquez, 2000, Lista de peces marinos del Caribe mexicano, An. Inst. Biol. Univ. Nac. Auton. Mex. Ser. Zool. 71(2):143–177.

Hypoplectrus castroaguirrei. This new species was described by L. F. Del Moral Flores, J. L. Tello-Musi, and J. A. Martínez-Pérez, 2011, Revista de Zoología 22:1–10, from reefs off the coast of Veracruz, Mexico.

Hypoplectrus chlorurus. Added to the list based on record from Chinchorro Bank, Mexico (R. M. Loreto, M. Lara, and J. J. Schmitter-Soto, 2003, Bull. Mar. Sci. 73(1):153–170).

Hypoplectrus gemma. Occurrence in Mexico reported by A. Aguilar-Perera and A. N. Tuz-Sulub, 2010, Pan-American J. Aquatic Sci. 5:143–146. Identification as this species, rather than another closely related new species (*H. maya*; not yet recorded from Mexico), confirmed by P. S. Lobel (personal communication, 2011).

Hypoplectrus indigo. Recorded from Mexican waters by several authors, most recently from Chinchorro Bank, by R. M. Loreto, M. Lara, and J. J. Schmitter-Soto, 2003, Bull. Mar. Sci. 73(1):153–170.

Hypoplectrus providencianus. Added to the list as being reported along the Mexican Caribbean coast, and most recently on the basis of observations from Chinchorro Bank, off southern Quintana Roo (R. M. Loreto, M. Lara, and J. J. Schmitter-Soto, 2003, Bull. Mar. Sci. 73(1):153–170). Common names from Carpenter (2003b).

Hypoplectrus randallorum. This new species, described from Belize by P. S. Lobel, 2011, Zootaxa 3096:1–17, was reported to occur throughout the Caribbean and the Florida Keys. Common name in English suggested by author.

Liopropoma aberrans. Reported from northern Gulf of Mexico, off Alabama, at 102-m depth and off North Carolina at 96-m depth (A. M. Quatrini, S. W. Ross, K. J. Sulak, A. M. Nacaise, T. L. Casazza, and G. D. Dennis, 2004, Southeast. Nat. 3(1):155–172). Common name proposed by R. Claro and L. Parenti, 2001, The marine ichthyofauna of Cuba, Appendix 2.1, Pages 33–57 *in* R. Claro, K. C. Lindeman, and L. R. Parenti, editors, Ecology of the marine fishes of Cuba, Smithsonian Institution Press, Washington, D.C.

Liopropoma carmabi. Occurrence in Mexico based on ANSP 123875 (identified by P. C. Heemstra), collected from Palancar Reef, Cozumel Island (J. J. Schmitter-Soto, personal communication, 2007).

Parasphyraenops incisus. Added to the list based on a 55-mm specimen (NCSM 35959, the largest yet recorded) collected off North Carolina, in September 2001, at a depth between 57 and 100 m (A. M. Quattrini, S. W. Ross, K. J. Sulak, A. M. Nacaise, T. L. Casazza, and G. D. Dennis, 2004, Southeast. Nat. 3(1):155–172). Common name suggested by G. D. Johnson and W. F. Smith-Vaniz, 1987, Bull. Mar. Sci. 40(1):48–58.

Page 133

Rypticus carpenteri. This new species, closely related to and previously confused with *R. subbifrenatus*, was described by C. C. Baldwin and L. A. Weigt, 2012, Copeia 2012(1):24. It is known from Florida, from Belize, and throughout the Caribbean. Adults probably occur on the Caribbean coast of Mexico where, to date, it is known from a larval specimen (J. J. Schmitter-Soto, personal communication, 2012).

Rypticus subbifrenatus. See *R. carpenteri*.

Page 134

Lipogramma anabantoides. Reported from Mexico by R. G. Gilmore, 1997, Bull. Mar. Sci. 60:782–788, but this distribution was inadvertently omitted from the 2004 list.

Lipogramma evides. Depth of occurrence above 200 m not definite (type specimens collected off Arrowsmith Bank, Mexico, in an otter-trawl haul covering a depth range of 146–265 m).

Lipogramma regium. Added to the list by being videotaped at a depth of 102 m in the northern Gulf of Mexico, off Alabama (A. M. Quattrini, S. W. Ross, K. J. Sulak, A. M. Nacaise, T. L. Casazza, and G. D. Dennis, 2004, Southeast. Nat. 3(1):155–172).

Opistognathus brochus. New to the list. Described by W. A. Bussing and R. J. Lavenberg, 2003, Rev. Biol. Trop. 51(2):534.

Opistognathus fossoris. New to the list. Described by W. A. Bussing and R. J. Lavenberg, 2003, Rev. Biol. Trop. 51(2):539.

Opistognathus megalepis. Depth occurrence above 200 m not definite (type specimens collected off Arrowsmith Bank, Mexico, in an otter-trawl haul covering a depth range of 146–265 m).

Opistognathus punctatus. *Opistognathus mexicanus* was placed in synonymy of *O. punctatus* by W. A. Bussing and R. J. Lavenberg, 2003, Rev. Biol. Trop. 51(2):529–550, and is deleted from the list. Common names used for *O. mexicanus* in the 2004 list are transferred to *O. walkeri* in the present list.

Opistognathus walkeri. New to the list. Described by W. A. Bussing and R. J. Lavenberg, 2003, Rev. Biol. Trop. 51(2):537. See *O. punctatus* regarding common names.

Page 135

Ambloplites rupestris. Established in Mexico (Miller et al., 2006).

Lepomis auritus. Although listed as native in the 2004 list, it was noted in the appendix that this species may be introduced to Canada. The Committee on the Status of Endangered Wildlife in Canada (COSEWIC) concluded that it is native to New Brunswick (2008, Cosewic assessment and update status report on the redbreast sunfish *Lepomis auritus* in Canada, COSEWIC, Ottawa). It has been introduced and established in Mexico (Miller et al. 2006).

Lepomis gulosus. The Committee on the Status of Endangered Wildlife in Canada (COSEWIC) concluded that this species is native (2005, COSEWIC assessment and update status report on the warmouth *Lepomis gulosus* in Canada, COSEWIC, Ottawa).

Lepomis humilis. The Committee on the Status of Endangered Wildlife in Canada (COSEWIC) concluded that this species was introduced (2008, COSEWIC assessment and update status report on the orangespotted sunfish *Lepomis humilis* in Canada, COSEWIC, Ottawa).

Lepomis megalotis. Common name in Spanish is changed to reflect local use (D. A. Hendrickson, personal communication, 2008). See *L. peltastes*.

Lepomis microlophus. Introduced and established in Mexico (Miller et al. 2006).

Lepomis peltastes. Removed from synonymy of *L. megalotis* by R. M. Bailey, W. C. Latta, and G. R. Smith, 2004, Misc. Publ. Mus. Zool. Univ. Mich.192:1–215. Common names in English and French refer to distribution of the species.

Lepomis punctatus. Introduced and established in Mexico (Miller et al. 2006).

Micropterus dolomieu. Introduced and established in Mexico (Miller et al. 2006).

Micropterus henshalli. This newly recognized species, endemic to the Mobile basin, was removed from the synonymy of *M. punctulatus* by W. H. Baker, C. E. Johnston, and G. W. Folkerts, 2008, Zootaxa 1861:57–67.

Micropterus punctulatus. See *M. henshalli*.

Micropterus salmoides. Using allozymes and mitochondrial DNA sequence data, T. W. Kassler, J. B. Koppelman, T. J. Near, C. B. Dillman, J. M. Levengood, D. L. Swofford, J. L. VanOrman, J. E. Claussen, and D. P. Philipp, 2002, Pages 291–322 *in* D. P. Philipp and M. S. Ridgway, editors, Black bass: ecology, conservation, and management, American Fisheries Society, Symposium 31, Bethesda, Maryland, concluded that *M. floridanus* should be recognized as a species separate from *M. salmoides*. However, no specimens were analyzed from the broad area of intergradation recognized with morphological data by R. M. Bailey and C. L. Hubbs, 1949, Occas. Pap. Mus. Zool. Univ. Mich. 516:1–40, and allozyme data of D. P. Philipp, 1983, Trans. Am. Fish. Soc. 112:1–20. The taxonomy remains unclear.

Pomoxis annularis. Introduced and established in Mexico (Miller et al. 2006).

Pomoxis nigromaculatus. Introduced and established in Mexico (Miller et al. 2006).

Percidae. Several hypotheses of phylogenetic relationships among darters have been published since the 2004 list: B. L. Sloss, N. Billington and B. Burr, 2004, Mol. Phylogenet. Evol. 32:545–562; N. C. Ayache and T. J. Near, 2005, Bull. Peabody Mus. Nat. Hist. 50(2):327–346; T. J. Near and B. P. Keck, 2005, Mol. Ecol.

14:3485–3496; R. L. Mayden, R. M. Wood, N. J. Lang, C. B. Dillman and J. F. Switzer, 2006, Pages 20–39 *in* M. L. Lozano-Vilano and A. J. Contreras-Balderas, editors, Studies of North American desert fishes in honor of E. P. (Phil) Pister, conservationist, Universidad Autónoma de Nuevo León, Monterrey, Mexico; N. J. Lang and R. L. Mayden, 2007, Mol. Phylogenet. Evol. 43:605–615; C. M. Bossu and T. J. Near, 2009, Syst. Biol. 58(1):114–129; J. C. Bruner, 2011, Pages 5–84 *in* B. A. Barton, editor, 2011, Biology, management, and culture of walleye and sauger, American Fisheries Society, Bethesda, Maryland; T. A. Smith, T. C. Mendelson and L. M. Page, 2011, Heredity 107(6):579–588; Near et al., 2011, Syst. Biol. 60(5):565–595. However, the only disagreements among genera recognized concern *Crytallaria* and *Nothonotus*. Bruner (2011) treats *Crystallaria* as a subgenus of *Ammocrypta*; all others treat *Crystallaria* as a genus. Most have continued to treat *Nothonotus* as a subgenus of *Etheostoma* (Sloss et al. 2004; Ayache and Near 2005; Mayden et al. 2006; Lang and Mayden 2007; Bruner 2011; Smith et al. 2011); however, Near and Keck (2005), Bossu and Near (2009), and Near et al. (2011) treat *Nothonotus* as a genus. In all of these studies, *Ammocrypta* and *Crystallaria* were found to be sister taxa, making the genus-level decision based on monophyly arbitrary. Relationships of *Nothonotus* to other clades vary with the gene analyzed (e.g., three different relationships among major clades were hypothesized by the three genes analyzed by Near et al. [2011]). Given the disagreements among studies and data sets, we retain the genera recognized in the sixth edition of the list (2004). Family common names in English and French are expanded to emphasize the fact that more than 90% of species in this family are darters.

Page 136

Crystallaria asprella. See *C. cincotta*.

Crystallaria cincotta. This new species, formerly in *C. asprella*, was described by S. A. Welsh and R. M. Wood, 2008, Zootaxa 1680:64. It is endemic to the Ohio River drainage but extirpated from most of its former range and known only from the lower Elk River system in central West Virginia.

Etheostoma akatulo. This new species, formerly in *E. stigmaeum*, was described from the Caney Fork River system, Tennessee, by S. R. Layman and R. L. Mayden, 2009, Copeia 2009(1):158.

Etheostoma atripinne. Evidence for recognizing this species, endemic to the Cumberland River drainage in the Nashville basin, Tennessee, and regarded as a subspecies of *E. simoterum* in the 1991 (p. 90) and 2004 editions, was given by S. L. Powers and R. L. Mayden, 2007, Bull. Ala. Mus. Nat. Hist. 25:10–12. The common name Cumberland snubnose darter was used by Powers and Mayden (2007) and in the 1980 and earlier editions of the list. See *E. simoterum*.

Etheostoma autumnale. This new species, described by R. L. Mayden, 2010, Copeia 2010(4):727, and previously referred to *E. punctulatum*, is endemic to the White, Current, Eleven Point, and Little Red River systems of the Arkansas River drainage in southern Missouri and northern Arkansas. Common name from Mayden (2010).

Etheostoma brevispinum. Previously considered a subspecies of *E. flabellare*, *E. brevispinum* was recognized as a species found in southern Virginia, North Carolina, and northern South Carolina by R. E. Blanton and G. A. Schuster, 2008, Copeia 2008(4):851.

Page 137

Etheostoma cinereum. See *E. maydeni*.

Etheostoma erythrozonum. This new species, formerly in *E. tetrazonum*, was described from the Meramec River drainage, Missouri, by J. F. Switzer and R. M. Wood, 2009, Zootaxa 2095:2. Common name from Switzer and Wood (2009).

Etheostoma flabellare. See *E. brevispinum*.

Page 138

Etheostoma lemniscatum. This new species, formerly in *E. percnurum*, was described from Big South Fork Cumberland River, Kentucky and Tennessee, by R. E. Blanton *in* R. E. Blanton and R. E. Jenkins, 2008, Zootaxa 1963:20.

Etheostoma marmorpinnum. This new species, formerly in *E. percnurum*, was described from Little River (Tennessee River drainage), Tennessee by R. E. Blanton and R. E. Jenkins, 2008, Zootaxa 1963:15.

Etheostoma maydeni. This new species, formerly considered a population of *E. cinereum* from the Cumberland River drainage of Tennessee and Kentucky, was described by S. L. Powers and B. R. Kuhajda *in* S. L. Powers, B. R. Ku-

hajda and S. R. Ahlbrand, 2012, Zootaxa 3277:52.

Etheostoma mihileze. This new species, described by R. L. Mayden, 2010, Copeia 2010(4):722, and previously referred to *E. punctulatum*, is endemic to the middle Arkansas River drainage in northwestern Arkansas, northeastern Oklahoma, southeastern Kansas, and southwestern Missouri. Common name from Mayden (2010).

Etheostoma nigrum. See *E. susanae*.

Page 139

Etheostoma occidentale. This new species, described by S. L. Powers and R. L. Mayden, 2007, Bull. Ala. Mus. Nat. Hist. 25:15, and previously referred to *E. simoterum*, was described from streams of the western Highland Rim of the Cumberland River drainage, Kentucky and Tennessee. Common name from Powers and Mayden (2007). See *E. simoterum*.

Etheostoma orientale. This new species, described by S. L. Powers and R. L. Mayden, 2007, Bull. Ala. Mus. Nat. Hist. 25:16, and previously referred to *E. simoterum*, was described from streams of the eastern Highland Rim of the Cumberland River drainage, Kentucky and Tennessee. Common name from Powers and Mayden (2007). See *E. simoterum*.

Etheostoma percnurum. See *E. lemniscatum*, *E. marmorpinnum*, and *E. sitikuense*. *Etheostoma percnurum* is now restricted to Copper Creek, Clinch River drainage, Scott County, Tennessee.

Etheostoma planasaxatile. This new species, described by S. L. Powers and R. L. Mayden, 2007, Bull. Ala. Mus. Nat. Hist. 25:14, and previously referred to *E. simoterum*, was described from the Duck River system, Tennessee. Common name from Powers and Mayden (2007). See *E. simoterum*.

Etheostoma punctulatum. The range of *E. punctulatum*, as now restricted, is limited to tributaries of the Missouri River in south-central Missouri. See *E. autumnale* and *E. mihileze*.

Etheostoma simoterum. Previously considered to be distributed throughout the Tennessee River drainage and Cumberland River drainage below Cumberland Falls, this species as now defined is restricted to the upper Holston River system (Tennessee River drainage) and the upper Big Sandy River system (Ohio River basin). S. L. Powers and R.

L. Mayden, 2007, Bull. Ala. Mus. Nat. Hist. 25:10, based on morphological and molecular investigations, elevated *E. atripinne* to species and described *E. occidentale*, *E. orientale*, *E. planasaxatile*, and *E. tennesseense* as new species in the *E. simoterum* complex. These species are diagnosed by nuptial male coloration, meristics, morphometrics, and variation at two mitochondrial loci. R. C. Harrington and T. J. Near, 2011, Syst. Biol. 61:63–79, supported the elevation of *E. atripinne* and distinctiveness of *E. planasaxatile* but suggested that *E. tennesseense* is conspecific with *E. simoterum* and that *E. occidentale* and *E. orientale* are conspecific with *E. atripinne*. As the latter study did not examine and test diagnostic characters of nuptial male coloration and other morphologically diagnostic characters outlined by Powers and Mayden (2007), we elect to recognize the six species either described or elevated by those authors. *Etheostoma simoterum* retains the recently used common name Snubnose Darter (Tennessee snubnose darter was the name appearing in lists prior to 1991). See *E. atripinne*, *E. occidentale*, *E. orientale*, *E. planasaxatile*, and *E. tennesseense*.

Page 140

Etheostoma sitikuense. This new species, formerly in *E. percnurum*, was described from Citico Creek (Tennessee River drainage), Tennessee, by R. E. Blanton *in* R. E. Blanton and R. E. Jenkins, 2008, Zootaxa 1963:17.

Etheostoma stigmaeum. See *E. akatulo*.

Etheostoma susanae. Endemic to the upper Cumberland River drainage, Kentucky and Tennessee, this form was also included in the 2004 list. However, the taxon intergrades with *E. nigrum nigrum* in the upper Kentucky River, Kentucky (W. C. Starnes and L. B. Starnes, 1979, Copeia 1979(3):426–430) and is recognized by some authors as a subspecies of *E. nigrum* (e.g., Page and Burr 2011).

Etheostoma tennesseense. This new species, described by S. L. Powers and R. L. Mayden, 2007, Bull. Ala. Mus. Nat. Hist. 25:12, and previously referred to *E. simoterum*, was described from the Tennessee River drainage above Duck River in Tennessee, Alabama, and Virginia and the Bluestone River of the upper Ohio River basin, Virginia. Common name from Powers and Mayden (2007). See *E. simoterum*.

Etheostoma tetrazonum. See *E. erythrozonum*.

Gymnocephalus cernua. M. Kottelat and J. Freyhof (2007) corrected the spelling of the species name as used in the 2004 list (i.e., *G. cernuus*). The name *cernua* was used for this species prior to its formal description by Linnaeus, who treated *cernua* as a noun in apposition.

Percina apristis. Formerly recognized as a subspecies of *P. sciera* and restricted to the Guadalupe River system, Texas, R. H. Robins and L. M. Page, 2007, Zootaxa 1618:51–60, gave reasons for recognizing *apristis* as a species.

Page 141

Percina bimaculata. This newly recognized species, endemic to the Susquehanna and Potomac River drainages, was removed from the synonymy of *P. caprodes* by T. J. Near, 2008, Bull. Peabody Mus. Nat. Hist. 49:3–18. An older name for this species, *Perca* (*Percina*) *nebulosa* Haldeman, 1842, is preoccupied by *Perca nebulosa* Rafinesque, 1814.

Percina caprodes. See *P. bimaculata*. *Percina caprodes fulvitaenia* Morris and Page, 1981, was recognized as *P. fulvitaenia* in the 2004 list based on taxonomy used by B. A. Thompson, 1997, Occas. Pap. Mus. Nat. Sci. La. State Univ. 73:1–34. However, Thompson provided no data on *fulvitaenia*, and M. A. Morris and L. M. Page, 1981, Copeia 1981(1):95–108, provided evidence for integradation of *P. c. fulvitaenia* with *P. c. caprodes* and *P. c. semifasciata*.

Percina crypta. This new species was described from the Chattahoochee and Flint River systems in Georgia and Alabama by M. C. Freeman, B. J. Freeman, and N. M. Burkhead *in* M. C. Freeman, B. J. Freeman, N. M. Burkhead, and C. A. Straight, 2008, Zootaxa 1963:28.

Percina kusha. This new species, restricted to the headwaters of the Coosa River in Georgia and Tennessee, was described by J. D. Williams and N. M. Burkhead *in* J. D. Williams, D. A. Neely, S. J. Walsh, and N. M. Burkhead, 2007, Zootaxa 1549:4.

Percina macrocephala. See *P. williamsi*.

Percina sciera. See *P. apristis*.

Page 142

Percina sipsi. This new species, known only from the Sipsey Fork of the Black Warrior River in the Bankhead National Forest in northwestern Alabama, was described by J. D. Williams and D. A. Neely *in* J. D. Williams, D. A.

Neely, S. J. Walsh, and N. M. Burkhead, 2007, Zootaxa 1549:12.

Percina smithvanizi. This new species, found above the Fall Line in the Tallapoosa River system in eastern Alabama and western Georgia, was described by J. D. Williams and S. J. Walsh *in* J. D. Williams, D. A. Neely, S. J. Walsh, and N. M. Burkhead, 2007, Zootaxa 1549:15.

Percina williamsi. This new species, restricted to the upper Tennessee River drainage of Tennessee, Virginia, and North Carolina and formerly in *P. macrocephala*, was described by L. M. Page and T. J. Near, 2007, Copeia 2007(3):606.

Cookeolus japonicus. Expansion of distribution. The occurrence of this species in Mexico was inadvertently omitted from the 2004 edition. J. E. Fitch and S. J. Crooke, 1984, Proc. Calif. Acad. Sci. 43 (19):301–315, in a revision of eastern Pacific catalufas (Priacanthidae) reported on (as *C. boops*) a number of specimens from Mexico off Baja California at Alijos Rocks and the Revillagigedo Islands. Voucher specimens exist in several museums, including CAS, LACM, SIO, and USNM. It is a circumglobal species in tropical seas and, in addition to the two localities already mentioned for the eastern Pacific, has been recorded from the southeastern Gulf of California to Peru, as well as the oceanic Isla del Coco and Isla Malpelo (Robertson and Allen 2008).

Priacanthus arenatus. Name in Spanish corrected (gender) from catalufa ojón to catalufa ojona.

Apogon dovii. Diacritic mark was inadvertently omitted in author's name; correction of year of publication.

Apogon gouldi. Range extended into United States based on a collection off North Carolina (NCSM 35956) from a depth of 97 m (A. M. Quattrini, S. W. Ross, K. J. Sulak, A. M. Nacaise, T. L. Casazza, and G. D. Dennis, 2004, Southeast. Nat. 3(1):155–172).

Page 143

Caulolatilus princeps. Caulolatilus hubbsi, included in the 2004 list with some reservation, is shown to be a junior synonym of *C. princeps* by R. N. Lea and R. F. Feeney, in press, Galapagos Research.

Page 144

Carangidae. Change in sequence of this family follows analysis of molecular data by K. N. Gray, J. R. McDowell, B. B. Collette, and J. E. Graves, 2009, Bull. Mar. Sci. 84(2):183–198, which agreed with published morphological studies.

Carangoides orthogrammus. Listed as *Caranx orthogrammus* in the 2004 list. W. F. Smith-Vaniz *in* Carpenter (2003b:1427) and W. F. Smith-Vaniz and Carpenter, 2009, Fish. Bull. 105(2):207–233, discuss the problem with dentition as the only character to distinguish certain genera and species traditionally assigned to *Caranx* and, in the interest of nomenclatural stability, advocate current usage until carangid generic limits and phylogenetic relationships are better resolved. This species also occurs in the Indo-Pacific where the recommended change agrees best with current usage.

Page 145

Pseudocaranx dentex. Listed as *Caranx dentex* in the 2004 list. W. F. Smith-Vaniz *in* Carpenter (2003b:1427) and W. F. Smith-Vaniz and Carpenter, 2009, Fish. Bull. 105(2):207–233, discuss the problem with dentition as the only character to distinguish certain genera and species traditionally assigned to *Caranx* and, in the interest of nomenclatural stability, advocate current usage until carangid generic limits and phylogenetic relationships are better resolved. This species also occurs in the Indo-Pacific where the recommended change agrees best with current usage.

Page 146

Coryphaenidae. For species of Coryphaenidae, the common names mahi-mahi (with variations in spelling) and dorado are also used in commerce.

Remora albescens. This species was placed in *Remora* in the 2004 edition based on the study of B. O'Toole, 2002, Can. J. Zool. 80:596–623. Analysis of molecular data by K. N. Gray, J. R. McDowell, B. B. Collette, and J. E. Graves, 2009, Bull. Mar. Sci. 84(2):183–198, supports this conclusion. *Remorina,* where *albescens* has often been placed, is a junior synonym of *Remora.*

Page 147

Lutjanus guttatus. Common name in Spanish changed to reflect more prevalent use in western Mexico.

Page 148

Diapterus brevirostris. A. F. González-Acosta, P. Béarez, N. Álvarez-Pliego, J. De la Cruz-Agüero, and J. L. Castro-Aguirre, 2007, Cybium 31(3):369–377, showed that *D. brevirostris* is separate from *D. peruvianus* (Cuvier, 1830) (as in the 2004 list) and is the species found in our area.

Diapterus rhombeus. Expansion of distribution. It has been found in the Loxahatchee and Indian rivers, Florida (R. G. Gilmore, personal communication, 2011). All Florida records are from brackish water.

Eugerres awlae. Added to the list based on A. F. González-Acosta, J. De la Cruz-Agüero, and J. L. Castro-Aguirre, 2007, Bull. Mar. Sci. 80:109–124, who resurrected this species from the synonymy of its sympatric congener *E. plumieri* and verified its occurrence in the southwestern Gulf of Mexico, the Caribbean coast of the Yucatan Peninsula (Quintana Roo, Mexico), Honduras, Costa Rica, Venezuela (holotype), and the West Indies. Some previously published records for *E. plumieri* (thought to be a species complex) in South Carolina, southern Florida, and perhaps southern Brazil may represent, in part, *E. awlae* (González-Acosta et al. 2007). *Eugerres awlae* inhabits shallow coastal waters and brackish mangrove lagoons and often enters freshwaters of river mouths. González-Acosta et al. (2007) also verified the occurrence of *E. plumieri* in Atlantic Mexico, Guatemala, Jamaica, and Puerto Rico but cast doubt on its occurence in the United States, as previously published by other authors, and called for confirmation of those records. Thus, the occurrence given for *E. plumieri* in the present list (A-F:UM) may need modification in the future. Likewise, González-Acosta et al. (2007) cast doubt on the occurrence of *E. brasilianus* in Mexican waters based on examination of specimens from the West Indies, Belize, Costa Rica, Panama, Colombia, and Brazil (type locality). We choose to keep *E. brasilianus* in the present list pending future studies/confirmations.

Eugerres brasilianus. See *E. awlae.*

Eugerres plumieri. See *E. awlae.*

Haemulidae. Two species formerly included in the Inermiidae have been added. One of these (*Inermia vittata*) is the generic type, and Inermiidae thus becomes a junior synonym of Haemulidae.

Page 149

Emmelichthyops atlanticus. In an analysis of mitochondrial and nuclear DNA, M. D. Sanciango, L. A. Rocha, and K. E. Carpenter, 2011, Zootaxa 2966:37–50, recovered *E. atlanticus*, placed in the family Inermiidae in the 2004 list, within Haemulidae. See *Haemulon vittatum.*

Genyatremus dovii. Transferred from *Anisotremus* by J. J. Tavera, A. A. Pizarro, J. De la Cruz-Agüero, and E. F. Balart, 2011, J. Zool. Syst. Evol. Res. DOI: 10.1111/j.1439-0469.2011. 00622.x.

Genyatremus pacifici. Transferred from *Anisotremus* by J. J. Tavera, A. A. Pizarro, J. De la Cruz-Agüero, and E. F. Balart, 2011, J. Zool. Syst. Evol. Res. DOI: 10.1111/j.1439-0469. 2011.00622.x.

Haemulon californiensis. In an analysis of mitochondrial and nuclear DNA, M. D. Sanciangco, L. A. Rocha, and K. E. Carpenter, 2011, Zootaxa 2966:37–50, transferred this species from *Xenistius* to *Haemulon.*

Haemulon macrostomum. Occurrence in Mexico based on J. J. Schmitter-Soto, L. Vásquez-Yeomans, A. Aguilar-Perera, C. Curiel-Mondragón, and J. A. Caballero-Vázquez, 2000, Lista de peces marinos del Caribe mexicano, An. Inst. Biol. Univ. Nac. Auton. Mex. Ser. Zool. 71(2):143–177.

Haemulon vittatum. In an analysis of mitochondrial and nuclear DNA, L. A. Rocha, K. C. Lindeman, C. R. Rocha, and H. A. Lessios, 2008, Mol. Phylogenet. Evol. 48:918–928, transferred this species, placed in Inermiidae in the 2004 list, from *Inermia* to *Haemulon.* The family Inermiidae is accordingly deleted from the list. See Haemulidae.

Page 150

Pomadasys ramosus. Added to the list based on a record (UMMZ 92114) from Veracruz (Miller et al. 2006:350 [where the footnote should be consulted]). Although there are no records from the United States, the common name in English was applied by Miller et al. (2006).

Calamus calamus. Recorded in Mexican waters by J. J. Schmitter-Soto, A. Cruz-Martínez, R. Herrera, and A. Hernández, 2007, Los peces de la costa sur de Quintana Roo: una década de cambios, Technical report, Mesoamerican

Barrier Reef Fund, Chetumal, Quintana Roo, Mexico.

Diplodus argenteus. Listed without comment under this name in the 2004 list. R. de la Paz, 1975, Trav. Docum. ORSTOM 45:1–96, had earlier determined this species to comprise two subspecies geographically separated by the Amazon River outflow, of which the typical form is restricted to southern Brazil south to Argentina and the northern form (*D. a. caudimacula*) ranges from northern Brazil north to Florida (including Mexico). Carpenter (2003c) maintained this arrangement, but J. L. Castro-Aguirre, H. S. Espinosa-Pérez, and J. J. Schmitter-Soto, 1999, Ictiofauna estuarino-lagunar y vicaria de México, Editorial Limusa-Noriega/IPN, Mexico City, had, with little explanation, treated *caudimacula* as a species. Although future research may confirm species distinctness, we continue to include both forms under *D. argenteus.*

Page 151

Bairdiella icistia. The occurrences of *B. icistia* and *Cynoscion xanthulus* have been changed regarding their presence in the land-locked Salton Sea of southern California (previously listed as "F[I]:U-PM"). These and most other introduced fishes there have been extirpated due principally to increasing salinity of its waters (46.5 parts per thousand in May 2006). These two species of sciaenids, along with the now-extirpated haemulid *Anisotremus davidsonii*, were successfully introduced as sport fishes into a lesser-saline Salton Sea from the Gulf of California between 1949 and 1956 (Source: Pacific Institute, www.pacinst.org).

Corvula batabana. Formerly *Bairdiella batabana*; placed in *Corvula* by L. N. Chao, 2003, Sciaenidae, Pages 1583–1653 *in* Carpenter (2003c).

Corvula sanctaeluciae. Formerly *Bairdiella sanctaeluciae*; placed in *Corvula* by L. N. Chao, 2003, Sciaenidae, Pages 1583–1653 *in* Carpenter (2003c).

Cynoscion xanthulus. See *Bairdiella icistia.*

Page 152

Micropogonias furnieri. Added to the list based on its presence in the St. Lucie River, Florida (R. G. Gilmore, personal communication, 2011).

Odontoscion dentex. Occurrence in Mexican waters most recently noted by J. J. Schmitter-Soto, A. Aguilar-Perera, S. Avilés-Torres, R.

Herrera P., J. A. Caballero V., C. L. Campos B., and N. Carvajal H., 1998, Distribución y abundancia de la ictiofauna arrecifal en la costa sur de Quintana Roo, Technical report, Consejo Nacional de Ciencia y Tecnología/El Colegio de la Frontera Sur, Chetumal, Quintana Roo, Mexico.

Odontoscion xanthops. Genus inadvertently misspelled *Odontosion* in the 2004 list.

Ophioscion imiceps. New to the list. Occurs from southern Mexico to Ecuador (Robertson and Allen 2008; D. R. Robertson, personal communication, 2011).

Paralonchurus rathbuni. New to the list. Occurs from Sinaloa, Gulf of California (e.g., CAS 24216 and 41719; SIO 65-104; GCRL 2585) to Peru (Robertson and Allen 2008 [where listed from Nayarit to Peru]; D. R. Robertson, personal communication, 2011).

Page 154

Kyphosus saltatrix. Originally described by Linnaeus in 1758 as *Perca saltatrix*, then referred to by Linnaeus in 1766 as *Perca sectatrix*— both accounts referring to the Bermuda Chub, family Kyphosidae, as noted by Eschmeyer (2012). The correct name is *Kyphosus saltatrix* (Linnaeus, 1758).

Page 155

Elassoma evergladei. See *E. okefenokee.*

Elassoma gilberti. This new species, formerly in *E. okefenokee* and found in northwestern Florida and southwestern Georgia, was described by F. F. Snelson, Jr., T. J. Krabbenhoft, and J. M. Quattro, 2009, Bull. Fla. Mus. Nat. Hist. 48:119–144. Common name was suggested by those authors.

Elassoma okefenokee. The original description of *E. evergladei orlandicum* Lönnberg, 1894, involved syntypes of both *E. okefenokee* and *E. evergladei* but was obviously based on *E. okefenokee* Böhlke, 1956 (thus a senior synonym). However, the name was considered to be unavailable under the provisions of Article 23.9.1.1 of the International Code (C. R. Gilbert, 2004, Cal. Acad. Sci. Annotated Lists of Fishes 33). F. F. Snelson, Jr., T. J. Krabbenhoft, and J. M. Quattro, 2009, Bull. Fla. Mus. Nat. Hist. 48(4):119–144, later showed that because the name *orlandicum* appeared in a paper by R. L. Barney and B. J. Anson, 1920, Ecology 1:241–256, it is available according to the International Code. To resolve the situation, Snelson et al. (2009) designated one of the syntypes of *E. evergladei* as lectotype of *E. evergladei orlandicum*. See *E. gilberti*.

Cichlidae. In the 2004 list, we continued to place most New World species in *Cichlasoma*, even though this genus was shown by Kullander (1983) to be endemic to South America. In this edition, we use genera that have been accepted by recent workers, even though phylogenetic support often is lacking or results are not universally accepted. A few species in our area remain in *Cichlasoma* because there is no other accepted genus. We also add a second and widely used common name in English for the family.

Amatitlania nigrofasciata. Formerly *Cichlasoma nigrofasciatum*. Placed in *Amatitlania* by J. J. Schmitter-Soto, 2007, Zootaxa 1603:1-76. Change in name in Spanish suggested by J. J. Schmitter-Soto (personal communication, 2011) because it is the name in wide use in Honduras, where the species is native.

Page 156

Amphilophus citrinellus. Formerly *Cichlasoma citrinellum*. Placed in *Amphilophus* by K. J. Roe, D. Conkel, and C. Lydeard, 1997, Mol. Phylogenet. Evol. 7:366–376; J. R. Stauffer and K. R. McKaye, 2002, Cuadernos de investigación de la Universidad Centroamericana 12:1–18; and others.

Amphilophus macracanthus. Formerly *Cichlasoma macracanthum*. A species of uncertain relationships, it was placed in *Astatheros* by K. J. Roe, D. Conkel, and C. Lydeard, 1997, Mol. Phylogenet. Evol. 7:366–376, and by G. A. Concheiro-Pérez, O. Rícan, G. Ortí, E. Bermingham, I. Doadrio, and R. Zardoya, 2007, Mol. Phylogenet. Evol. 43:91–110. However, Kullander (2003) considered *Astatheros* to be a synonym of *Amphilophus*, a decision followed by Miller et al. (2006).

Amphilophus nourissati. Formerly *Cichlasoma nourissati*. Placed in *Amphilophus* by Kullander (2003) and Miller et al. (2006), although there is no published supporting phylogeny.

Amphilophus robertsoni. Formerly *Cichlasoma robertsoni*. A species of uncertain relationships, it was placed in *Astatheros* by K. J. Roe, D. Conkel and C. Lydeard, 1997, Mol. Phylogenet. Evol. 7:366–376, and by G. A. Conchoeiro-Pérez, O. Rícan, G. Ortí, E. Berming-

ham, I. Doadrio, and R. Zardoya, 2007, Mol. Phylogenet. Evol. 43:91–110. However, Kullander (2003) considered *Astatheros* to be a synonym of *Amphilophus*, a decision followed by Miller et al. (2006).

Amphilophus trimaculatus. Formerly *Cichlasoma trimaculatum*. Placed in *Amphilophus* by G. A. Concheiro-Pérez, O. Rícan, G. Ortí, E. Bermingham, I. Doadrio, and R. Zardoya, 2007, Mol. Phylogenet. Evol. 43:91–110.

Cichlasoma beani. The genus *Cichlasoma* was restricted to a small group of South American species by Kullander (1983). This species does not belong in that genus, but there is no hypothesis on generic placement. See Kullander (2003) and Miller et al. (2006).

Cichlasoma bimaculatum. See *C. beani*.

Cichlasoma grammodes. See *C. beani*.

Cichlasoma istlanum. See *C. beani*.

Cichlasoma nebuliferum. Although placed in *Paraneetroplus* by Kullander (2003) and later in *Theraps* by Miller et al. (2006), the continuing uncertain generic relationships of this species resulted in its provisional inclusion in *Cichlasoma* in the 2004 list. C. D. McMahan, A. D. Geheber, and K. R. Piller, 2010, Mol. Phylogenet. Evol. 57:1293–1300, based on analysis of mitochondrial and nuclear DNA relationships of more than two dozen Central American and Mexican cichlid species, determined that this species that falls outside the two clades considered by them to comprise the genera *Paraneetroplus* and *Theraps*. It is therefore provisionally retained in *Cichlasoma*.

Cichlasoma urophthalmus. The genus *Cichlasoma* was restricted to a small group of South American species by Kullander (1983). This species does not belong in that genus and was placed in *Nandopsis* by C. D. Hulsey, F. J. García de León, Y. Sánchez Johnson, D. A. Hendrickson, and T. J. Near, 2004, Mol. Phylogenet. Evol. 31:754–764. However, that assignment has not been followed by others (e.g., Miller et al. 2006; P. Chakrabarty, 2007, Misc. Publ. Mus. Zool. Univ. Mich. 198:1–31).

Cryptoheros chetumalensis. This new species from Mexico, Guatemala, and Belize was described by J. J. Schmitter-Soto, 2007, Zootaxa 1603: 37. It was split from *C. spilurus*, which appeared in the 2004 list as *Cichlasoma spilurum*, which does not occur in Mexico.

Herichthys bartoni. Formerly *Cichlasoma bartoni*.

Placed in *Herichthys* by C. D. Hulsey, F. J. García de León, Y. Sánchez Johnson, D. A. Hendrickson, and T. J. Near, 2004, Mol. Phylog. Evol. 31:754–764.

Herichthys carpintis. Formerly *Cichlasoma carpintis.* Placed in *Herichthys* by C. D. Hulsey, F. J. García de León, Y. Sánchez Johnson, D. A. Hendrickson, and T. J. Near, 2004, Mol. Phylogenet. Evol. 31:754–764, and P. Chakrabarty, 2006, Mol. Phylogenet. Evol. 39:619–627.

Herichthys cyanoguttatus. Formerly *Cichlasoma cyanoguttatum.* Placed in *Herichthys* by C. D. Hulsey, F. J. García de León, Y. Sánchez Johnson, D. A. Hendrickson, and T. J. Near, 2004, Mol. Phylogenet. Evol. 31:754–764.

Herichthys deppii. Formerly *Cichlasoma deppii.* Placed in *Herichthys* by G. A. Concheiro-Pérez, O. Rícan, G. Ortí, E. Bermingham, I. Doadrio, and R. Zardoya, 2007, Mol. Phylog. Evol. 43:91–110.

Herichthys labridens. Formerly *Cichlasoma labridens.* Placed in *Herichthys* by C. D. Hulsey, F. J. García de León, Y. Sánchez Johnson, D. A. Hendrickson, and T. J. Near, 2004, Mol. Phylogenet. Evol. 31:754–764.

Herichthys minckleyi. Formerly *Cichlasoma minckleyi.* Placed in *Herichthys* by C. D. Hulsey, F. J. García de León, Y. Sánchez Johnson, D. A. Hendrickson, and T. J. Near, 2004, Mol. Phylogenet. Evol. 31:754–764.

Herichthys pantostictus. Formerly *Cichlasoma pantostictum.* Placed in *Herichthys* by C. D. Hulsey, F. J. García de León, Y. Sánchez Johnson, D. A. Hendrickson, and T. J. Near, 2004, Mol. Phylogenet. Evol. 31:754–764.

Herichthys steindachneri. Formerly *Cichlasoma steindachneri.* Placed in *Herichthys* by C. D. Hulsey, F. J. García de León, Y. Sánchez Johnson, D. A. Hendrickson, and T. J. Near, 2004, Mol. Phylogenet. Evol. 31:754–764.

Herichthys tamasopoensis. Formerly *Cichlasoma tamasopoensis.* Placed in *Herichthys* by C. D. Hulsey, F. J. García de León, Y. Sánchez Johnson, D. A. Hendrickson, and T. J. Near, 2004, Mol. Phylogenet. Evol. 31:754–764.

Parachromis friedrichsthalii. Formerly *Cichlasoma friedrichsthalii.* Placed in *Parachromis* by Kullander (2003) and Miller et al. (2006), although there is no published supporting phylogeny.

Parachromis managuensis. Formerly *Cichlasoma managuense.* Placed in *Parachromis* by Kullander (2003), and Chakrabarty, 2006, Mol. Phylogenet. Evol. 39:619–627.

Parachromis motaguensis. Formerly *Cichlasoma motaguense.* Placed in *Parachromis* by Kullander (2003), and Chakrabarty, 2006, Mol. Phylogenet. Evol. 39:619–627.

Parachromis salvini. Formerly *Cichlasoma salvini.* Placed in *Parachromis* by G. A. Concheiro-Pérez, O. Rícan, G. Ortí, E. Bermingham, I. Doadrio, and R. Zardoya, 2007, Mol. Phylogenet. Evol. 43:91–110.

Paraneetroplus argenteus. Formerly *Cichlasoma argenteum.* Placed in *Vieja* by G. A. Concheiro-Pérez, O. Rícan, G. Ortí, E. Bermingham, I. Doadrio, and R. Zardoya, 2007, Mol. Phylogenet Evol. 43:91–110, and in *Paraneetroplus* by C. D. McMahan, A. D. Geheber, and K. R. Piller, 2010, Mol. Phylogenet. Evol. 57:1293–1300, based on analysis of mitochondrial and nuclear DNA relationships of Central American and Mexican cichlid species. Because *P. bulleri*, type species of *Paraneetroplus* Regan, 1905, is nested within a group of species referred to the genus *Vieja* Fernández-Yépez, 1969 (McMahan et al. 2010), *Vieja* is placed in the synonymy of *Paraneetroplus*.

Paraneetroplus bifasciatus. Formerly *Cichlasoma bifasciatum.* See *P. argenteus.*

Paraneetroplus breidohri. Formerly *Cichlasoma breidohri.* See *P. argenteus.*

Paraneetroplus bulleri. Formerly *Cichlasoma bulleri.* See *P. argenteus.* Also placed in *Paraneetroplus* by Kullander (2003) and C. D. Hulsey, F. J. García de León, Y. Sánchez Johnson, D. A. Hendrickson, and T. J. Near, 2004, Mol. Phylogenet. Evol. 31:754–764.

Paraneetroplus fenestratus. Formerly *Cichlasoma fenestratum.* See *P. argenteus.*

Paraneetroplus gibbiceps. Formerly *Cichlasoma gibbiceps.* See *P. argenteus.* Also placed in *Paraneetroplus* by Kullander (2003), and C. D. Hulsey, F. J. García de León, Y. Sánchez Johnson, D. A. Hendrickson, and T. J. Near, 2004, Mol. Phylogenet. Evol. 31:754–764.

Paraneetroplus guttulatus. Formerly *Cichlasoma guttulatum.* See *P. argenteus.*

Paraneetroplus hartwegi. Formerly *Cichlasoma hartwegi.* See *P. argenteus.*

Paraneetroplus melanurus. Formerly *Cichlasoma synspilum.* C. D. McMahan, C. M. Murray, A. D. Geheber, C. D. Boeckman, and K. R. Piller, 2011, Zootaxa 2833:1–14, synonymized *P. synspilus* with *P. melanurus.* See *P. argenteus.*

Paraneetroplus regani. Formerly *Cichlasoma regani.* See *P. argenteus.*

Paraneetroplus zonatus. Formerly *Cichlasoma zonatum.* See *P. argenteus.*

Rocio gemmata. This new species was described from Quintana Roo by S. Contreras-Balderas and J. J. Schmitter-Soto in J. J. Schmitter-Soto, 2007, Zootaxa 1603:61.

Rocio ocotal. This new species was described from Laguna Ocotal, Chiapas, by J. J. Schmitter-Soto, 2007, Zootaxa 1603:59.

Rocio octofasciata. Formerly *Cichlasoma octofasciatum.* Placed in the genus *Rocio* by J. J. Schmitter-Soto, 2007, Zootaxa 1603:1–76.

Theraps heterospilus. Formerly *Cichlasoma heterospilum.* Placed in *Theraps* by C. D. McMahan, A. D. Geheber, and K. R. Piller, 2010, Mol. Phylogenet. Evol. 57:1293–1300, based on analysis of mitochondrial and nuclear DNA relationships of more than two dozen Central American and Mexican cichlid species.

Theraps intermedius. Formerly *Cichlasoma intermedium.* See *T. heterospilus.*

Theraps irregularis. Formerly *Cichlasoma irregulare.* See *T. heterospilus.* Also placed in *Theraps* (type species of the genus) by Kullander (2003) and Miller et al. (2006).

Theraps lentiginosus. Formerly *Cichlasoma lentiginosum.* See *T. heterospilus.* Also placed in *Theraps* by G. A. Concheiro-Pérez, O. Rícan, G. Ortí, E. Bermingham, I. Doadrio, and R. Zardoya, 2007, Mol. Phylogenet. Evol. 43:91–110.

Theraps pearsei. Formerly *Cichlasoma pearsei.* See *T. heterospilus.*

Theraps rheophilus. Formerly *Cichlasoma rheophilus* (sic, should have been *rheophilum*). Closely related to *T. lentiginosus.* Validity of species questioned by Kullander (2003), which Eschmeyer (2012) interpreted to amount to synonymization. Although species' status not addressed by McMahan et al. (see citation in entry above for *T. heterospilus*), Miller et al. (2006:375–376) regarded it as a valid species, based on examination of specimens from the type locality.

Theraps ufermanni. Formerly *Cichlasoma ufermanni.* See *T. heterospilus.*

Thorichthys affinis. Formerly *Cichlasoma affinis.* Placed in *Thorichthys* by Miller et al. (2006).

Thorichthys callolepis. Formerly *Cichlasoma callolepis.* Placed in *Thorichthys* by C. D. Hulsey, F. J. García de León, Y. Sánchez Johnson, D.

A. Hendrickson, and T. J. Near, 2004, Mol. Phylogenet. Evol. 31:754–764.

Thorichthys ellioti. Formerly *Cichlasoma ellioti.* Placed in *Thorichthys* by K. J. Roe, D. Conkel, and C. Lydeard, 1997, Mol. Phylogenet. Evol. 7:366–376.

Thorichthys helleri. Formerly *Cichlasoma helleri.* Placed in *Thorichthys* by C. D. Hulsey, F. J. García de León, Y. Sánchez Johnson, D. A. Hendrickson, and T. J. Near, 2004, Mol. Phylogenet. Evol. 31:754–764.

Thorichthys meeki. Formerly *Cichlasoma meeki.* Placed in *Thorichthys* by K. J. Roe, D. Conkel, and C. Lydeard, 1997, Mol. Phylogenet. Evol. 7:366–376.

Thorichthys pasionis. Formerly *Cichlasoma pasionis.* Placed in *Thorichthys* by Miller et al. (2006).

Page 158

Thorichthys socolofi. Formerly *Cichlasoma socolofi.* Placed in *Thorichthys* by Miller et al. (2006).

Tilapia zillii. Introduction to Mexico was inadvertently omitted from the 2004 list. Several publications have noted its occurrence there, including H. Espinosa-Pérez, M. T. Gaspar-Dillanes, and P. Fuentes-Mata, 1993, Listados faunísticos de México III, Los peces dulceacuícolas mexicanos, Instituto de Biología, UNAM, Mexico, D.F., and Minckley and Marsh (2009, see references cited therein).

Damalichthys vacca. Placed in *Rhacochilus* in the 2004 list; however, G. Bernardi and G. Bucciarelli, 1999, Mol. Phylogenet. Evol. 13(1):77–81, indicate that this species belongs in *Damalichthys.*

Hypsurus caryi. Transferred to *Embiotoca* by G. Bernardi, 2009, Fish Biology 74:1049–1055. However, in a revision of the family Embiotocidae, F. H. Tarp, 1952, State of Calif., Dept. of Fish and Game, Fish Bull. No. 88, Sacramento, noted a number of morphological differences between these two genera, and we prefer to recognize both genera.

Page 159

Labridae. Several recent molecular analyses (e.g., M. W. Westneat and M. E. Alfaro, 2005, Mol. Phylogenet. Evol. 36:370–390) agree with morphological studies from the 1980s and 1990s that found Labridae to be paraphyletic without the inclusion of species formerly in

Scaridae. Genera of species in our area that were formerly placed in a now-deleted Scaridae are *Calotomus, Cryptotomus, Nicholsina, Scarus*, and *Sparisoma*.

Page 160

Halichoeres bivittatus. L. A. Rocha, D. R. Robertson, J. Roman, and B. W. Bowen, 2005, Proc. Royal Soc. B 272:573–579, showed that the Slippery Dick is divisible into two species, well separated genetically but morphologically indistinguishable, with near total geographic and ecological separation. The northern form is largely confined to coastal areas of the United States (from Cape Hatteras southward) and closely adjacent northeastern Mexico, whereas the southern form typically ranges from the Florida Keys and the Bahamas southward throughout the West Indies, southern Mexico, and Central America to northern South America. Both forms occur in the Florida Keys and Bermuda, where they are separated ecologically, most notably by temperature. The supposed type locality of *Labrus bivittatus* ("Indian Ocean") is obviously erroneous, so precise allocation of the name *bivittatus* is presently impossible.

Halichoeres burekae. This new species was described from the western Gulf of Mexico, from Texas and Mexico, by D. C. Weaver and L. A. Rocha, 2007, Copeia 2007(4):800.

Halichoeres cyanocephalus. Occurrence in Mexico based on J. W. Tunnell, Jr., A. A. Rodríguez, R. L. Lehman, and C. R. Beaver, 1993, An ecological characterization of the southern Quintana Roo coral reef system, Texas A&M University, Center for Coastal Studies, Corpus Christi.

Page 161

Scarus taeniopterus. Noted in Mexican waters by several authors, most recently by J. J. Schmitter-Soto, A. Aguilar-Perera, S. Avilés-Torres, R. Herrera P., J. A. Caballero V., C. L. Campos B., and N. Carvajal H., 1998, Distribución y abundancia de la ictiofauna arrecifal en la costa sur de Quintana Roo, Technical report, Consejo Nacional de Ciencia y Tecnología/El Colegio de la Frontera Sur, Chetumal, Quintana Roo, Mexico; and J. J. Schmitter-Soto, A. Cruz-Martínez, R. Herrera, and A. Hernández, 2007, Los peces de la costa sur de Quintana Roo: una década de cambios, Mesoamerican Barrier Reef Fund, Technical report, Che-

tumal, Quintana Roo, Mexico. (J. J. Schmitter-Soto, personal communication, 2007).

Stethojulis bandanensis. New to the list. Observations of this distinctively colored and widespread Indo-Pacific wrasse in Mexican Pacific waters were reported by B. C. Victor, G. M. Wellington, D. R. Robertson, and B. I. Ruttenberg, 2001, Bull. Mar. Sci. 69(1):279–288. In Mexico, these observations (mainly during the 1990s) were made at the Revillagigedo Archipelago of Mexico, the cape region of the Baja California peninsula, and northward to the central Gulf of California, Baja California Sur. It also has been recorded at localities in the tropical eastern Pacific south of Mexico (e.g., Robertson and Allen, 2008). Recent observations at the Islas Marías in the southeastern Gulf of California and at Isla Espíritu Santo in the southwestern gulf were reported by B. E. Erisman, G. R. Galland, I. Mascareñas, J. Moxley, H. J. Walker, O. Aburto-Oropeza, P. A. Hastings, and E. Ezcurra, 2011, Zootaxa 2985:26–40.

Page 162

Lycenchelys sarsii. This North Atlantic and Arctic species is added based on B. W. Coad and J. D. Reist, 2004, Can. Manuscr. Rep. Fish. Aquat. Sci. 2674. Common names are in reference to Michael Sars, Norwegian theologian and biologist.

Lycodes akuugun. This new species was described from the Aleutian Islands at depths ranging from 121 to 460 m by D. E. Stevenson and J. W. Orr, 2006, Copeia 2006(1):78.

Lycodes eudipleurostictus. The addition of this species is based on specimens from Arctic and Atlantic Greenland from depths of 188–1,187 m reported by P. R. Møller, J. G. Nielsen, S. W. Knudsen, J. Y. Poulsen, K. Sünksen, and O. A. Jørgensen, 2010, Zootaxa 2378:1–84. It is also known from Arctic Canada and Alaska, but from depths greater than 200 m.

Lycodes gracilis. This species was elevated from a subspecies of *L. vahlii* by H. Carl, 2002, Steenstrupia 27(1):65–81, as noted by C. M. Mecklenburg, P. R. Møller, and D. Steinke, 2011, Mar. Biodiv. 41:109–140. Distribution is based on P. R. Møller, J. G. Nielsen, S. W. Kundsen, J. Y. Poulsen, K. Sünksen, and O. A. Jørgensen, 2010, Zootaxa, 2378:1–84.

Lycodes luetkenii. This species was noted from Greenland at depths of 100 to 900 m by P. R. Møller, J. G. Nielsen, S. W. Knudsen, J. Y.

Poulsen, K. Sünksen, and O. A. Jørgensen, 2010, Zootaxa 2378:1–84, and from Canada by B. W. Coad and J. D. Reist, 2004, Can. Manuscr. Rep. Fish. Aquat. Sci. 2674.

Page 163

Lycodes marisalbi. This Arctic species is added based on B. W. Coad and J. D. Reist, 2004, Can. Manuscr. Rep. Fish. Aquat. Sci. 2674.

Lycodes seminudus. This Arctic species is added based on B. W. Coad and J. D. Reist, 2004, Can. Manuscr. Rep. Fish. Aquat. Sci. 2674.

Lycodes vahlii. See *L. gracilis.*

Page 164

Lumpenopsis clitella. This new species was described from waters off southern California at 54 m by P. A. Hastings and H. J. Walker, Jr., 2003, Copeia 2003(4):804.

Lumpenopsis hypochroma. The genus *Allolumpenus* was considered a junior synonym of *Lumpenopsis* by P. A. Hastings and H. J. Walker, Jr., 2003, Copeia 2003(4):808. *Allolumpenus hypochromus* of previous lists is replaced by this new name combination.

Page 165

Anarrhichthys ocellatus. R. F. Feeney, R. N. Lea, S. Dyer, and S. Gietler, 2007, California Fish and Game 93(1):52–55, documented this species from the waters off northern Baja California, Mexico.

Page 166

Xenocephalus egregius. Recognized as *Gnathagnus egregius* in the 2004 list, but V. G. Springer and M.-L. Bauchot, 1994, Proc. Biol. Soc. Wash. 107(1):79–89, showed *Xenocephalus* Kaup, 1858, to be a senior synonym of *Gnathagnus* Gill, 1861.

Axoclinus storeyae. This name is applicable to the species appearing in the 2004 list as *Axoclinus carminalis.* See *Enneanectes carminalis.*

Enneanectes carminalis. D. G. Smith and J. T. Williams, 2002, Zootaxa 105:1–10, demonstrated that the tripterygiid fish to which the species name *carminalis* (Carmine Triplefin) has long been applied does not belong in the genus *Axoclinus,* as previously supposed (sixth edition, p. 161). Rather, by virtue of Vernon Brock's earlier (1940, Stanford Ichthyol. Bull. 2:29–35) neotype designation, *carminalis* is referable to the genus *Enneanectes* and is applicable to the species (i.e., is a senior syn-

onym) treated in the sixth edition as *E. sexmaculatus* (Delicate Triplefin). The next available name for the Carmine Triplefin is *Axoclinus storeyae.*

Page 167

Dactyloscopus byersi. See *D. heraldi.*

Dactyloscopus elongatus. Originally described as a subspecies of *D. fimbriatus* but recognized as a species by P. A. Hastings and V. G. Springer, 2009, Zootaxa 2120:3–14. *Dactyloscopus fimbriatus* occurs in Central and South America and is deleted from the list, but the common names applied to it in the 2001 list (with correction of spelling for the name in Spanish) are maintained for *D. elongatus.*

Dactyloscopus fallax. Described by C. E. Dawson, 1975, Nat. Hist. Mus. Los Angel. Cty. Sci. Bull. 22, as a subspecies of *D. pectoralis* but treated as a species ranging from the southeastern Gulf of California to Ecuador by P. A. Hastings and V. G. Springer, 2009, Zootaxa 2120:3–14. Common name in English suggested by P. A. Hastings (personal communication, 2010).

Dactyloscopus heraldi. Originally described as a subspecies of *D. byersi* endemic to the southwestern coast of the Baja California peninsula (tip of the peninsula northwestward to Bahía San Juanico) but recognized as a species by P. A. Hastings and V. G. Springer, 2009, Zootaxa 2120:3–14. Common name in English suggested by P. A. Hastings (personal communication, 2010).

Dactyloscopus insulatus. Described by C. E. Dawson, 1975, Nat. Hist. Mus. Los Angel. Cty. Sci. Bull. 22, as a subspecies of *D. pectoralis* but treated as a species endemic to the Revillagigedo Archipelago of Mexico by P. A. Hastings and V. G. Springer, 2009, Zootaxa 2120:3–14. Common name in English suggested by P. A. Hastings (personal communication, 2010).

Dactyloscopus pectoralis. Genus inadvertently misspelled *Dacyloscopus* in the 2004 list. This species was considered by C. E. Dawson, 1975, Nat. Hist. Mus. Los Angel. Cty. Sci. Bull. 22, to be comprised of three subspecies, all of which occur in Mexico. P. A. Hastings and V. G. Springer, 2009, Zootaxa 2120:3–14, recognized the three taxa as species, with *D. pectoralis* restricted to the Gulf of California and the southwestern coast of the Baja California peninsula. See *D. fallax* and *D. insulatus.*

Myxodagnus opercularis. Distributed in the Gulf of California and at the Revillagigedo Archipelago of Mexico. See *M. walkeri*.

Myxodagnus walkeri. Originally described as a subspecies of *M. opercularis* but treated as a species ranging from the southeastern Gulf of California (Nayarit) to Costa Rica by P. A. Hastings and V. G. Springer, 2009, Zootaxa 2120:3–14. Common name in English suggested by P. A. Hastings (personal communication, 2010).

Platygillellus rubrocinctus. Presence in Mexico (Isla Mujeres of the Yucatan Peninsula) noted by C. E. Dawson, 1982, Bull. Mar. Sci. 32(1): 14–85.

Page 168

Hypsoblennius invemar. Spelling of author's name corrected from Acero to Acero-P.

Page 169

Labrisomus albigenys. Inadvertently omitted from the 2004 list. Added based on a collection from Cayos Arcos, Campeche Banks, Mexico (FMNH 59875) and which was reported by V. G. Springer, 1959, Publ. Inst. Mar. Sci. Univ. Tex. 5:417–492.

Malacoctenus hubbsi. See *M. polyporosus*.

Malacoctenus mexicanus. Originally described as a subspecies of *M. margaritae* occurring in the Gulf of California southward to Acapulco, Mexico, but treated as a species by P. A. Hastings and V. G. Springer, 2009, Zootaxa 2120: 3–14. *Malacoctenus margaritae* is restricted to Panama and Costa Rica and is deleted from the list. Common name in English suggested by P. A. Hastings (personal communication, 2010).

Malacoctenus polyporosus. Originally described as a subspecies of *M. hubbsi* found along the coast of the southeastern Gulf of California from near Mazatlán southward to Acapulco but treated as a species by P. A. Hastings and V. G. Springer, 2009, Zootaxa 2120:3–14. Common name in English suggested by P. A. Hastings (personal communication, 2010).

Page 170

Paraclinus walkeri. Change in orthography of name in English to agree with geographic name in Mexico (from San Quintin Blenny).

Starksia langi. This new species, decribed by Castillo and Baldwin *in* C. C. Baldwin, C. I. Castillo, L. A. Weigt, and B. C. Victor, 2011, ZooKeys 79:53, and previously considered part of *S. sluiteri*, is known from Quintana Roo, Mexico (UF 209342). *Starksia sluiteri* occurs outside our area and is deleted from the list.

Starksia sangreyae. This new species, decribed by Castillo and Baldwin *in* C. C. Baldwin, C. I. Castillo, L. A. Weigt, and B. C. Victor, 2011, ZooKeys 79:27, and previously considered part of *S. atlantica*, is known from Quintana Roo, Mexico (UF 209760). *Starksia atlantica* occurs outside our area and is deleted from the list.

Page 171

Starksia starcki. Occurrence in Mexico at Xahuayxol, Mexican Caribbean (ECOCH 2513), based on J. J. Schmitter-Soto, L. Vásquez-Yeomans, A. Aguilar-Perera, C. Curiel-Mondragón, and J. A. Caballero-Vázquez, 2000, Lista de peces marinos del Caribe mexicano, An. Inst. Biol. Univ. Nac. Auton. Mex. Ser. Zool. 71(2):143–177.

Starksia weigti. This new species, decribed by Baldwin and Castillo *in* C. C. Baldwin, C. I. Castillo, L. A. Weigt, and B. C. Victor, 2011, ZooKeys 79:37, and previously considered part of *S. lepicoelia*, is known from Quintana Roo, Mexico (UF 209340, UF 209629, UF 209755). *Starksia lepicoelia* occurs outside our area and is deleted from the list.

Chaenopsidae. J. J. Schmitter-Soto, L. Vásquez-Yeomans, A. Aguilar-Perera, C. Curiel-Mondragón, and J. A. Caballero-Vázquez, 2000, Lista de peces marinos del Caribe mexicano, An. Inst. Biol. Univ. Nac. Auton. Mex. Ser. Zool. 71(2):143–177, listed *Lucayablennius zingaro* (Böhlke, 1957) (Arrow Blenny, tubícola flecha) because of its highly probable presence in Mexico (present in adjacent Bacalar Chico, Belize). We do not list it pending actual locality records.

Acanthemblemaria hastingsi. This new species, endemic to the Gulf of California, Mexico, was described by H.-C. Lin and G. R. Galland, 2010, Zootaxa 2525:55.

Chaenopsis roseola. The common name given in the 2004 edition, freckled pikeblenny, is changed to Flecked Pikeblenny as proposed in the original description by P. A. Hastings and R. L. Shipp, 1981, Proc. Biol. Soc. Wash. 93(4):876.

Page 172

Hemiemblemaria simula. Recorded in the Mexican Caribbean by E. Núñez Lara, 1998, Factores que determinan la estructura de la comunidad de peces arrecifales en el sur del Caribe mexicano: un análisis multivariado, Master's thesis, Centro de Investigación y de Estudios Avanzados del Instituto Politécnico Nacional, Mérida, Yucatan, Mexico.

Protemblemaria bicirrus. Correction of spelling of specific name from 2004 list (*P. bicirris* is an unjustified emendation).

Stathmonotus hemphillii. Original spelling ends with -*ii*.

Stathmonotus tekla. Formerly considered a subspecies of *S. stahli* (P. A. Hastings and V. G. Springer, 1994, Smithson. Contrib. Zool. 558) but elevated to species by P. A. Hastings and V. G. Springer, 2009, Zootaxa 2120:3–14, based on consistent differences in numbers of caudal rays, dorsal spines, and precaudal vertebrae. *Stathmonotus stahli* is restricted to the southeastern Caribbean Sea and is accordingly deleted from the list. The common names Eelgrass Blenny and tubícola anguila are transferred from *S. stahli* to *S. tekla*.

Acyrtops beryllinus. Occurrence in Mexico based on a specimen (IBUNAM-P 5605) in the fish collection of the Instituto de Biología at the Universidad Nacional Autónoma de México.

Page 173

Tomicodon eos. Ampersand added between authors' names.

Tomicodon reitzae. See *T. rupestris*.

Tomicodon rupestris. Added to the list based on J. T. Williams and J. C. Tyler, 2003, Smithson. Contrib. Zool. 621:1–26. Specimens of *T. rupestris* and *T. reitzae* from Mexico are in the Milwaukee Public Museum (R. Mooi, personal communication, 2004). Common names for *T. rupestris* are those used in the 2004 list for *T. fasciatus*, a species that does not occur in our area.

Page 174

Eleotridae. According to C. E. Thacker, 2009, Copeia 2009(1):93–104, gobioids in our area would be classified as follows: Eleotridae would remain the same; Gobiidae (gobies) would contain the genera *Aboma*, *Aruma*, *Barbulifer*, *Bathygobius*, *Bollmannia*, *Chriolepis*, *Coryphopterus*, *Elacatinus*, *Enypnias*, *Evermannichthys*, *Ginsburgellus*, *Gobiosoma*, *Gobulus*, *Gymneleotris*, *Lophogobius*, *Lythrypnus*, *Microgobius*, *Neogobius*, *Nes*, *Oxyurichthys*, *Palatogobius*, *Parrella*, *Priolepis*, *Proterorhinus*, *Psilotris*, *Pycnomma*, *Rhinogobiops*, *Risor*, *Varicus*, *Cerdale*, *Clarkichthys*, *Microdesmus*, and *Ptereleotris* (i.e., genera of the Gobiidae plus those of the Microdesmidae and Ptereleotridae of the 2004 list); and a new family Gobionellidae (gobionellids) would be recognized with the genera *Acanthogobius*, *Awaous*, *Clevelandia*, *Ctenogobius*, *Eucyclogobius*, *Evermannia*, *Evorthodus*, *Gillichthys*, *Gnatholepis*, *Gobioides*, *Gobionellus*, *Ilypnus*, *Lepidogobius*, *Lethops*, *Quietula*, *Sicydium*, *Tridentiger*, *and Typhlogobius* (C. E. Thacker, personal communication, 2009). The family name Oxudercidae may be the oldest available name for this latter clade (A. C. Gill, personal communication, 2009); however, as of this time, Case 3464 from R. E. Watson before the International Commission on Zoological Nomenclature, proposes to suppress Oxudercidae Günther, 1861, and conserve Periophthalmidae Gill, 1863. Also, if the phylogenetic conclusions of Thacker were followed, the above-listed families along with Apogonidae and Pempheridae (families in our area) would all be placed in Gobiiformes. While we recognize that the classification used in our listing of North American species does not reflect what is known of gobioid systematics based on the work of C. E. Thacker and several other researchers (e.g., C. E. Thacker and D. M. Roje, 2011, Syst. Biodivers. 9(4):329–347), changes have not been made pending further studies and general acceptance by gobioid systematists.

Gobiidae. *Elacatinus evelynae*, *E. genie*, and *E. horsti*, which were included in the 2004 list, are deleted on the authority of P. L. Colin (2010, Zootaxa 2370:36–52), who determined that the first two species do not occur in our area of coverage and that the alleged record of *E. horsti* from Florida is based on a misidentified specimen of *E. xanthiprora*. J. J. Schmitter-Soto, L. Vásquez-Yeomans, A. Aguilar-Perera, C. Curiel-Mondragón, and J. A. Caballero-Vázquez, 2000, Lista de peces marinos del Caribe mexicano, An. Inst. Biol. Univ. Nac. Auton. Mex. Ser. Zool. 71(2):143–177, listed *E. dilepis* (Robins & Böhlke, 1964) (as "*Gobiosoma dilepsis*"[sic]) (orangeside goby, gobio naranja) because of its highly probable presence in Mexico (present in adjacent Bacalar Chico, Belize) and *E. horsti* (Metzelaar, 1922); however, these species are not listed for Mexico pending actual locality records. See Eleotridae.

Antillogobius nikkiae. This new genus (diagnosed by J. L. Van Tassell and L. Tornabene) and new species (described by Van Tassell and P. L. Colin) of seven-spined gobies were described in Van Tassell, Tornabene, and Colin, 2012, Aqua, International Journal of Ichthyology 18(2):61–94. The species has been collected or observed at several localities in the Caribbean Sea and the Bahamas, most frequently at depths around 100 m. Its occurrence in Mexico is based on observations at Banco Chinchorro, Quintana Roo, off the eastern part of the Yucatan Peninsula.

Awaous banana. As alluded to in the 2004 edition of the list (Appendix 1, pp. 245–246), controversy over species nomenclature in this genus continues. Some, including Miller et al. (2006) and Minckley and Marsh (2009), recognize *A. tajasica* (Lichtenstein, 1822) as a valid species on the Atlantic slope of the Americas, with *A. transandeanus* (Günther, 1861) being the name applicable to all Pacific American populations. However, Watson, 1996, Ich. Explor. Freshwaters 7(1):1–18, earlier showed that *A. tajasica* is restricted to Brazil south of the Amazon River. Watson also determined that the name *A. banana* is applicable to all other western Atlantic populations and that these are indistinguishable from eastern Pacific populations, previously called *A. transandeanus*. We here follow Watson, as the definitive revisionary study.

Barbulifer mexicanus. The spelling of one of the authors' names is corrected (with apology) from Larsen to Larson.

Page 175

Bathygobius antilliensis. This new species was described by L. Tornabene, C. Baldwin, and F. Pezold *in* L. Tornabene, C. Baldwin, L. A. Weigt, and F. Pezold, 2010, Aqua, International Journal of Ichthyology 16(4):146, and was previously confused with *B. curacao*. It is largely confined to insular areas of the tropical western Atlantic and has been recorded from the Florida Keys. It occurs in Belize and almost certainly in adjacent Mexico (although as yet unrecorded).

Bathygobius geminatus. This new species was described by L. Tornabene, C. Baldwin, and F. Pezold *in* L. Tornabene, C. Baldwin, L. A. Weigt, and F. Pezold, 2010, Aqua, International Journal of Ichthyology 16(4):151, and was previously confused with *B. curacao*. It has been identified only from Florida and Puerto Rico.

Bathygobius lacertus. This species from the western Atlantic was removed from the synonymy of *B. soporator* by L. Tornabene, C. Baldwin, L. A. Weigt, and F. Pezold, 2010, Aqua, International Journal of Ichthyology 16(4):154–156. Originally described from Cuba, it ranges from the Florida Keys southward throughout the Caribbean, including Mexico.

Bathygobius soporator. See *B. lacertus.*

Bollmannia boqueronensis. Name in Spanish added based on occurrence in Mexico at Alacranes Reef Marine Park off the eastern part of the Yucatan Peninsula, reported by R. Moreno-Mendoza, C. González-Salas, A. Aguilar-Perera, A. Gallardo-Torres, and N. Simoes, 2011, Mar. Biodiv. Rec. 4:1–4, and as discussed by Van Tassell et al. 2012 (see *Antillogobius nikkiae* for the citation).

Coryphopterus kuna. An adult of this species has been recorded near Palm Beach, Florida (B. C. Victor, L. Vásquez-Yeomans, M. Valdéz-Moreno, L. Wilk, D. L. Jones, M. R. Lara, C. Caldow, and M. Shivji, 2010, Zootaxa 2346: 53–61). Larvae, but no adults, were recorded off Quintana Roo, Mexico, by these same authors.

Coryphopterus lipernes. Recorded from Mexico by R. M. Loreto, M. Lara, and J. J. Schmitter-Soto, 2003, Bull. Mar. Sci. 73(1):153–170.

Page 176

Coryphopterus tortugae. Validity of this species, which had been confused with *C. glaucofraenum* and was questionably included in the 2004 list, has been confirmed by C. C. Baldwin, L. A. Weigt, D. G. Smith, and J. H. Mounts, 2009, Smithson. Contr. Mar. Sci. 38:111–138.

Ctenogobius saepepallens. Recorded from Mexico by R. M. Loreto, M. Lara, and J. J. Schmitter-Soto, 2003, Bull. Mar. Sci. 73(1):153–170.

Elacatinus jarocho. This new species was described from Ahogado de Guilligan, Gulf of Mexico, off Veracruz state, by M. S. Taylor and L. Akins, 2007, Zootaxa 1425:46.

Elacatinus lobeli. This species, closely related to

E. oceanops, was described by J. E. Randall and P. L. Colin, 2009, Zootaxa 2173:32, based on specimens from Belize and Honduras. Occurrence in Mexico confirmed by J. J. Schmitter-Soto (personal communication, 2011). See *E. oceanops*.

Elacatinus oceanops. The Neon Goby has been reported nominally from the Yucatan Peninsula several times, most recently by J. J. Schmitter-Soto, L. Vásquez-Yeomans, A. Aguilar-Perera, C. Curiel-Mondragón, and J. A. Caballero-Vázquez, 2000, An. Inst. Biol. Univ. Nac. Auton. Mex. Ser. Zool. 71(2):143–177. However, a closely related species, *E. lobeli*, recently was described by J. E. Randall and P. L. Colin, 2009, Zootaxa 2173:32, based on specimens from Belize and Honduras. The authors did not examine specimens of the new species from the Yucatan but indicated that *E. oceanops* is restricted to Florida, and it is assumed that Yucatan material attributed to *E. oceanops* was based on *E. lobeli*. This has been confirmed by J. J. Schmitter-Soto (personal communication, 2011).

Elacatinus redimiculus. This new species was described from La Banquilla Reef, Gulf of Mexico, off Veracruz state by M. S. Taylor and L. Akins, 2007, Zootaxa 1425:48.

Elacatinus xanthiprora. See Gobiidae.

Page 177

Gillichthys detrusus. Resurrected from the synonymy of *G. mirabilis* by C. C. Swift, L. T. Findley, R. A. Ellingson, K. W. Flessa, and D. K. Jacobs, 2011, Copeia 2011(1):93–102. It is endemic to the northernmost Gulf of California and Colorado River delta where it is sympatric with *G. mirabilis*.

Gymneleotris seminuda. Correction of spelling of specific name in the 2004 list (from *seminudus*).

Page 178

Neogobius melanostomus. C. A. Stepien and M. A. Tumeo, 2006, Biol. Invasions 8:61–78, recognized this species in *Apollonia*, as *A. melanostoma*. However, further work has recognized *Apollonia* as a subgenus of *Neogobius*, of which *N. melanostomus* is the type (M. E. Nielson and C. A. Stepien, 2009, Mol. Phylogenet. Evol. 52:84–102).

Proterorhinus semilunaris. C. A. Stepien and M. A. Tumeo, 2006, Biol. Invasions 8:61–78, using mitochondrial DNA sequence data, found that *P. marmoratus* (Pallas, 1814), as

previously recognized, is divisible into two species, of which *P. marmoratus* occurs in brackish or saltwater and *P. semilunaris* is confined to freshwater. Based on this, they determined that all introduced populations in the United States and Canada are identifiable as *P. semilunaris*, and *P. marmoratus* is deleted from the list. Common name in English is that used by Stepien and Tumeo (2006).

Quietula guaymasiae. Parentheses were inadvertently omitted from around the authors' names in the 2004 list; it was described in *Gillichthys*.

Page 179

Robinsichthys arrowsmithensis. New to the list. Although depth of occurrence above 200 m not definite (holotype and a paratype were collected at remote Arrowsmith Bank, Quintana Roo, Mexico, in a vertical trawl haul covering a depth range of 92 to 586 m), we choose to include this species as most likely occurring at the upper end of that range and straddling our 200-m depth limit (as we have done for the grammatid *Lipogramma evides*, the bythitid *Calamopteryx robinsorum*, and the opistognathid *Opistognathus megalepis*) and because we know of no New World gobiid that occurs only below 200 m.

Page 180

Acanthurus tractus. M. A. Bernal and L. A. Rocha, 2011, Zootaxa 2905:63–68, based on pigmentation and mitochondrial DNA sequence data, found that *A. bahianus* is divisible into two species. *Acanthurus tractus* occurs in the northwestern Altantic southward to northern South America, and *A. bahianus* is confined to the South Atlantic. The common names Ocean Surgeon and cirujano pardo are retained for *A. tractus*, the species in our area of coverage.

Ctenochaetus marginatus. New to the list. This wide-ranging species is known from scattered localities in the central Pacific eastward to the tropical eastern Pacific, where it occurs from Costa Rica to Colombia and all of the oceanic islands (including Mexico's Revillagigedo Archipelago) except the Galapagos (Robertson and Allen 2008; D. R. Robertson, personal communication, 2011).

Sphyraena borealis. *Sphyraena picudilla*, recognized in the 2004 list, was considered a synonym of *S. borealis* by W. F. Smith-Vaniz,

B. B. Collette, and B. E. Luckhurst, 1999, Fishes of Bermuda: history, zoogeography, annotated checklist, and identification keys, American Society of Ichthyologists and Herpetologists, Special Publication 4, Miami. Common name in English changed by dropping geographic modifier, which is no longer necessary.

Sphyraena qenie. Added to the list based on occurrence at Islas Marías in the southeastern Gulf of California (B. E. Erisman, G. R. Galland, I. Mascareñas, J. Moxley, H. J. Walker, O. Aburto-Oropeza, P. A. Hastings, and E. Ezcurra, 2011, Zootaxa 2985:26–40) and from the Pacific coast of central Mexico (P. Humann and N. DeLoach, 2004, Reef fish identification: Baja to Panama, New World Publications, Jacksonville, Florida).

Page 181

Evoxymetopon taeniatus. We continue to accept Poey rather than Gill as the author of this species based on our interpretation of T. Gill, 1863, Proc. Acad. Nat. Sci. Phila. 15:224–229 (following Article 50.1.1 of the International Code).

Page 182

Istiophoridae. We follow B. B. Collette, J. R. McDowell, and J. E. Graves, 2006, Bull. Mar. Sci. 79(3):455–468, in recognizing the genera *Istiompax* and *Kajikia*.

Istiompax indica. Formerly *Makaira indica* (Cuvier, 1832). See Istiophoridae.

Kajikia albida. Formerly *Tetrapturus albidus* Poey, 1860. See Istiophoridae.

Kajikia audax. Formerly *Tetrapturus audax* (Philippi, 1887). See Istiophoridae.

Makaira nigricans. B. B. Collette, J. R. McDowell, and J. E. Graves, 2006, Bull. Mar. Sci. 79(3):455–468, concluded that the Blue Marlin is a worldwide species and that *M. mazara* (Jordan & Snyder, 1901), recognized in the 2004 list as the Indo-Pacific blue marlin (marlin azul del Indo-Pacífico), is a synonym.

Tetrapturus georgii. This species has been known from the western Atlantic within our area for several years where it was often confused with the White Marlin, *Kajikia albida* (e.g., L. Beerkircher, F. Arocha, A. Barse, E. Prince, V. Restrepo, J. Serafy, and M. Shivji, 2009, Endangered Species Research 9:81–90; R. Hanner, R. Floyd, A. Bernard, B. B. Collette, and M. Shivji, 2011, Mitochondrial

DNA 22(S1):27–36). J. E. Graves (personal communication, 2009) has observed it being caught and released inside Delaware Canyon over the continental shelf and also from a photograph of a specimen caught inside Hudson Canyon from less than 200-m depth.

Page 183

Schedophilus medusophagus. Listed as *Centrolophus medusophagus* in the 2004 list. Generic change based on R. L. Haedrich, 2003 [dated 2002], Centrolophidae, Pages 1867–1868 in Carpenter (2003c). Also, date of description corrected.

Schedophilus pemarco. New to the list. One specimen, collected in Bear Cut, Virginia Key, Florida, 9 March 1968 (UF 142519), was identified by R. H. Robins. The common and scientific names are an acronym for Pêcherie Maritime au Congo.

Nomeus gronovii. Presence in Pacific Mexico confirmed by specimens from the Gulf of California at Scripps Institution of Oceanography and the Instituto de Biología, Universidad Nacional Autónoma de México.

Page 184

Osphronemidae. Change in family placement for *Trichopsis vittata* from Belontiidae follows L. Rüber, R. Britz, and R. Zardoya, 2006, Syst. Biol. 55(3):374–397.

Channa argus. Although known from United States prior to publication of the 2004 list, it was not included because of lack of evidence of permanent establishment. T. M. Orrell and L. Weigt, 2005, Proc. Biol. Soc. Wash. 118(2): 407–415, documented reproduction in Maryland. It has been recorded in Mexico and Canada, but establishment has not been verified.

Caproidae. See Zeiformes.

Pleuronectiformes. Change in sequence position of Bothidae follows Nelson (2006), and that work should be consulted for relevant literature.

Page 185

Cyclopsetta querna. Parentheses were inadvertently omitted from around the authors' names in the 2004 list.

Etropus ciadi. This new species was described by A. M. van der Heiden and H. G. Plascencia-González, 2005, Copeia 2005(3):470–478, from shallow depths (8–40 m) in the Gulf of California, Mexico. Common names proposed by A. M. van der Heiden (personal communication) based on intermediacy in physical appearance between the new species and the other two members of the genus in the Gulf of California (*E. crossotus* and *E. peruvianus*).

Page 186

Embassichthys bathybius. Listed for Mexico in the 2004 list based on a record presumed to be from the Pacific coast of northern Baja California (LACM 37464-1, at 36.639° N, 119.414° W, 900–1,000 m). However, this locality is off southern San Diego County, California, and is at a depth below our limit of coverage. We are aware of no record of this species from Mexico.

Microstomus kitt. New to the list. Recorded from the southwestern coast of Greenland by P. R. Møller, J. G. Nielsen, S. W. Knudsen, J. Y. Poulsen, K. Sünksen, and O. A. Jørgensen, 2010, Zootaxa 2378:1–84.

Page 187

Monolene maculipinna. Correction of author and year of publication (from Norman, 1933).

Page 188

Trinectes inscriptus. Occurrence in Mexico based on specimens from Quintana Roo, housed at ECOCH (J. J. Schmitter-Soto, 1999, Southwest. Nat. 44:166–172; J. J. Schmitter-Soto, personal communication, 2008).

Trinectes paulistanus. Parentheses were inadvertently omitted from around the author's name in the 2004 list.

Page 189

Melichthys vidua. New to the list. Widespread in the Indo-Pacific, occurring from eastern Africa to Panama. In the eastern Pacific, it is known mainly from the oceanic islands, including the Revillagigedo Archipelago of Mexico (Robertson and Allen 2008; D. R. Robertson, personal communication, 2011).

Page 190

Acanthostracion polygonius. Correction of spelling of specific name (from *polygonia*).

Page 191

Chilomycterus antennatus. Presence in Mexico confirmed by J. A. Caballero-Vázquez, H. C. Gamboa-Pérez, and J. J. Schmitter-Soto, 2005, Hidrobiologica 15(2 Especial):215–226.

Chilomycterus reticulatus. Parentheses were inadvertently omitted from around the author's name in the 2004 edition. J. M. Leis, 2006, Memoirs of Museum Victoria 63(1):77–90, treated *C. atringa* as a *nomen dubium* because *Diodon atringa* Linnaeus is unidentifiable. However, *D. reticulatus* Linnaeus is clearly identifiable and should be used for this species (in *Chilomycterus*). *Chilomycterus atringa*, spotted burrfish, as appearing in the 2004 list, is no longer valid. Following Leis (2006), the species from the Atlantic is *C. reticulatus*, which is thought to have a circumglobal distribution.

Diodon eydouxii. J. M. Leis, 2006, Memoirs of Museum Victoria 63(1):77–90, documents this species in the eastern Pacific from the equator to 20° N, plus a California record from Los Angeles Harbor. There are several records of this pelagic species from Mexican Pacific and U.S. Atlantic waters (north to Virginia), but all are from surface waters over depths greater than 200 m.

Appendix 2
Names Applied to Hybrid Fishes

Many fish species hybridize in nature and others have been crossed in the laboratory or in fish hatcheries. Scientists routinely refer to hybrids by the names of both parental species, as for example, *Luxilus cornutus* × *Notropis rubellus*, a fairly commonly occurring natural cyprinid hybrid. This hybrid combination when first collected was not recognized as such and was described as a new species, *N. macdonaldi* Jordan & Jenkins, 1888. Following Article 23(h) of the International Code of Zoological Nomenclature, 3rd edition, 1985 (and Article 23.8 of the 4th edition, 1999), scientific names based on hybrids have no nomenclatural validity, and *N. macdonaldi* is, therefore, an unavailable name.

Hybrid fishes generally are not given common names. In a few instances, hybrids have been recognized and named by anglers, and several are listed in such sources as P. T. Fuller, L. G. Nico, and J. D. Williams, 1999, Nonindigenous fishes introduced into inland waters of the United States, American Fisheries Society, Special Publication 27, Bethesda, Maryland, and the 2001 World Record Game Fishes published by the International Game Fish Association. Others have become important in fish management or are marketed from aquaculture fisheries and have been accorded common names. The U.S. Food and Drug Administration has required specific labeling of such cultured fishes being sold in consumer markets.

Although various authors give the male or the female first, when parental sexes are known, we follow the systematists' practice of listing parental species alphabetically. Hybrid moronids of unknown parentage are called "wipers."

In the table below, we list the parental species (arranged by family) and common name applied to the hybrid fish for those that are established in fishery literature. We stress that this is not a list of all hybrid fishes known from our area.

PARENTAL SPECIES	COMMON NAME

Salmonidae-trouts and salmons

Oncorhynchus clarkii × *O. mykiss*	cutbow trout
Salmo trutta × *Salvelinus fontinalis*	tiger trout
Salvelinus fontinalis × *S. namaycush*	splake

(The cross of *S. namaycush* × splake has the name "backcross," which we acknowledge can cause confusion.)

Esocidae-pikes and mudminnows

Esox lucius × *E. masquinongy*	tiger muskellunge

Moronidae-temperate basses

male *Morone americana* × female *M. saxatilis*	Virginia bass
female *Morone americana* × male *M. saxatilis*	Maryland bass
female *Morone chrysops* × male *M. saxatilis*	sunshine bass
male *Morone chrysops* × female *M. saxatilis*	palmetto bass
male *Morone mississippiensis* × female *M. saxatilis*	paradise bass

Centrarchidae-sunfishes

Lepomis macrochirus × *Micropterus salmoides*	blue bass

Percidae-perches and darters

Sander canadensis × *S. vitreus* .... saugeye

Cichlidae-cichlids and tilapias

Oreochromis mossambicus × *O. urolepis* .... red tilapia

Pleuronectidae-righteye flounders

Parophrys vetulus × *Platichthys stellatus* .... forkline sole

PART III

References

Most references to literature cited in Appendix 1 of Part II are in abbreviated form as in previous editions, omitting the title but giving other information to identify the publication. References cited repeatedly are listed below and cited in the text by author(s) and year of publication.

Carpenter, K. E., editor. 2003a [dated 2002]. The living marine resources of the western Central Atlantic. Volume 1: Introduction, mollusks, crustaceans, hagfishes, sharks, batoid fishes and chimaeras. FAO Species Identification Guide for Fishery Purposes and American Society of Ichthyologists and Herpetologists Special Publication No. 5. Food and Agriculture Organization of the United Nations, Rome.

Carpenter, K. E., editor. 2003b [dated 2002]. The living marine resources of the western Central Atlantic. Volume 2: Bony fishes part 1 (Acipenseridae to Grammatidae). FAO Species Identification Guide for Fishery Purposes and American Society of Ichthyologists and Herpetologists Special Publication No. 5. Food and Agriculture Organization of the United Nations, Rome.

Carpenter, K. E., editor. 2003c [dated 2002]. The living marine resources of the western Central Atlantic. Volume 3: Bony fishes part 2 (Opistognathidae to Molidae), sea turtles and marine mammals. FAO Species Identification Guide for Fishery Purposes and American Society of Ichthyologists and Herpetologists Special Publication No. 5. Food and Agriculture Organization of the United Nations, Rome.

Coad, B. W., and J. D. Reist. 2004. Annotated list of the Arctic marine fishes of Canada. Canadian Manuscript Report of Fisheries and Aquatic Sciences 2674.

Eschmeyer, W. N., editor. 2012. Catalog of fishes electronic version. Available: http://research.calacademy.org/research/ichthyology/catalog/fishcatmain.asp. (Accessed over several years during the work of the Committee).

Kottelat, M., and J. Freyhof. 2007. Handbook of European freshwater fishes. Kottelat, Cornol, Switzerland, and Freyhof, Berlin, Germany.

Kullander, S. O. 1983. A revision of the South American cichlid genus *Cichlasoma* (Teleostei: Cichlidae). Naturhistoriska Riksmuseet (Swedish Museum of Natural History), Stockholm.

Kullander, S. O. 2003. Family Cichlidae (cichlids). In R. E. Reis, S. O. Kullander, and C. J. Ferraris, Jr., editors. Check list of the freshwater fishes of Central and South America. Edipucrs, Porto Alegre, Brazil.

Mecklenburg, C. W., T. A. Mecklenburg, and L. K. Thorsteinson. 2002. Fishes of Alaska. American Fisheries Society, Bethesda, Maryland.

Mecklenburg, C. W., P. R. Møller, and D. Steinke. 2011. Biodiversity of Arctic marine fishes: taxonomy and zoogeography. Marine Biodiversity 41:109–140.

Miller, R. R., W. L. Minckley, and S. M. Norris. 2006 [dated 2005]. Freshwater fishes of Mexico. University of Chicago Press, Chicago.

Minckley W. L., and P. C. Marsh. 2009. Inland fishes of the greater Southwest: chronicle of a vanishing biota. University of Arizona Press, Tucson.

Moyle, P. B. 2002. Inland fishes of California. University of California Press, Berkeley.

Nelson, J. S. 2006. Fishes of the world, 4th edition. John Wiley & Sons, New York.

Page, L. M., and B. M. Burr. 2011. A field guide to freshwater fishes of North America north of Mexico, 2nd edition. The Peterson Field Guide Series. Houghton Mifflin Harcourt, Boston.

Reis, R. E., S. O. Kullander, and C. J. Ferraris, Jr., editors. 2003. Check list of the freshwater fishes of South and Central America. Edipucrs, Porto Alegre, Brazil.

Robertson, D. R., and G. R. Allen. 2008. Shorefishes of the tropical eastern Pacific online information system. Version 1.0. Smithsonian Tropical Research Institute, Balboa, Panama. Available: www.stri.org/sftep. (November 2012).

Scott, W. B., and E. J. Crossman. 1973. Freshwater fishes of Canada. Bulletin of the Fisheries Research Board of Canada 184.

Editions of the Names List
(given in chronological order)

Chute, W. H. (chairman), R. M. Bailey, W. A. Clemens, J. R. Dymond, S. F. Hildebrand, G. S. Myers, and L. P. Schultz. 1948. A list of common and scientific names of the better known fishes of the United States and Canada. American Fisheries Society, Special Publication 1, Ann Arbor, Michigan (and Transactions of the American Fisheries Society 75:355–398).

Bailey, R. M. (chairman), E. A. Lachner, C. C. Lindsey, C. R. Robins, P. M. Roedel, W. B. Scott, and L. P. Woods. 1960. A list of common and scientific names of fishes from the United States and Canada, 2nd edition. American Fisheries Society, Special Publication 2, Ann Arbor, Michigan.

Bailey, R. M. (chairman), J. E. Fitch, E. S. Herald, E. A. Lachner, C. C. Lindsey, C. R. Robins, and W. B. Scott. 1970. A list of common and scientific names of fishes from the United States and Canada, 3rd edition. American Fisheries Society, Special Publication 6, Washington, D.C.

Robins, C. R. (chairman), R. M. Bailey, C. E. Bond, J. R. Brooker, E. A. Lachner, R. N. Lea, and W. B. Scott. 1980. A list of common and scientific names of fishes from the United States and Canada, 4th edition. American Fisheries Society, Special Publication 12, Bethesda, Maryland.

Robins, C. R. (chairman), R. M. Bailey, C. E. Bond, J. R. Brooker, E. A. Lachner, R. N. Lea, and W. B. Scott. 1991. Common and scientific names of fishes from the United States and Canada, 5th edition. American Fisheries Society, Special Publication 20, Bethesda, Maryland.

Nelson, J. S. (chair), E. J. Crossman, H. Espinosa-Pérez, L. T. Findley, C. R. Gilbert, R. N. Lea, and J. D. Williams. 2004. Common and scientific names of fishes from the United States, Canada, and Mexico, 6th edition. American Fisheries Society, Special Publication 29, Bethesda, Maryland.

Edition of the World List

Robins, C. R. (chairman), R. M. Bailey, C. E. Bond, J. R. Brooker, E. A. Lachner, R. N. Lea, and W. B. Scott. 1991. World fishes important to North Americans, exclusive of species from the continental waters of the United States and Canada. American Fisheries Society, Special Publication 21, Bethesda, Maryland.

Personal Communications

A. Acero P., Universidad Nacional de Colombia (Instituto de Ciencias Naturales), Cerro Punta Betín, INVEMAR, Santa Marta, Colombia

H. L. Bart, Jr., Tulane University Museum of Natural History, Belle Chasse, Louisiana

D. S. Clark, St. Andrews Biological Station, St. Andrews, New Brunswick, Canada

B. B. Collette, National Marine Fisheries Service Systematics Laboratory, National Museum of Natural History, Washington, D.C.

J. E. Craddock, Woods Hole Oceanography Institute, Woods Hole, Massachusetts

B. E. Erisman, Scripps Institution of Oceanography, University of California-San Diego, La Jolla

W. N. Eschmeyer, Florida Museum of Natural History, University of Florida, Gainesville

A. C. Gill, Macleay Museum and School of Biological Sciences, University of Sydney, New South Wales, Australia

R. G. Gilmore, Jr., Estuarine, Coastal and Ocean Science, Vero Beach, Florida

J. E. Graves, School of Marine Science, Virginia Institute of Marine Science, College of William and Mary, Gloucester Point

K. E. Hartel, Museum of Comparative Zoology, Harvard University, Cambridge, Massachusetts

P. A. Hastings, Scripps Institution of Oceanography, University of California-San Diego, La Jolla

P. C. Heemstra, South African Institute for Aquatic Biodiversity, Grahamstown, South Africa

D. A. Hendrickson, Texas Memorial Museum and Section of Integrative Biology, University of Texas, Austin

S. Herman, Fish and Wildlife Division, Sustainable Resource Development, Government of Alberta, Rocky Mountain House, Alberta

N. D. Holland, Scripps Institution of Oceanography, University of California-San Diego, La Jolla

R. Miller, Maurice Lamontagne Institute, Mont Joli, Quebec

R. D. Mooi, The Manitoba Museum, Winnipeg, Manitoba

E. J. Pfeiler, Centro de Investigación en Alimentación y Desarrollo, A.C.-Coordinación Guaymas, Guaymas, Sonora, Mexico

K. R. Piller, Department of Biological Sciences, Southeastern Louisiana University, Hammond

J. A. Lopez, University of Alaska Museum, Fairbanks

C. B. Renaud, Canadian Museum of Nature, Ottawa, Ontario

D. R. Robertson, Smithsonian Tropical Research Institute, Balboa, Panama

C. R. Robins, Ichthyology, Natural History Museum, The University of Kansas, Lawrence

C. Scharpf, Baltimore, Maryland

J. J. Schmitter-Soto, El Colegio de la Frontera Sur, Chetumal, Quintana Roo, Mexico

D. G. Smith, Division of Fishes, National Museum of Natural History, Washington, D.C.

J. D. Stelfox, Fish and Wildlife Division, Sustainable Resource Development, Government of Alberta, Cochrane, Alberta

D. E. Stevenson, National Marine Fisheries Service, Alaska Fisheries Science Center, Seattle

C. E. Thacker, Natural History Museum of Los Angeles County, Los Angeles

H. J. Walker, Jr., Scripps Institution of Oceanography, University of California-San Diego, La Jolla

Index

B

I

Q

X